Places of Their Own

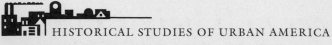 HISTORICAL STUDIES OF URBAN AMERICA

Edited by Kathleen N. Conzen, Timothy J. Gilfoyle, and James R. Grossman

ALSO IN THE SERIES

Places of Their Own

African American Suburbanization in
the Twentieth Century

Andrew Wiese

The University of Chicago Press · *Chicago and London*

Andrew Wiese is associate professor of history at San Diego State University.

The University of Chicago Press, Chicago 60637
The University of Chicago Press, Ltd., London
© 2004 by The University of Chicago
All rights reserved. Published 2004
Printed in the United States of America
13 12 11 10 09 08 07 06 05 04   1 2 3 4 5

ISBN: 0-226-89641-2

Library of Congress Cataloging-in-Publication Data

Wiese, Andrew.
    Places of their own : African American suburbanization in the twentieth century / Andrew
Wiese.
        p. cm. — (Historical studies of urban America)
Includes bibliographical references and index.
    ISBN 0-226-89641-2 (alk. paper)
    1. African Americans — Social conditions — 20th century. 2. Suburbanites — United States —
History — 20th century. 3. Suburbs — United States — History — 20th century. 4. African
Americans — Economic conditions — 20th century. 5. United States — Social conditions — 20th
century. 6. Social classes — United States — History — 20th century. 7. United States — Economic
conditions — 20th century. 8. United States — Race relations. I. Title. II. Series.
E185.86 .W436 2003
307.74'089'96073 — dc21

                                                                                              2003012588

⊗ The paper used in this publication meets the minimum requirements of the
American National Standard for Information Sciences — Permanence of Paper
for Printed Library Materials, ANSI Z39.48-1992.

To María

Contents

Acknowledgments

IN ONE FORM or another, this book has been with me since I was a college student. In the time that has passed, I have incurred debts too many to mention and too substantial ever to repay.

Most important among my creditors are the suburbanites who shared their time, their stories, and their trust with me. Deserving special mention are Grace Bolden, Stephen and Ruby Hall, Lula Hitchcock, the late Essie Kirklen, Paula Mays, Keith Moore, and the late William Wheeler. For the grace and openheartedness they extended to me, I am forever grateful.

Financial support from many institutions was indispensable to the completion of this project. A Richard Hofstadter Fellowship from Columbia University supported this work as a dissertation. Grants from the Walter Reuther Archives at Wayne State University, the Historical Society of Southern California, and the Herbert Hoover Presidential Library defrayed the cost of research. At San Diego State University, a Faculty Development Program grant subsidized travel to collections in Atlanta, and two Research, Scholarship and Creative Activity grants afforded leaves from teaching during which I wrote substantial portions of the manuscript. I also received assistance from the National Endowment for Humanities at two critical junctures; a 1994 Summer Seminar grant brought me to the University of Kansas, where I began reworking my dissertation, and a Fellowship for College Teachers in 2002 made it possible for me to complete the manuscript.

Just as consequential was the generosity of friends and family, who made a place for me in their homes while I researched, wrote, or presented my work. Jack and Christina Alfandary, Chuck Baker, Charles Bares, Michael Clancy, Dee and Bill Clancy, Louis and Jackie English, Joyce LeMelle, Elizabeth Nicolaides, Becky Nicolaides and David Weisenberg, Laura and Corey Patrick, Christopher Stark and Mary Corbin Sies, Maria and T. R. Turner, and Hawk Smith and Yinka Akinsulure-Smith, there is a light on in the spare bedroom for you, and the sheets are turned down.

Teachers, mentors, and colleagues nourished this project from its infancy. Alan Nagel and Sandra Barkan at the University of Iowa provided compelling models of a scholarly life; at Columbia University, the late James Shenton, Elizabeth Blackmar, Alan Brinkley, Marc Weiss, Saskia Sassen, and especially Kenneth Jackson challenged me through words and deeds to conceptualize this study in the broadest possible terms. At Barnard College, the late William McNeil, Herbert Sloan, Rosalind Rosenberg, and Ester Fuchs afforded me an office, encouragement, and a computer to begin. Ann Schofield, Angel Kwolek-Folland, Peter Mancall and Lisa Bitel, William Tuttle, and David Katzman welcomed me to the University of Kansas and touched my work and my life in unforgettable ways. I owe a special thanks to David Katzman, who helped me become a better writer. I also feel lucky to have met Michael French, whose friendship and intellectual companionship have made life in San Diego so much more agreeable. At San Diego State University, I received support and encouragement from many colleagues. I am especially grateful to Raymond Starr and Frank Stites, who helped me adjust to a new city; to Matt Kuefler and Cristina Rivera-Garza, who provided models of wit and productivity despite the workload; and to Lisa Cobbs-Hoffman, Joanne Ferraro, and Harry McDean for their sound advice and mentorship along the way. I owe a special thanks to Ted Kornweibel and Bill and Aimee Lee Cheek, who read and reviewed a draft of the manuscript.

Like all academic projects, this one rests on a foundation that other scholars have built. My footnotes may be read as a long and grateful acknowledgment, but I wish to confirm my special debt to the scholarship of James Borchert, Lizabeth Cohen, Robert Fishman, Clifford Geertz, Steven Gregory, Richard Harris, David Harvey, Dolores Hayden, Bruce Haynes, Kenneth Jackson, Earl Lewis, George Lipsitz, John Logan, Becky Nicolaides, Harold Rose, Robert Self, Carol Stack, Thomas Sugrue, and Henry L. Taylor Jr. In ways both subtle and obvious, their ideas were signposts that helped me find my way. A number of scholars also commented on material that became part of this manuscript. Through their criticisms, Alan Brinkley, Lizabeth Cohen, Spencer Crew, Robert Fairbanks, Robert Fishman, Thomas Hanchett, Kenneth Jackson, Angel Kwolek-Folland, Earl Lewis, Katherine Newman, Darlene Roth, Quintard Taylor, Mark Weiss, Leslie Wilson, and William H. Wilson strengthened this project in innumerable ways. Four other scholars made unique contributions. I was planning a senior thesis and actually looking for someone else when I poked my head into Henry Taylor's office for directions in 1986. More than an hour later I emerged with a bibliography, methodologies, questions, and the conviction that the African American suburb I hoped to study was part of

something much larger. With his help and encouragement, I have been building on this groundwork ever since. I am also grateful to Richard Harris, whose
exceptionally creative and thorough scholarship made a safe place for the study
of working-class suburbs and whose friendship has led to numerous insights
through the years. Mary Corbin Sies urged me to investigate more explicitly
the theories that underlay my work, initiating a dialogue that continues to bear
fruit. Lastly, Becky Nicolaides has been my friend, ally, and collaborator since
we shared an address and a view of the Hudson River in the late 1980s. Her
exclamation-filled encouragements were unfailing and, to me, invaluable.

I was fortunate to receive professional and technical assistance from many
people. At the University of Chicago Press, Robert Devens, Elizabeth Branch
Dyson, and Erin DeWitt shepherded the book through production with pre-
cision and good humor. James Grossman set high expectations for this book,
and he had faith that I could approach them. Carla Anderson, John Archer,
Christopher Clarke-Hazlett, and Timothy Crimmins went out of their way to
share photographs. Amy Williams of the Library of Congress, Photographs
and Prints Division, provided able assistance in finding and reproducing material from their collections. Charlotte Brooks generously granted permission
to use a montage of her photographs for the cover. Kathy Holcomb tran-
scribed my Atlanta interviews, and Kelly Camps compiled bibliographic material for chapter 9. Tom Ferenger and Jon Rizzo, extraordinarily professional
staff members at San Diego State's Instructional Technology Services department, helped me prepare photographs and illustrations. Harry D. Johnson,
staff cartographer for SDSU's Department of Geography, created maps with
evident pride of craftsmanship.

Several people deserve special recognition. More than anyone, Ted Wheeler
deserves credit for setting and keeping me on the road that led to this book. As
coach, mentor, and friend for more than twenty years, he has served as an ex-
emplar of humanism and personal integrity. He challenged me to investigate
race and inequality by going home to the suburbs, and he offered ceaseless advice—usually by phone before seven in the morning—to listen carefully and
to trust my instincts. My parents, Jim and Nancy Wiese, have been my biggest
fans since before I can remember. They encouraged my every pursuit with the
same loving enthusiasm. They know how long this project has been brewing
and how much I gave up in the meantime. Finally, this book is dedicated to
my wife, María Ibarra, who read every word, challenged my assumptions,
took me to the beach whether I needed it or not, and asked with arched eye-
brows, "Did you eat?" Her love was the best reason of all to put my pencil
down and send this book to the publisher.

Introduction

I'm gonna move way out to the outskirts of town.

—William Weldon and Andy Razaf (1942)[1]

SPRING SUNLIGHT dapples onto the lawns of Melbenan Drive in west suburban Atlanta. Two dozen brick homes sit back from the street; behind them wooden decks and living-room windows open onto an expanse of pine trees. Residents returning from work swing European sedans through brick gateposts and step from their cars in polished shoes and business attire. They walk to their front doors past azaleas, sculptured evergreens, and magnolias in blossom. When they have disappeared, a leisurely calm returns to the street. For millions of Americans, this is the suburban dream: detached single-family homes on spacious lawns and a quiet street, middle-class neighbors, a place to raise children, a private refuge from the public world. The scene is similar to thousands of suburban streets in the United States, yet Melbenan Drive and neighborhoods like it in almost every major metropolitan area are distinctive in one important respect: the middle-class home owners on this street are African Americans.

In recent decades, neighborhoods such as these have multiplied across the United States. Between 1960 and 2000, the number of African Americans living in suburbs grew by approximately 9 million, representing a migration as large as the exodus of African Americans from the rural South in the mid-twentieth century.[2] By 2000, more than one-third of African Americans — almost 12 million people — lived in suburbs. By virtue of numbers alone, black suburbanization had become one of the most important demographic movements in the twentieth-century United States, and it had established the suburbs as an indispensable context for the study of African American life.

This transit also signaled significant historical change in American society. The suburban boom heralded the emergence of a new black middle class, larger and more economically secure than any black elite in the past. It revealed, too, a shift in long-standing patterns of inequality: a loosening of the shackle between race and class and a breaching of residential barriers that for generations had barred African Americans from the most economically vibrant localities and confined them to areas where locational disadvantages reinforced racial inequity. At the same time, suburbanization reflected the legacy of segregation and racial inequality that had long shadowed the metropolitan landscape. Levels of suburban segregation declined slowly after 1960, but most new suburbanites settled within a few minutes' drive of more mature black communities.[3] The places to which they moved often suffered from higher-than-average property taxes, financially strapped public schools, and slower rates of property appreciation than predominantly white suburbs. Even as it reflected a shifting class structure within black America, suburbanization reinforced the significance of race in American life.

Despite the magnitude of this migration and its obvious connections to the past, black suburbanites remain a "people without history," to borrow a phrase from anthropologist Eric Wolf.[4] Social scientists, journalists, and urban studies scholars have documented many aspects of the recent migration — its demographic and fiscal characteristics, patterns of segregation, and housing quality — but these inquiries have paid limited attention to the period before 1960.[5] Largely missing, too, are careful analyses of change and continuity in African Americans' aspirations, their housing politics, or the varied meanings of a suburban home.[6] Moreover, emphasis on recent suburbanization by the middle class has obscured the pivotal role that working-class families played in establishing a foundation for subsequent migration, and it conceals the geographical continuity that defined black suburban settlement since the turn of the twentieth century. Finally, by separating recent suburbanization from its history, this scholarship reinforces a perception of the suburbs as essentially "white territory," implicitly supporting a line of argument that blames recent suburbanites for abandoning "the black community" and hastening the decline of central cities.[7]

Recent work by historians and historical sociologists — most of it appearing since the mid-1990s — has begun to correct these oversights. Case studies of individual suburbs and suburban areas have explored various aspects of black suburbanization since the turn of the century. These include its linkages to suburban employment, real estate development, migration, domestic ideology, and the production of social difference.[8] Works by Henry Taylor, William H. Wilson, Bruce Haynes, and Shirley Ann Wilson Moore, especially, incorporate careful ethnographic detail to reveal the diverse interior life of black suburban communities over time. Necessarily, these case studies focus narrowly in geographic or chronological scope, concentrating on the dynamics of individual places. Most avoid extended comparison with other suburbs or patterns of metropolitan development.[9] Until recently, the dearth of academic literature and the lack of topical focus have inhibited synthesis. The time has come to examine African American suburbanization as a discrete historical process bound up with the wider history of both African Americans and the nation's urban areas.

The importance of history is clear in places like West Atlanta. An observer with a sense of the past may easily discern the traces linking neighborhoods like Melbenan Drive to a lengthy history of African American struggles for space on the edge of town. Place-names that dot the city's west side — such as Washington Park, Fountain Heights, Chennault Street, Calloway Drive, J. B. Harris Manor, and others — disclose a century of black activism in the real estate market. Moreover, they reveal a chain of African American settlement stretching outward in time and space from the compact black neighborhoods of Jenningstown and the environs of Atlanta University, established outside the city after the Civil War, to the winding streets and opulent homes of recent subdivisions on the margins of Fulton County.[10] Evoking the memory of black developers and dignitaries, these appellations recall a social history of upward mobility imprinted on the green and rolling terrain. By the same token, other landmarks — the location of parks, highways, and public housing projects, urban renewal sites, and demapped streets blocking passage between areas that were once white and those that were black — reveal the assiduous resistance with which whites met African American decentralization. The struggle over space on the outskirts of Atlanta was a long-standing historical process linking African American social, cultural, and political history to the growth of the metropolis at large.

Though the details vary by time and place, wherever African Americans moved to suburbs in large numbers after 1960, the outlines of such struggles are visible. Black communities established by one generation served as the geographic and social foundation for the next. In suburban areas across the United States, black suburbanization was a cumulative process linked through time and space by contested racial struggle and the desire of black families to create places of their own. Marked by the geographical persistence of race,

African American suburbanization reflected and reinforced an ongoing process of racial formation. Just the same, choices in suburban landscape, location, and lifestyle bolstered distinctions that African Americans drew among themselves. As among whites, suburbanization played an important role in the making of African American identities in the twentieth century.

The Literature of Suburbanization

In addition to recovering black history in the suburbs, this book challenges historians to think and write about suburbs in a different way. For more than forty years, suburbanization has been one of the most fertile topics of research among U.S. urban historians. Since Sam Bass Warner Jr.'s 1962 landmark study, *Streetcar Suburbs*, historians have detailed the physical, social, and political development of suburbia. They have explored the role of transportation, the real estate industry, local boosters, and the federal government in creating the suburban pattern, and they have probed the desires and fears of middle-class Americans that made the suburban home a keystone of the American dream.[11] For all this diversity, however, historians have taken a rather narrow view of the suburbs.

With a few exceptions, historians have focused on suburbs of elite and middle-class whites, and they have defined suburbs according to the attributes of these communities.[12] Kenneth Jackson, whose 1985 book, *Crabgrass Frontier*, remains a standard in the field, argues that America's distinctive landscape can be summarized as follows: "Affluent and middle-class Americans live in suburban areas that are far from their work place, in homes that they own, and in the center of yards that by urban standards elsewhere are enormous."[13] For Jackson, home ownership, low population density, and middle-class commuting from dormitory neighborhoods are essential to the definition of suburbanization. Middle-class suburbia is not merely a physical landscape, however. As Robert Fishman explains, "Suburbia . . . expresses values so deeply embedded in bourgeois culture that it might also be called the bourgeois utopia."[14] At the root of the physical pattern of middle-class suburbia, then, is a cultural landscape, a set of ideas including an idealization of family life, leisure, feminine domesticity, and union with nature that are deeply rooted in Anglo-American culture.

Usually unspoken is the corresponding assumption that suburbs are white in racial composition. Scholars such as Jackson and Fishman are mindful of the diversity of American suburbia. Jackson, in particular, is a fierce critic of the racism that excluded blacks and other minorities from most suburban areas. Nonetheless, he concludes that suburbanization was a process in which African Americans played little part before the 1970s. Most Americans — indeed, most historians — have adopted this exclusive image as the model for all suburbs. Whether the term evokes images of Big Wheels and minivans, political conservatism, architectural conformity, or restrictive gender roles, in common parlance "suburb" is still likely to be understood to mean a white community. Following the logic of this equation, there are many people who assume that if visible numbers of black (or poor) people lived in a community, it was not a suburb.[15] Given this characterization, it is not surprising that black suburbs have received little attention.

The truth is, however, historians have done a better job excluding African Americans from the suburbs than even white suburbanites. Scholarly neglect notwithstanding, African Americans lived in and moved to suburbs through-out the twentieth century, and black communities served as a social and spatial basis for expanded suburbanization over time. During the Great Migration of the 1910s and 1920s, one in six African American migrants to the urban North moved to a suburb. In the South, black residence on the urban fringe was even more widespread; in fact, it was characteristic of the region before World War II. By 1940 more than a million African Americans lived in sub-urban areas, and suburbanites represented one-fifth of the black population in the metropolitan United States.[16] Black families resided in wealthy commuter suburbs such as New Rochelle, New York; Montclair, New Jersey; and Web-ster Groves, Missouri; industrial satellites such as Homestead, Pennsylvania, and Fairfield, Alabama; and "all-black" residential suburbs such as Robbins, Illinois; Glenarden, Maryland; or Lincoln Heights, Ohio. During the 1940s and 1950s, the number of African Americans in suburbs surged by almost a million, including several hundred thousand people who became suburban forerunners on the West Coast, and the suburban history of the period was marked by black attempts to overcome racial barriers and white attempts to sustain them. By the time civil rights–inspired suburbanization accelerated after 1960, there were more than 2.5 million African Americans in the suburbs, plus millions of others who lived in outlying neighborhoods that were inside the borders of a central city. The social and spatial inroads that these families made served as a template for the urban exodus to come.[17]

Analysis of African American suburbanization also contributes to a more diverse picture of the class composition of American suburbs. Although African Americans never constituted more than 5 percent of the U.S. sub-urban population before 1960, they were part of a much larger and equally neglected group of blue-collar suburbanites who formed the majority in many suburbs through midcentury.[18] In 1940, geographer Richard Harris demonstrates, skilled workers were more likely than professionals to be suburbanites in three of the nation's six largest metropolitan areas, and at the national level, blue-collar families proved as likely to be home owners (often in the suburbs) as members of the white-collar middle class. Furthermore, Harris argues, many of them expressed distinct class-based suburban ideals and lifeways, including intensive economic uses of housing.[19] In contrast to the middle-class model, the metropolitan fringe before 1945 comprised a variegated landscape that included factories, workers' housing, and ethnic enclaves as well as middle-class commuter suburbs.

For historians, the presence of hundreds of thousands of African American suburbanites, plus millions of other working-class people in the suburban fringe, poses a challenge to write suburban histories that include the range of Americans who lived on the city's edge, and it suggests that we need to re-conceptualize suburbanization to encompass the *whole* expansion of American cities beyond their bounds, not just the celebrated decentralization of the white middle class.

Expanding African American History

In addition to challenging prevailing paradigms in urban and suburban history, *Places of Their Own* complements a substantial literature in African American history that focuses on black agency and the texture of everyday life.[20] By treating suburban homes and neighborhoods as arenas of struggle, this book links African American social and political history through the everyday politics of housing. While a number of scholars have examined African Americans' responses to urban landscapes and the ways they adapted them to their own use, surprisingly few historians have examined the meanings of housing, homes, or landscape.[21] Most have treated the built environment as a confining reality that African Americans did little to shape. Expanding scholarly purview to include suburban communities reveals that African Americans not only shaped and defended residential neighborhoods, but they often produced them from the ground up. In pre–World War II suburbs such as Inkster, Michigan, and Lawnside, New Jersey, African Americans built homes of their own on a do-it-yourself basis. By contrast, black developers in the postwar South built scores of suburban subdivisions in planned "Negro expansion areas" gained through political negotiation with local whites, and since the

1980s, new construction for "upscale, well-educated African Americans" has become a major activity in many metropolitan areas.[22] Widening the focus of black history to include the suburbs makes it essential to ask about the landscapes to which African Americans aspired, the sorts of homes they desired, what they struggled to create, and what they would have preferred if they had the choice, not to mention how and why these preferences changed over time.

Places of Their Own

Tracing the history of African Americans in suburbs also raises unavoidable questions about race, class, and space in the twentieth century. Since the 1980s, a growing number of scholars have explored the social production of identity—especially identities of race, class, gender, and sexuality. Scholars have demonstrated that identities are not fixed but, as anthropologist Steven Gregory writes, "are constructed through social practices that 'position' people as subjects within complex hierarchies of power and meaning."[23] Thus, identity formation is an inherently political process in which the state as well as everyday social interaction play important roles.[24]

In the twentieth-century United States, race and class formation were fundamentally spatial processes as well.[25] Though scholars reveal the fluidity and contingency of social identity, as *historical* distinctions, race and class emerged in the form of devastating material and spatial inequality—differences marked on bodies and inscribed in the land: sun-leathered skin and bent postures, decrepit housing, substandard schools, and shorter lives. The legacy of these inequities, concrete differences among living people, gave life to persistent racial and class identities through time.[26]

On the one hand, race and class subordination branded urban and suburban space. Residential locations were not neutral with respect to social resources. Rather, they reflected positions in a sharply drawn hierarchy of metropolitan spaces that had compounding advantages or disadvantages for those who lived in them. Excluded from metropolitan locations with the greatest advantages—for example, high-income neighbors, a robust tax base, strong public schools, rapidly climbing property values—and restricted to those with the fewest, African Americans faced persistent spatial inequalities. Racism not only limited black access to employment, credit, and public facilities, but it ensured that most African Americans lived in a racially separate and materially unequal world. Housing discrimination hemmed them in, efforts to segregate schools and other public facilities affected people regardless of class, and other distinctly spatial practices—such as redlining, commercial disinvestment, industrial polluting, and political gerrymandering—compounded race and class inequalities, imposing a burden on everyone who lived in black neighborhoods and limiting the empowering potential of black space.[27] Even as jim crow diminished in politics, employment, and public accommodations after midcentury, residential segregation, with its associated "black tax," remained a predominant feature in cities as well as suburbs. Spatial inequalities reinforced the close link that African Americans experienced between race and class status for much of the century, contributing to a consolidation of their political interests around racially defined places.[28]

Against this backdrop, African Americans struggled to create places of their own. In metropolitan areas dominated by whites, they sought to use suburban space to their advantage, to satisfy their needs as well as their aspirations. This intention operated at many levels. For some, the place in question was a home that they owned, evidence of permanence, a marker of achievement, and the satisfaction of a long-deferred dream in the black South. For others, suburban space represented a means to economic subsistence, even independence: a lot with a spreading garden, chickens in the yard, and a house they had built with the help of friends and neighbors. For many, it was a black community, a place of social comfort and cultural affirmation if not racial pride, a "safe space" in which to nurture families and educate children, a symbol of resistance to white supremacy and a foundation for politics, if not economic and political power. For most suburbanites, too, home was a place of refuge, a shelter from the pressures of white racism.[29] In important ways, therefore, black suburbanization was a movement set in juxtaposition to the wider society.

For African Americans, the meaning of domestic spaces such as homes and neighborhoods drew from many sources. These included a history and culture rooted in the South, memories as well as media representations, economic exigencies as well as relations of status, rivalry, and attachment within black communities. Suburban spaces also gained meaning in relation to their social and economic context. Before World War II, as African American migrants weathered the transition to an urban industrial economy, working-class families went to extreme lengths to purchase property. In many suburbs, they sacrificed urban services, rented spare rooms, and some even built houses of their own to bring the cost of a suburban home within reach. They grew gardens and kept domestic animals so that they could have fresh food and avoid depleting limited cash. Proximity to work was also an important factor, and in many communities, women's labor was the economic foundation for suburban life. Finally, African American suburbanites sought to live in family-based communities, but the family of greatest emphasis was usually extended. In an era of urban migration, working-class African Americans created spaces secluded from white racism as well as the world of wages and market insecurity.

By the same token, as economically more secure blacks moved to the suburbs after World War II, the landscape and social life that they created reflected sensibilities they shared as emerging members of the American middle-class. At the same time, racial discrimination undermined this union. Middle-class families reaffirmed their class status vis-à-vis other blacks, but they also perceived their efforts to overcome racial barriers as acts of racial progress. By moving to suburbs, many of them signaled an implicit assertion of equality, challenging white supremacy, which was a central element of the white middle-class vision of suburbia. Like prewar suburbanites who had used their homes as shelter from the insecurities of wage labor under industrial capitalism, members of a rising black middle class valued their homes and neighborhoods as places of shelter, not only from the natural elements but from the challenges that beset them as members of a group defined by race and class.

Ironically, increased racial integration after 1960 tended to strengthen social divisions on the basis of race as well as class. If they moved to mostly white areas to safeguard economic interests that they shared with middle-class whites, many black suburbanites reported feeling isolated and uncomfortably aware of "subtle and sometimes not so subtle white antagonism," which reinforced a feeling of difference.[30] Increased exposure to whites made them more likely than other blacks to encounter racism directly.[31] As a result, moving to mostly white suburbia often served to heighten rather than diminish African Americans' sense of racial identity, inspiring many suburban families to seek out extraterritorial black spaces, maintaining social and cultural ties with black communities and peers regardless of the distance. Many, too, sought to enforce these connections more directly, by moving to communities that were both middle class and African American.

Organization of the Book

This book is organized in three chronological sections that narrate the process of African American suburbanization in the twentieth century. Part 1, which is divided into three chapters, examines the years from 1900 to 1940. These decades witnessed a surge of African American migration to metropolitan

areas. Outside the South, especially, black urban neighborhoods grew un-
precedentedly. At the same time, black suburban communities, fed by the arrival of working-class southerners seeking jobs and homes, germinated and
grew. Chapter 1 examines the suburbs where African Americans lived and
moved, their regional and economic variations, and their place in the larger
universe of American suburbia. Chapter 2 links the growth of suburban communities to the Great Migration, exploring the process of migration and the
variable influences of race, class, gender, and culture that shaped it. Chapter 3
investigates the migrants' aspirations for better places to live, tracing the outlines of an African American suburban dream that was rooted in the experience of working-class southerners in transition to an urban, industrial society.

Part 2 addresses the 1940s and 1950s, which were a period of transition in
African American suburban history. While the number of black suburbanites
doubled, the socioeconomic standing of the new migrants changed. By the
end of the 1950s, the majority of new suburbanites were members of a growing black middle class. Chapter 4 explores one important factor underlying
this shift, the explosion in white suburbanization and the varied means that
whites used to realize their vision of suburbia as a place for "Caucasians only."
Chapter 5 investigates the economic and political currents that worked against
this grain: the growth of a small but significant black middle class, intensifica-
tion of the struggle for "democracy in housing," and, to a limited extent, federal support for African American housing. Chapter 6 analyzes shifts in suburban ideology and the spatial production of identity that accompanied the
rise in middle-class suburbanization. Chapter 7 illuminates regional variation,
exploring the planning and political negotiation that led to a process of "separate suburbanization" in the South.

The two chapters in part 3 examine African American suburbanization
in the context of the civil rights mobilizations of the 1960s and early 1970s
(chapter 8) and the period of economic restructuring, wealth polarization,
and urban crisis that followed (chapter 9). In these years, black suburbanization became a truly mass movement, outstripping rates of growth among
whites and amounting to a total migration as large as any in African American
history. By the end of the century, suburbia, once a symbol of white supremacy
and exclusion, had become a fundamental setting for African American life.

Chapter 1

The Outskirts of Town
The Geography of Black Suburbanization
Before 1940

AT THE END of World War II, on the cusp of a mass migration that would remake the nation's suburbs, social scientist Carey McWilliams offered a jarring portrait of the landscape surrounding the nation's third largest city. Depicting "the main highways leading into Los Angeles," he described a cinematic procession of billboards and hand-lettered signs marking "canary farms, artificial pools for trout fishing, rabbit fryers, dogs at stud, grass-shack eating huts, psychic mediums, real-estate offices, filling stations, vacant-lot circuses, more rabbit farms, roadside peddlers, hobby shops, hemstitching, store-front evangelists, bicycles to rent, and frogs for sale." For McWilliams, a public intellectual seeking the pulse of the region, these signs were emblems of "the city's improvised economy" and the "curious spectacle of a large metropolitan city without an industrial base," but for the urban historian looking back through six decades of suburban sprawl, they raise intriguing questions about the nation's prewar suburbs, posing a stark contrast with the image of suburbia as the manicured province of the middle class. How common were these disorderly spaces, not quite urban or rural? Who lived there and why? What does their presence mean for the way we understand suburbanization?[1]

A few years before McWilliams examined the City of Angels, a cadre of young photographers employed by the federal government documented equally striking scenes on the margins of numerous U.S. cities. Interspersed with their photographs of ranch hands, farmworkers, and small-town streetscapes, the photographers of the depression-era Farm Security Administration revealed an unkempt and heterogeneous landscape at the margins of Ameri-

Fig. 1.1 *Real Estate Office Near Detroit, Michigan.* John Vachon, 1941.
Hand-lettered advertisements for low-cost building allotments were a signature
of blue-collar suburbia through the mid-twentieth century. In the wartime United
States, informal housing markets flourished, fueled by the boom in defense industries
and fed by rural and small-town migration. (Courtesy of the Library of Congress,
Prints and Photographs Division, FSA/OWI Collection, LC-USF34-063741-D
DLC)

can cities. Photographs by Carl Mydans, John Vachon, Marion Post Wolcott,
and Ben Shahn captured a suburbia of smokestacks, cemeteries, scrub trees,
and rutted streets; a suburbia of steel mills, worker cottages, trailer camps,
gap-toothed subdivisions, makeshift housing, and vegetable gardens all co-
existing with the prim residential blocks of the middle class. Like many social
realists of their day, these artists were attracted by the juxtaposition of urban
capitalism with the rural landscape and the people who inhabited it. Despite
this bias, their photographs provide ample evidence that the ragged suburban
borderland McWilliams depicted on the rim of Los Angeles characterized
many parts of metropolitan America.[2]

Contemporary observers were well aware of the diversity that characterized the nation's suburbs. The most important prewar study, Harlan Doug-

Fig. 1.2 *Typical Half-Built House at Steel Subdivision, Hamilton County, Ohio.*
Carl Mydans, 1935. Prewar suburbia included a range of residential neighborhoods,
from neat middle-class subdivisions to unplanned communities such as this Cincinnati suburb, where owner-builders produced a rough-hewn streetscape. (Courtesy
of the Library of Congress, Prints and Photographs Division, FSA/OWI Collection,
LC-USF33-TO1-000307-M5 DLC)

lass's *The Suburban Trend* (1925), asserted that "suburbs so manifestly differ
from one another that even the most general account of their character . . .
could not ignore the fact." He grouped suburbs in two main categories,
residential and industrial (of which the latter were more common), naming a
profusion of suburban types: "rich and poor suburbs," "planned and unplanned suburbs," "resort suburbs," "exclusive American industrial suburbs,"
"old people's suburbs," and "exclusive suburbs of the very rich" as well as
"a fringe of unwilling suburbs where the city started to expand but failed."
After World War I, Douglass pointed out, a "veritable suburban hegira of
the very poor" had produced a host of "foreign industrial suburbs," "Negro
suburbs," residential suburbs of "poorly paid workers," and sundry metropolitan "mill villages," which he declared "the characteristic suburbs of the
Piedmont region."[3]

Other witnesses disclosed similar variety. In a survey of Flint, Michigan,
Walter Firey described what he believed was a "typical" suburban landscape
comprised of "platted suburbs, small acreages, larger part-time farms and
trailer camps." Even Ernest Burgess, the University of Chicago sociologist

Fig. 1.3 *Steel Plant and Workers' Houses, Birmingham, Alabama.*
Marion Post Wolcott, 1939. Suburban factories were the economic anchor for
thousands of early suburbanites. Even in the shadows of a mill, suburban workers
often cultivated the landscape, using domestic space in economically productive
ways as a means of insulation from the marketplace. (Courtesy of the Library of
Congress, Prints and Photographs Division, FSA/OWI Collection, LC-USF
34-051864-D DLC)

whose concentric zone theory became the dominant model for understanding
suburban history, openly admitted that suburbs in Chicago's "commuters'
zone" "range the entire gamut from an incorporated village run in the interests of crime and vice, such as Burnham, to Lake Forest, with its wealth, culture, and public spirit." Taken together, these sources attest that the vast and
largely forgotten suburbia captured on film at the end of the depression was
not an artifact of the economic catastrophe, the war boom, or artistic license
but was a central feature of North American urban history.[4]

Only recently have scholars begun to recover and reaffirm this view. In a
book and a series of important articles, geographer Richard Harris has demonstrated that suburbanization by blue-collar workers was widespread in the
United States and Canada.[5] Using large census samples dating to 1850, political scientist Todd Gardner confirms that patterns of high- and low-status
residence in the urban United States correlated more closely with metropoli-

tan size than with location in a city or suburb. "As late as 1940," Gardner writes, "the suburbs were generally of lower status than central cities in all but the most populous metropolitan areas."[6] Even in a city like Chicago, where blue-collar suburbanites were the minority, the families of freight handlers, tool makers, and stackers of wheat—not to mention steelworkers, railroad laborers, and domestic servants—lived in modest suburbs ranging from Chicago Heights, Blue Island, Maywood, and Melrose Park to parts of Evanston, Glencoe, and North Chicago. Ethnic suburbanites, too, were numerous: Poles in Cicero and Posen, Czechs in Berwyn, Italians in Stone Park, Jews in Skokie, and African Americans in Robbins, Evanston, Phoenix, and East Chicago Heights.[7]

As these examples confirm, African Americans indeed lived in suburbs before World War II. By 1940 a million and a half lived in areas defined by the U.S. Census as suburban, which included "thickly settled" districts adjacent to cities of 50,000 people or more. Complicating the numbers was the Census Bureau's decision to draw metropolitan boundaries along county lines, which inflated the total in the South. Many of the region's 1 million black "suburbanites" were farmers whose numbers were actually declining due to out-migration and urban displacement. Even so, there were hundreds of thousands of African Americans in settled residential areas outside southern cities where they held urban jobs much as their white counterparts. Outside the South, matters are simpler. In the North and West, a wave of black suburbanization coincided with the Great Migration of the 1910s and 1920s. Between 1910 and 1940, the number of black suburbanites in the northern and western states grew by 285,000, which represented approximately 15 percent of black population growth in metropolitan areas of these regions. By 1940 nearly 500,000 African Americans lived in suburban areas outside the South. Blacks constituted less than 5 percent of the total U.S. suburban population, but as many as one in five African Americans living in metropolitan areas resided in the suburbs.[8]

Working-Class Suburbs

In contrast to the stereotype of suburbs as bedrooms for the white middle class, African American suburbs before 1940 were predominantly blue-collar communities in which residents often worked as well as lived. On average, suburbanites had less education and lower incomes than African Americans in central cities, and a higher proportion worked in low-skilled jobs. Most

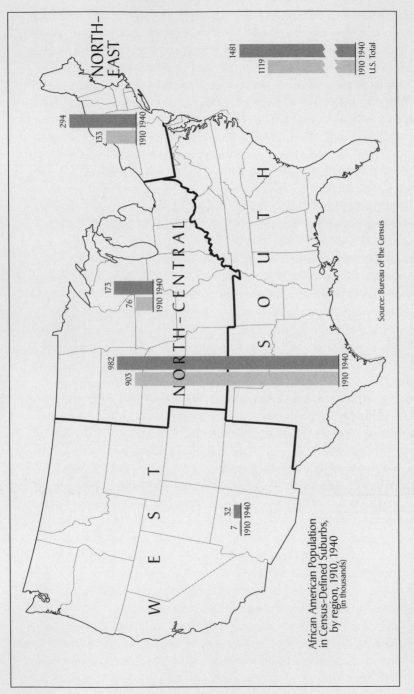

NORTH-
EAST

294 | 133
1910 1940

173 | 76
1910 1940

982 | 903
1910 1940

32 | 7
1910 1940

NORTH-CENTRAL

S O U T H

W E S T

1481 | 1119
1910 1940
U.S. Total

African American Population
in Census-Defined Suburbs,
by region, 1910, 1940
(in thousands)

Source: Bureau of the Census

Fig. 1.4   Suburban African Americans, by Region, 1910 and 1940. (Map by Harry D. Johnson)

black suburbs were also visually unlike middle-class white suburbs, occupying cheap, often nuisance-prone land. Many were geographically isolated, cut off by railroad tracks or other physical barriers, reflecting in almost every case a history of black struggle to acquire and hold space. Suburban housing ranged from tenements filtered down from European immigrants to "small, cheaply constructed cottages" and owner-built "shacks" as well as commodious bungalows contracted for upwardly mobile families.[9] Many black suburbs also lacked basic infrastructure: paved streets, sewers, gas, electricity, or city water. Surveying a class of southern suburbs in 1930, historian Carter G. Woodson noted that "in most of them there are only a few comfortable homes, a small number of stores, a church or two, a school, and a post office. The population is not rich enough to afford taxes to lay out the place properly, pave the streets, and provide proper drainage and sanitation."[10] In many cases, poor services reflected the neglect of white officials; in others, residents resisted improvements as a way to cut costs, prioritizing homes they could afford over services they could not. In contrast to the well-groomed suburbs of the white middle class, most early black suburbs were unplanned, unregulated, and unpretentious working-class communities.

The Landscape of Black Suburbia: The South

A review of black suburbia logically begins in the South, where for almost a century after the Civil War, the great majority of African Americans lived. Though most southern blacks in the early twentieth century were farmers who lived in rural areas, the region was home to important urban African American communities from the mid-nineteenth century forward. Metropolitan migration accelerated after the turn of the century, so that by 1920 a quarter of southern blacks lived in urban places. In larger cities, such as New Orleans, Birmingham, Memphis, Houston, and Atlanta, African Americans constituted between 25 and 40 percent of the population. African Americans labored on the docks and in the rail yards and small factories that brought trade to the region. They worked on the street crews and construction teams that built its infrastructure, they provided services to businesses and private citizens, and they lived in every section of the urban South.[11]

Black residential dispersal was characteristic of southern cities. Before the end of slavery and long before the extension of utilities or public transportation, free black families and urban slaves inhabited the edges of town, where they were removed from daily surveillance by whites but close enough to town to hold urban jobs.[12] Many settled in rustic "urban clusters" on the sub-urban frontier, occupying marginal, thus inexpensive, land in rail corridors, river bottoms, or simply out "in the piney woods."[13] According to Charles Knight, who explored the racial geography of urban Virginia in the 1920s, "a stranger with a topographical map of the city could, by tracing the ravines and steep slopes, locate a large number, perhaps a majority of the Negro residents within the corporate limits."[14] Knight's observation derived from Lynchburg, but his analogy captured the state of affairs in cities and suburbs across the South.

After emancipation, the number and variety of suburban black settlements multiplied. As migration swelled urban communities, developers subdivided peripheral land, selling lots to African Americans, usually in places where blacks had established a foothold. The Biddleville section of Charlotte, North Carolina, illustrates the accumulative nature of African American suburban settlement in the postbellum South. At the end of the Civil War, northern mis-sionaries established the Biddle school for freedmen and freedwomen on the northwestern edge of the city. In 1871 the school's first president bought fifty-five acres of adjacent property and sold building lots to African Americans. Displaced plantation laborers and prewar residents of Charlotte bought land, building small frame houses of various designs. By 1890 Biddleville was home to about two hundred black adults, several churches, a black-owned grocery store, and a small cemetery. Although a few residents worked on nearby farms, most walked the two miles to Charlotte for work each day, making the com-munity a modest black commuter suburb.[15]

Patterns were similar elsewhere. Landowners opened new allotments bordering a nucleus of black settlement—a school, workplace, or cluster of old plantation housing—marketing them explicitly to black purchasers. In Lexington, Kentucky, African Americans settled in a dozen clusters through-out the city before 1890, several of which had evolved as subdivisions on the urban fringe. Black families in Durham, North Carolina, and Atlanta, Georgia, lived in half a dozen settlements on the cities' edges, and Charlotte's Biddleville was one of at least five outlying black neighborhoods that ringed that city. The legacy of these developments was apparent decades later. As sociologist Charles S. Johnson reported in the 1940s, in smaller cities and towns, "practically all the Negro neighborhoods . . . are located at the edge of town," where "there are usually no white areas beyond them."[16] Small or large, by the turn of the century, most southern cities had a variety of black "urban clusters," "rim villages," or "newtowns" scattered among white neigh-borhoods, farms, and millworks on the margins of town.[17]

As southern cities grew, many such communities were absorbed into the central city, where they contributed to a checkerboard pattern of white and black neighborhoods.[18] Others, Carter Woodson observed, remained "natural suburbs settled by Negroes who transact practically all of their business in the cities."[19] Residents worked in the homes of neighboring whites or in outlying factories or farms; others walked to town for jobs, shopping, and social life. Baseball giant Hank Aaron recalled his childhood in the early 1940s in Toulminville, Alabama, near Mobile in details that would have equally well described life in the fringe settlements earlier in the century:

> There were only two or three houses on Edwards Street when we moved there [in 1942]. It was wide open, with a dairy on the corner and country things on every side of us—cows, chickens, hogs, cornfields, sugarcane, watermelon patches, pecan groves, and blackberry thickets. The streets were just mudholes that cars were always getting stuck in. We took our water from a well, and for heating and cooking we brought in whatever wood we could find. Sometimes we'd strip it off an old abandoned farmhouse. There were no lights in our house—not even windows. A kerosene lamp was all we needed. The bathroom was an outhouse in the backyard.[20]

While they were not agricultural communities, these places retained, in Woodson's words, a "decidedly rural" flavor.[21] Families supplemented incomes with gardens and domestic livestock. Aaron's father worked in a shipyard, but his son remembered "almost never" eating "anything that was store-bought. . . . We tried to keep a hog in the backyard to kill every year, and everything else came from the garden." Poverty, too, was seldom distant. During periods of his father's unemployment, Aaron recalled, "we were practically vegetarians before we ever heard of the word."[22] As in Toulminville, trees and underbrush often separated houses in these areas. Since city officials rarely provided adequate services, streets were unpaved, and the limits of black neighborhoods were easily recognizable by "where the sidewalk ends."[23] As in contemporary cities of Latin America, Africa, and Asia, the urban poor in the late-nineteenth and early-twentieth-century South were as likely to live on the outskirts of town as in its center.

The Landscape of Black Suburbia: The North and West

In contrast to the checkerboard pattern of neighborhoods that had emerged in the urban South by the early twentieth century, comparatively few African

Americans lived on the fringes of northern or western cities before World War I. Most of those who did lived in "older, densely settled suburbs" linked to decentralizing employment in manufacturing or domestic service.[24] A handful held older tenure in semi-rural communities that traced their roots to the nineteenth-century struggle to end slavery.[25] Others were not independent householders at all, but lived in the homes of white employers. For the most part, the urban fringe was white territory. Not until the Great Migration did large numbers of African Americans begin moving to suburbs outside the South.

Within this continental expanse, however, historical differences shaped regional diversity. In the whole region west of Nebraska, there were just 7,000 black suburbanites in 1910, fewer than in a midsize border city such as Cincinnati. Forty percent lived in the Los Angeles and San Francisco areas. Fully 10 percent resided in Pasadena, California, with its "Millionaires' Row" and a compact neighborhood of black and other nonwhite service workers nearby.[26] Outside Pasadena and a few other suburbs, though, the West played little role in the story of black suburbanization before World War II.

Circumstances differed somewhat in the Midwest and Northeast. In the area stretching from Kansas City to Boston, there were slightly more than 200,000 black suburbanites in 1910. Two general patterns prevailed, reflecting the history of African Americans in different parts of this region.[27] Almost half of northern suburbanites, 93,000 people, lived in a 200-mile arc sweeping from Philadelphia to the tip of Long Island. This section of the Mid-Atlantic seaboard offered the closest parallels with the southern and border states. The legacy of slaveholding and abolitionist activity combined with comparatively strong migration to the area before World War I laid the basis for a large number of historic black communities.[28] Throughout most of the remaining northern states, black settlements were fewer and farther between. Important black communities had developed during the nineteenth century in cities such as Cincinnati, Detroit, and Chicago, but suburban residences were confined to a relative few places.

Metropolitan Philadelphia exemplifies the Mid-Atlantic pattern. A 1915 survey of "living conditions among colored people in towns in the outer part of Philadelphia and in other suburbs" documented African American communities in forty-one suburbs within a twenty-five mile radius of city hall. These included the "thickly settled" black community of 5,000 people in Chester on the Delaware River as well as hamlets of a dozen or more families in Haddonfield, Merchantville, and Willow Grove Heights, where African Americans "buy the lots and erect the houses themselves."[29] It included enclaves of black service workers in tony suburbs such as Darby and Ardmore, neighborhoods of steelworkers near the mills at Manayunk and Coatesville, and the independent black municipality of Lawnside, New Jersey, established by freed slaves before the Civil War.

As elsewhere in the country, racial restrictions governed black settlement in Philadelphia's suburbs. In Swarthmore it was "practically impossible [for blacks] . . . to rent or buy, except in one section where one land owner rents and sells to colored people. Many colored people who work in Swarthmore live in Morton and commute every day." Meanwhile, "in Rutledge, the town next to Morton, are found many colored servants, but none are permitted to reside in this town." In most cases, black families lived in marginal or isolated enclaves "just outside," "adjoining," or "one mile out" from town, and the names that locals used to denote black settlements—"Hammer Hollow" and "Quiggley's Hill" in Devon, "up on the hill" in Berwyn and Ambler— reflected the social as well as physical distance that separated these communities from the remainder of town.[30] By the 1960s, sociologists Leonard Blumberg and Michael Lalli reported, the legacy of early suburban settlement was visible in more than sixty "little ghettoes" in the suburbs that

> are now, or were in the recognizable past, areas of marginal location with respect to residential development. . . . Often they were cut off by railroad tracks, swamps, or highways. In one case, a two-block long stone wall was built reputedly to mark "the line." . . . They are permitted locations for a negatively valued population.[31]

Over time, similar devaluations of African American residential areas created suburban landscapes branded physically with the emblems of racial inequality.

Typical of the remaining northern states was Chicago. In 1910 the city was home to 44,000 African Americans, the third largest black population outside the South after New York and Philadelphia. Just 5,000 blacks lived in the surrounding metropolitan ring, congregating in a small number of suburbs where they found jobs as well as homes. One-fifth lived in Evanston, a wealthy commuter suburb north of the city that employed a large number of domestic service workers. Another fifth lived in Harvey, Aurora, and Joliet, three industrial satellites where steel and railroad employment had attracted communities of several hundred people. As many as 10 percent resided as live-in servants in white homes, and most of the rest lived in independent households scattered among half a dozen other suburbs. In contrast to the segregated

Fig. 1.5 *House in Negro Section, Detroit, Michigan.* John Vachon, 1941.
Sharp physical barriers ringed most early black suburbs, giving physical semblance
to the color line. A white developer built the wall behind this home at the insistence
of Federal Housing Administration officials before they would insure an adjacent
subdivision. A park, public land, arterial roads, demapped streets, and an industrial
strip formed the remaining borders of the black Eight-Mile-Wyoming neighborhood, which straddled the Detroit city limits. Tangible features such as these were
the handwriting of racial distinction in the suburban landscape. (Courtesy of the
Library of Congress, Prints and Photographs Division, FSA/OWI Collection,
LC-USF 34-063747-D DLC)

communities that would emerge by midcentury, most of Chicago's black suburbanites shared neighborhoods with working-class whites—mostly European immigrants—but their concentration in low-rent areas laid the foundation for racially segregated communities that would emerge by the outset
of World War II.[32]

The crucial event in this history was the acceleration of black migration
after 1915. Much as outlying settlements in the South had seen repeated addition since the Reconstruction era, small, isolated suburban communities
formed the groundwork for expanding suburban populations in the decades
that followed. Despite regional variation, most new suburbanites settled in

four types of suburbs, loosely defined by the dominant sources of local employment, residents' socioeconomic status, and their mode of access to land and housing. Suburban industrial towns, domestic service enclaves in affluent suburbs, and rustic, unplanned subdivisions were the most common. In the South and border regions, too, a small number of upwardly mobile families found space in tidy bungalow suburbs, reflecting trends in the wider middle-class suburbia.

Industrial Suburbs

The largest number of Great Migration–era suburbanites gravitated to gritty industrial suburbs, especially those that were home to auto making, metal manufacture, railroads, and meatpacking, which were the four principal employers of black industrial labor before World War II. In the Chicago area, the black suburban population climbed from 5,000 to 25,000 between 1910 and 1940. By the later date, 30 percent of suburban blacks lived in six industrial satellites: Waukegan, Aurora, Maywood, Joliet, Harvey, and Chicago Heights, each of which was reliant on the making or shaping of steel. In the Detroit area, more than 10,000 African Americans lived in five automobile and steel suburbs, and they made up almost 40 percent of the black suburban population. In metropolitan Pittsburgh, where smoke-belching mills anchored a dozen satellite steel towns, 45 percent of African Americans lived outside the central city.[33]

This blueprint also pertained in the South, where it was accentuated by the older dispersal of black residential areas. Depression-era surveys revealed dozens of outlying African American neighborhoods "close to occupants' source of employment," including roundhouses, rail yards, fertilizer factories, dry docks, steel mills, slaughterhouses, cotton compresses, and sundry other "industrial plants."[34] In the region's most industrialized city, Birmingham, Alabama, African Americans lived in "small islands scattered all over the city" but especially in the vicinity of local mills and mines.[35] In Titusville, Ensley, and North Birmingham, black workers lived hard by the mills of the Tennessee Coal, Iron and Railroad Company and the American Cast Iron Pipe Company. On the south side, African Americans lived in mining hamlets, such as Oxford and Rosedale, and to the southwest, the steel mills and coal mines of Bessemer attracted thousands of families, making it home to one of the largest black suburban communities in the South. By 1940 African Americans lived in a dozen "long established communities and industrial suburbs" across the metropolitan area.[36] In these places, as in industrial cities across the Northeast and Midwest, decentralized manufacturing anchored a widespread black suburban landscape prior to World War II.[37]

Underlying this pattern was the decentralization of American manufacturing after the turn of the century. Responding to growing markets, new methods of mass production, and a desire for greater control over labor and local government, industry shifted production to new factories at the outer edge of U.S. urban areas.[38] "Huge industrial plants are uprooting themselves bodily from the cities," wrote economist Graham Taylor in 1915. "With households, small stores, saloons, lodges, churches, schools clinging to them like living tendrils, they set themselves down ten miles away in the open."[39] The result was a boom in industrial suburbs wedded to the central city through urban "switching yards and belt lines," dependent on metropolitan markets for goods, labor, and services and linked to the city as satellites in relation to an urban center of gravity.[40]

Living conditions in what Taylor called the "civic by-products of industrialism" depended on their size, age, and extent of development by the time African Americans began migrating in large numbers.[41] In the oldest, black families fared poorly, jostling for space with destitute European immigrants in disadvantageously located neighborhoods. Along the rail sidings, steep hills, hollows, or riverbanks adjacent to the mills, they suffered not only from "old houses in poor condition" but from "smoke nuisance," "fumes," and a constant din of trucks, trains, and industrial machinery.[42] In Chester, Pennsylvania, the second oldest European settlement in the Keystone State, hundreds of families occupied "antiquated" row houses and century-old rear tenements along the Delaware River. In Elizabeth, New Jersey, recent migrants squeezed into the aging port district, where sociologist Ira De A. Reid found scores of people living in structures that were "unfit for human habitation."[43]

Newer and smaller suburbs varied more widely. In the steel towns of the Monongahela River Valley near Pittsburgh, African Americans eked out a mean living in the mills, a fact reflected in stifling population densities, high rents, and low rates of home ownership — though even in these places, a minority of families escaped the riverside wards, buying tidy homes on the hillsides and forest fringes above town.[44] In other factory suburbs, where neighborhoods were not limited by the topography of a river valley or built to bursting with the tenements of earlier generations, housing quality and rates of home ownership were usually higher, and small-town amenities persisted. In Maywood, Joliet, and Harvey, Illinois; East Chicago, Indiana; Fairfield, Alabama; Highland Park and River Rouge, Michigan; Berkeley, California;

and Plainfield and Rahway, New Jersey, African Americans sank roots in relatively new neighborhoods, and many found opportunities to purchase homes of their own. Rates of home ownership in these suburbs in 1940 ranged from a low of 17 percent in East Chicago to a high of 52 percent in Berkeley.[45]

To be sure, few industrial suburbs exhibited the "suburban style" that historian Robert Fishman described as "the pattern of tree-shaded streets, broad open lawns, substantial houses set back from the sidewalks . . . prosperous family life and union with nature."[46] Instead, many resembled aging city neighborhoods more than middle-class suburbs. Nonetheless, during the early twentieth century, these places reflected the main processes of American suburbanization: the decentralization of homes, families, and jobs away from an urban core. To the families who worked and lived in them, they offered advantages easily obscured by the broken windows and vacant mills that characterized them at the century's end; among these were the possibility of steady work and wages impossible in the rural South. As in central cities, work at the heart of the industrial economy linked agricultural migrants with the progress of the nation and provided incomes that began their integration into a growing consumer society. Further, taxes on industrial property supported comparatively high levels of service, schooling, and teacher salaries. Finally, the scale of many industrial suburbs preserved an atmosphere of neighborly churches and small-town social life that many had left behind in the South.

Domestic Service Employment Suburbs

These "little giant[s] of industry" were not the only suburbs to attract black families before World War II.[47] By the 1910s chic residential suburbs prospered along the rail and trolley lines leading from virtually every American city. Chicago's North Shore, Philadelphia's Main Line, and New Jersey's Watchung Mountains, not to mention Atlanta's Druid Hills, Baltimore's Roland Park, or the Park Cities north of Dallas, were but a few precincts in a landscape synonymous with luxury and economic privilege. Nonetheless, many elite suburbs were remarkably heterogeneous in comparison with the automobile suburbs of a later era.[48] Dependence on rail commuting and the scarcity of alternative transportation limited the flow of goods, services, and labor to many such places. As a result, suburbs known for wealthy commuters often housed bustling communities of shopkeepers, mechanics, industrial workers, and the servants who made it possible to live comfortably in the palatial homes that made these places famous. Like the auto and steel suburbs

Fig. 1.6   Separated by U.S. Highway 1 from the opulent neighborhoods where many of them worked as domestics, African Americans in Coral Gables, Florida, and the adjoining section of Coconut Grove occupied shotgun houses and other modest frame dwellings, which were typical of black neighborhoods in the urban South. Street paving and utilities were installed much later. (Courtesy of John Archer, 2000)

that ringed Detroit, Chicago, and Pittsburgh, moneyed commuter suburbs — many of the nation's wealthiest and best-known addresses — represented both home and workplace for thousands of low-paid workers and their families.[49]

As the Great Migration proceeded, African Americans made up a growing number of these workers. Neighborhoods of black service workers were ubiquitous in the South; as an observer of Richmond, Virginia, noted in the 1930s, "every high grade white section has a Negro settlement nearby."[50] In other parts of the country, "typical early affluent suburbs," such as Pasadena and Evanston; Montclair, New Jersey; and New Rochelle, New York, housed black communities that were among the largest in these states, and African Americans often constituted a larger percentage of the population than in the cities that they surrounded.[51] The nation's premier suburban region, Westchester County, New York, was home to 23,000 African Americans by 1930.[52]

The geography of settlement in affluent suburbs reflected the inequality inherent to domestic service as well as the distinctive social relationships it engendered. Elites monopolized the most attractive sections of town, their wide lawns and spacious homes reflecting their own suburban ideology. Domestic workers settled in cheaper sections nearby, places undesirable to middle-class whites and as yet unregulated by public or private land-use restrictions.[53] Black precincts in Westchester County, New York, exemplified the residential geography of domestic service: New Deal–era surveys located African American neighborhoods in "low land," "hollows," "hillsides," and pockets of "old houses cut into small units for Negro use" along the railroad tracks.[54] When it rained, the water found its way to the places where black people lived. In similar fashion, African American communities grew in "main line" suburbs from Long Island to Los Angeles.

Unplanned Subdivisions – make shift suburbs.

In addition to settling in suburbs where they worked, thousands of African American migrants moved to strictly residential suburbs that promised primitive services, semi-rural surroundings, and the opportunity to own a home. In 1932 a panel of experts on "Negro Housing" acknowledged the existence of a whole class of residential neighborhoods in "outlying territories where Negroes are able to buy cheap land and build for themselves homes from whatever materials they can find, often a room or two at a time." Describing a subdivision near Houston, the committee wrote, "There is another class of people buying out six or eight miles from town. There is an acreage division out there which they sell in 1-acre tracts, and a good many people have gone out there. . . . The type of people who buy have their work in town and do not make enough to own and run a car, but they hear the cheap prices quoted and jump at it. . . . It is just land out in the country" without gas, water, or paved streets.[55]

As the Great Migration unfolded, inexpensive allotments sprang up on the outskirts of cities across the country. "In every city," sociologist T. J. Woofter reported in 1928, "small outlying settlements are growing up where land is cheaper, and where Negroes can afford small houses and use street cars or automobiles to reach their working places."[56] Reflecting the operation of a low-cost housing market that was largely eradicated after World War II, most such places developed in unincorporated or unregulated sections of the metropolis where lot owners could build houses and use property with a

minimum of restrictions. By 1940 nearly every city that attracted a stream
of black migrants counted at least one such community among its suburbs.
Cities such as Cleveland, Detroit, and Philadelphia gave birth to a half dozen
or more, but even small cities like Columbus, Ohio (population 306,000),
had as many as four peripheral subdivisions where working-class black families bought land and built homes during this period. Youngstown, Ohio
(population, 211,000), had two.[57]

In many such subdivisions, families accumulated "sweat equity" by building their own houses. An owner-builder near Nashville described the process:

> I had a little Christmas savings and we had bought up some good
> lumber, so I decided to make a little start. I just meant to put up two
> little rooms and a shed on the back of the lot and then build the house
> I wanted in the front as I got the money. I went to a lumber yard and
> outlined everything to them and told them as soon as I got the Christ-
> mas savings in November I would pay them if they would let me have
> the lumber at that time. I got the lumber, and the man I got to frame it
> up for me said since I had so much lumber it would be cheaper to just
> build the kind of house I wanted at once, so we started. After I framed
> it up, the money ran out and I had to let it stand for five or six months
> before I could get a top on it. When I was working on the house I
> had a regular job, and I would get up at four o'clock in the morning
> and work on it until seven, then go home to breakfast and to work; I
> would come from work and come right back over here and work until
> dark. . . . People would pass by and wonder why I did not finish the
> house; I thought that was a silly thing for them to ask because they
> ought to have known that if I had had the money I would have finished
> it . . . but I just kept going, and as soon as I would get a little ahead I
> would get something else to put on it and work a little more.[58]

Over time, residents built houses, churches, and small stores in much the
same fashion. Local authorities usually provided schools but little else; utilities arrived years later. In fact, some early suburbanites opposed improvements in order to avoid paying for them. Despite inauspicious beginnings,
many of these places developed into lasting black communities, offering opportunity to tens of thousands of African Americans to purchase homes of
their own in a quiet place removed from the central city.[59]

Fig. 1.7   *New Houses Going Up on the Outskirts of Detroit, Michigan.*
John Vachon, 1941. Owner building was a common practice among working-class
Americans in the early twentieth century. Photographer John Vachon captured two
white men building a home in a low-cost subdivision near Detroit in the early
1940s. The fruits of similar activity are visible in the background. (Courtesy of
the Library of Congress, Prints and Photographs Division, FSA/OWI Collection,
LC-USF34-063690)

Bungalow Suburbs   [handwritten: sponsored/industrial make shift suburbs]

In addition to these distinctly blue-collar suburbs, real estate developers also
opened a number of well-groomed residential subdivisions for the nation's
diminutive black middle class. Most arose in the South, where proportionally
large black populations and the historic dispersal of black residences facilitated
access to suburban real estate.[60] Many adjoined black colleges, which were
themselves often located on the outskirts of town, ensuring an aura of middle-
class respectability as well as a ready market among the local faculty and staff.
[handwritten: think Dillard on Xavier] Some grew inside the city limits or in sections later annexed to the city, but almost all were situated at the outer edges of urban development at the time of
their construction. In the developing jim crow society of the prewar South,

Fig. 1.8   The Fountain Heights subdivision opened in the late 1930s on the western edge of Atlanta near Atlanta University. Developed by a consortium of black businessmen, it attracted members of the black middle class. The subdivision included many features associated with bungalow suburbs of the era, such as ample lots and setbacks, modern utilities, a distinctive street layout, and ornamental public space. (Photograph by Andrew Wiese, 1997)

they represented a step on the road to racially separate cities from core to periphery.[61]

In Richmond, Virginia, the University Realty Company, a black-owned concern, opened Frederick Douglass Court for middle- and upper-income African Americans in the mid-1920s. Located at the edge of town near Virginia Union University "within easy walking distance of a street car line," the sixteen-acre development offered 30-by-135-foot building lots for $675 to $825. Buyers could elect to hire their own contractor or pay the developer to build a home for them. The company offered three models ranging from a six-room two-story frame house without central heat to a fully equipped six-room stucco house with built-in refrigerator, sun parlor, and front porch. An early photograph of the development shows a row of two-story houses set back neatly from the street with a small strip of grass and a short sidewalk to the front steps.[62]

In Charlotte, a white entrepreneur, W. S. Alexander, developed a "beautiful Negro suburb" called Washington Heights in 1913. Alexander advertised the development as a suburb of "tone and character" with "beautiful streets convenient to churches and schools." Within a decade, many of the city's black elite had purchased ample 50-by-150-foot lots and built, according to historian Thomas Hanchett, "wooden one-story cottages trimmed in simple but fashionable bungalow style."[63]

Like Douglass Court, Washington Heights was located at the end of a trolley line adjacent to a black college (Johnson C. Smith University) in a section of town attractive to educated and professional blacks. Mamie Garvin Fields, who moved to a "perfect honeymoon house" in the area in 1914, recalled the atmosphere of upward mobility that pervaded the neighborhood. Its "progressive" residents "believed in education and . . . believed in buying property. Especially," she said, "they wanted to own their own homes."[64] As newlyweds, the Fields rented their first house from a local professor who built it for income, but its amenities were characteristic of the nation's booming middle-class suburbs. "Set back from the street," Fields remembered, "it had a good-sized yard in front and a planted path leading up to the door, which was between two windows with flower boxes. Very romantic, like a picture out of a magazine." Inside, the house had "a parlor, dining room, kitchen and two bedrooms, all on one floor — just enough for a young couple and any guest we wanted to have."[65] The neighborhood matched middle-class white suburbia in its voluntaristic atmosphere as well. Residents established a local neighborhood association to advocate for civic improvements. Developers also built a collection of nearby stores that served as a neighborhood center.[66] Inside the city limits or out, such places reflected a continent-wide phenomenon of residential expansion into the undeveloped fringe through the subdivision of bare land and the construction of new single-family housing. Except for the race of the buyers, there was little to distinguish them from hundreds of suburban subdivisions constructed for middle-class whites before the Great Depression.

Conclusion

Before World War II, black suburbia encompassed a conglomeration of neighborhoods, hamlets, and municipalities comprising more than a million people. With the exception of the southern streetcar suburbs, most black suburbanites were working-class people, restricted by race to low-paying work in industry, personal service, and outdoor labor. The majority were southerners, migrants who had fled or forsaken the terrain of their childhood and whose social position and cultural inclinations had brought them together in new places.

But were these places suburbs? From the perspective of writers who have defined suburbs according to the standards of the white middle class and elite, the answer has often been "no." I take a different view. Despite the neat logic of a definition rooted in class and race, this description leaves too much at the urban margins unexplored. Unwittingly or not, it also reinforces the very biases that underlay the growth of restrictive suburbs to begin with. In the twentieth-century United States, the idea of suburbs as white and middle- or upper-class space, places where a "better" class of people lived, played an important part in sustaining the spatial advantages that adhere to these places still. Rather than focusing on this limited set of suburbs, I am interested in the many ways that metropolitan society and landscapes developed over time. In the last century, this history has been characterized by the decentralization of people and functions away from historic urban cores, a process that sociologist Ernest Burgess described in the 1920s as "the tendency [of cities] to overflow, and so to extend over wider areas, and to incorporate these areas into a larger communal life." It is this entire process that I refer to as suburbanization.[67] Strictly speaking, then, suburbs include the multiplicity of communities that this process produced. However, because of the importance of local governments in shaping space, as well as for the practical reason that the most readily available census data follow political boundaries, I use the term "suburb" in a more conventional sense to refer to incorporated and unincorporated places on the outskirts but outside the limits of a larger city. There are pitfalls to defining suburbs from the perspective of process more than place, of course; the almost impossible diversity of the areas such a definition encompasses is perhaps its most daunting. Nonetheless, the history of African American suburbanization suggests the merits of exploring the metropolitan past in a more comprehensive and inclusive way than before.

Regardless of race or class, African Americans participated in the process of urban decentralization in the early twentieth century, and they contributed to a landscape that was diverse in population, economic function, and physical appearance. The communities they built reflected the outlines of older racial geographies as well as the changing location of employment, the availability of land, and shifting race relations. Just as apparent, the places they made were intentional communities, reflecting the agency of men and women who believed that they could make better lives on the outskirts of the city than in its center. Distinctive insofar as they diverged from white and middle-class norms, they were very much a part of the suburban trend that produced the race- and class-stratified metropolitan world in which Americans still lived almost a century later.

Chapter 2

"Who Set You Flowin'?"

The Great Migration, Race, and Work in the Suburbs

I'm goin' to Detroit, get myself a good job.
Tried to stay around here with the starvation mob.
I'm going to get me a job up there in Mr. Ford's place,
Stop these eatless days from starin' me in the face.

> —blues lyric (1920s)[1]

Oh, my Lord, how was I going to live if I didn't work?

> —Laura Scantleberry, retired domestic worker, New Rochelle, New York (1980)[2]

MAY 21, 1920, was a date that Mallie Robinson would remember for the rest of her life. From a railway platform in Cairo, Georgia, she and her five children boarded a train bound for California. The trip was no small step for a woman raised on a cotton plantation who disliked even going into town, but Robinson had few options. Her husband had run off the summer before. The plantation landlord blamed her for the breach of contract and evicted her, which in the race- and gender-stratified agricultural economy of the region could have spelled disaster. Robinson turned to her kinfolk for help. Her half-brother Burton had moved to California during World War I, finding work as a gardener in Pasadena. A visit home convinced Mallie that her future lay there. "If you want to get closer to heaven," Burton told his Georgia kin, "visit California."[3] When he left, a group of relatives began laying plans to join him. When they had saved enough money for tickets, the Robinsons, Mallie's sister Cora Wade and her husband Sam and their children, a brother, and several others — thirteen people in all — set out for the Golden State.[4]

With its orange groves, translucent skies, and enveloping views of the San Gabriel Mountains, Pasadena was "the most beautiful sight of my whole life," Robinson wrote.[5] Less obvious to the new arrival was the "vast economic disparity and racial segregation" intrinsic to the city.[6] Pasadena was the richest municipality in the United States in 1920, but it was also home to a growing army of minority service workers — Mexicans, Japanese, and African Americans — who harvested its oranges, tended its rose gardens, polished its silver, and otherwise maintained the leisurely lifestyles of its upper crust.[7]

Like many new arrivals, the Robinsons spent their first weeks with kin; Burton's three-room flat near the railroad tracks at the heart of Pasadena's growing black community was their first shelter. After Mallie and her brother-in-law, Sam Wade, found work, the group secured larger quarters, a bungalow with a yard on Glorietta Street in a mostly black section on the northwest side. Like Mallie's job as a domestic, their residential options reflected the earmark of race on local society. As the number of migrants grew, whites restricted them to a physically demarcated band of settlement west of downtown. "North Fair Oaks [Avenue], that was the dividing line between blacks and whites," Robinson's daughter Willa Mae remembered. "We lived over there on the black side . . . and we couldn't even cross to this side, the white side."[8] Within these limits, the Robinsons set down roots. The older children enrolled in school. Mallie and Sam worked long hours, scrimping to save their earnings, while Cora watched the youngest children. Eventually, the family pooled its money, buying an unpretentious frame house on Pepper Street a few blocks away where the Robinson children grew to adulthood, and the youngest of them, Jackie, became the man who would break the color line in baseball.

Mallie Robinson's migration narrative illustrates the interplay between human agency and social structures that marks the history of African American migrations. Economic conditions gave momentum to her journey, impelling her flight from declining southern agriculture and attracting her to Pasadena, a booming suburb of Los Angeles. In both regions, racial proscriptions structured the labor market, limiting the type of work available to her as a black female: sharecropper in Georgia, maid in Pasadena. Racism limited where she could live, shop, seek medical help, or send her children to school. Yet within these constraints, her journey reflected individual circumstance,

Fig. 2.1   Claypool residence, Pasadena, California, ca. 1910. Home to
Los Angeles commuters and wealthy migrants from colder climes, Pasadena's
topography reinforced its race and class divisions. From their veranda, the Claypool
family enjoyed a view of the San Gabriel Mountains as well as the neighborhoods
where the suburb's large service workforce lived. (Courtesy of the Archives at the
Pasadena Museum of History)

perception, and choice: a dying marriage, the certainty that "her four boys
and one girl would never rise above their parents' status in the South," and the
conviction that she would have to make it on her own — for she had resolved
that no man would again raise a hand to her children.[9] Likewise, her decision
reflected the overriding importance of kinship in southern black life and the
discrete geography that her own social network had assumed. She received information and assistance from her half-brother. Various family members made
the trip west together, sharing housekeeping and resources until they could
get on their feet. Once in Pasadena, they moved up the housing ladder from
an apartment to a comfortable bungalow with a yard. However much their
decisions were shaped by forces beyond their control, black southerners like
Mallie Robinson made the most of limited choice, moving through the world
around them and transforming both themselves and the places where they
set down.

As a migration story, Robinson's tale also reveals the juncture between suburbanization and the mass movement known as the Great Migration. During the 1910s and 1920s, more than a million African Americans left the South, while thousands of others relocated to urban areas within the region. Of those who quit the South, as many as one in six settled in suburbs, as did many who stayed behind.[10] Like other migrants, most of the new suburbanites were working-class people who moved "direct from the South."[11] Raised in the countryside and small towns of the region—places like Live Oak, Florida; Bell Haven, North Carolina; Perry County, Alabama; Magnolia, Arkansas; and Kosciusko, Mississippi—they were sharecroppers, students, schoolteachers, and service workers, people from all walks of African American life. They relocated to metropolitan areas as members of extended families and communities bound by ties of affection and elements of a southern black culture characterized by a "helping ethic," the centrality of kinship, and the insatiable desire for economic independence.[12] Nascent suburbanites like the Robinsons formed an important but largely ignored component of the Great Migration.

The Great Migration

Historians generally regard 1916 as a turning point in African American history, the first year in a concentrated exodus from the rural South that would change the nation and the place of black people in it. Between 1916 and 1918, over 400,000 black men and women moved to urban areas outside the South, initiating more than a decade of intensive urban migration. Like most historical dates, 1916 was less a precise breakpoint than a shift in momentum and direction in an ongoing social process. Since the collapse of Reconstruction in the 1870s, African Americans had been a people in motion, seeking peripatetically to improve their lives. Movement from plantation to plantation, seasonal forays to lumber camps and sawmills, and a gradual shift toward urban areas marked southern black history of the late nineteenth century. Growing numbers, too, left the region altogether: more than 20,000 for Kansas in the 1870s, a larger number to Oklahoma in the 1890s, and a steady flow along the rail and steamship lines of the eastern seaboard. All in all, more than 220,000 African Americans left the South in the three decades before 1910, and the proportion in urban areas rose from approximately 20 to 27 percent.[13]

Driving these migrants were crippling social and economic conditions in the South: its plantation agriculture and the certainty of mass poverty that entailed plus the straitjacket of race, second-class citizenship with a lifetime guarantee. "The chance long looked for to move out" was World War I, which led to the suppression of European immigration and a spiraling demand for U.S.-made war materials.[14] As the tide of immigrant labor receded, large manufacturers sent agents south, enticing trainloads of workers to needy rail yards, munitions plants, and steel mills. Quickly, direct recruiting became unnecessary as "glowing accounts from the North" spread throughout the black South.[15] Race papers like the *Chicago Defender* and *Pittsburgh Chronicle* published editorials promoting the benefits of northern life, and migrants' own letters and visits home provided convincing evidence of how much better things were. What migrants found in metropolitan areas rarely matched their expectations, but the contrast with what they knew was spark enough to light a fire in the imagination of young men and women across the region.[16]

The people whose journeys took them to the suburbs moved for many of the same reasons as other migrants: higher-paying work, a less oppressive racial climate, the opportunity for self-improvement, or simply "general better conditions," the catch-all comparison between southern certainty and northern hope.[17] Sam Butler came to Evanston, Illinois, from Cokesbury, South Carolina, with his wife's cousin in 1922. "Many others were leaving the South then; work was scarce and the pay was lower," he recalled. "Those that left home . . . would come back visiting and tell how things were . . . in the North. So, naturally, we're going to go. So when I got a chance to come North, I came."[18] W. A. Wheeler, a chauffeur from Lafayette, Georgia, recounted a similar story:

> There were some boys that I worked with in Kenilworth [Illinois] who came here as butlers, and they came down for a funeral. . . . And they told me, "Boy, you staying here? Why in the hell don't you get out of here?" And so, . . . I decided I wanted to go. He says, "If you go, I'll see that you get a job." And I already knew they had good jobs. I got packed and I got in the car with one of them. . . . I wasn't married at that time. . . . So, I got in the car. I drove all night in this guy's car.[19]

For Butler and Wheeler, economic opportunities beckoned, but their journeys also represented acts of self-transformation. As Wheeler acknowledged, "In the South, you could get by as long as you stayed a boy . . . but I wanted to be a man for a long time."[20]

For Cora Watson, a schoolteacher who moved to Evanston from Greenwood, South Carolina, in 1914, it was her children's future that commanded her attention; the salient issue was education. "I had a lot of relatives in South Carolina," she said.

> Some of them went to New York, some went to Evanston. They came back to visit in South Carolina and told us how much better these places were. . . . White and colored could go to the same schools, they said. . . . I was grown, married and had children then. . . . I said if white and colored can go to the same school, that's for me. . . . I brought my two oldest children with me.[21]

Similar to the meaning that urban migrants attributed to integrated streetcars and black traffic officers, biracial schools served Watson as a symbol of opportunity for her children, the potential for personal mobility and the possibility that black people might be treated with dignity. Despite her relatively secure social position, these prospects were enough to change her life's course.

If common conditions set migrants in motion, ties of family and acquain-(family) tance provided bonds that made suburbs into specific destinations. Migrants' social networks served as conduits for information about jobs, housing, and local mores, providing crucial assistance in planning — what to bring, how much to save, pitfalls to avoid — and offering shelter for migrants when they arrived. Family ties also furnished expanded social contacts, emotional and financial support, and a familiar atmosphere in which a bit of home had gone before.[22]

John Gaskin's journey from Camden, South Carolina, to New Rochelle, New York, in the 1930s illustrates both the urge among young African Americans to leave the South as well as the logic of social networks that determined where they landed. Gaskin recalled:

> I was young, single, and leaving home for the first time and for good. I had relatives living in Boston, so I went to live with them. I met a couple of gentlemen from my home who I worked with in Boston for the summer, but they lived in New Rochelle. They asked me to come to New Rochelle. So I did because I didn't like Boston. . . . When I first came to New Rochelle, I was living with people from my home. Some of them had been classmates of mine. So it was like being at home because I knew them before.[23]

For Gaskin, the availability of paid employment allowed him to survive in New Rochelle, but it was his connection to friends and kinfolk that gave his journey its unique shape.

Southern social ties played a similar role in migration to the West. Like Mallie Robinson, who followed her brother's lead, Mrs. John Wright recalled that her parents had migrated from Georgia to Pasadena in stages after a friend of her father's returned home for a visit. The friend

> liked the place very much, and since my dad was a great friend of his, he told him, why not move out here and find out just what it was, because the privileges here were much better than they were in Georgia. So he thought he would take a chance. So he came out here first to look around to see whether he would like it or not, and he did, and he found a job and a place to stay, and so when he had enough money, he sent for the rest of the family.[24]

For these people, migration to northern and western suburbs reflected a calculation of unfamiliar but enticing opportunity weighed against the realities of the jim crow South. Their experience as black southerners shaped and gave momentum to their travels, and their journeys followed a framework rooted in networks of kith and kin that they had built in black communities across the region.

White Responses to the Great Migration

Despite their efforts to liberate themselves from racial and economic restrictions, African Americans were not free to settle in urban or suburban areas as they pleased. Instead, the Great Migration coincided with white efforts to restrict black mobility in social, economic, and spatial terms. In cities and suburbs alike, the arrival of black migrants provoked new initiatives in land-use planning, education, and public space designed to secure black inequality and white privilege. Racism restricted their occupations and opportunity for advancement; it governed the hours, conditions, and wages of their labors; it checked their use of public facilities; and it limited their ability to move in space, to shop, play, worship, and make homes.

Though black households had long been relegated to marginal places in the nation's metropolitan areas, the late nineteenth and early twentieth century represented a turning point in the history of race and the restriction of urban space. Before the 1890s, there had been few attempts to strictly segregate urban territory on racial lines. Nonetheless, concurrent with southern white efforts to enact comprehensive restrictions on African American voting rights and to formalize segregation in public accommodations, whites across the country began seeking means to draw race more sharply into the metropolitan landscape. The Great Migration initiated an unrelenting struggle to use, control, and define metropolitan space that would shape American life for the remainder of the century.

Southern and border cities such as Baltimore, Richmond, and Louisville, among the first to experience escalating black migration, led the way. Local officials enacted ordinances in the early 1910s that restricted blacks and whites to separate zones in the city. African Americans immediately challenged racial zoning, and the Supreme Court invalidated the practice in 1917. Nonetheless, officials in the South as well as in more northerly communities experimented with racial zoning for several decades, giving both formal and informal sanction to whites who sought to establish boundaries beyond which blacks could not pass.[25]

Whites also sought private means to achieve residential segregation. At the 1909 inaugural meeting of the National Association of Real Estate Boards, also known as the Realtors, and the 1910 National Conference on City Planning, delegates promoted private real estate covenants and deed restrictions that prohibited purchase or occupancy of property by "any person other than of the Caucasian race."[26] By 1914 the Realtors had adopted a code of ethics enjoining members from "introducing into a neighborhood . . . members of any race or nationality . . . whose presence will clearly be detrimental to property values," and Realtor-sponsored textbooks propounded the claim that nonwhites devastated the value of property.[27] Leading builders and lenders reinforced these initiatives, steadfastly refusing to provide housing for African Americans outside a few segregated districts. By the 1920s, racial segregation had become standard practice throughout the formal real estate industry, and the ideas, or "representations," of space that underlay it would exert lasting influence in the metropolitan United States.[28]

The Suburban Trend

American suburbs played a key part in this movement to racialize urban space, that is, to link specific places to an evolving racial hierarchy, limiting access, cementing advantage and disadvantage, and defining locations and their residents in separate and unequal terms. The reasons were varied. At the edges of urban expansion, the newest suburbs provided a clean slate for development according to the latest fashion. In addition, entrepreneurs during this period began to consolidate formerly separate aspects of real estate development — land subdivision, service installation, and the construction and sale of homes — into unified operations, heralding the rise of "community builders" who exercised unprecedented power over future development.[29] During the suburban building boom of the 1920s, these entrepreneurs wrote segregation into the metropolitan fabric more effectively and comprehensively than ever before. Developers used deed covenants to govern future land use, controlling the cost, size, location, and style of housing that could be constructed, its occupancy by single or multiple families, and the race and ethnicity of inhabitants, and they consistently promoted the idea that racial homogeneity was essential to the security of property values.[30] Concurrently, suburban governments, smaller and more responsive to local demands than big-city officials, experimented with restrictive land-use planning: zoning and subdivision regulations, health and safety ordinances, and building codes governing the cost of new construction and the uses to which it could be put. Completing the circle, white suburbanites themselves made it difficult, if not dangerous, for nonwhites to set up housekeeping. House bombings and arson against black families became common means to prevent blacks from settling among whites, even in comfortably middle-class areas such as Cleveland Heights, Ohio, and White Plains, New York.[31] As the suburbs boomed, white people purchased not merely homes but a concept of space in which racial segregation and white superiority were taken for granted; in the process, hundreds of municipalities grew up as "closed cities," effectively "shut against Negroes."[32]

Patterns of race restriction in Los Angeles, a leader in the suburban trend, exemplified national predilections. Beginning early in the century, suburban officials and real estate brokers competed to attract white residents, promising ironclad restrictions against racial diversity. Real estate agents in Pasadena, which was already heterogeneous in population, extended race-restrictive covenants throughout the city to prevent black families from moving beyond established areas, and whites in some neighborhoods resorted to force to stop blacks from moving in.[33] Newer suburbs sought to exclude nonwhites altogether. Restrictions in affluent communities such as Beverly Hills were legion, extending to Latinos, Asians, and Jews, but modest residential suburbs in the industrial belt south of the city, such as Lynbrook, Compton, Willowbrook, and Bell Gardens, were also restricted to whites.[34] In South Gate, a suburb "where the working man is welcomed," restrictive covenants openly excluded African Americans and Asians. The local paper reported in 1926:

> Home Gardens [later part of South Gate] is distinctly a white man's
> town. No one but Caucasians may own or lease real estate here. . . . A
> goodly percentage of our people were born south of the Mason and
> Dixon line . . . [and] one of the controlling factors in their choice of a
> location was the racial restrictions.[35]

Likewise, residents of Lomita, just south of the black community in Watts, posted yard signs in the mid-1920s warning African Americans "to stay out," and in Manhattan Beach, "Ku Klux Klan pressure" led local officials to condemn black-owned property and "close the beach to their swimming as well as occupancy."[36] "By the end of the twenties," writes historian Lawrence DeGraaf, "virtually all black residents had been terrorized out of the city."[37]

As went Los Angeles, so went the nation. Through a combination of discrimination in real estate, banking, and public policy as well as the tangible threat of violence, racial segregation became the rule in the nation's suburbs by 1940. Still, like all trends, the uniformity that Realtors and community builders so sought proved elusive. In built-up areas, African Americans and whites still lived intermingled with one another, and in the vast urban hinterland, as yet unincorporated and unregulated, land use remained largely a matter of individual choice. In these places, a wide variety of development ensued, including subdivisions built for African Americans and others open to anyone with a few dollars for a down payment. Nevertheless, the prevailing trend favored segregation. In the 1930s when the federal government intervened to stabilize the collapsing real estate market, new government agencies, staffed with representatives of the real estate industry, became the basis for a federal housing bureaucracy in which racial homogeneity was a central value. Methods of comprehensive planning and discrimination perfected in many suburbs during the teens and twenties, thus, set precedents that would guide developers and public officials through the mass suburban explosion after World War II.

Industrial Suburbs: Detroit's Downriver District

Within these national outlines, local circumstances shaped distinctive suburban communities. Since early black suburbanites were as likely to work in the suburbs as in the central city, the structure of suburban labor markets proved essential to the process of suburbanization. Paid labor affected the kinds of communities that African Americans could create, limiting the cost and location of homes and impinging on economic security and mobility.

Racial stratification in the labor market ensured that most black suburbanites were confined to low-waged work, but polarized job opportunities for men and women also gave rise to gendered patterns of suburban migration. Jobs laid a foundation for settlement, but they also delimited opportunities, affecting the attractiveness of one community over another and governing the types of workers most likely to step off the train.

The suburbanization of manufacturing in Detroit's Downriver region illustrates the interplay between suburban employment, race, and black migration. As automotive and allied industries boomed during the 1910s and 1920s, dozens of firms opened or expanded facilities along the Detroit and Rouge Rivers southwest of the city in the suburbs of Dearborn, River Rouge, Ecorse, Wyandotte, and Trenton.[38] Local enterprises included the biggest shipbuilder on the Great Lakes, two of the largest metal makers in the region, and the largest factory complex on the planet, Ford Motor Company's River Rouge auto plant in Dearborn, which was a thousand-acre facility capable of rolling out seven thousand cars per day and employing up to 100,000 workers.[39] Before 1940 ore-bearing barges crowded Downriver waterways, and the makers of steel, autos, chemicals, screw machine products, truck chassis, and metal stampings churned out a tide of durable goods that secured the region's claim as one of the most industrialized on earth.[40]

As industry boomed, Downriver communities attracted thousands of blue-collar suburbanites. Factories fouled the environment, but they provided just the sort of jobs that most residents had left their homes to find, whether they hailed from Appalachia, eastern Europe, or the black belt of Alabama. Local manufacturers meant local jobs, and residence in the area ensured convenient access to scores of industrial employers.[41] Area firms also furnished a deep tax base from which to pay for services. By the late 1920s, suburban officials had extended water, electricity, sewers, and gas, as well as paving and lighting, throughout most of the Downriver suburbs. Children attended brand-new schools, and the "handsome" River Rouge High School, which served River Rouge and Ecorse, ranked among the finest in the state.[42] Additionally, local people believed that these "small town[s] on the edge of a big city" were "ideal for residences" due to the availability of low-cost land for sale to blue-collar workers.[43] In Dearborn, the miracle city of the twenties, the population mushroomed from 2,500 to 50,000 in ten years. Nearby, Ecorse and River Rouge more than doubled in size, reaching 12,000 and 17,000 people by 1930.[44]

As in suburban Los Angeles, race played a central role in the formation of Downriver society. Detroit's southwestern suburbs were notoriously hostile

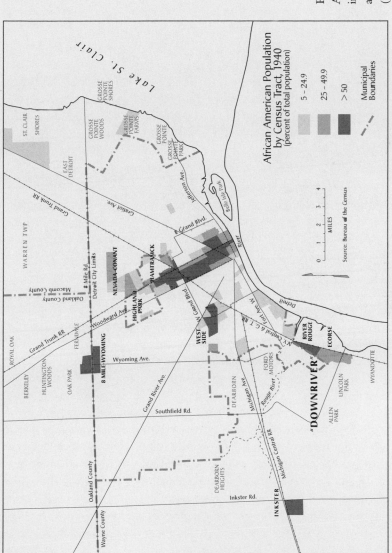

Fig. 2.2
African Americans
in Detroit, Michigan,
and Suburbs, 1940.
(Map by Harry D. Johnson)

African American Population
by Census Tract, 1940
(percent of total population)

5 – 24.9
25 – 49.9
> 50

Municipal
Boundaries

Source: Bureau of the Census

0   1   2   3   4
MILES

Lake St. Clair

ST. CLAIR
SHORES

GROSSE
POINTE
SHORES

GROSSE
POINTE
WOODS

GROSSE
POINTE
FARMS

GROSSE
POINTE

GROSSE
POINTE
PARK

EAST
DETROIT

WARREN TWP.

Grand Trunk RR

Gratiot Ave.

Jefferson Ave.

Belle Isle Park

River

Detroit

E. Grand Blvd.

8 Mile Rd.

Oakland County
Macomb County

Detroit City Limits

NEVADA-CONANT

HAMTRAMCK

HIGHLAND
PARK

Woodward Ave.

FERNDALE

Grand Trunk RR

ROYAL OAK

BERKELEY

HUNTINGTON
WOODS

OAK PARK

8 MILE-WYOMING

Wyoming Ave.

W. Grand Blvd.

WEST
SIDE

N.Y. Central & C.T.I. RR

RIVER
ROUGE

ECORSE

WYANDOTTE

"DOWNRIVER"

LINCOLN
PARK

ALLEN
PARK

FORD
MOTORS

Rouge River

Fort Ave. W.

Michigan Ave.

DEARBORN

Grand River Ave.

Southfield Rd.

Oakland County

Wayne County

DEARBORN
HEIGHTS

Inkster Rd.

Michigan Central RR

INKSTER

Fig. 2.3 Rouge River, southwest Detroit, and Dearborn, Michigan, ca. 1920s. The Rouge River snaked through one of the most industrialized regions on earth, passing Ford Motors' River Rouge plant, visible through the smoke in the upper right. Lacking the bucolic atmosphere of elite suburbia, Detroit's Downriver suburbs attracted thousands of blue-collar families who seized the chance to buy homes in the vicinity of well-paying industrial employment. The New York Central Railroad, which bisected River Rouge into white and black worlds, can be seen entering the suburb at the left center. (Courtesy of the Burton Historical Collection, Detroit Public Library)

to blacks. Early on, Dearborn and Wyandotte established reputations as "no Negro" towns.[45] Home to tens of thousands of European immigrants and white migrants from the upper South, these suburbs became crucibles for the formation of a militant white working-class identity. Despite the employment of 10,000 African Americans at Ford by the mid-1920s, Dearborn police prevented blacks from venturing about town, and African Americans advised that one "better not be caught there, especially after sun down."[46] In 1930 just forty-three African Americans lived in Dearborn (perhaps all of them as live-in domestics).

Wyandotte presents a similar history. As the local paper professed in 1937, "Wyandotte has never been a pleasant place for Negroes. In years gone by, colored people who tried to effect a residence here were either compelled or induced to leave town. One time, many years ago, a colored man was killed here. . . . Since then, colored people have shunned the town as a place of residence."[47] Local news clippings demonstrate that Wyandotte's reputation was well deserved. In 1916 a mob attacked a rooming house whose owner had admitted a black tenant, in 1923 whites forced a carload of blacks from the road and robbed them, and in 1937 a mob tried to lynch a black prisoner at the city jail. Not surprisingly, just four of Wyandotte's 30,000 residents in 1940 were black.[48]

Despite these hazards, African Americans found their way to the Downriver area. Essential to the process was a thriving low-cost housing market, which flourished in the absence of formal land-use restrictions throughout much of the area before 1945.[49] Between 1915 and 1919, half a dozen real estate companies subdivided and sold inexpensive building lots on the west side of River Rouge, just a mile from Dearborn. Most of the vendors were family businesses with small pieces of property for sale locally and in nearby suburbs. Several of them were from long-standing families. All of them were white, and they all sold bare land with minimal investment or restriction on its use. In at least two cases, the lack of restrictions extended to race.[50] "As early as 1916," a local history reported, "seven pioneer black families . . . from the South" bought property and began building houses. Upward of thirty African American households were in residence by 1920, mixed among a white, mostly immigrant, majority.[51] By the time River Rouge incorporated in 1922, a few hundred African Americans were living on the west side of town. With black home owners in residence and landowners determined to sell to them, white officials were ill prepared to halt the migration. The city adopted a modest building code with incorporation, but the first opportunity to control land use through subdivision regulation, a building code, zoning, or police power had passed.[52]

As in other African American suburbs of the period, most of River Rouge's new suburbanites were working-class southerners. Eighty-nine percent of the suburb's seventy black adults in 1920 were southern-born, half from Alabama. Eighty-three percent of men worked in manufacturing—mostly in auto and metal fabricating—and 70 percent reported an unskilled occupation, a manifestation of the prevailing pattern in American industry.[53] In contrast, few black women worked outside the home, confining their workday to the considerable task of making homes in the raw landscape of the suburb's west side. Twenty percent of adult women were in the paid workforce in 1920, compared to 33 percent in Detroit, but they represented just 12 percent of the paid black workforce.[54] Dependent on racially restricted male factory labor, migrants to River Rouge constituted the foundation of a black suburban industrial working class.

Ford Motor Company's decision to shift its production line to Dearborn in the early twenties cemented the trend. The company's black workforce ballooned from 2,500 to 10,000 between 1920 and 1926.[55] West-side property owners, recognizing an opportunity, marketed the area directly to African Americans. Hundreds of families bought land and set up housekeeping west of the New York Central Railroad tracks, meanwhile developers opened additional subdivisions in a contiguous section of Ecorse, to the south. According to a 1926 study, contractors and buyers operated freely, hammering up "single family houses and shacks." Less than half had basements, and a third relied on an outhouse in the backyard. Many homes were "built with the idea that they will be temporary shelters until the family gets established. Basements are not dug, the structure is flimsy and subject to early deterioration. Many of the houses are constructed by the owners who are seldom skilled in the carpentry trade."[56] From these inauspicious beginnings, the black population of these two suburbs climbed to 3,500 in 1930, by which time African Americans constituted a majority on the west side and 15 percent of the local population.[57]

Although whites in River Rouge and Ecorse gave way to black efforts to build homes with less apparent resistance than whites in nearby communities, race no less marked the suburbanization process.[58] The subdivisions where African American families settled were physically isolated from the rest of town by a wide railroad corridor. Crossed by through streets at only a few points over a length of several miles, the rift of the New York Central Railroad was a physical barrier that split the suburbs in two. Initially, economic need characterized settlement on the west side. As low-wage workers, African Americans and eastern European immigrants bought what they could afford and employed property in similar class-based ways. Nonetheless, race soon became the defining feature of the area, assuming an increasingly spatial character. As black migration increased and immigrants' economic position improved, whites drifted away from the west side, and the tracks became a kind of racial Maginot Line. East-side restaurants, taverns, and theaters refused to serve blacks. African Americans were not welcome at east-side parks, playgrounds, or other recreational facilities. Elementary schools were segregated, the city hospital afforded separate treatment to black patients, and the metropolitan charity board established separate community centers for east- and

Fig. 2.4 *House on Ninth Street, Ecorse, Michigan, November 1984.* Carla Anderson. Typical of many homes west of the tracks in Ecorse and River Rouge, this house illustrates the modest residential landscape that black as well as white families produced in the Downriver region's low-cost subdivisions. (Courtesy of Carla Anderson)

west-side children.[59] Residential segregation was almost complete, and it endured for half a century. In 1940, 1,800 African Americans lived in Ecorse, but not one resided east of the tracks. In River Rouge, fewer than ten lived among 15,000 east-side whites. Thirty years later, whites in River Rouge could recall only one black family, reputedly "the first in 50 years," who had lived on the east side, and they had been intimidated into leaving.[60]

For their part, African Americans in River Rouge and Ecorse created a community of their own, building on networks of kin and friends that had facilitated their migration to the area. By the mid-1920s, separate Baptist, Methodist, and Pentecostal churches served as the basis for Downriver social and spiritual life. Choirs, devotional societies, and guest ministers visited from other black communities in the metropolitan area. Local groups hosted fashion shows, fish fries, barbecue dinners, and other events to boost fellowship and raise funds.[61] By the late 1930s, black teachers instructed students at two mostly black elementary schools, a black police officer patrolled the streets, and black staff administered two community centers sponsored by the metropolitan charity board.[62] A range of small businesses responded to the need for services and leisure-time outlets. Albert Talley and Emma Peterson styled hair. Frank Roundtree operated a filling station on Palmerston Avenue near the McFall Brothers Funeral Home, and Andrew Cook and Benjamin Gordan operated beer gardens where crowds of men and women gathered to drink, dance, and socialize. Black grocers sold produce, and on Sunday afternoons, worshipers from St. John's AME Church could walk down the block to the restaurants of Minnie Webb and Lacey Abner.[63] For the black southerners who had moved to Detroit for a job in "Mr. Ford's place," the River Rouge–Ecorse community represented a familiar social environment. By the early 1940s, the New York Central tracks marked the end of one world and the beginning of another, as though the color line had been scrawled across these suburbs with a steam shovel.

Work, Gender, and Migration

If the shadow of race was clear in patterns of suburban settlement, the distinctive nature of black employment also shaped a highly gendered process of suburbanization. Where large factories dominated the skyline, as in suburban Detroit, men often made up 75 to 90 percent of the black suburban workforce, and as many as 90 percent worked in industrial settings.[64] Likewise, men outnumbered women in the population of industrial suburbs, frequently by large margins. In a sample of twelve such suburbs in 1920, for instance, men made up 55 to 60 percent of the black population (see table 2.1).[65] Though disparities receded as African American women joined men and formed families, the proportion of women in the labor force remained below the average in most cities or other suburbs. In short, factory suburbs were magnets for male-led industrial migration.

Lackawanna, New York, represented an extreme case of sexually unbalanced suburbanization spawned by the opening of industrial jobs, but its history reflects the importance of gender and the labor market in suburban migration more generally. Situated south of Buffalo, Lackawanna came into existence after the Bethlehem Steel Company began building a mill on the Lake Erie shoreline in 1901. With a motley collection of company housing and frame boardinghouses adjacent to the "smoking blast furnaces and rolling mills of the Bethlehem Steel Company," Lackawanna was a one-industry

Table 2.1: Sex Distribution among African Americans in Industrial and
Domestic Service Suburbs, 1920

Suburb	Black Population	Percent Male	Percent Female
Industrial Suburbs			
Homestead, PA	1,814	67%	33%
East Chicago, IN	1,424	61%	39%
Coatesville, PA	1,881	60%	40%
Chicago Heights, IL	731	59%	41%
Lackawanna, NY	269	57%	43%
Chester, PA	7,125	55%	45%
Joliet, IL	701	55%	45%
Hamtramck, MI	2,022	55%	45%
Mixed Suburbs			
Aurora, IL	627	51%	49%
Passaic, NJ	586	50%	50%
White Plains, NY	995	49%	51%
Service Suburbs			
Hackensack, NJ	1,153	47%	53%
Orange, NJ	3,621	47%	53%
Berkeley, CA	507	46%	54%
Englewood, NJ	1,138	46%	54%
Yonkers, NY	1,940	46%	54%
Evanston, IL	2,522	45%	55%
Pasadena, CA	1,084	44%	56%
New Rochelle, NY	2,637	42%	58%
East Orange, NJ	2,378	41%	59%
Montclair, NJ	3,467	41%	59%
Mount Vernon, NY	1,298	36%	64%

Source: U.S. Census of Population: 1920, vol. III, *Composition and Character of the Population by States* (Washington, D.C., 1922), 118, 261, 263, 297, 488, 645–47, 690–95, 866–70.

town, dependent on the company for employment, fiscal security, and political leadership.[66] In 1920 the city's African American population reflected these circumstances in an especially palpable way. Although a few dozen black families had lived there before World War I, the company recruited nearly 200 African American men in the fall of 1919 as strikebreakers during the Great Steel Strike.[67] When census takers canvassed the community a few months later, they found 250 black residents, 57 percent of them male. The majority lived in "the old village," a section of "dingy, smoke blackened" company housing at the north end of town.[68] Ninety-five percent worked in the steel mills, and four out of five reported his occupation as "steelworker," the undifferentiated category of "men in greasy overalls" who "performed the dirtiest, heaviest, hottest, most dangerous tasks" in the mills.[69] By contrast, women represented less than 10 percent of the black workforce, including a plurality who kept house for male boarders.[70] Despite variations among suburbs, as in Lackawanna, unskilled male factory workers represented the archetypal black suburbanite in U.S. industrial suburbs.

Lackawanna was not alone in the prevalence of male factory workers nor the paucity of employment for women. The factory and railroad jobs that dominated most industrial suburbs were closed to women. Further, the blue-collar composition of the population limited opportunities for domestic work, which was the mainstay of black female labor at the time. Homestead, Pennsylvania, a steel satellite of Pittsburgh, is a case in point. The social scientist Margaret Byington observed in 1910, "Women and children rarely work outside the home since the steel plant and machine works cannot use them and there are no other industries in town." Furthermore, in a community "where there are not marked differences in financial status and by far the larger number of housewives do all their own work, there is not much opportunity to obtain any form of domestic service by the day."[71] Consequently, women represented just 10 percent of Homestead's black workforce in 1920, rising to 15 percent twenty years later. In this respect, Homestead differed little from many industry-dependent suburbs, where women rarely surpassed 25 percent of the black labor force before World War II.[72]

One avenue that *was* available to women in suburbs like Homestead and Lackawanna was keeping lodgers. The limited number of jobs for women and the surplus of single men made housekeeping for tenants financially inviting. In some factory towns where housing construction trailed population growth, mill managers recruited black householders to accept boarders, paying landlords directly with funds deducted from the tenant's wages. In Homestead, where men outnumbered women two to one in 1920, 40 percent of black households contained at least one paying tenant. In households headed by women, the figure exceeded 70 percent, and "boarding house keeper" was the largest job category among women.[73]

As much as gendered work and demographic patterns reflected the structure of suburban employment, the disproportionate number of working-age men and women, virtually all of whom were migrants, reflected decisions that black southerners made about where to settle. For men, the attraction of industrial suburbs was clear. According to educator Alain Locke, "Mass entrance into American industry" represented a "new vision of opportunity" for many black southerners who had formerly sought economic independence through farm ownership.[74] During flush economic times, suburban factory towns were places where newcomers could find comparatively high-paying work easily. For men with long-term goals, too, industrial suburbs promised greater opportunities to improve their economic position than many other places. Though job discrimination confined the majority of black industrial workers to hard, dangerous, and poorly paid positions, "the open shop, heavy industries" that dominated such suburbs offered, according to historian Peter Gottlieb, "the best chances for male migrants to advance above unskilled work."[75] For men, then, industrial suburbia supported a gendered dream of upward mobility.

One potential drawback was that these places offered few chances for women to contribute to household wages through paid employment, a fact that may have suppressed migration by some families and single women. For many men and women, however, these circumstances must have appealed to their preferences relating to gender and family responsibilities. Male migrants who scouted for job opportunities in industrial suburbs and later sent for wives and children could not have failed to notice the shortage of employment for women, nor does it seem likely that many wives were unaware of the situation before arriving. Although Homestead's Byington attributed the pattern to structural conditions as opposed to "any theory as to women's sphere," the male-dependent household economies that developed in many mill suburbs may well have reflected a distinctive vision of gender roles among the black men and women who settled there from homes in distant states.[76]

Patterns of leisure in industrial suburbs also may have appealed to a particular conception of black manhood. Reflecting the dominance of young men in the population, Gottlieb points out, factory suburbs afforded numerous opportunities for men to relax in masculine company in "pool halls, boarding houses and black-owned barber shops" as well as on "the street corners and stoops of increasingly black and male neighborhoods."[77] Such suburbs boasted an abundance of organized sports, including baseball, basketball, and football teams; boxing matches; and track-and-field meets that appealed particularly to male participants and spectators.[78] The Homestead Grays, the legendary baseball team of the Pittsburgh mill suburb, marked the town not only as a site of national economic might but as a landmark on the map of black masculine imaginations. Men's leisure spaces in suburbs such as Homestead and Lackawanna extended to a range of saloons, cigar stores, beer gardens, dance halls, bookmakers, and card rooms, as well as brothels and what one observer called "other outposts of the 'sporting life.'"[79] For male migrants who had left the South because "they want[ed] to be men," the masculine world of work and leisure in these suburbs reaffirmed an image of hard-working, autonomous, and physical black manhood.[80]

Male-dominated manufacturing work affected local life in another important way. Like the smoke that hung in the air, the rhythms of industrial labor, symbolized by the periodic scream of the factory whistle, ruled the local environment. During boom times, the mill towns roared with life, factories ran three shifts, and crowds of denim-clad workers ebbed and flowed at the plant gates. On payday, these suburbs assumed a carnival atmosphere. Standing-room crowds packed the movie houses; shoppers thronged local stores; saloons filled with men and women, drinking, dancing, and playing cards; and the streets echoed with the sounds of music and laughter.[81] In Bessemer, Alabama, a white writer observed with a mixture of astonishment and contempt that on "'big pay-day' . . . hilarious Negroes throng the shops, cafes, and entertainment spots in the Negro section . . . [and] Negro miners put on a show of easy spending in sheer pride of occupation."[82] By contrast, periodic economic slowdowns led workers to seek opportunity elsewhere, leaving vacant apartments, quiet streets, and empty bar stools. As a visitor to Madison, Illinois, explained, because it was "the home of millworkers, the community rises or falls with the fortunes of the steel industry."[83]

Domestic Service Suburbs

At the far end of the suburban spectrum from the soot-stained mill towns were leafy enclaves of the white elite and upper-middle class. As exemplars of bourgeois family life "free from the bustle, noise and crowded conditions of the great metropolis," the nation's elite suburbs are well known and widely studied.[84] Missing from most accounts, however, is the fact that many of these suburbs were significant sites of paid labor.[85] In what one publicist called "the best suburban cities," affluent whites' desire for a leisurely lifestyle led to the employment of thousands of paid domestic workers, most of whom lived very nearby, often in households of their own.[86]

Despite the relative lack of scholarly attention to paid labor in affluent suburbia, service workers were a conspicuous segment of the suburban labor force. The wealthiest suburbanites employed whole staffs of domestic workers, including butlers, governesses, and various other indoor and outdoor workers.[87] Large numbers of middle-class suburbanites, too, employed some form of domestic help. In the South, these workers historically were black; elsewhere, African Americans formed a growing proportion of the service labor force by the 1920s. Men and women who worked as maids, gardeners, cooks, chauffeurs, day workers, hired hands, and "wash ladies" performed labor that was essential to creating the cultivated landscapes and leisurely social life that epitomized bourgeois suburbs before World War II.

A survey of thirty-three affluent suburbs with more than 250 black employees in 1940 reveals the importance of domestic service in elite suburbia. Two-thirds of these communities, including many of the most fashionable addresses in the United States, were home to separate African American neighborhoods. In all of them, service workers constituted between 10 and 25 percent of the working population. In Montclair, Orange, and Englewood, New Jersey; Mount Vernon and New Rochelle, New York; and Evanston, Illinois, domestic and kindred service workers actually formed a larger proportion of the population than either professional or managerial employees, the two highest categories of white-collar work. In all six, female domestics outnumbered male professionals.[88]

Other black workers, while not directly employed in middle-class households, were equally bound to the economy of residential affluence. Thousands of women toiled in commercial laundries, and others did wash from their own homes. Men and women worked in private clubs, restaurants, and hotels catering to white suburbanites, and every large service suburb spawned black-owned businesses that served white clients: caterers, movers, employment agents, painters, and others. Finally, many families subsisted on services that they supplied to domestic workers—especially housing, laundry, and child care.[89]

As these examples suggest, the sexual division of labor in "high-class suburban communities" gave rise to a singular economic profile.[90] The largest part of the service workforce in such suburbs was female. Whereas women represented one-third of the black paid labor force nationwide in 1920, women in affluent suburbia often made up 40 to 50 percent of the black workforce.[91] In suburbs such as Mount Vernon and New Rochelle, New York, female wage earners outnumbered men. "Due to the servant situation," women also formed a disproportionate share of the black population, often reaching 55 percent or more (see table 2.1).[92] Thus, in addition to unpaid economic roles managing households, keeping boarders, tending gardens, and sustaining local community life, women earned as much as half of the wage income available to African American families, an unprecedented figure for urban American women in the early twentieth century.[93]

In contrast to the "wonderful" opportunities for women, men had greater difficulty finding stable and well-paying work in domestic service suburbs.[94] A sample of 1920 census schedules from eight suburbs indicates that between 20 and 40 percent of employed men worked in domestic or kindred service. Chauffeurs held top jobs, but men also worked as cooks, gardeners, and hired men in private households or as porters, elevator operators, waiters, and care-takers for local hotels and clubs. Contrasting with the emphasis that histori-ans have placed on industrial labor as the spark for male migration, few men worked in industrial settings. The proportion of men employed in manu-facturing ranged from less than 1 percent in Pasadena to as much as 22 per-cent in Montclair, New Jersey.[95] The greatest number — usually 40 to 50 per-cent — worked as common laborers, shoveling, sweeping, and carrying loads in coal and lumber yards; driving trucks; carting goods; or maintaining city streets. These jobs were likely to be short term, poorly paid, and sensitive to economic fluctuation. "There being little work for men," observed a resident of Mount Vernon, "laborers usually take what they can get," and during the depression, men faced "displacement [by whites] from even these meek and lowly positions."[96] Rather than reflecting greater opportunity, the diversity of men's occupations symbolized the insecurity and haphazardness of their employment.

Gender and Migration to Affluent Suburbia

In suburbs where female migrants formed a major proportion of the pop-ulation, gender and race also intermingled to shape distinctive communities and migration patterns. Especially for young women striking out alone and for women with children, elite suburbs offered ample employment, immedi-ate opportunities for lodging, and an enveloping community of women in similar circumstances. Smaller and more intimate than central cities, they were generally safer destinations for women traveling alone.[97] They were also cheaper and potentially more convenient to employment than most black neighborhoods in the city. Domestic servants could board with employers, saving money to send home or spend on a place of their own. Once black women began settling, of course, they themselves became attractions for new arrivals. For women who needed or wanted to earn a wage, service suburbs were popular destinations.[98]

As in suburbs where the factory whistle governed daily activity, rhythms of women's domestic employment set their own community cadence. In Westchester County, New York, like many suburban areas, thousands of domestic servants had Thursday afternoon and Sundays off. Consequently, much of the calendar of black suburban social life was compressed into two days of the week. In addition to church-related activities, women conducted Thursday meetings of a variety of social, philanthropic, and religious organizations. They went to the movies, shopped, sought romance, cleaned their own homes, spent time with their children, and visited friends and relatives. Willie Carrington of New Rochelle recalled, "Since most of the people were domestics and off on Thursday, there was always something going on in the churches, including dinners. Even though Thursday was their day off, they spent most of the day cooking dinner and serving it to each other and they enjoyed it. It was a social outlet too."[99] Likewise, Caldonia Martin of Evanston remembered that "Thursday night was the night the colored people went out to have a good time, because the maids were off then."[100] In Chagrin Falls Park, Ohio, where Wednesday was the domestics' day off, a former domestic worker recollected that during the depression groups of women gathered at Stella Denson's canteen, where they could listen to music from the jukebox, buy a bottle of beer, and "tease the men" who didn't have any money.[101] Like payday in the mill towns, "maids' day off" was a shaping feature of African American social life in these suburbs, regardless of where people worked.

For women without immediate family ties, the predominance of black women also cushioned migration to unfamiliar places and provided channels of mutual aid that were vital to the establishment and persistence of black communities. Claudia Robinson, a domestic worker in Mount Vernon, New York, recalled her first day on the job and the community of women that welcomed her. "I didn't know anyone," she remembered.

> The next day, I went out and walked around. There was a girl up the street and her name was Nannie and we got acquainted. So that Thursday she said, "Come and go to my house today." So I did. Her sister had a big house on 8th Avenue and 4th Street. Lovely people. That is how I got in with the people in Mount Vernon, through them.[102]

In Evanston a group of socially established black women reached out to newcomers by creating a residential home for single women and live-in servants. In the mid-1920s, members of Evanston's Iroquois League, with the help of white churchwomen, purchased a "beautifully modern" three-story building, which they operated as a "house for girls"; it included private rooms for fifteen workingwomen and public space for domestic workers who "needed a place to go on their days off."[103] "Within its cheery walls," one of the founders declared, "you would no doubt be surprised to know how many spend their Thursday and Sunday" or "to know the sacrifice some women have made for this home." "Lifting as we climb," Iroquois League members acted on the helping impulse that had united African American families and communities in the South, extending it to a new community of female "strangers with no place to stay."[104]

For workingwomen with children, too, feminine communities eased the burden of child care. Women like Bertha Sturdivant of New Rochelle, New York, left their children with relatives in the South when they moved north. Others whose social networks preceded them brought their children and relied on "aunts and grandparents," close friends, or neighbors to watch their children while they worked.[105] Ann Howard of Mount Vernon recalled that a couple she called Mama and Papa Green had "helped" with her children while she worked in a local laundry.[106] Mallie Robinson of Pasadena left her four younger children at home with her sister during her first years in the suburb, while she did "wash, ironing, floors and windows" for white families.[107] As in many domestics' families, however, it became the responsibility of older children to care for their siblings as they grew up. Some suburban women paid for child care by the hour, day, or week, though in most cases, low pay precluded this option. In most suburbs, African American families "got around the problem of children," as one retired domestic worker put it, through reliance on reciprocal networks of kinfolk and close friends.[108]

Finally, the gendered division of labor in industrial and domestic service suburbs left its mark on black migration itself. Black women were often pioneer migrants to domestic service suburbs and, like other pioneers, became anchors for continuing chains of migration. Mary Ann Courtney left Virginia in 1907, "traveled around, living in different cities," and moved to Mount Vernon, New York, by herself in 1915. A friend who worked as a domestic in nearby Bronxville arranged a job for her, and she started work the day after arriving. Claudia Robinson also moved to Mount Vernon alone. She was between jobs in Poughkeepsie when she heard about a live-in job in the suburb. She came by car, got the job, and moved in that very night. Her husband followed later, and after a time the couple established a household of their own. In neighboring New Rochelle, Bertha Sturdivant also preceded her husband and children to the suburb. She came up from Raleigh, North Carolina, in 1916, leaving two children with her mother-in-law, but her family followed once she had gotten established. Likewise, John Smith of New Rochelle followed an aunt who was the pioneer in his family. Shortly after Smith turned seventeen, during World War I, his aunt arranged a job for him on a coal delivery truck in New Rochelle and "sent for me to come up" from Virginia. "I probably could have started some place else," he mused, "but I came here, and have been here ever since."[109] Attracted by the availability of domestic and personal service employment, African American women led the way to affluent suburbs, establishing a basis for continued migration.

Not only did domestic service work offer the opportunity for African American women to become suburban pioneers, but black women's employment created a self-perpetuating cycle of kin-based female migration and recruitment into domestic service. The number of black women in the paid workforce "who were gone before we were up and did not return until we were in bed" created a labor vacuum within black households.[110] Some women tried to minimize the problem by living in with employers or by boarding or sharing housekeeping with other women, but domestics who were married or had children often turned to their kinfolk for assistance. Initially, some women left their children with relatives in the South, but staying on required a more permanent solution. Women recruited siblings and other female kin from the South to help care for their children and assist with housework. At the same time, unpaid work in the homes of relatives often served younger southern women as a period of "apprenticeship" before they found paid household work of their own — thus perpetuating the cycle of migration and expanding it deeper into social networks throughout the South.[111]

Osceola Spencer's migration from West Point, Mississippi, to Evanston suggests how such gendered migration chains worked. Spencer's aunt married a man from Evanston and moved there in 1912. Several years later, the aunt recruited Spencer's younger sister to come to Evanston to care for her young children. Soon, Spencer's parents and another sister also joined the "pioneers" in Evanston. Having come up for a visit, they "found out how much liberty there was in Evanston compared with what it was in West Point. . . . They said, 'just like heaven'" and decided to stay permanently. By the time Spencer became pregnant with her first child in 1918, her closest female kin had moved north, so she went to Evanston to stay with her mother and sisters. While she was there, Mississippi expanded its military draft, and her husband, who was now eligible, "caught the next train to Evanston."[112]

The Spencers never moved back to the Magnolia State. In ways such as these, domestic service employment interacted with the needs of black family life and shaped manifestly gendered chains of migration to the suburbs.

Once they had settled, African American women created families of their own, which served to establish permanent roots in the suburbs. Oral histories as well as obituaries are filled with enumerations of suburban families such as Selma Smith's "seven children . . . twenty-three grandchildren . . . fifty-two great-grandchildren" or Bertha Sturdivant's seventy-five descendants in the vicinity of Mount Vernon and New Rochelle. With four generations of family in Mount Vernon, Bertha Sturdivant was "Mother Sturdivant" to those who knew her. By the 1970s women such as these, who had come to the suburbs as domestic servants, had become the progenitors of black communities that were deeply interwoven with ties of kinship and affection that had their roots in the migration of a black woman from the South.[113]

Although suburbs differed on the basis of gender, African Americans in affluent suburbia faced a racially stratified labor market that confined them to a handful of "uncertain and poorly paid jobs."[114] "There was only one thing you could do," said Alice Bugg of Pasadena, "either cook or wash or iron. There was no other work."[115] Especially galling to black taxpayers was bias in public employment. In Pasadena, which followed the standard pattern, the city government excluded African Americans from all but a handful of unskilled, outdoor jobs in the city's garbage and parks departments. The *California Eagle* noted as late as 1940 that "the City . . . does not hire a single [black] policeman, fireman, regular day-time school teacher, meter reader, or any other type of employment for the utilities; no, not even a janitor or an elevator boy in the city hall." So entrenched was resistance to hiring African Americans in "white" departments of the city government, NAACP president Ruby McKnight Williams recalled acidly, "We had to picket City Hall to get janitors."[116]

"The submerged employment status of the colored population" was only one element of racial subordination in local life.[117] As numbers of African American suburbanites grew, white institutions adopted exclusive or segregative policies. School boards drew district boundaries to create racially segregated schools.[118] Boy Scout troops, parks and playgrounds, beaches, swimming pools, stores, taverns, and theaters segregated or excluded blacks.[119] Montclair, New Jersey, an elegant railroad suburb of Newark and New York City, was typical. The Reverend D. C. Rice remembered the suburb in the 1920s as "a community with segregated hospitals, housing, theaters and a segregated school system with all white teachers . . . a colored YMCA . . . colored churches, a colored dance hall and colored barbershops."[120] A continent away in Pasadena, conditions were almost identical. Jackie Robinson recalled that suburbanites like himself "saw movies from segregated balconies, swam in the municipal pool only on Tuesdays, and were permitted in the YMCA on only one night a week. Restaurant doors were slammed in our face."[121] "They let us in alright," concluded Robinson's brother, Mack, "but they wouldn't let us live."[122]

Domestic Service Suburb: Evanston, Illinois

Evanston, Illinois, a commuter suburb of Chicago, illustrates more concretely the relationship between work, race, and community building in the elite suburbs before World War II. Lying just north of the city on Lake Michigan, Evanston began to attract white commuters before the turn of the century. Ancient beach ridges offered compelling views, lake breezes moderated the summer heat, and after 1883 improved rail service provided convenient access to the central business district. As prosperous Chicagoans adopted the commuting habit, they transformed Evanston from a quiet college town of 4,200 in 1880 to a bustling commuter suburb of 25,000 by 1910.[123]

Though wealthy whites were the suburb's most influential residents, Evanston's African American community was as old as the village itself. Black settlers arrived in the 1850s, while Chicago was still a muddy boomtown, and by 1880, 125 African Americans lived in the suburb. They held jobs ranging from the skilled trades to personal service, but as Evanston and nearby suburbs drew white commuters, the availability of domestic work attracted a growing number of migrants. By 1910 Evanston's black community had swelled to 1,100 people, and the suburb was the domestic service hub for Chicago's affluent North Shore. It had also developed migration chains linking it with black communities in the South. As the Great Migration poured black southerners into the Chicago area during the next three decades, African American Evanston grew sixfold.[124]

The economic foundation for this black community was labor in domestic and personal service. By 1940 African Americans composed one-third of Evanston's sizable service labor force, and domestic work was the dominant job category among black Evanstonians, especially women.[125] Contrary to the norm among white suburbanites of the era, more than half of black women in Evanston worked outside the home. As many as 80 percent did domestic work

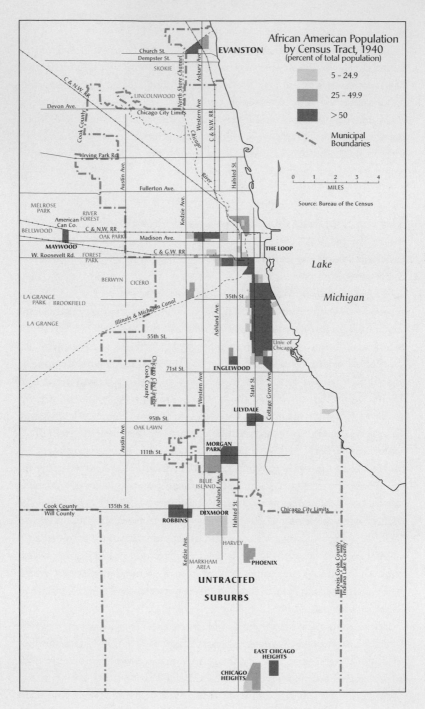

Fig. 2.5   African Americans in Chicago, Illinois, and Suburbs, 1940.
(Map by Harry D. Johnson)

or laundry.[126] Throughout the 1920s and 1930s, the daily migration of black women from west side to east side and back again was one of the familiar tides of Evanston life, and long before reverse commuting became a national phenomenon, black women waited each morning for the northbound train to take them away from the city and deeper into the North Shore suburbs.[127] Black men held a wider range of jobs, though service employment accounted for a plurality of male occupations before World War II. Unlike the predominance of industrial work in Chicago and nearby factory suburbs, more than 40 percent of African American men worked in domestic and kindred services in 1920, while just 10 percent held industrial jobs. Chauffeurs, porters, and janitors headed the list of men's occupations. Like many black communities of its size, Evanston also supported a small professional elite, as well as a number of skilled workers and local entrepreneurs, but domestic and personal service overshadowed all other fields.[128]

Race relations in Evanston followed outlines characteristic of the nation's elite suburbs. As the number of African Americans grew, white Evanstonians began to redraw the local color line. The two local hospitals began to turn away black patients after the turn of the century, granting exceptions "only . . . if your [white] employer brought you." "Even if there was an emergency," resident James Avery recalled, "they sent you down to Cook County."[129] The YMCA barred African Americans in 1914. Restaurants, hotels, and many stores "didn't serve the colored," while in other establishments, black customers could shop but were forbidden to try on merchandise.[130] The suburb's scout troops banned African Americans, and all but one city park forbade black children from using the playground equipment. Northwestern University, too, was a leader in segregation, excluding black students from its dormitories after the turn of the century and after 1914 forbidding them from taking physical education courses on campus or swimming in the university pool.[131] Finally, Evanston cinemas required black patrons to sit in the "roost," or balcony. By 1920 white Evanston had established informal racial restrictions that mimicked patterns of jim crow segregation in the South. "There were no signs such as 'whites only,'" recalled three senior citizens, "but everyone knew where they were allowed and not allowed to be."[132]

White Evanstonians pursued similar practices in education and housing. As black Evanston grew, the school board established a policy of flexible districting that allowed officials to shift district limits to encompass black community expansion, the effect of which was to concentrate black children in one elementary school.[133] The suburb's white real estate establishment also standardized practices of informal racial zoning that made neighborhood school segregation easier. By the mid-1920s, one resident reported that there was "no doubt that there are confined limits within which Negroes may come to live in Evanston."[134]

In contrast to many suburbs that sought to exclude African Americans altogether, the distinctive social relationships among whites and blacks in suburbs like Evanston produced unusual housing market practices. Since hundreds of African Americans owned local property by 1910 and black workers were indispensable to elite life, Evanston brokers, contractors, and lenders conceded "a certain, well-defined Negro section" for black households while restricting access to the remainder of town.[135] Leading members of Evanston's real estate fraternity financed the construction and purchase of scores of new homes for African Americans on the west side. Meanwhile, they excluded blacks elsewhere through various formal and informal arrangements.[136] In developing sections of north and southwest Evanston, white builders firmly refused to sell or rent to African Americans.[137] In existing neighborhoods, residents acted collectively to block black expansion. To the south of the suburb's black district, residents established the West Side Improvement Association in 1922 "to preserve [the neighborhood] as a place for white people to live."[138] As part of the plan, they formed a "syndicate" to buy properties that were at risk of being sold to African Americans or otherwise subsidizing their purchase by whites. In 1926, recognizing that "our purse was not long enough" to hold the color line on a case-by-case basis, property holders signed a restrictive covenant legally binding them not to sell or rent to "Negroes." On the basis of this covenant, the group went to court in 1933 to evict a black family who had rented a house in the neighborhood.[139] Through these and other means, local whites ensured that there was no area of African American expansion outside west Evanston between 1910 and 1945, despite black population growth of almost 5,000.

More intrusive than the exclusion of African Americans from white neighborhoods, local officials and real estate agents also took steps to expel black families from neighborhoods where they already lived, in effect pushing the community westward and away from the center of town.[140] In 1921 Evanston passed the first comprehensive zoning ordinance in Illinois. Despite planners' expressed concern for residential preservation, the new code zoned almost every block where blacks lived outside west Evanston—most of them near the railroad tracks or the edges of downtown—for industrial or commercial use.[141] Steered by municipal land-use policy, public and private development during the next thirty-five years replaced scores of black-occupied homes and apartments with commercial facilities.[142] Over time, racial struggle over space resulted in the dislocation of black Evanston to the west. By the end of the century, just one street of African American homes and the stately buildings of Evanston's three oldest black churches provided the only reminder that the heart of the suburb's black community was once east of the railroad tracks.

By 1940 it was a simple matter to trace the limits of black Evanston. To the west and north, the community ended abruptly at the banks of a wide drainage canal. To the east, black neighborhoods came to a halt at the Chicago & Northwestern Railroad tracks, with a small node projecting eastward on two streets to the elevated commuter line. On the south, Church and Emerson Streets formed "the dividing line" between white and African American neighborhoods.[143] Eighty-four percent of African American households in Evanston lived within these limits, and the core of the neighborhood was 95 percent black. Beyond these bounds, African American families lived in a few pockets of older homes purchased before 1900, but on the eve of World War II, suburban Evanston was nearly as segregated as the city of Chicago.[144]

In Evanston and suburbs like it, race was not merely a social distinction but a spatial reality whose dimensions and meaning were well understood by residents on both sides of the color line. Ted Wheeler, a Georgian who moved to the suburb as a teenager in 1947, recognized the connection between spatial and social inequality that was written in the suburb's racial boundaries: "You remember what Martin Luther King said about Chicago being the most segregated city in America?" Wheeler recalled. "In Evanston that meant that none of the brothers ever crossed that canal [to northwest Evanston] unless they were carrying a white man some food."[145] For African American suburbanites in the Great Migration era, *what* they were allowed to be and *where* they were allowed to be were two sides of the same coin.

Conclusion

Although scholars have paid limited attention, suburbs attracted an important share of black migration during the 1910s and 1920s. Like migrants who settled in cities, the new suburbanites were blue-collar southerners who sought to improve their lives by moving through space. They came to the suburbs for jobs and to join others who had gone before them. In new surroundings, they rebuilt familiar communities, interwoven with ties of kinship and association rooted in the South. Even so, suburban migrants made choices that distinguished them, settling in a variety of suburban places, where the structure of the labor market shaped distinctive communities.

In suburbs as well as cities, migrants' arrival provoked novel efforts on the part of whites to restrict access to public and private space. Discrimination in the real estate market, backed by legal and extralegal restrictions, blocked African American access to most suburban areas. Instead, migrants moved to a few suburbs where the availability of employment, the presence of an earlier African American community, or the lack of land-use controls opened a door to settlement. Most such areas were poorly situated, prone to flooding, industrial pollution, or some other nuisance. Often they were isolated, physically and socially, from the rest of town, a process that was exacerbated by the spread of segregation and exclusion in public facilities. The result was a racial hierarchy of separate and unequal suburban territory — racialized space — that reinforced racial and economic inequality in social life.

In such a context, it is easy to forget African Americans' own aspirations for the places they would live. But as important as racism, work, gender, and family were in shaping suburban life, they only partially explain African Americans' decisions about where to settle and how to live. Black suburbanites also expressed normative ideas about housing, landscape, and social life that affected the kinds of communities they made. Despite differences among suburbs, early suburbanites exhibited similar attitudes about home ownership, economy, and domestic production that shaped the way they used space. They were more likely than central city residents to be home owners, and they often used their homes as means to economic subsistence. Many also avoided cities explicitly, preferring environments that mixed elements of urban and rural life. As they had demonstrated by leaving the southern communities of their youth, early suburbanites molded the world around them to meet their hopes as well as their needs. In suburbs as well as cities, they sought to manipulate space to achieve their own aims.

Chapter 3

Places of Their Own
An African American Suburban Dream

In the South where most of our people come from, nearly everybody who is anybody owns something. "A little home of my own someday" idea is in the minds of little children, and when they become grown-ups, they are property owners.

> —*New York Age* (1927)[1]

It's better to live in a "shack" that's your own than to abide in a palace that belongs to another.

> —*Baltimore Afro-American* (1927)[2]

IN 1959 a writer from the *Cleveland Plain Dealer* visited a small African American community near Cleveland called Chagrin Falls Park. He described a landscape of small houses, large gardens, frame churches, and cinder-block stores as well as overgrown lots and cannibalized automobiles. To the reporter's eye, the 700 inhabitants lived in a "shantytown," but among those he interviewed were men and women who described "the Park" as a community where they had built better lives for themselves. Representative of these was Magnolia Strickland, a native of Georgia who praised the community for its open space, fresh air, gardens, and the opportunity to own a home. "I think I bettered my condition," Strickland said. "I got five rooms; they all got heat from an oil furnace. I got an electric stove and hot and cold running water from my well—and it's all paid for. . . . I couldn't have done all that in Cleveland."[3]

The divergent views of Strickland and the reporter illustrate common reactions to early black suburbs. To outsiders—journalists, city planners, white neighbors, and many middle-class blacks—these places were "slums," "poverty pockets," or in the case of Chagrin Falls Park a "curse."[4] Academic observers, too, saw these communities as little more than "rural slums" or "little ghettoes" that belonged outside the legitimate suburbanization process.[5] To residents, however, these neighborhoods represented something altogether different; they were home, places where people had bought land, built houses, nurtured families, and created communities. Moreover, Strickland's comments suggest that residents wanted many of the same things as other suburbanites, including homes of their own, bucolic landscapes, and family-centered community life. Yet they also pursued a distinctive residential ethic: a set of values and practices that affected how they perceived and used domestic space. Slums to some, these places were also suburbs shaped by the experience, aspirations, and income of the black families who made them home.

The emphasis that Strickland and her neighbors placed on the aesthetic as well as material benefits of their domestic situation underscores the importance of residential choice among black suburbanites. Evident as the point may seem, few historians have explored the domestic preferences that shaped how and where African Americans lived. While paying careful attention to the impact of white suburban ideologies on the metropolis, urban historians have largely ignored African Americans and other people of color. Scholars of African American history, by contrast, have examined many facets of black agency, but most have overlooked mores related to housing, landscape, and the use of space.[6] Focusing on central cities—aging tenements, crowded apartments, high rents, and real estate discrimination—most scholars until recently have treated the physical environments in which blacks lived as a fixed backdrop that people confronted but did little to create.[7] Approaching suburbanization from the perspective of Magnolia Strickland, however, illustrates that African Americans' choices about how and where to live reflected not only the location of a job but social, economic, and aesthetic predilections that they brought with them from the South. Strickland and her neighbors indicate that middle-class whites were not the only Americans who sought to better their lives by moving to the suburbs.

Despite differences in the communities where they settled, early black suburbanites moved to suburbs for many of the same reasons as nonblacks. Suburban jobs and the appeal of suburban social networks were among them. So, too, were cheap land, fuel, and transportation (especially widespread automobile ownership) and a relative lack of building restrictions at the edge of town. Further, many of the normative values associated with the middle-class "suburban dream," such as the emphasis on detached single-family houses in a semi-rural environment, were widely shared among Americans in the early twentieth century. In short, black suburbanites responded to the same social, ideological, and structural forces that encouraged urban decentralization in general.

All the same, class, race, and culture influenced discrete patterns of suburban life. Facing low wages and unstable employment, African American workers used suburban property as a means of adapting to urban capitalism. In this respect, they heeded class-based imperatives that they shared with other Americans. Regardless of race, blue-collar workers were more likely than middle-class suburbanites to view their homes as a basis for economic survival — as a source of income through renting rooms, as a supplement to wages through gardening and backyard livestock, and, in the years before the welfare state, as irrevocable shelter in times of unemployment, sickness, or retirement. They were less likely than the middle class to view a house as an appreciating asset that they would later sell, and they were more likely to "underconsume" in order to obtain a home of their own, habits that included owner building, self-provisioning, delaying service improvements, and sacrificing children's education for additional wages.[8] Consequently, working-class immigrants in many parts of North America were *more* likely to own their own homes than native-born middle-class whites, a pattern that was especially pronounced on the suburban fringe.[9] For millions of blue-collar Americans before World War II, suburban homes represented a means to economic security and shelter from a hostile economic environment.

Like other Americans, black suburbanites also internalized images of ideal places to live, drawing inspiration not only from elite-oriented visions of suburban arcadia but from southern history and cultural inclinations they shared with other black migrants. Despite the diversity of early suburbs, working-class African Americans expressed recognizable values in regard to housing, home ownership, economic independence, open space, and family life. Where there was vacant land, they worked to buy it and build homes. Even in the most congested suburbs, they grew gardens, kept domestic livestock, and used domestic space to generate income. They relied on extended families for economic as well as emotional support, and many explicitly rejected city living, preferring, instead, rustic landscapes reminiscent of the region from which most had come. Lastly, they gravitated to black communities not only because of racial restrictions but because of the comfort and connection they felt among people like themselves. Taken together, these preferences reflect a coherent vision of better living in the metropolitan United States, what we would rightly call a working-class African American suburban dream.[10]

To explore this vision, this chapter examines the case of one African American suburb, Chagrin Falls Park, Ohio, placing it in the context of dozens of black suburbs before World War II. Although the community was small, it is an apt choice for analysis. As an unplanned subdivision, it represented an important category of suburban settlement, but more important, the lifeways characteristic of this community and places like it were common in black suburbs of all kinds. Furthermore, because Chagrin Falls Park was an unincorporated suburb developed from scratch by working-class black families, it reveals migrants' values and aesthetics with a minimum of overt intervention by whites. Black suburbanization in Chagrin Falls Park is not the last word, but it points toward new avenues for research in African American and urban history.

Unplanned Suburb: Chagrin Falls Park, Ohio

During the spring of 1921, an agent of the Home Guardian Corporation of New York walked into the Cleveland offices of Samuel Rocker, publisher of the *Jewish World*, a Yiddish-language newspaper. Home Guardian had recently subdivided a suburban tract southeast of the city called Chagrin Falls Park. The agent proposed to Rocker that the *Jewish World* offer lots in Chagrin Falls as subscription premiums.[11] By June 1921 full-page advertisements in the *World* announced the premiums, and readers began buying lots.[12] Developed with a minimum of investment and no restrictions, the subdivision had no sewers, water lines, or electricity, and its streets were little more than dirt lanes. Perhaps because of poor services, the buoyant expectations of Rocker and Home Guardian went unfulfilled. Lots sold slowly, and in 1924 Home Guardian sold the remainder of its lots to white real estate agents Grover and Florence Brow, who began a thirty-year career selling Chagrin Falls Park lots — mostly to African Americans in the city of Cleveland.[13]

In marketing rustic building lots to African Americans, the Brows replicated the decision of real estate agents in dozens of American cities. Despite the professionalization of real estate practice and the spread of land-use planning, low-cost land markets serving working-class families endured in the United States and Canada before World War II.[14] African Americans represented a small but important segment of these markets. During the

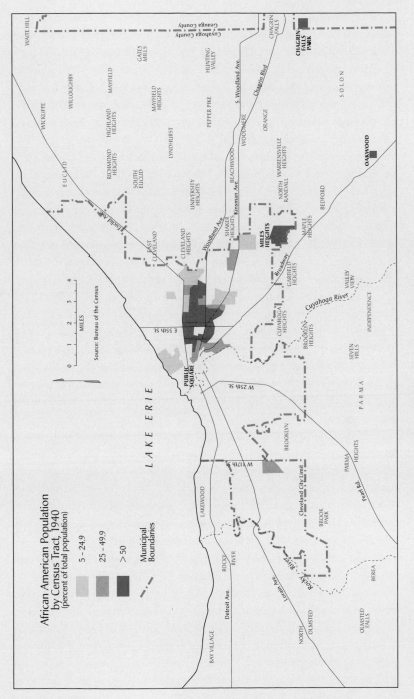

African American Population
by Census Tract, 1940
(percent of total population)

5 – 24.9

25 – 49.9

>50

Municipal
Boundaries

Source: Bureau of the Census

MILES

0   1   2   3   4

LAKE ERIE

PUBLIC SQUARE

Fig. 3.1   African Americans in Cleveland, Ohio, and Suburbs, 1940. (Map by Harry D. Johnson)

1910s and 1920s, black newspapers brimmed with advertisements for lot subdivisions like Chagrin Falls Park. Between 1921 and 1927, New York's black press advertised subdivisions in no less than fourteen suburbs, in addition to homes and lots in a dozen more.[15] Black papers such as the *Chicago Defender*, *California Eagle*, *Pittsburgh Courier*, *Cleveland Gazette*, and *Baltimore Afro-American* published advertisements for local allotments as well as subdivisions as far away as Egg Harbor and New Brunswick, New Jersey; Gainesville, Florida; and Washington, D.C.[16]

Regardless of the region or race of the subdivider, their sales pitches were remarkably similar, reflecting agents' best understanding of their market. Insofar as families bought, these ads may offer clues to the desires of black suburbanites during the Great Migration. Reflecting migrants' southern origins, ad after ad offered a slice of country life: open space for fruit trees, garden plots, chickens, and other small livestock. Notably, they promised elements of the country in combination with urban amenities: proximity to urban jobs, convenient transportation, and community facilities such as churches, schools, and stores. In a few cases, ads appealed to race pride explicitly, encouraging readers to "join hands with your own people" by buying lots in a black subdivision.[17] More often, they linked suburbanization to race uplift by naming subdivisions after heroes in the freedom struggle, such as Booker T. Washington, Frederick Douglass, or Abraham Lincoln. Promoting a borderland between urban and rural living, with the image of racial progress at center stage, agents above all promised the opportunity "for colored people to own a home."[18]

Although the Brows's sales pitch is not recorded, they made inexpensive suburban land available to working-class black Clevelanders. Prices of Chagrin Falls Park lots fluctuated during the 1920s from $60 to $200—two weeks' to two months' salary for the average black factory worker in Cleveland. By contrast, similar parcels in the city ran to several hundreds of dollars, and house prices reached into the thousands. African Americans began purchasing lots from the Brows after 1924, and a small number began to build houses in this semi-rural subdivision. Ironically, lot sales picked up after 1929 as real estate prices collapsed during the depression. By the mid-1930s, Florence Brow sold lots in the Park for as little as $25, and black families who had managed to save money were able to purchase at a bargain. Even more important, many early white purchasers let their taxes fall delinquent during the 1930s, and scores of black Clevelanders purchased lots at the Geauga County Sheriff's auction, some for as little as $2 a piece.[19]

The people who bought lots and built homes in Chagrin Falls Park were

Fig. 3.2   Advertisement for a black subdivision in Oakwood, Ohio, not far
from Chagrin Falls Park. Ads for low-cost building lots in rustic subdivisions were
common in the pages of the nation's black press during the Great Migration.
(*Cleveland Gazette*, June 14, 1924)

primarily working-class black Clevelanders who had migrated from the South
(predominantly Georgia, Alabama, and Tennessee). Of household heads who
settled in the Park between 1924 and 1945, 60 percent had worked in unskilled labor or personal service in Cleveland before moving to the Park. Fully
a third had been common laborers. Most settlers relocated to the Park as mature married couples — most were in their late thirties or forties — having lived
in Cleveland for a number of years before moving to the suburbs. Just 5 percent owned homes before moving to the Park — a home-ownership rate less

than half the average in the neighborhoods from which they moved. On the whole, original Park residents represented a cross section of black Cleveland weighted toward the lower end of the economic ladder.[20]

Having purchased bare lots in Chagrin Falls Park, black families built homes and community institutions in a fashion similar to working-class European immigrants in a number of cities. Clara Adams described her husband's efforts:

> When they had the sheriff's sale, he went up there and bought these three lots. He built on two lots a little three-room house. He had friends to help him. The funny part about it, he was on WPA at that time and he was talking about building a house. I said, "How you gonna build a house? You haven't got any money." And he said, "I got $50." And I said, "$50?" 'Cause that tickled me, him talking about building a house on $50. But he said, "Well, if you never start anything, you never get anything."[21]

Buyers with greater resources hired builders, and a few rented or bought houses vacated by early white residents, but most newcomers, like Adams, came out on the weekends or evenings and built their own homes.[22] To cut costs, many used scrap lumber, and they extended construction over long periods, building what they could afford and then waiting until the next few paychecks to proceed. Where family labor or carpentry skills proved insufficient, many builders employed the muscle of friends and neighbors. An ethic of neighborly aid pervaded the community during the early years of building. One resident, whose mother built her own house, remarked that "most everybody could do some kind of fixing, and everybody kind of helped everybody."[23] Another woman, who was a young adult when her father built in the Park, remembered, "The neighbors dug the basement by hand, and my father and another man that lived down the street built the house. Everything was done as we went. We paid for the stuff as we went along."[24] In some cases, the products of these labors were little more than tar-paper shelters or rickety "nautilus houses" that grew larger each year as a family's income allowed.[25]

In spite of rudimentary conditions and the challenge of owner building, Chagrin Falls Park gained population. The 1930 census enumerated just 57 African American residents, who were interspersed with a smaller number of whites. By 1940 the census tallied 200 African Americans in the Park (most whites had moved on), but the Second World War spurred a period of rapid growth that marked the community's heyday. After the war, Chagrin Falls

Fig. 3.3   Stephen and Ruby Hall built this Chagrin Falls Park house in the late 1930s with the help of Mrs. Hall's parents and other relatives. In the backyard were a cast-iron pump, chicken coop, vegetable garden, and an outhouse. (Photograph by Andrew Wiese, 1998)

Park was a bustling settlement with four churches, numerous social clubs, several small nightspots, beauty parlors, stores, and an automobile service station. The community's most notable public buildings were a two-room elementary school, a cinder-block firehouse, and a brand-new community center, built with local donations and volunteer labor. By 1950 Chagrin Falls Park was home to more than 700 black residents, and the community boasted a home-ownership rate of 70 percent, considerably higher than the 52 percent in neighboring middle-class Chagrin Falls, where many Park residents worked as domestic servants for whites.[26]

Owner building was just one factor that reduced the cost of a suburban home for residents of the Park. Living at the limits of their income, residents avoided the cost of utilities by doing without. Like many such communities, Chagrin Falls Park had no paved streets, electricity, gas, water lines, sewers, garbage collection, or local fire protection throughout its early years. Residents lit with kerosene or coal oil, they dug wells and backyard privies, and they cooked over coal or wood stoves. Families burned or hauled their own garbage (or fed it to the pigs that many kept), and they struggled frantically when a home or church caught fire. Electricity arrived in the Park in 1936, when the township school board built a new (and de facto segregated) elementary school in the community, though it would be decades before some residents connected. The school board also drilled the first deep well in the community, and some residents relied on the schoolhouse pump to supply drinking water. Other services followed slowly. In 1946 the Park welcomed its first paved street, and a group of local men had established a volunteer fire company. A survey that year revealed that 40 percent of local wells faced imminent danger of seepage from septic tanks and backyard privies, though families were left to respond to the problem on an individual basis. Sanitary conditions in the Park remained a recurrent problem until the township government laid sewers and storm drains in 1974, although even then a substantial number of residents opposed construction for fear that the tax assessment would price them out of their homes. As late as the 1980s, there were a few older residents of Chagrin Falls Park who lived in homes without running water.[27]

Although the longevity of primitive services in Chagrin Falls Park represented an extreme, limited public service and regulation were characteristic of working-class suburban areas before World War II. Indeed, the ubiquity of unrestricted development was one of the reasons that cities and suburbs enacted land-use planning in the first place. Most suburbs did not enact zoning laws until the 1940s, however, and even those that did had no influence over development outside their boundaries. Hence, the unincorporated fringe was the native environment of working-class suburbia.

In African American suburbs, however, race often acted as a brake on future improvements. Discrimination in employment and lending kept black suburbs poor and poorly housed, even as working-class white suburbs installed public improvements and rose in income after World War II. Racism also made it unlikely that neighboring suburbs would annex, extend services, or share schools with these communities. Where black neighborhoods were located within larger suburbs, poor services reflected municipal neglect as much as residents' economy, serving as a means to mark the color line. Either way, the rustic environment of many black suburbs tended to reinforce over time the entanglement of race and space, solidifying for whites an equation between black people, poverty, and substandard housing. Poor conditions became the rationale for redlining, municipal avoidance, and inattention. As a result, rudimentary services persisted for much longer in early black suburbs than most comparable white communities.[28]

Within incorporated suburbs, too, land-use restrictions often remained uneven before World War II. Suburbs with large working-class populations, especially, often balked at strict enforcement of building codes and opposed taxation to pay for extensive services.[29] Suburbs known for wealthy commuters also enforced building and sanitary codes selectively. In Evanston, Illinois, and Pasadena, California, officials issued permits for cheap owner-built homes, and some families delayed service hookups even where sewers and water mains ran down the middle of the street.[30] Throughout the Philadelphia area, black sections of elite suburbs retained unpaved streets into the 1960s.[31] In these suburbs, land-use regulations served to reinforce racial inequality more than a uniform landscape; racism as much as thrift was responsible for rudimentary services in black neighborhoods. Even so, working-class families took advantage of municipal laxity to carve footholds in the suburbs at low cost.

In addition to foregoing services, residents of Chagrin Falls Park and other suburbs extended their incomes by growing vegetables and raising small livestock. Ruby Hall recalled that her father "wanted a place where he could have a garden to help with the food, and he got him hogs and killed them in the wintertime. A lot of people was doing the same. So people had them a lot of chickens and gardens. A lot of people had been farmers, so they knew how to farm."[32] Throughout the early years of community growth, residents relied on gardens to supply fresh food in the summer and to produce surplus for the winter.[33] Like Mrs. Hall's father, many residents supplemented their diets with animal produce as well. Chickens were abundant, but residents also kept geese and ducks, and occasionally a hog or two. A few residents, like Horace Lumpkin, raised animals to sell (or turned corn into alcohol), and others sold garden produce in small stores that dotted the community.[34] Residents also put the nearby landscape to economic use, cutting wood for fuel, picking fruit, and hunting. One woman remarked, "All this was woods back up in here, and people didn't care whose woods it was, and they thinned that woods out and burned it up."[35] While urban African Americans of the same income level suffered during years of economic hardship, residents of suburbs like Chagrin Falls Park at least had the cushion of home produce to keep starvation from the door.

Even in prosperous times, the challenge of making a living in a community distant from city employment placed a burden on families in Chagrin Falls Park. As low-skilled and low-paid workers, residents acutely felt fluctuations in the business cycle. Several early residents worked in a nearby iron foundry but were forced to find other work when it closed in the mid-1920s. Men often commuted to jobs in Cleveland or nearby suburbs. One man noted, "We went through a whole lot . . . just to be out here . . . [but] there wasn't no

Fig. 3.4 Residents of Chagrin Falls Park created a rustic landscape that included modest homes, large gardens, livestock pens, and plenty of open space. This landscape (ca. 1940) reflected a vision of suburban life that emphasized domestic production, thrift, and family security, while exposing a lingering ambivalence about urban industrial life. (Courtesy of the Estate of Elizabeth Meade Smith)

thought of this not being home. This was home. Once we got here, this was it. Whatever it took to get back here, that's what we did."[36] Trolley service from Cleveland to Chagrin Falls ceased in 1924, but workers could catch a bus to the city from several neighboring suburbs. Some men drove or carpooled, while other men spent the week in the city and weekends in the Park with their families. Luck Walker worked at American Steel & Wire in Cleveland and drove himself and several other Park men to and from the city each day. Henry MacMiller and his brother-in-law Frank Young were among several Park men who worked for the Cleveland Department of Sanitation and who carpooled in MacMiller's auto. Al Turner, on the other hand, worked with his wife as caretaker for a whites-only social club in a nearby suburb.[37] Facing a restrictive job market, limited incomes, and a commute of more than fifteen miles to the most reliable sources of employment, black men in the Park risked a great deal more than their middle-class white counterparts for a home in the suburbs.

Given the insecurity of male employment, women's wage work was vital to the survival of Chagrin Falls Park and suburbs like it. Middle-class white suburbanites could generally afford to live on the salary of a male breadwinner. The limited research on working-class white suburbanites suggests, too, that few married women worked outside the home.[38] In contrast, working-class black families who aspired to a home in the suburbs often relied on the income of two or more adults. While men typically commuted to distant jobs, women found work as domestic servants for white families just a mile away in the village of Chagrin Falls. The 1940 census reported 29 percent of Park women as employed outside the home, but other sources suggest that women's wage labor played an even more important role than this figure implies.[39] All twelve of the early female settlers of the Park interviewed in 1986 reported having worked as domestic servants, cooks, or laundresses at one time during their years in Chagrin Falls Park. Moreover, service was the occupation of their mothers, aunts, and sisters in the Park. Tellingly, women who worked exclusively as housewives were identified as such. One elderly man noted proudly that his wife had not had to work outside the home.[40] A 1983 community survey supported this conclusion; seventy-nine percent of female seniors who had lived in the community for longer than thirty years listed a current occupation or the category "retired" as opposed to "housewife," when asked to list their occupation.[41] Even if the census revealed less than a third of women in the labor force at enumeration time, a higher percentage appear to have been employed at crucial times during their lives — periods of male unemployment, for example, or during periods of property accumulation and home building.

In addition to doing wage work, women in suburbs of all kinds stretched incomes through various forms of domestic production: tending gardens, sewing, taking in roomers, or operating small business ventures. In Chagrin Falls Park, women did laundry or sewing for local whites, and several daughters remember their mothers rendering soap from lard and selling the product to neighbors or families in "the Falls."[42] Several women in the Park ran small stores. Nellie Lawrence, who was the community's midwife, opened a store in a tar-paper structure in the 1940s selling products ranging from coal oil to candy and fresh produce. Lottie Lewis and Estella Denson ran small canteens with jukeboxes and space for dancing. In addition to increasing women's influence within the community, women's work — inside and outside of homes — provided a vital source of income for black families who wanted to purchase land, build homes, and relocate from the city. In contrast to the middle-class emphasis on suburban homes as sites of consumption, property in working-class suburbs was a site of essential domestic production, much of it by women.

Women in Chagrin Falls Park also appear to have played even broader public roles than women in white suburbs — regardless of class.[43] That role included waged employment and a myriad of unpaid economic tasks as well as active participation, if not leadership, in local politics and public affairs. During the 1940s, residents of the Park organized a number of campaigns for local improvement, including the establishment of a political organization, a move for municipal incorporation, a desegregation suit against the township school board, and efforts to construct a local community center and a fire station. Women took leading roles in all but the latter effort.

The surviving minutes of the Geauga County Negro Republican Club (May 1940–April 1941) offer several examples of women's public roles in Chagrin Falls Park. Established in 1940, the Republican Club rallied voters, secured patronage jobs through the County Republican Party, and transported voters to the polls on election day as well as sponsoring a local baseball team and other social activities. Within the club, women fulfilled a variety of "traditional" gender roles: they chaired the sick committee and the social committee, performed musical numbers that opened and closed each meeting (though a man always led the opening prayer), and their comments tended to emphasize social service, health, education, and children. Even before World War II began to siphon young men from the community (though most of the club's members were above draft age), women filled three of the five positions on the club's executive committee. Women were nearly equal contributors to the club's frequent collections. Finally, when the club appointed official delegations — to visit the offices of the County Republican Party or the editor of the *Cleveland Call and Post*, the city's black newspaper — women shared these responsibilities.[44] Though women in many suburbs participated in child- and family-related service activities, women's political participation in Chagrin Falls Park suggests an even broader latitude for public action in early African American suburbs.

This same pattern was evident after the war. When residents petitioned the township for incorporation as a village in 1946, a woman led the initiative, and two women served on the three-person committee that presented the case to the township board of trustees.[45] That same year, a delegation from Chagrin Falls Park addressed the Cleveland Branch of the NAACP to press for desegregation of the Park elementary school. Eleven of fourteen representatives were women. Two years later, when residents established a local community center, half of the founders were women.[46]

The activities of the irrepressible Essie Kirklen suggest the range of women's roles in Chagrin Falls Park. In the years before 1945, Mrs. Kirklen

Fig. 3.5   Women in suburbs such as Chagrin Falls Park wore many hats, including those of mother, breadwinner, and extended family member. Nellie Lawrence, who moved to Chagrin Falls Park to join family in 1939, served the community for many years as its midwife and became a surrogate "grandmother" to many local children. (Courtesy of Mrs. Fannie Detwyler and Monica Detwyler-Spivey)

not only taught Sunday school at the Church of God, but she also helped lay the church's foundation and swung a hammer in the church rafters.[47] She raised a son and the children of relatives, earning an income for a time through day work in white homes. She purchased building lots at the county sheriff's auction, rented property, and pitched a hand while neighbors built homes. She kept minutes for the Republican Club and promoted the establishment of the community center, and in 1946 Kirklen led the failed campaign for municipal incorporation. Kirklen was an extraordinary individual, but her vita suggests that there was space in suburbs like Chagrin Falls Park for women to play broader public roles than in suburbs of either middle-class or working-class whites. In a suburb with limited economic resources in which men earned uncertain incomes at distant jobs, the needs of community building itself may have structured distinctive gender roles within African American families, offering assertive women the opportunity to shoulder responsibilities that were less available elsewhere.

Toward a Working-Class African American Suburban Vision

The most important reason early residents gave for settling in Chagrin Falls Park was the desire to own a house and property. Among early settlers, the value of property ownership ran so deep that it needed almost no explanation. Ruby Hall, for example, noted that families like hers moved to the Park because "wasn't nobody could buy in the city." Others seemed to take it for granted that working-class people would buy property when the chance presented itself. Describing the events that led to her move in 1940, Clara Adams recalled, "I had a couple of days [of work] per week out in Euclid [another suburb], and I met Mrs. Love who was living out here. She was telling me about the lots and how you would get them for four and five dollars. . . . I told my husband about this, and so he wanted to meet her. She told him about how he could go to the sheriff's sale in Chardon and get these lots. So when they had the sheriff's sale, he went up there and bought three lots." To Ruby Hall, the reason people struggled to build a community in an isolated section of suburban Cleveland was simple. "Everybody at that time," she said, "wanted a little place of their own."[48]

The desire for a place of one's own, historians have shown, has been a central feature of American suburbanization since the nineteenth century. Exactly what different groups wanted and why remains a subject for debate. Middle-class whites, for example, often invested home ownership with images of mas-

The history of the origin of the Church of God

The origin of the Church of God ,was on this wise
Rev;J.V.Goodwin came out and had a tent meeting ,and put up
a tent in 1933 and had meeting allthat summer in the tent
And orginize the Church.and in the Fall and winter had meeting
in Sis.Kirklen little house.Then Purchase some lots,and all
agreed to build a Church.
We bought a 10 room house in Cleveland and tore it down and
began to build,the men dug the basement and the women laid the
brickand stones.And we had meeting in the basement until the
top was finish.The women who laid the stones were Sis.Sallie Denson
Sis.Leatha Smith,Sis.Roberta Lloyd.One,s that hope to put up the
Rafters were Sis.Kirklen Sis,Smith and Sis.Lloyd and Bro.Roy and
HarryPulley.Bro.Royand Bro.Harry Pulley were the Builders
And differend one"s donated Windows The men of the Community
poured the cement for the floor in the basement the community donated
cement and lime.And Rev.Goodwin got the sand on the river
 Rev.Goodwin Plastered the Church And we sold Fruit ,Quilts,
Chichens and eggs to raise money to help on the building and the
Children pulled nails out of the lumber
Omembers who were in the organizing the Church were
Sis.Sallie Denson
Sis,Leatha Smith
Sis,Florence Hayes
SiS.Jossie Yougg
Sis.Cecil Greggs
Sis.Roberta Lloyd
Sis&Bro.Luke Walker
Bro.& Sis.James Lacey
Bro.H. Mc-Miller
Bro .Albert Bolden
Bro. Hatch
Bro.Joe Brown

Other members came in later

Fig. 3.6 "The History of the Origin of the Church of God," Chagrin Falls Park,
Ohio. Essie Kirklen, no date. The detailed description of shared labor in this church
history suggests the varied roles that women played in building black communities in
blue-collar suburbs like Chagrin Falls Park.

culine independence, female domesticity, and idealized nuclear families, not
to mention long-term capital appreciation and superior educational advantages to ensure the heritability of their success. Working-class whites, on the
other hand, more often valued home ownership for its everyday economic
usefulness as well as for economic security over the long run.[49] African Americans, too, sought to use space for their own ends, placing high value on home
ownership as well as detached housing, family-based communities, and bucolic environments. Yet in each case, they approached these as people with a
history and experiences that set them apart. Looking at these aspirations more
carefully reveals the outlines of a working-class black suburban vision rooted

in settlers' experience in the South as well as their expectations for life in urban areas.

As black southerners, suburbanites' value for property ownership had a long history. In the aftermath of the Civil War, property ownership was indissolubly linked with freedom in the aspiration of former slaves. Throughout the late nineteenth and early twentieth centuries, property ownership persisted among the chief values of blacks in the rural South.[50] As the *New York Age* editorialized, "Nearly everybody who is anybody" in the South "owns something."[51] Proprietorship symbolized hard work and ambition in a way evident to every member of the community. It provided a basis for upward mobility, shelter for immediate and extended families, and a foundation in a society that systematically marginalized African Americans. Lastly, it meant a greater degree of independence, which is to say freedom, than any form of tenancy. Although historians such as James Grossman argue that the ideal of upward mobility through urban industrial labor gradually supplanted the value of independent land ownership as the Great Migration progressed, rural southerners who boarded trains for northern cities did not discard older values as easily as excess baggage. Peter Gottlieb suggests as much in his study of black migrants to Pittsburgh, arguing that the difficulty most blacks faced in finding and purchasing housing contributed to a lasting ambivalence about northern life. Anthropologist Carol Stack has revealed more recently that the desire to own property, even at the expense of modern utilities, is among the values that have drawn many African Americans back to the rural South since 1970.[52]

The strength of this value was evident in the African American press, which actively celebrated the benefits of home ownership. Throughout the period of the Great Migration, newspapers both inculcated and reinforced the ideal of home ownership among their readers. Writers evoked concerns ranging from the importance of "sunlight, air and sanitary surroundings for the health and moral status of your family" to the more parochial interests of urban renters. As one 1927 advertisement exclaimed, "We can hardly believe the man who wrote 'Home Sweet Home' was ever put out in the street by his landlord."[53] Others sought to link home buying to individual success as well as racial progress. In the view of a Baltimore real estate agent, "Every home owner is looking forward to independence and prosperity. Every home owner is interested in his wife, his family, his race and his community. If you are not a member of this big happy, well-to-do family, then it's time you were waking up."[54]

Despite limited means, African Americans in Cleveland jumped at the chance to buy property. Some may have relinquished this dream over time, but others clearly did not. Chagrin Falls Park resident Nellie Lawrence was a case in point. As her daughter explained, Mrs. Lawrence had been a sharecropper all her life—"did all the work, give 'em half the profits." Consequently, she "always wanted to be in a home of her own."[55] For migrants such as these, communities like Chagrin Falls Park offered the prospect of upward mobility through urban labor without the sacrifice of long-held desires for independent property ownership. Hence, for a significant group of African American migrants before World War II, suburbanization combined the best of both worlds.[56]

In addition to fulfilling historic desires for property ownership, a house of one's own represented an economic strategy for many early suburbanites. Owner building itself was the most obvious example, as families expended their own labor power to defray the largest expense they faced. There was no single pattern. Some families built everything by themselves or with the help of friends, but many engaged some combination of paid and unpaid labor over an extended period. Rather than purchasing shelter as a commodity through savings or future earnings, residents created "sweat equity" by investing their own labor in the production of new homes.

Owner building and other economic uses of property were common class-based strategies of urban survival in the early twentieth century. Gardens and livestock helped families economize. Proprietorship allowed them to escape central city rents, and domestic spaces provided rental income that supported economic mobility and helped families weather hard times. Regardless of race or ethnicity, domestic production was a characteristic feature of working-class suburbia.[57]

This was particularly true of black suburbs, where evidence of self-provisioning and other economic uses of property was omnipresent across the range of suburban types. In Homestead, Pennsylvania, Margaret Byington reported in 1910 that African American and white immigrant steelworkers used yards for gardening and raising small livestock whenever they could. Likewise in Pasadena, residents remembered that "everyone had their own garden in the backyard, and everybody had chickens and eggs."[58] In World War II Richmond, California, black women in the city's sprawling defense housing projects regularly kept kitchen gardens, where they grew okra, collards, butter beans, sweet potatoes, and other vegetables. By growing familiar foods, they not only supplemented their incomes and diet but, through exchanges or gifts of fresh produce, reinforced community bonds and preserved tangible links to their heritage as African American southerners.[59]

Black suburbanites not only grew food in the backyard; they also utilized interior spaces as a source of income. Women took in laundry, sewing, or piecework, and, as one New York suburbanite noted, "There were rooms in the house which could be rented to get extra money."[60] In Chagrin Falls Park, Estella Denson not only ran a small canteen in her house, she and her husband built an addition to their home that they rented to recent arrivals. Essie Kirklen initially rented space from another family when she moved to Chagrin Falls Park, and once she became settled, she, too, occasionally took in boarders to supplement her income. Clara Adams's husband built their own home as well as three additional houses, which the Adamses kept as rentals.[61] Socially and economically, home ownership in suburbs like Chagrin Falls Park supported upward mobility for many African American families. Magnolia Strickland spoke to precisely this point. Looking back from 1959, she remembered that her twenty years in Chagrin Falls Park had not been easy, but they had been worth the struggle. Measuring the distance she had traveled from the rural South by the amenities of her Chagrin Falls home, she concluded, "I couldn't have done all that in Cleveland."[62]

Rental uses of domestic space were especially common in larger black suburbs, where builders inscribed the practice in the landscape by building or converting houses for two or more families. In Evanston, Illinois, for example, two-flats were the specialty of the suburb's leading black construction firm, whose partners, as residents, were well aware of the predilections of their neighbors and friends. By 1930, 40 percent of houses on the west side of town, where builders had erected four hundred new housing units during the 1920s, were occupied by two families.[63] In such suburbs, property rental not only helped families pay their mortgages, supporting desires for home ownership in the short term; it was also a means to economic independence over a lifetime as many of these properties continued to produce income for black home owners through the rest of the century.

In addition to supporting economic autonomy and upward mobility, values representing suburbanites' best hopes, home ownership reflected migrants' insecurity in the urban economy. Although wage relations had expanded in the South during the late nineteenth and early twentieth centuries, millions of southern blacks worked as tenant farmers, largely outside the cash economy. With expanded industrial job opportunities for blacks during World War I, thousands of young southerners left this life behind — often moving to nearby towns and cities before making the leap north. High wages promised access to a world of new consumer goods, but the transition to a cash economy could also be traumatic. As wageworkers at the bottom of the metropolitan labor market, African American migrants suffered greatly during slumps in the economy. Dependence on an urban wage could spell disaster in the event of unemployment, sickness, or injury. Hence, like many European immigrants as well as native-born whites, some black migrants responded to the process that historian Joe Trotter calls "proletarianization" by holding on to familiar patterns of economic survival.[64] Household production in the suburbs was a cushion against the market and a middle ground between rural and urban life.

A number of contemporary observers drew this same connection, contrasting suburbanites' "rural" strategies with "progressive" or "modern" city life. In Detroit a black social worker argued critically in 1926 that residents of black suburbs often "slip into old southern rural ways of doing things." A black real estate agent in the same study agreed, noting that in the suburbs, "there is no opportunity for a type of development which would enable them to adjust to an urban environment."[65] To the contrary, it appears that many early suburbanites were doing just that. For laboring families who understood privation firsthand, these strategies weren't backward; they were adaptive and practical. More than one resident of Chagrin Falls Park remarked pointedly that they had seen hard times, but they had never gone hungry. While many southern migrants embraced the market and consumer culture—perhaps, as Lizabeth Cohen argues, more avidly than their working-class ethnic counterparts—others were clearly chastened by the experience, and some sought a lifestyle in the suburbs that gave them access to urban opportunities without requiring complete dependence on the market.[66] Evidence from black suburbs suggests that migrants brought with them diverse ideas about survival and mobility in the northern metropolis as well as considerable ambivalence about the urban economy.

In other ways, too, black suburbanites adapted to life in the North by bringing parts of the South with them.[67] As chapter 2 illustrates, black suburbanites followed intricate migration chains to the suburbs. The kinship network of early Chagrin Falls Park resident Sallie Denson suggests the ways that extended family supported the development of suburban communities. Mrs. Denson, a widow, moved to the Park in the late 1920s and built a cinderblock house on Geneva Street with the help of her grown children. By the early 1930s, five of these children—Essie, Edith, Cornelia, Letha, and Pete—had relocated from Cleveland to Chagrin Falls with their spouses. Two other sons, John and Willie, lived in the Park with their wives for a short time before returning to Cleveland. By 1940 Essie's sister-in-law and her husband had also settled, as had two of Mrs. Denson's nephews and their wives. These wives, Annie and Mattie Pounds, attracted cousins Shepherd Beck and Nellie Lawrence to settle with their families in Chagrin Falls by the early 1940s.[68] The

Denson family had among the most extensive kin relations in the Park, but other early residents followed a similar pattern, settling with or joining family already living there.[69] By the 1940s a strong network of kin-based suburbanization had created a web of familial relationships that bound residents to one another as a community. In a suburb where incomes and jobs were insecure, transportation inconvenient, and voluntary cooperation important for survival as well as progress, extended families were a bulwark against hardship and a foundation for upward mobility. In contrast to the middle-class suburban model of the era, characterized by child-centered nuclear families, suburbanization for African Americans in Chagrin Falls Park strengthened the bonds of extended families and friendships that stretched through Cleveland to roots in the South.[70]

In addition to visions of home and family, residents of Chagrin Falls Park expressed normative ideas about landscape that reflected their experience in the South and shaped the community they built in the suburbs. "My family heard about a place where they could buy them some land which reminded them of home," one woman said. "They all came from the South, and they had lived in Cleveland for many years, but they never forgot their home. They wanted a little place where they could have chickens and different little things and a little farm life and gardens."[71] Weighing the sacrifice of city services against the benefits of country living, Clara Adams, who relocated with her husband in 1940, claimed:

> I didn't mind it [giving up a modern apartment in Cleveland]. When we came out here it was just so nice and quiet. You didn't hear nothing but the birds in the morning singing nice. It was where I could have a garden, and I liked that. So it wasn't hard at all. Plus, I was used to the country. That's where I was raised up, so it didn't bother me at all. I didn't like *in* the city—too congested. I liked *out*. I like the fresh air, and it's nice and quiet.[72]

Magnolia Strickland echoed these sentiments, noting, "I think I bettered my conditions. I had a nice new house to live in. I had nice, fresh air, and you could have vegetables and a garden."[73] Based on preferences such as these, residents let side lots grow thick, cultivated extensive gardens, and planted fruit trees and even pine trees from "down home." In the evenings, they sat on front porches they had built and surveyed the quiet. Like middle-class suburbanites, they created a bucolic landscape of residence in union with nature, but with a difference. For early Park settlers, the prospect of fresh air, birdsong, open space, and "a little farm life and gardens" outweighed the desire for modern conveniences that were fundamental to middle-class suburbanization.[74] Their landscape was more rustic, but it was no less suburban.

Coupled with the attractions of country living, many Park settlers also explained their relocation in terms of repulsion from the city. "I was determined not to live in Cleveland," said Fanny Detwyler.[75] Mrs. Detwyler brought her mistrust of urban living directly from the North Carolina countryside, and she avoided the city altogether in her journey to Chagrin Falls Park. Other early residents, however, sought upward mobility through migration to Cleveland and other cities, and they found the experience wanting. Congestion, poverty—especially during the depression—and what some perceived as the atmosphere of immorality that plagued certain city neighborhoods spurred many early Park residents to seek a better place to live. Magnolia Strickland remarked, "I wanted to move out here, I wanted to move anywhere, because East 61st and Thackery was no good."[76] Stephen Hall stressed that many people—like himself—came because of rum running and rent parties in Cleveland's crowded east side—"especially a person that had a family and they didn't believe in none of that stuff."[77] Truck driver Shepherd Beck explained his decision in terms of sleep. "I was working the road, and I'd come home and all the children from the neighborhood was playing ball in my yard and yelling. How am I gonna sleep? I said, 'I'm gonna find me someplace quiet.'"[78] The place he found was Chagrin Falls Park.

Residents of other suburbs drew similar contrasts between city and suburb, expressing environmental preferences that matched those in Chagrin Falls Park. Georgian Lessie Smith was one of many residents of Evanston, Illinois, who contrasted the small-town atmosphere and open spaces of the suburb with the "congestion" and "roughness" of Chicago. Cora Watson, who migrated to Evanston in the 1910s, had hesitated to leave Greenville, South Carolina, even as members of her family relocated to Chicago. "I didn't want to live in a large city," she said. "And then they told me about Evanston." Likewise, Bernice Brown of Englewood, New Jersey, reported that her family had settled there "because this was one of the best areas for making a living, yet it had a resemblance to country life."[79] Alice P., whose parents migrated from South Carolina to the New Jersey suburbs, concurred: "For blacks, living in Englewood or Hackensack was better than living in Paterson or Newark . . . and it *certainly* was better than living in New York City."[80] Examples of suburbanites' preference for a "rural atmosphere" or their "sincere dislike for the rapid city life" could be multiplied to sustain the same point.[81] Thousands of black suburbanites objected to the quality of life in many city neighborhoods, desiring environments reminiscent of the small towns and countryside from which most had come. Low incomes and housing discrimination often thwarted these designs, but where they could, black families shaped their surroundings to suit their ideals as well as their needs.

Beyond the legacy of southern landscape, race and shared elements of southern culture shaped the process of early black suburbanization in other ways as well. Racism as well as African Americans' efforts to overcome it ensured that most black suburbanites lived in a segregated world. Discrimination limited black incomes and prevented families from buying property in all but a few areas of the metropolis — often marginal land beset by environmental nuisance. Bias in mortgage lending encouraged working-class black families to build their own homes and to use property in economically productive ways. Although informal home building was common among working-class white suburbanites, it was a choice African Americans made from even fewer options. Race also shaped early suburbanization from the inside. Suburbanites' passion for home ownership sprang from a venerable black tradition in the South. Patterns of family migration and settlement followed lines that were common among African American migrants, and women's economic activity in many suburbs reflected the wider economic participation of black women in the wage economy. Necessity and choice reciprocated dialectically, but clearly some women chose to settle in suburbs because they were good places to live as well as to work.

If race and racism shaped early black suburbanization, suburban life itself tended to reinforce migrants' racial identities. Held at arm's length by white suburbanites, African Americans relied on their own resources. They established separate institutions, worshiped in separate churches, and socialized in a predominantly black milieu. Politically, they organized to overcome racial inequality as members of race- and place-based communities. In Chagrin Falls Park, black men rode to work together and labored with other blacks in segmented occupations — in the foundry at American Steel & Wire or at the back of a garbage truck with the Department of Sanitation. Women who worked as domestics had closer connections with local whites, but at best these relationships left racism unchallenged. Religious groups from the Park visited black churches in nearby suburbs such as Twinsburg and Miles Heights, and ministers from these communities as well as Cleveland preached guest sermons in local churches. The local Echo Singers performed in black communities throughout the region. The Park baseball team played black "nines" from all over northeastern Ohio, and when the Republican Club hosted an August fish fry, black families from Cleveland and its suburbs crowded Woodland Avenue with their automobiles and "walked in that dust like it was gold dust."[82] Encouraged by persisting white racism as well as their own perception of accomplishment, residents of such places as Chagrin Falls Park forged a distinct sense of themselves as both African Americans and suburbanites.

Although early African American suburbanites confronted the challenge of urbanization as black people with a unique history and culture, they also followed patterns that were common among working-class suburbanites generally, and they shaped landscapes that shared many features with a wider working-class suburbia. Faced with similar economic circumstances, they responded to urban industrial capitalism in part by withdrawing from it. They valued home ownership for many of the same reasons, pursuing similar strategies of economic subsistence including owner building, vegetable gardening, and other productive uses of domestic space. Working-class suburbanites responded to the urban economy in similar ways whether they were Mexican immigrants in East Los Angeles; Polish workers in Milwaukee or Detroit; blue-collar immigrants from the British Isles in Toronto or Hamilton, Ontario; or African Americans in Chagrin Falls Park.[83]

Conclusion

Even as suburbs like Chagrin Falls Park peaked in population, structural conditions that had nurtured them began to change. Rapid white suburbanization after World War II led to the extension of land-use controls to formerly unregulated areas. Zoning and building ordinances curtailed informal home building and raised the price of a suburban home for working-class and poor families. Racist application of these regulations, too, closed the door on future development in many places, and the enforcement of sanitary codes led to the demolition of existing black housing and restrictions on domestic production. A number of suburbs also resorted to urban renewal as a means of isolating, or even expelling, suburban black communities.[84]

At the same time, federal intervention in the housing market and the development of a welfare state eased some of the economic insecurity that had shaped early working-class suburbanization. This was especially true for working-class whites, but the same trends also affected African Americans. The extension of social security and unemployment insurance to a growing number of black workers as well as black entrance into unions in the 1940s promised the kinds of economic security that suburban home ownership had provided before the war. Further, the establishment of federal mortgage programs accommodated the dreams of home ownership for millions of blue-collar families without the hardships of owner building. Comparatively few blacks or other minorities participated in these programs; even so, tens of thousands of modestly priced new homes were constructed for African Americans during the late 1940s and 1950s, and Federal Housing Administration insistence on racial segregation ensured that most were built near existing black areas — usually older black suburbs. While home ownership became marginally more available to middle-income black families and black home-ownership rates inched upward, poor families were increasingly priced out of the market. Within a decade of the war, regulation of the suburbs had foreclosed a wide range of working-class suburban outlets, and federal subsidies limited the number who were willing or able to make the move. By the mid-1950s, the stream of black migrants to the suburbs shifted perceptibly toward the black middle class.

Semi-rural suburbs like Chagrin Falls Park weathered these changes poorly. The Park tripled in population during the 1940s, reaching a peak of nearly 900 in 1960 as a new wave of black southerners hit the city. However, population dwindled thereafter. As African American living standards improved, black expectations for life in an "affluent society" expanded, and strategies of working-class subsistence that had served prewar suburbanites failed to support a standard of living satisfactory to most urban-born African Americans. Pioneer suburbanites preferred a lifestyle reminiscent of the South, but their children and grandchildren often perceived these places as the boondocks. Moreover, they had greater options. By the 1990s, population in Chagrin Falls Park had shrunk to less than 500, and the average income was the lowest in Geauga County.[85] Even so, dozens of elderly men and women lived independently in homes that they owned.

Even though many early suburbs suffered depopulation and chronic poverty, the history of these places belies the mystique of suburbia as the preserve of elite and middle-class whites. In the years before 1950, thousands of central city blacks moved to suburbs. Long ridiculed as "poverty pockets" and "suburban slums," the communities where they settled were often poor, but they were fully part of the national trend toward urban decentralization known as suburbanization. At the same time, they reflected a vision of residential, family, and community life that was at once suburban, working class, and African American. This vision, as much as economic necessity, shaped the landscape of American suburbia in the same fashion as the well-documented dreams of middle-class whites.

Early residents of Chagrin Falls Park and other suburbs valued home ownership less as a long-term capital investment or as shelter for an idealized nuclear family than for its usefulness in cutting costs, providing supplemental income, and limiting dependence on a fragile wage. Equally important, home ownership was a basic symbol of status in African American communities of the South and a marker by which to measure upward mobility in the city. To the southerners who migrated to the suburbs, home ownership was a long-deferred dream that they were willing to sacrifice much to achieve.

Early suburbanites also expressed preferences for a bucolic landscape, but their ideal included unrefined open space, elaborate gardens, small livestock, and the familiar food and routine that these implied. In these suburbs, the cackle of chickens was more common than the sound of a lawn mower. Women's participation in the economic and civic life of Chagrin Falls Park and many suburbs further distinguished them from white suburbs of the same era, and the familial values that facilitated suburban settlement placed higher merit on kinship networks than on isolated nuclear families. Extended families allowed women to work outside the home without worrying about the care of their children. They provided conduits for information about employment and economic support during times of need. Further, the complex networks of family and friendship that characterized suburban society laid a foundation for intimate, stable, and controllable community life that differed from both central city black neighborhoods and the highly mobile and individualistic nuclear family–based society of middle-class white suburbia. To a greater or lesser extent, similar patterns can be discerned in early black suburbs of all kinds.

Lastly, early suburbanites shared a common displeasure with the quality of life in many city neighborhoods. They sought environments reminiscent of the southern small towns and countryside where they had grown up. Low incomes and white racism routinely thwarted these designs, but where they could, black suburbanites shaped domestic space to suit their preferences, as well as their needs, creating suburbs that combined country pleasures with proximity to urban jobs and the cultural and social opportunities of the city.

Chapter 4

"Forbidden Neighbors"

White Racism and Black Suburbanites, 1940–1960

Fig. 4.1   "In a speech against Negro home owners, Chairman James Newell (*center*) tries to rouse hastily formed 'Levittown Betterment Committee.'" Burton Glinn, 1957. Residents of Levittown, Pennsylvania, protest the purchase of a home by the William Myers family. In an era of mass suburbanization, white suburbanites formed a bulwark of resistance to black suburbanization. (Courtesy of Burton Glinn Magnum Photos)

IN AUGUST 1946 officials of Woodmere, Ohio, approached black Cleve-lander Eddie Strickland on the site of a new home he was building in the suburb and arrested him for the "illegal use of used lumber." Strickland, who had been at work on the house since February, had completed the first story when the village constable intervened, objecting ostensibly to Strickland's use of secondhand boards for subflooring material. Threatened not only with arrest but with the loss of his labor and investment, Strickland was exasperated. Speaking to a reporter from Cleveland's black weekly, the *Call and Post*, he argued that his lumber was "better than new." Moreover, in the context of wartime restrictions on building materials, construction with used lumber was a common practice in Cleveland and many suburbs. Finally, Strickland appealed to his rights as a property owner—and implicitly to his rights as an American. Standing amidst his half-finished home in the dusty overalls of a black workingman, Strickland's emotions welled up inside him. "This is my lot and my property," he fumed, "and I'm going to build a home on it or die in the attempt."[1] Strickland never got the chance to keep his promise. After an eighteen-month court battle, Woodmere officials triumphed, blocking Strickland and several other black property owners from building or completing homes on land they owned in the suburb.[2]

Eddie Strickland's confrontation with Woodmere officials raises a variety of substantive issues beyond the immediate struggle over local building regulations in a Cleveland suburb. First, Strickland's arrest came in the middle of a three-year struggle between black property owners and white villagers who were determined to prevent the suburb's black population from growing. In a national context, moreover, Strickland's arrest reflected the expansion of municipal land-use regulations, more aggressive policing of the suburban rim by local governments, and growing racial exclusivity in the suburbs—even in those designed for the working class. In outline and outcome, events in Woodmere reveal that suburban land became a focus of racial struggle in the postwar United States. In the postwar era, whites of various social classes united along racial lines to restrict the benefits of suburban living to "Caucasians only."

At the same time, Strickland's unsuccessful attempt to build a suburban home for his family indicates that the appeal of suburban living remained strong among blue-collar African Americans after the war. Even more than before, African Americans of every description sought homes in suburban areas. Despite obstacles placed in their way, the black suburban population swelled by almost a million during the 1940s and 1950s.[3] Furthermore, Strickland's emotional defense of his home and his rights illustrates that in Woodmere and other suburbs, white officials faced aggressive and politically conscious African Americans who were willing to risk arrest and even violence for a suburban home. On the eve of the southern civil rights movement, African Americans throughout the nation used every available means to assert their right to housing of their choice. Combined with desires for better homes and neighborhoods, African Americans' willingness to challenge the status quo placed them on a collision course with whites in the suburban housing market.

A closer look at the struggle over building rights in Woodmere suggests the intensity and outlines of a larger racial contest over suburban land in the wartime and postwar United States. Before 1940, Woodmere had been an unincorporated area five miles east of the Cleveland city limits. Unregulated building by blue-collar whites of various ethnicities gave the area a reputation as a "poor man's neighborhood." Less charitable observers described it as a "shanty town."[4] By the early 1940s, several affluent areas nearby had incorporated as separate suburbs with boundaries carefully skirting the dirt streets of Woodmere. In 1945 what remained was a square mile of unincorporated land, most of it wooded, in the midst of large estates, horse farms, and municipalities angling for high-priced subdivisions.[5] About this time, black Clevelanders began purchasing home sites in the area. They received permits from county officials in Cleveland and began building their own homes much as working-class families had done in many other suburbs before the war. By 1944 as many as fifteen black families were living in Woodmere, and a number of others were building houses on a do-it-yourself basis.

The first hint of trouble was a wave of unexplained fires, which damaged African American–owned homes and building sites in 1944. Telephone conversations overheard on the local party line revealed growing resentment among some whites over the number of African Americans building in the area. Later that year, residents held a referendum for incorporation, which led to the formation of the Village of Woodmere. For more than a year, black families continued building while a political coalition amenable to owner-builders held sway on the village council. In 1946, however, the coalition collapsed, and in a series of irregular meetings, the council passed a building code aimed at restricting do-it-yourself builders, among whom blacks were a prominent group. The code mandated a maximum one-year time limit for the construction of new homes, forbade secession of work for any period longer than forty-eight hours, and prohibited the use of secondhand building materials. Finally, the code required builders to post a $1,000 bond to ensure compliance. Not only was the latter provision uncommon in Cuyahoga County, but the bond in blue-collar Woodmere was five times larger than the next highest bond in the county—a $200 pledge required in the upper-income suburb of University Heights.[6]

Subsequent events indicated that the framers of Woodmere's building code had more in mind than simply improving construction standards. Upon passage of the ordinance, the village building commissioner revoked previously issued county building permits, and local police arrested a group of black home builders who refused to submit to the ordinance. In addition to Strickland, police "restrained" Charles Taylor of Cleveland after he erected a Quonset hut on property he owned in the village, and they cited veteran Edward Taylor after he laid a concrete foundation for a home (on the Fourth of July, no less) without a permit. Meanwhile, white builders reportedly continued to work unmolested.[7]

The struggle ended in 1948 when a Cleveland judge upheld the convictions and supported Woodmere's right to regulate residential construction by local ordinance. Although the fate of Strickland and his peers is unknown, Woodmere's new restrictions made it increasingly difficult for families like theirs to relocate to the community. By lifting construction standards (and allegedly enforcing regulations in a discriminatory manner), Woodmere officials raised the cost of home building in the village and substantially limited settlement by working-class blacks. Moreover, the passage of similar building restrictions throughout the county helped limit the number of African American suburbanites in the Cleveland area. The trend had an apparently chilling effect on the attendance of blacks at the weekly land auction in Cleveland, where a number of families had formerly purchased suburban land for delinquent taxes. By 1950 the *Call and Post* decried what it described as a "countywide system of barring Negro home builders in suburban areas by irregular building regulations."[8] Where arson had failed to stem black home building, local government proved an effective weapon in the contest for suburban space.

Far from being an isolated event, Strickland's confrontation with authorities in Woodmere reflected a national trend toward regulation of the suburban fringe that hastened the decline of working-class suburbanization in the postwar decades.[9] In Cleveland and other metropolitan areas, the proliferation of suburban municipalities led to the extension of land-use regulations to formerly unregulated areas. Zoning and building codes curtailed informal building and inflated the cost of a suburban home. Racist application of these regulations closed the door on development for blacks, and the enforcement of sanitary regulations led to the demolition of existing black housing and restrictions on domestic production. A number of suburbs also used urban renewal authority to isolate or even expel suburban black communities. By 1960 the proliferation of white suburbs and the explosion of suburban land-use restrictions had effectively curtailed working-class community building of the sort that had characterized African American suburbanization since World War I.

"Forbidden Neighbors"

As events in Woodmere reveal, white racism continued to play a leading role in shaping African American suburbanization. Many whites projected their deepest fears about crime, disorder, health, status, and sexuality on to African Americans.[10] Moreover, whites typically conflated psychological expressions of racial fear with more straightforward economic anxieties and assumptions of social privilege. Among their greatest concerns was that "property values will experience a severe drop" with the arrival of black neighbors.[11] Such was the established opinion of white real estate agents, appraisers, home builders, and lenders. Real estate textbooks presented the hypothesis as fact, and for whites who may have had reason to doubt, the dilapidation of city and suburban neighborhoods where many African Americans lived provided apparent proof to cement the link.[12] Although numerous studies of race and property values refuted any causal link between integration and property values, whites who had invested their savings and staked future financial security on their home remained unconvinced.[13] Combined with violent fantasies about the social consequences of racial integration—especially images of rape and miscegenation—economic fear led millions of whites to view black neighbors as something like Visigoths at the gates of Rome.[14]

Finally, for many working- and middle-class whites—especially immigrants and their children, whose adaptation to American society involved the adoption and manipulation of its racial hierarchies—the coming of African Americans threatened their efforts to rise in status and stability in white American society. As a number of historians have pointed out, suburbanization was closely related to the making of race and class identities in the postwar period. Federal entitlements such as the GI Bill and mortgage insurance programs made it possible for millions of Americans of European descent to attain key symbols of middle-class status, such as a college education, proprietorship of small businesses, and ownership of a new home. Moreover, they encouraged families to measure their class status in terms of their position as consumers rather than as workers.[15] At the same time, George Lipsitz points out, "the suburbs helped turn European Americans into 'whites' who could live near each other and intermarry with relatively little difficulty. But this white 'unity' rested on residential segregation and on shared access to housing and life chances largely unavailable to communities of color."[16] For millions of "not yet white ethnics," segregation was a ticket to social and economic mobility. To live in a neighborhood with blacks, by contrast, was to lose hard-won gains, to be associated with "blackness," and potentially to be trapped at the bottom rung of the American social ladder. In this context, African Americans were "forbidden neighbors" in almost every white neighborhood in postwar America.[17]

To defend their neighborhoods, whites created a gauntlet of discriminatory practices that limited African Americans' access to the housing market. As early as the 1910s, white real estate agents had created Realtors organizations and pledged to uphold a code of ethics that prevented them from being party to transactions that permitted blacks to move into white neighborhoods. Similarly, white financial institutions almost uniformly refused to lend money to African Americans to buy property outside "established Negro areas," and they charged a premium for credit inside as well. Further, white home builders took the view that racial segregation was a "social problem" not a "housing problem," staunchly defending their right to refuse to sell or rent homes to African Americans and other minorities.[18] At the neighborhood level, whites formed home-owners' associations whose chief goal was to prevent African American "infiltration" or "invasion." These groups were instrumental in organizing white neighborhoods to enact race-restrictive covenants, which prohibited the sale or rental of property to "other than Caucasians." As the U.S. Commission on Civil Rights concluded, housing discrimination involved the "deliberate exclusion" of blacks and other minorities "at all levels of the housing and home finance industries."[19]

The example of baseball legend Jackie Robinson illustrates the barriers facing African Americans in the suburban real estate market. When Jackie and Rachel Robinson began searching for a home near New York in 1956, they found themselves entirely shut out. Robinson, who led the Brooklyn Dodgers to the world championship that year and whose reputation for personal integrity was well known, was unable to buy a satisfactory home in the suburbs of the city where he was most celebrated. Eventually, the Robinsons found a house across the state line in Stamford, Connecticut, "due to the strong efforts" of several white families there. However, their travail reveals the difficulty that faced less fortunate families. "We were put through the usual bag of tricks right in this state," Robinson said:

At first we were told the house we were interested in had been sold just before we inquired, or we would be invited to make an offer, a sort of a sealed bid, and then we'd be told that offers higher than ours had been turned down. Then we tried buying houses on the spot for whatever price was asked. They handled this by telling us the house had been taken off the market. Once we met a broker who told us he would like to help us find a home, but his clients were against selling to Negroes. Whether or not we got a story with the refusal, the results were always the same.[20]

In the market for suburban housing, the Robinsons, like thousands of others, were simply "Negroes" marked by race as second-class citizens or worse. For families without like resources or social connections, entrance into the white housing market proved a Herculean endeavor.

Where such barriers proved insufficient, however, white suburbanites routinely engaged in acts of terrorism to prevent the settlement of African Americans in their neighborhoods. In the late 1940s and 1950s, African American attempts to move out of "arbitrarily restricted areas" produced what historian Arnold Hirsch called "an era of hidden violence," as whites in city and suburban neighborhoods met breaches in the color line with a guerrilla war of death threats, property destruction, and physical violence.[21] When it came to race, arson was as suburban as the backyard barbecue grill during much of the postwar period.[22]

Government, too, was deeply supportive of racism in the housing market. Through the late 1940s, white property holders vigorously enforced deed covenants that restricted the sale or rental of property to "Caucasians only," and American courts upheld the practice.[23] Moreover, the chief federal agencies responsible for housing followed standard real estate industry practice in discriminating against African Americans and other minorities. This was not surprising, since as future Housing and Urban Development secretary Robert Weaver noted, "the very financial and real estate interests which led the campaign to spread racial covenants and residential segregation" were appointed to run them.[24] The Federal Housing Administration and its companion Veterans Administration program stimulated home construction by insuring or guaranteeing individual home loans against default. By limiting risk for private lending institutions and assuring that builders who built to agency standards would have a ready market of buyers, these agencies helped millions of families purchase homes. During the 1940s and 1950s, the FHA alone issued mortgage insurance on almost a third of new homes, meanwhile rates of home ownership blossomed from 44 percent in 1940 to 62 percent of American households by 1960.[25]

As late as 1950, however, both agencies required that neighborhoods be racially segregated in order for homes to qualify. FHA appraisers were instructed to consider the "adverse racial influences" affecting neighborhoods before approving mortgage insurance or construction loans. Until 1948, the FHA's *Underwriting Manual* advised that "racial intermingling in housing is undesirable per se and leads to a lowering of value."[26] Through the late 1940s, agency handbooks also advised home builders to incorporate race-restrictive covenants in their sales contracts, providing easy-to-copy samples in the appendix of each volume. In the view of open-housing advocate Charles Abrams, the FHA had "adopted a racial policy that could have been culled from the Nuremberg laws." By the late 1950s, only 2 percent of the homes built with FHA support since World War II were occupied by African Americans or other minorities.[27]

Just as important as federal involvement in housing, local governments were strategic agents in preventing African Americans from moving freely to the suburbs. As whites migrated to suburbs by the millions in the 1940s and 1950s, they quickly established new municipal governments to provide services and control local affairs.[28] Through authority over building codes and permits, health and safety regulations, and zoning and subdivision requirements, these new suburbs exercised extensive control over land use and development within their borders. As political scientist Michael Danielson points out, local government "afford[ed] suburbanites a potential for exclusion which exceeds that usually available to the resident of the central city."[29] In contrast to the situation in city neighborhoods where residents represented a small fraction of central city voters, white suburbanites could command the prompt support of village governments in attempts to exclude nonwhites.[30]

The experience of Morris Milgram, a lifelong developer of integrated housing, sustains this conclusion. Milgram recounted a litany of obstacles that suburban governments used to stop his projects. In one Philadelphia suburb, he wrote, officials greeted a project

> warmly . . . until word reached them . . . that the development would be integrated. At that point, [they] indicated a preference for lots of about half an acre. When we agreed to go along with that, they demanded lots of closer to one acre. . . . Our board then voted to accept an alternate site which the village indicated would win their approval, a site between an all-white and an all-black area in the center of the town.

However, the village failed to improve the black area as promised, and the FHA gave such low valuations on our proposed housing that the second site, like the first[,] had to be sold.

In other instances, "authorities demanded much bigger sewer and water ties than they had before they received word of our plans for integration, as well as much more expensive road paving. In still another instance, the ground was suddenly needed for the building of a high school." So routine were these impediments that Milgram advised other developers of open housing to maintain a policy of strict secrecy regarding their intended clientele.[31]

Developers of "open occupancy" housing on the West Coast faced similar difficulties. Following Ford Motor Company's decision to relocate an assembly plant from Richmond, California, which had a sizable black community, to predominantly white Santa Clara County, the American Friends Service Committee and the United Auto Workers Union made plans to sponsor a subdivision near the factory that would be open to the company's black workforce. Almost immediately, the project ran into opposition. Local and county officials blocked four separate site proposals before the developers were able to find a workable site. One was re-zoned for industrial use soon after the developer made his plans public. In a second suburb, officials refused a building permit for the proposed site. Officials up-zoned a third parcel to require larger lots than auto workers might easily afford, whereupon the developer resigned in disgust. A second developer, Joseph Kaufman, met similar resistance. Having selected a site in Milpitas, Kaufman ran into trouble with the owner of an adjacent parcel, who refused permission to connect with sewer lines running under his property. Next, county sanitation officials adopted a new pricing formula that raised sewer costs for this particular project sixfold. When Kaufman went ahead undeterred, the neighbor filed suit to block him from using a drainage ditch that adjoined his property. Only when Kaufman and his backers had purchased the adjacent parcel from its owner and swallowed the costs of municipal intransigence was the project able to proceed. Against these odds, Kaufman completed 156 homes, and residents began moving into Santa Clara's first truly integrated postwar subdivision in 1954.[32]

Kaufman's experience demonstrates both the variety and efficacy of opposition from local governments and well-placed property holders. Opponents delayed the project by two years, imposing a host of unforeseen costs that most builders would have been unable to afford. The delays alone would have killed most projects, since developers generally relied on borrowed money, working with a limited cash flow. Kaufman only succeeded because of the commitment and clout of his sponsors. The UAW and AFSC absorbed added costs, including legal fees, and used their influence with state officials at crucial moments in the approvals process to pressure local authorities to keep the project alive. Lacking similar assistance, even the most committed of builders found it almost impossible to build open housing in municipalities opposed to their plans.

Discrimination by local governments was especially effective in the industrial cities of the Northeast and Midwest, where historic and geographic factors exacerbated racial exclusion. Since there were fewer pockets of African American residence or land ownership outside the South, there were fewer areas of the urban fringe in which development for African Americans might proceed uncontested by whites. It is "a fundamental fact," wrote federal housing advisor George Snowden, "that good and well-located sites for housing of nonwhites are simply not available in most instances. . . . [I]t's a sad commentary that it's more true in the North and Middle West. For the most part, quality locations have been preempted and are available for white occupancy only."[33] Ironically, migrants' attraction to larger industrial cities heightened the difficulties they faced. In cities like Detroit, Chicago, Newark, and Philadelphia, there was comparatively little vacant land left for development inside the city limits. Because these cities had grown explosively before 1929, most of the land suitable for development was located outside the central city, where it fell under the jurisdiction of suburban officials who had even less reason to mind the needs of poorly housed African Americans than officials in central cities.

Finally, although housing discrimination affected African Americans of every class, the proliferation of suburbs and land-use regulations disproportionately affected families with low to moderate incomes. Even as racial bias came under legal assault soon after the war, discrimination based on income gathered momentum. Under pressure from the FHA and the financial institutions that bought long-term mortgages, concerns with the stability of property values reached a fever pitch after the depression. Home owners came to depend on the real estate mantra that values would rise, relying on homes as vehicles for accumulating wealth. One consequence was the hardening of opposition to anything or anyone that might be perceived as a threat to housing values, including people with less money. Suburbs not only ruled against informal home building, but increasingly they zoned out apartments, mobile homes, and modest tract housing of the kind that thousands of white suburbanites had purchased in the first years after the war. In the New York suburbs, zoning decisions more than doubled the average lot size required for a new home during the 1950s.[34] As a result, unincorporated and unregulated suburban territory, which had been the native habitat of working-class suburbanites before the war, became increasingly scarce. This was also true in a variety of predominantly black suburbs, where rising economic status among suburban migrants invigorated a class-based home-ownership politics, leading to the passage of building and sanitary restrictions after the war.[35] At the same time, exclusion became increasingly effective as the number of white suburbs and suburbanites multiplied. As suburbs sprawled outward, they pushed the unregulated rural fringe further from the central city, making it less accessible to blue-collar African Americans, who faced the double injury of discrimination in suburban employment as well as housing.[36] In combination with widespread race bias, discrimination based on income made it increasingly difficult for working-class blacks to find homes in the suburbs after World War II.

Racial Cleansing in the Suburbs

In addition to using municipal regulations to exclude African Americans, suburban officials exercised discretionary powers to move or eliminate those who were already there. Sterling Tucker of the National Urban League observed in 1962, "There appears to be a tendency for suburban areas seeking to rid themselves of unsightly areas, usually occupied by Negroes, to ordain a new public use for the land and to remove the families without providing specific relocation arrangements elsewhere in the immediate communities."[37] Like many suburban efforts at racial exclusion, this trend disproportionately affected working-class blacks, who had formed the majority of black suburbanites before the war. Beginning in the 1940s, many suburbs took steps to demolish and redevelop existing black communities.[38]

Events on Long Island, New York, illustrate the role of urban renewal in reshaping the suburban landscape. White Long Islanders sought not only to exclude African Americans but to displace many who were already there. As in other areas of the mid-Atlantic seaboard, small working-class black communities dotted the landscape of Long Island prior to World War II, some dating to the early nineteenth century when freed slaves had intermarried with Native Americans and established agricultural settlements.[39] Others reflected the activity of real estate agents who sold unimproved building lots during the Great Migration. In still other suburbs, neighborhoods of black domestic workers had developed along the tracks of the Long Island Railroad, where they were a short commute from the large homes and estates that hugged the Island's shores, and in various locales southern migrant farmworkers lived in seasonal housing, which often served as a steppingstone to more permanent accommodations nearby.[40] By the 1940s, Long Island exhibited a range of housing and neighborhood types evident among African Americans in the suburban Northeast.

After World War II, rapid white suburbanization put pressure on existing land-use patterns — including the Island's racial geography. Between 1940 and 1960, the population of Nassau and Suffolk Counties mushroomed from 604,000 to 1,961,000.[41] As space-hungry white New Yorkers lined up to purchase new tract homes, the price of land multiplied, and suburban officials increasingly perceived working-class black communities as impediments to growth. Coalitions emerged in villages and townships across the Island that were bent on "clean[ing] up" the neighborhoods in which the majority of blacks lived. In some suburbs that meant "cleansing" them of African Americans altogether.[42]

Pressure to redevelop or eliminate black communities manifested itself in several ways. Municipalities such as Glen Cove, Long Beach, and Rockville Centre strengthened local housing codes, condemning scores of dilapidated rental properties and evicting black tenants, many of whom were unable to find new housing elsewhere in town.[43] Similarly, zoning changes reclassified working-class residential areas — so-called "slum pockets" — for commercial use, leading to the eventual displacement of inexpensive housing by businesses and other nonresidential users.[44]

More invasive was urban renewal, state and federal programs that provided municipal governments with the resources to rebuild sections classified as "slums." Following the lead of central cities, numerous suburbs employed urban renewal powers to demolish and rebuild existing black communities. On Long Island alone, Rockville Centre, Glen Cove, Long Beach, Freeport, Roslyn, Hempstead, Inwood, Huntington, Manhasset, and Port Washington initiated urban renewal programs aimed at older black neighborhoods.[45] In these areas, white suburbanites harnessed the power of the state to redraw the color line and defend privileges associated with class and race.

The case of Freeport, a suburb of commuters and resort homes on the south shore of Long Island, is illustrative. In Freeport, the target of public action was a neighborhood near the Long Island Railroad tracks called Bennington Park. Job opportunities in domestic labor had attracted blacks to the neighborhood after the turn of the century when wealthy whites from New York began building large homes in the suburb.[46] Although some Bennington Park residents built or purchased their own homes, the majority rented cheaply constructed houses and apartments built by speculators seeking to profit from African American housing demand. Between 1930 and 1950, Freeport's black population grew by more than a thousand, leading to crowding and the deterioration of living conditions in Bennington Park. Landlords subdivided older homes, overtaxing local facilities. By 1946 a New York State Housing Commission described the neighborhood as "the worst rural slum in the state," and among Freeport whites, pressures to redevelop the area increased.[47]

"The slums in Bennington Park have been an eyesore in Freeport for many years," wrote one observer. "Many of the homes in that area are absolutely lacking in sanitary facilities, and some do not have running water. The tenants have to get their supply from outdoor pumps. . . . As a result of the living conditions in the area, moral conditions are bad and to be brief, the whole mess needs cleaning up."[48] More to the point for many whites, Freeport's "slums developed right on its main street where no casual visitor can miss them. Shacks that were worn out a quarter of a century ago straddle a section that could pay high taxes as business property."[49]

In spite of these arguments, voters rejected a referendum in 1946 to initiate a slum-clearance program, apparently fearing that the construction of public housing would lead to rising property taxes and a new influx of black families. Nonetheless, proponents of redevelopment revived the issue in 1949. After a two-year campaign by the press and local civic leaders, Freeport voters approved plans for a local redevelopment authority in 1951. Leaders of the effort urged that Bennington Park be demolished in order to build "a better home for all Americans." For some of them, better housing was certainly a paramount concern, but even Freeport's most liberal organizations emphasized the economic good that demolition of Bennington Park would do the community. The American Veterans Committee noted, "We can't promote Freeport as a garden spot if people have to see a slum."[50] For Freeport whites, poverty and substandard housing became synonyms for the black community as a whole. Viewing the matter through this lens, most agreed that it should be removed. Although Bennington Park voters themselves had rejected the 1946 referendum by a two-to-one margin, the proponents of slum clearance courted Freeport's small black middle class on the second go-around. Many of them, hoping that renewal would improve housing conditions in their community, supported the measure. With their involvement, the referendum passed, and Freeport sent a redevelopment plan to Washington for approval in 1952.

Eventually, the city knocked down the two hundred fifty dwellings in Bennington Park and replaced them with one hundred units of low-income housing on an out-of-the-way site a short distance away. Meanwhile, the village redeveloped Bennington Park for commercial and light industrial use. By the 1990s the site was home to a car dealership and U-Store-It rental units surrounded by an eight-foot hurricane fence.[51]

Although the abuses of urban renewal as "Negro removal" in central cities have been widely documented, events in Freeport illustrate that the practice was not confined to cities.[52] Throughout the postwar period, numerous suburbs used state and federal funds to demolish African American communities and redevelop them for other uses. In New York, which had the nation's largest state redevelopment program, more than a dozen suburbs employed public authority to displace or relocate black communities after the war. In Rockville Centre, slum clearance caused a decline in that village's small black population during the 1940s. Oscar van Purnell, a black resident who had initially supported the effort, later regretted having been tricked by "swift and gifted politicians." Rather than rebuilding the black community, he recalled, officials were "very successful in taking some of the land [where African Americans had lived] and building factories, office buildings, and the most disturbing thing, a tennis court." As in Freeport, African Americans displaced from the site scrambled to find housing, though in Rockville Centre, hundreds were forced to leave town. On the bright side, van Purnell noted sarcastically, "they did have a very fine tennis court."[53] Regarding urban redevelopment efforts in general, sociologists John Logan and Harvey Molotch point out the way contrasting visions of space interact with power along class as well as racial lines. "Poor people," they write, "are not in a position to effectively claim that their neighborhood, *as used by them*, is either a national resource or useful for attracting capital."[54] In large part, suburban officials on Long Island shared this bias; black neighborhoods to them had little or no civic value.

Elsewhere in the metropolitan area, suburbs such as Port Washington, Inwood, and Glen Cove on Long Island; Port Chester, Mount Vernon, and White Plains in Westchester County; and Englewood, New Jersey, demolished large parts of their black neighborhoods during the 1950s, replacing them, if at all, with lesser numbers of public housing units.[55] The trend reached a peak in the 1960s when officials in Westchester County slated nearly forty-two hundred units of "slum" housing for demolition—most of it in areas where African Americans were living or moving—proposing to build just seven hundred units of public housing in their place. In cities and suburbs

Fig. 4.2   Public housing in White Plains, New York, rises over the surrounding neighborhood. Construction of this project in the 1960s facilitated the removal of African Americans from other parts of the suburb. Its location in a hollow upheld the traditional concentration of Westchester County's poor in low-lying areas. (Photograph by Andrew Wiese, 2000)

alike, slum clearance and urban renewal became tools to reshape the existing racial geography—at the expense of African American communities.[56]

Like the expansion of land-use regulations, suburban renewal had a disproportionate impact on working-class and poor blacks. Such families were most likely to live in the "dilapidated housing" and aging neighborhoods that officials slated for demolition. Elimination of these areas reduced the supply of affordable housing available to existing residents and newcomers alike, and since these areas often provided the first foothold for working families moving to the suburbs, their demolition foreclosed a pathway to further migration.[57] By the late 1950s, political and regulatory changes in the suburbs themselves—expanded land-use regulations and the selective use of slum clearance—had substantially curtailed suburban opportunities for working-class African Americans.

At a broader level, the 1940s and 1950s witnessed the establishment of a new regime of suburban land use, backed by the power of the local, state, and federal governments and rooted in a vision of metropolitan space in which white communities were seen as normative and African American places were aberrant, threatening, and negatively valued. This vision traced its heritage to the prewar period, but the sheer magnitude of white suburbanization and the input of federal authority made it novel, extending its reach not only across space but deep into the popular culture of the period. By the mid-1950s, "suburbia" had become a spatial metaphor for whiteness itself.

Chapter 5

Driving a Wedge of Opportunity

Black Suburbanization in the North and West, 1940–1960

We bought a house last year—
Amidst "the murmuring pine and the hemlock,"
The flowering dogwoods, the spreading yew,
The roses, chrysanthemums, blueberries, too.

We bought a house last year—
After looking at many,
Hearing "No's" loud and fierce,
After mortgage refusals
Pleadings "Money's too scarce"—
Or, just, "We don't want you,"
Or other things worse.

We moved *in* last year—
Amidst moving van's rumbles and usual clutter
And telephone wiring, utility men's mutter.
Amidst silent still neighbors
Except one tousled blond head
Whose tricycle trod, where his parents would dread!
Then, shouts from a distance—
"Don't go over there!"
The obvious enmity—
Borne out of fear!
"Don't walk on my land!" "Don't trespass!" "Don't speak!"
What building on sand! *Who* is mighty? Who, weak?

We bought a house last year—
Despite friction and fear.
We know we're not wanted
Except by a few
Who have courage to stand
On convictions felt true

But this house was our choice.
A home was our goal.
We had no intention of
Mortgaging our soul.

So, my child will stand straight
And firm, on his sod,
With courage, conviction
And faith, in our God!

          —Jean E. Moore[1]

IT TOOK Jim and Ann Braithewaite two years to find a home in the sub-urbs.[2] After transferring to Philadelphia in 1957, the family began looking for a house almost immediately. Meanwhile, they rented in "a predominantly Negro neighborhood" in the city. They dreamed of owning a detached split-level house with a big yard, which was common enough for couples with children in postwar Philadelphia, yet like thousands of African Americans, they searched in vain while white families moved to new suburban homes with relative ease.

The Braithewaites' struggle exemplified the experience of many African Americans after World War II. Although they were plainly middle class—she was a schoolteacher, he a mechanical engineer—with a combined income well above the metropolitan average, their race made them outcasts in the housing market. They answered newspaper ads, contacted real estate brokers, attended auctions, and made an estimated three hundred phone calls, but they met a "stone wall" of resistance. "We don't have any split-levels" or "That's already spoken for," brokers told them. Others were straightforward: "You're colored, aren't you? I can't do anything for you," said one.[3] Whatever the reaction, the results were the same. As African Americans, they were not welcome in any part of Philadelphia's white suburbia.

In "desperation," the Braithewaites recalled, they shifted strategy. With the help of a local fair-housing organization, they found a vacant lot whose owner was willing to sell to them. Though they had reservations about the location because it was "very close to a public school" and near an existing "Negro neighborhood," they hired a contractor and built a new home, inspecting progress at night, "hoping to prevent the accumulation of resentment" among their new neighbors. The family moved in, in October 1959, remaining fearful that "something cataclysmic" might happen. For "some time" they even avoided standing in front of the picture window, but the neighborhood remained quiet, thanks in part to the efforts of local Quakers who hosted a meeting to calm the neighbors and stayed with the family on their first night in the house. After months of frustration, the Braithewaites were suburbanites at last.

As a white-collar family, the Braithewaites symbolized a new wave of black suburbanization after the war. Whereas working-class families had dominated the prewar migration, middle-class African Americans — wealthier, better educated, and more likely to hold white-collar jobs than earlier suburbanites — began moving to suburbs in growing numbers. Bolstered by national economic expansion and the opening of new occupations, black family incomes rose. By the mid-fifties, the United States was home to a growing black bourgeoisie and a cohort of economically stable industrial workers whose members had the means to purchase suburban housing on a greater scale than ever before. As their numbers increased, families like these became the predominant suburban migrants by the mid-1950s. These decades represented a period of transition in a century-long process of black suburbanization. Working-class households remained a majority through the mid-1960s, but the momentum had shifted toward the nascent middle class.[4]

The Braithewaites' determination to buy a suburban home also signaled the arrival of a generation more willing than ever to challenge the racial status quo. On the eve of the mass action campaign for civil rights in the South,

African Americans across the country took up a contentious politics of housing, seeking shelter outside "established Negro areas" and pressing their rights through direct action and the courts.[5] Combined with the desire for better homes and neighborhoods, their eagerness to challenge racial barriers placed new pressure on suburban exclusivity, and it won small but significant gains.

Postwar black suburbanization also reflected input from a surprising source: the federal government. Many scholars have demonstrated that federal housing policies buttressed local efforts to exclude nonwhites from the suburbs and contributed substantially to rising levels of racial segregation and to the concentration of poverty in central cities.[6] Nonetheless, federal intervention also created new opportunities for African Americans to obtain suburban homes. During World War II, government agencies built tens of thousands of emergency housing units for black families in suburbs and outlying districts of central cities. Moreover, the mortgage programs administered by the FHA and VA assisted African Americans in buying or renting several hundred thousand new homes, many of which were in the suburbs. What is not in doubt was the federal role in strengthening the connection between race and space. By design, the vast majority of federally supported housing developments were racially segregated, and virtually all of them were built in the vicinity of existing black communities. Thus, the growing federal state affected African American suburbanization in expected and unexpected ways.

Despite the shift toward middle-class migration, which mirrored the trend among whites, African American suburbanization did little to undermine racial distinctions in midcentury America or the spatial form they assumed. As the Braithewaites' search for housing indicates, racism stalked black suburbanites after the war, transforming individual housing choices into explicit acts of racial protest and linking thousands of African Americans in a common racial struggle. "Traditional neighborhood restrictions" ensured that most black suburbanites settled in neighborhoods that were predominantly black or rapidly becoming so.[7] Most of the places where African Americans forced their way into the suburbs were a short distance from existing black neighborhoods. African Americans also organized to resist and overcome white supremacy. They relied for economic and emotional support on social networks rooted in black communities. Even in house hunting, families depended largely on other African Americans for information and assistance. Far from breaking down racial divisions, suburbanization during the 1940s and 1950s reinforced racial distinctions in the housing market and society.

Suburbanization by the Numbers

After decades during which African Americans had fought bitter piecemeal battles to become or remain suburbanites, the burst of black suburbanization after 1940 was a significant gain. Between 1940 and 1960, the number of black suburbanites in the United States grew by 1 million. Southern suburbs gained 328,000 people, even as central cities gobbled up thousands of square miles of suburban territory through annexation. Suburbs outside the South added almost 700,000. Gains were greatest in the Northeast and Midwest, where the black suburban population ballooned from 468,000 to 905,000. However, western suburbs also witnessed large gains for the first time, rising from just 32,000 to 274,000 and accounting for more than a quarter of black population growth in the region as a whole.[8]

The surge in suburbanization mirrored a dramatic demographic shift already under way across the country. During the 1940s and 1950s, more than 3 million African Americans left the rural South, resettling in urban and suburban areas throughout the country.[9] Migrants concentrated in the nation's largest metropolitan areas, a pattern evident in black suburbanization as well. Almost 60 percent of black suburban population growth in northern states accrued in the four largest metropolitan areas — New York, Philadelphia, Chicago, and Detroit — while the top ten areas accounted for almost 85 percent. Suburbanization in the West was even more compact, with fully three-quarters of black suburbanites moving to the two largest metropolitan areas — Los Angeles and San Francisco–Oakland.[10] As black central city populations grew, suburban numbers followed suit.

The Geography of Black Suburbanization

Despite rapid numerical gains, black suburbanization remained a geographically conservative process. Regardless of socioeconomic class, the great majority of new suburbanites settled within walking distance of extant communities, creating segregated nodes of settlement in or contiguous to existing black suburbs. Restricted by racism and sustained by social networks based in black communities, postwar suburbanites followed the topographic footprints of earlier migrants.

In this way, black migration to the suburbs illustrates the importance of the past in shaping subsequent suburbanization. As Charles Tilly writes, "Past social relations and their residues — material, ideological, and otherwise —

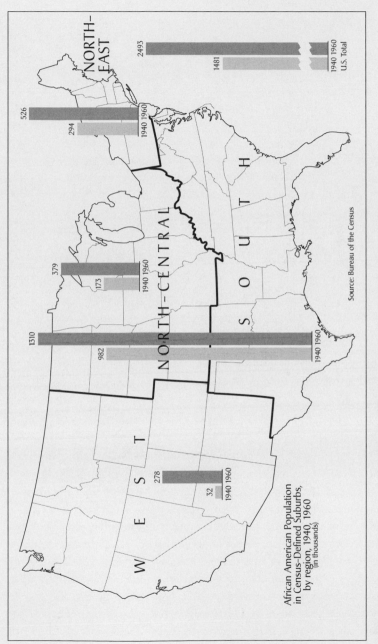

African American Population
in Census–Defined Suburbs,
by region, 1940, 1960
(in thousands)

NORTH–EAST

NORTH–CENTRAL

SOUTH

WEST

526
294
1940 1960

379
173
1940 1960

1310
982
1940 1960

278
32
1940 1960

2493
1481
1940 1960
U.S. Total

Source: Bureau of the Census

Fig. 5.1 Suburban African Americans by Region, 1940 and 1960. (Map by Harry D. Johnson)

Table 5.1: African American Suburban Population in Selected Metropolitan Areas, by Region, 1940–1960

	1940	1960	Change 1940–1960	% Change	Proportion of Regional Suburban Growth
North	**468,000**	**905,000**	**437,000**	**93%**	**100%**
New York	56,000	140,000	84,000	150%	19%
Detroit	26,000	91,000	65,000	250%	15%
Philadelphia	84,000	142,000	58,000	69%	13%
Chicago	25,000	78,000	53,000	212%	12%
West	**32,000**	**274,000**	**242,000**	**756%**	**100%**
Los Angeles	11,000	120,000	109,000	990%	45%
San Francisco	6,000	81,000	75,000	1250%	31%
South	**982,000**	**1,310,000**	**328,000**	**33%**	**100%**
Birmingham	70,000	84,000	14,000	20%	4%
Washington, D.C.	42,000	75,000	33,000	79%	10%
Miami	15,000	72,000	57,000	380%	17%
Baltimore	33,000	53,000	20,000	61%	6%
Atlanta	45,000	45,000	0[a]	0	0

[a] Atlanta annexed eighty-two square miles in 1952. African American population in the annexed area grew by approximately 22,000 between 1950 and 1960.

Source: U.S. Census of Population: 1960, vol. III, *Selected Area Reports,* part 1D (Washington, D.C., 1963), 3–5, 72, 87, 114, 121, 153–54, 173, 180, 191, 249, 253.

constrain present social relations, and consequently constrain their products as well."[11] Early black suburbanization, as an indivisibly social and spatial process, patterned what followed in a number of ways. Pioneer suburbanites maintained social relations with African Americans in nearby cities as well as communities of more distant origin. Through information and experiences passed along black social networks, suburbs became recognized landmarks in the mental geography of African Americans. Hence, prewar black suburbanites anchored continuing chain migrations. As time went by, early communities beckoned as places that were "open" to African Americans, places where new suburbanites could attend church, purchase familiar products, enjoy leisure time, and engage in social and political life among other African Americans, meanwhile avoiding the threat of violence and social ostracism that awaited them in much of white suburbia. Likewise, black suburban areas were among the few places where African Americans could freely buy or sell property, and many of them contained vacant land that was ripe for new development. After the war, they became focal points for new construction and beachheads for migration to surrounding areas.

The legacy of earlier suburbanization affected white behavior as well. While white suburban officials actively worked to demolish and redevelop existing black communities, another response was to isolate them in a kind of racial quarantine. Since the common wisdom in white real estate circles held that African Americans threatened property values, developers were hesitant to build housing for whites too close to black suburbs. Thus, white landowners and officials frequently let adjacent property lie fallow as a buffer between white and black neighborhoods. Occasionally, they also gave tacit consent to the construction of new housing for African Americans in these areas. Equally important, white suburbanites usually excluded black neighbors when they drew the boundaries of new municipalities. Fixing limits that prevented blacks from sharing local services fit the segregationist model of twentieth-century suburbia and contributed to persisting inequality in black-occupied territory, but it had the countereffect of ceding land-use control in unincorporated areas to property owners, who often seized on the opportunity to profit by selling to African Americans.

In another twist of racism, white fears of racial integration often produced a self-fulfilling prophecy of racial change in the vicinity of early suburban communities. Since there were many whites who dreaded settling or staying in neighborhoods near black communities for fear of eventual "invasion," homes in boundary neighborhoods often became difficult to sell to whites, increasing the likelihood that someone would sell across the color line. When they did, neighbors often dumped their houses on the market in a panic, provoking wholesale racial transition. In this way, too, the early presence of African Americans in the suburbs opened the door to further suburbanization—although in a highly circumscribed and spatially conservative pattern.

In a sense, race was a two-edged blade in the suburban housing market. Thousands felt its stroke in their exclusion from white communities, but in the territory around existing black neighborhoods, it carved footholds for future growth. The efforts of working-class blacks to make suburban homes before World War II laid a foundation on which middle-class suburbanites built after the war, connecting the newcomers to a history of black struggle in the suburbs and reinforcing racial continuity rather than disjuncture, even as a growing number of African Americans entered the middle class.

"*The Most Segregated City in America*"

Black suburbanization in Chicago exemplifies the cumulative race-governed pattern of settlement that prevailed in suburbs across the country, but especially in the industrialized Midwest and Northeast.[12] Between 1940 and 1960, the number of black suburbanites of the Windy City grew by 53,000, but just seven localities absorbed three-quarters of the increase. Each was home to an existing African American community. A closer look at three of these communities — Evanston, Maywood, and the environs of Robbins — illustrates processes of growth evident in greater Chicago and in suburbs across the region.[13]

Evanston's black community grew by 3,100 people during the 1940s and 1950s, an increase of 50 percent. Growth proceeded through a combination of new construction, intensified use of space within older black areas, and transfer of existing homes and apartments to African Americans in adjacent, formerly white, neighborhoods. On the western edge of Evanston's mostly black Fifth Ward, contractors built more than four hundred new homes, constructing housing on scattered lots as well as a handful of larger parcels along the drainage canal that bounded the suburb to the west. Among these were a dozen new units in a veterans housing project completed at the end of the war. In addition to new construction, approximately two-thirds of black Evanston's growth resulted through block-by-block transition in white neighborhoods adjoining the historic black core. Housing in these neighborhoods ranged from three-story Victorian buildings on Asbury Avenue to worker-built bungalows south of Evanston Township High School, which provided opportunities for African Americans of various incomes to purchase homes. In addition, black neighborhoods closer to the center of town witnessed the conversion of older homes into rental properties, often by black owners seeking to profit from the growth in black population.[14] As was true before the war, many of the new suburbanites were recent migrants from the South who came to find jobs and join family, but the suburb also attracted a growing number of middle-class families from Chicago. Growth in size and numbers notwithstanding, in 1960 black Evanston remained a racially segregated enclave on the west side of town.

In Maywood, an industrial and commuter suburb eleven miles west of the Loop, the black community grew by over 4,000 during the 1940s and 1950s, more than tripling the existing population. Established in the late nineteenth century with several rail links to the city, Maywood attracted African Americans during the Great Migration to work at the furnaces of the massive American Can Company, which loomed along the Chicago &

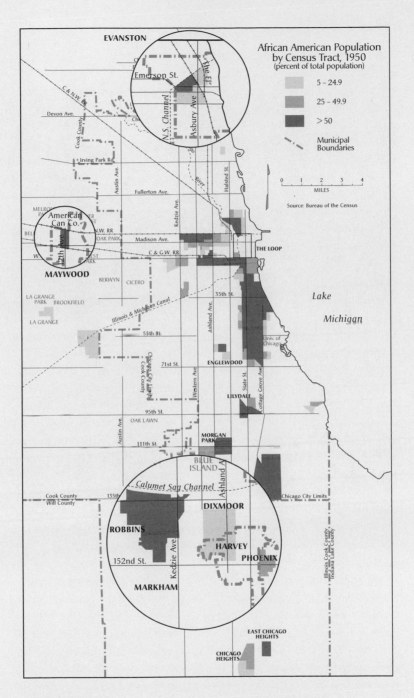

Fig. 5.2   African Americans in Chicago, Illinois, and Suburbs, 1950.
(Map by Harry D. Johnson)

Fig. 5.3   In-fill houses built on Evanston's west side after World War II reflect postwar fashion in their low-rise brick facades, but their slender profiles, confined by narrow lots, betray the roots of the subdivision in the blue-collar housing market of the 1910s. New homes made up approximately 40 percent of the additional housing occupied by African Americans in Evanston during the 1950s. (Photograph by Andrew Wiese, 2003)

Northwestern Railroad at the north end of town. In 1940, 1,200 blacks lived in what real estate appraisers viewed as an "old and shabby neighborhood" in the shadow of the can works.[15] As housing construction accelerated in newer suburbs after the war, white families began moving away from the soot and noise of the mill. African Americans replaced them, pushing into adjacent neighborhoods filled with "fine, large elm trees" and a mixture of frame bungalows and two-story houses.[16] In contrast to Evanston, where expansion resulted from a combination of new construction and neighborhood transition, almost 90 percent of black newcomers in Maywood moved into older housing units. However, the spatial consequences were much the same. African Americans wholly supplanted white families in the blocks surrounding the old Twelfth Avenue core. At the extremities of settlement, neighborhoods were integrated, though changing, but virtually all of Maywood's black residents remained confined to a segregated and sharply bounded black neighborhood at the center of town.[17]

    The largest arena for black suburbanization in postwar Chicago was a

Fig. 5.4 Brown Avenue, Evanston, Illinois. After World War II, African Americans expanded southward in Evanston, replacing white families in modest homes such as these, which were built by white immigrant and ethnic owners in the 1910s. (Photograph by Andrew Wiese, 1996)

cluster of suburbs south of the city, anchored by the black suburb of Robbins. As in Evanston and Maywood, African Americans had built homes in Robbins and in parts of neighboring Phoenix, Dixmoor, and west Harvey since World War I, creating a rustic landscape of small houses and outbuildings amidst the fields, factories, and marshes of the Calumet River basin.[18] After 1940, however, local populations expanded rapidly as contractors targeted the area for the construction of modest housing tracts for African Americans. These suburbs became magnets for development because they contained the only large parcels of land in the region that were open to African Americans. Moreover, because the communities had developed in unincorporated areas or were themselves incorporated as largely black municipalities, local whites lacked the regulatory tools to block development that they exercised in mostly white suburbs. During the 1940s and 1950s, Robbins welcomed the construction of more than twelve hundred new homes.[19] Many, following local tradition, were owner-built, but hundreds more were mass-produced in tidy subdivisions that juxtaposed sharply with the unpolished landscape that had characterized the suburb before the war.

Even more remarkable was new construction in Markham, an unincor-

Fig. 5.5   Postwar tract homes built for African Americans in Markham, Illinois. Developers constructed more than five hundred new homes in the area for a growing African American market, making it Chicago's fastest-growing black suburb after World War II. (Photograph by Andrew Wiese, 1988)

porated district just south of Robbins, where developers built more than five hundred "attractive . . . beautifully landscaped" frame-and-brick bungalows during the 1950s.[20] Although no blacks had lived in the area in 1950, Markham's black population swelled to 2,500 by 1960. By that time, African American population in the five suburbs had grown by 14,000, four-fifths of whom lived in new single-family homes. The landscape of these suburbs, formerly derided as shack towns and rural slums, took on a much more manicured look, including new subdivisions that were comparable to suburban housing tracts in many parts of the United States.[21]

In Chicago, as in other metropolitan areas, movement to the suburbs correlated with the expansion of home ownership. In Evanston, rates of ownership increased from 26 percent in 1940 to 43 percent by 1960. In Maywood, they more than doubled from 23 to 48 percent. The trend was even more pronounced in the vicinity of Robbins. Black home ownership, which had topped 50 percent in these rustic suburbs before 1940, ranged in 1960 from a low of 58 percent in Robbins to 79 percent in Dixmoor and a whopping 99 percent in the brand-new subdivisions of Markham.[22]

National trends followed a similar outline. Rates of nonfarm home ownership among all African Americans rose from 24 percent in 1940 to 39 percent in 1960 even as millions of people relocated from the rural South to urban areas. In the suburbs, however, home ownership climbed more sharply. In eight metropolitan areas with the largest black suburban populations, the number of black home owners increased sixfold—from 16,000 in 1940 to 105,000 in 1960—and the suburban home-ownership rate jumped from 32 to 51 percent. Long a cherished goal among African Americans, home ownership remained a central feature of black suburbanization after the war.[23]

Table 5.2:   African American Home Ownership in Cities and Suburbs, 1940–1960

Metropolitan Area	Home Owners, 1940	% Home Ownership	Home Owners, 1960	% Home Ownership
Chicago	5,717	7%	36,764	16%
Suburbs	1,754	28%	8,711	51%
Detroit	5,121	15%	50,498	39%
Suburbs	2,228	49%	10,126	56%
Los Angeles	5,495	30%	46,497	36%
Suburbs	1,344	48%	24,509	56%
Newark	379	3%	5,139	13%
Suburbs	861	17%	9,477	43%
New York City	5,086	4%	46,748	13%
Suburbs[a]	2,405	19%	12,961	42%
Philadelphia	6,600	10%	64,124	43%
Suburbs	3,438	32%	18,333	53%
St. Louis[b]	3,687	11%	20,586	29%
Suburbs	3,214	50%	6,826	59%
S.F.-Oakland	870	21%	21,912	32%
Suburbs	853	50%	14,381	51%
Suburban Total	16,097	32%	105,432	51%

[a] Bergen, Nassau, Suffolk, and Westchester Counties.
[b] St. Louis and East St. Louis cities combined.

Source: U.S. Census of Housing, vol. II, *General Characteristics,* parts 1–6, *Reports by States* (Washington, D.C., 1943), part 2, 214, 764; part 3, 576, 869; part 4, 146, 270, 860; U.S. Census of Housing: 1960, vol. I, *States and Small Areas,* part 1, *U.S. Summary* (Washington, D.C., 1963), 228–33.

The Postwar Boom and the Growth of the Black Middle Class

Underlying the expansion in black suburbanization was a rapid growth in African American incomes. Rising earning power laid the foundation for a greater black middle class and expanded the number of families who could afford well-built housing in the suburbs. Unlike earlier status-based black elites, this new group was larger in size—representing 20 percent of the black population—and economically situated in the same income and occupational categories as members of the white middle class. Although African Americans' economic position lagged behind that of whites, black incomes almost tripled during the 1940s and increased by another 50 percent during the 1950s.[24] Midway through the century, the number of nonfarm black households earning more than $3,000, the minimum necessary to buy a new contractor-built home with FHA financing, had risen to 19 percent from just 4 percent in 1940. In the urban North, nearly one-third of black families topped this mark, and in selected metropolitan areas, such as Los Angeles, as many as half of black families made that much.[25] Poverty remained a daily experience for millions of African Americans, but by the 1950s a growing number were entering new positions in the changing economy.

Several factors explain the expansion of African American incomes. First, World War II reignited black migration from the South. With the promise of better jobs beckoning, millions of young black southerners cut loose from the past, trading jobs in depressed southern agriculture for blue-collar occupations in urban areas where wages were higher. In addition, the generalized prosperity ignited by the war affected African Americans as well as others. Income for all workers rose during the period, and unemployment remained comparatively low. Pressure from civil rights organizations for a share of expanding public employment also unlocked limited opportunities for black workers in civil service and private-sector clerical work, which became one of the chief employers of black women by the 1960s. Finally, the expansion of African American urban communities created a growing market for black professionals and entrepreneurs who catered to black customers.[26]

As a result, the proportion of African Americans working in white-collar occupations rose from approximately 8 percent in 1940 to more than 13 percent in 1960, and the proportion of craftsmen, foremen, and kindred workers—the elite of the black working class—rose to 10 percent among black men.[27] Occupations such as these supported a middle-class status because they offered higher incomes and greater job security than was available to most black workers, which allowed families to save and invest money in ways that were distinct from those open to most working-class blacks. Equally important, improved opportunities for black women in the expanding clerical workforce, as well as in fields such as nursing, teaching, and government service, helped boost incomes and economic security for many African American families. Unlike their white counterparts, a larger proportion of black families, including many that considered themselves middle class, relied on dual breadwinners throughout the postwar period.[28] By the 1950s, there were a growing number of African American teachers, nurses, insurance agents, small business owners, civil servants, mail carriers, and stenographers, as well as skilled craft workers and foremen, who sought and could afford "moderately priced, decent housing" in the nation's suburbs without the hardships of informal building.[29]

Concurrent with the growth of the black middle class, however, opportunities for working-class families to move to suburbs narrowed, and patterns of working-class community building that had predominated before the war faced steady erosion. Rapid white suburbanization and the spread of land-use regulation sharply limited the availability of suburban land, especially for members of the working class. At the same time, the development of the federal welfare state and the entrance of black industrial workers into unions in the 1930s and 1940s marginally reduced the economic insecurity that had shaped working-class survival strategies before the war. Improved wage and benefit packages, pensions, and greater job stability enhanced the incomes of black industrial workers, and the extension of social security, unemployment insurance, and minimum wages offered limited economic assurances, which some African American families had sought through suburban home ownership and domestic production before the war. Working-class blacks not only faced increasing obstacles in moving to the suburbs, but some of them, at least, may have felt less compulsion to go. Working-class suburbanization persisted after the war — "mostly in the older Negro communities where housing is overcrowded and many times substandard," the columnist William Braden pointed out — but conditions that had once nurtured the phenomenon shifted during the 1940s and 1950s. As a result, the composition of suburban migration shifted steadily toward the middle class.[30]

Suburbanization and Civil Rights

An equally important influence on African American suburbanization after World War II was the growing struggle for civil rights. At the national level, the NAACP intensified its campaigns against segregation in public schools and race-restrictive covenants in housing. Activists lobbied Congress to pass civil rights legislation, such as a fair employment practices bill and anti–poll tax legislation, and they pressured the Truman administration to desegregate the armed services. Locally, African Americans in scores of communities challenged discrimination in employment, public accommodations, and municipal services. Rather than marking a quiescent interlude between the militancy of the early 1940s and the mass movement for civil rights after the mid-1950s, the decade after World War II produced swelling grassroots pressure for civil rights at both the local and national levels.[31]

Suburbs, too, witnessed intensified black political activity. Even before the Supreme Court invalidated de jure school segregation in *Brown v. Board of Education* (1954), black parents in suburbs such as Englewood and Asbury Park, New Jersey; New Rochelle, Yonkers, and Hempstead, New York; and Chagrin Falls Park, Ohio, raised legal challenges to de facto segregation in local schools. Dozens more followed suit before 1960.[32] Discrimination in public employment and services also provoked suburban protest. Residents of Evanston, Illinois, for example, pressured the local school board to hire its first black teachers in 1942. In 1945 and 1946, blacks publicly protested police harassment and proposals to construct whites-only housing for veterans.[33] In Pasadena, California, the local NAACP won a long battle against the practice of restricting blacks and other minorities at the municipal swimming pool to one day per week, so-called "International Day," after which the pool was drained and cleaned. After the war, the organization attacked discrimination at city hall and in downtown stores, which customarily refused to serve or hire African Americans. NAACP president Edna Griffin remembered, "There wasn't any place that blacks could go to and eat, not even a cafeteria."[34] Under California public accommodations law, Griffin and the NAACP filed suit against more than twenty local businesses in the late 1940s, forcing them to serve African American customers. "Every time I went in and they didn't serve me, I sued," Griffin recalled. "There was just no other way to breathe like a human being except through the courts."[35]

In other suburbs, the "need to breathe like a human being" inspired black residents to mobilize politically. Residents of "all-black" suburbs like Kinloch, Missouri, and Lincoln Heights and Urbancrest, Ohio, established municipal governments in the late 1940s to protect their own interests and control local affairs.[36] Elsewhere, black voters used the ballot and the courts to block threats from white neighbors. In North Richmond, California, suspicions that whites sought to "destroy our homes and sell our property to strangers" led voters to reject nearby Richmond's efforts to annex the area in the late 1940s.[37] In Inkster, Michigan, black residents filed suit to prevent local whites from de-annexing half of the suburb and taking most of the local tax base with them. By the mid-1950s, black activism in suburbs such as these opened up a new chapter in suburban race relations, creating a climate in which black families took new chances to become suburbanites.[38]

In cities and suburbs alike, the housing market was a key area of struggle. Discrimination in housing affected African Americans literally where they lived. It underlay the crowding and substandard conditions that plagued black neighborhoods. It impinged on desires for home ownership, hindered mobility and wealth accumulation, and limited basic rights to purchase and use private property. Housing discrimination also became a lightning rod for protest because, through the late forties, it remained a matter of public enforcement, implicating the state in the maintenance of racial segregation.[39] Unfair housing practices also became a major postwar issue because they directly affected the aspirations of middle-class and elite blacks, who elevated the issue through their control of civil rights organizations and the black press. While a growing number of families could afford to rent or buy housing outside of prewar ghettoes, they were prevented from doing so because of their race. Thus, housing discrimination reinforced race consciousness among middle-class blacks by tying their fates to ascribed racial characteristics just as it embedded their individual efforts to find shelter within a larger struggle for racial equality.[40]

Heightened consciousness about race and housing also points up important aspects of black politics in the postwar period. Historian Robert Self has called for scholars to reengage the history of postwar black politics as more than a prelude or prologue to the national struggle for civil rights, but as purposeful action with its own local and intermediate roots.[41] Focusing on political action in Corona, New York, anthropologist Steven Gregory also highlights the importance of place to politics, pointing toward the essential role that place-based political struggles played in shaping solidarities on the basis of race and class.[42] Examining the politics of housing reinforces the importance of these concerns, revealing the intensely local roots of black political action that engaged African Americans in a truly national struggle for equality in the postwar period.

On an institutional level, black housing politics coalesced in a movement for "open housing" that challenged established political institutions at the federal, state, and local levels. At the grassroots level, however, barriers in the housing market engaged hundreds of thousands of black citizens in acts of racial protest, transforming individual housing choices into political behavior with important ramifications for the meanings of race and class.

In the late 1940s and early 1950s, predominantly black civil rights organizations, such as the NAACP and the National Urban League, joined causes with a number of mostly white and liberal groups to advocate for a "free and democratic market for housing."[43] Organizations that coalesced under the banner of open housing reflected the spectrum of interests that anchored the liberal wing of the Democratic Party. They included national labor unions such as the AFL-CIO, the American Civil Liberties Union, the American Jewish Congress, the American Friends Service Committee and other liberal Protestant groups, and organizations of community relations and housing officials.[44]

The first target of these groups was the race-restrictive covenant. As African Americans transgressed prewar boundaries, moving into "forbidden" neighborhoods, white home owners scurried to enforce or enact restrictive covenants that would compel state and local courts to defend segregation. Within a year after the war, hundreds of black families across the United States fell victim to eviction cases involving what NAACP official Gloster Current called that "pernicious and undemocratic legal document," the race-restrictive covenant.[45] In July 1945 the NAACP initiated public action on behalf of "democracy in housing," gathering a caucus of national experts in Chicago to develop a strategy for confronting "the evils of segregation and racial restrictive covenants."[46] Over the next three years, conferees including NAACP legal experts Thurgood Marshall and Charles H. Houston, and lawyers representing black clients in covenant cases in various cities cooperated to bring restrictive covenant suits before the U.S. Supreme Court. The strategy paid off in 1948 when the Court ruled in the case of *Shelley v. Kraemer* that public enforcement of restrictive covenants was unconstitutional. The covenant victory served as a springboard for expanded efforts to change public and private practices in housing.[47]

In tandem with the covenant campaign, supporters of "democracy in housing" attacked discrimination by local housing authorities, state housing commissions, and the federal government, which represented the clearest examples of state-sponsored bias. In the aftermath of *Shelley*, open-housing proponents coalesced under an umbrella organization called the National Committee Against Discrimination in Housing. The group included among its directors leading liberal and civil rights advocates such as Walter Reuther of the United Auto Workers Union, Charles Abrams and Hortense Gabel of the New York State Committee Against Discrimination, Roy Wilkins of the Urban League, Loren Miller and Madison Jones of the NAACP, and Stephen Wise of the American Jewish Congress.[48] During the 1950s, the organization and its affiliate groups coordinated public pressure to persuade authorities in more than a dozen northern and western cities to abolish policies requiring racial segregation in public housing. In several cities and states, they secured legislation prohibiting discrimination in publicly supported private housing as well. By 1960 seventeen states and dozens of cities had enacted some form of legislation restricting discrimination in publicly assisted housing.[49]

At the federal level, open-housing advocates put pressure on the Federal Housing Administration to eliminate its most egregious discriminatory practices. In 1947 civil rights lobbyists convinced the FHA to revise its *Underwriters' Manual* by removing race as a category for property appraisal. After 1948 they impelled recalcitrant FHA and Veterans Administration officials to prohibit mortgage insurance in developments with race covenants enacted after February 15, 1950. Although the FHA continued to assist developers who refused to sell or rent to minorities, pressure from liberal groups during the Truman presidency encouraged the FHA to increase its efforts to supply housing for nonwhite families. By the mid-1950s, the FHA had taken concrete action to support the construction of new housing for African Americans, including assistance for a small number of open-occupancy housing developments.[50] Still, the agency did not offer unequivocal support for open housing until after passage of the national Fair Housing Act in 1968. At no time did it attempt to use its considerable clout to challenge everyday discrimination by builders, brokers, and lenders, but by the mid-1950s, the agency had reversed its exclusionary stance and made substantial investments toward expanding African American opportunities to purchase and rent housing.

"Black Pioneers"

At the local level, the foot soldiers of the open-housing movement were black families who had the means to leave segregated neighborhoods and the nerve to challenge the color line. These families, known in black communities as "pioneers," were also at the cutting edge of black movement to the suburbs.[51] In financial and ideological terms, pioneers represented a small but influential group within African American communities. Contemporary studies indicated that most pioneers were members of an economic and professional elite, well educated and experienced with white institutions and integrated settings.[52] Dorothy Jayne's study of "pioneer Negro families" in metropolitan Philadelphia reveals that more than half of male pioneers and almost one-third of women were "employed in professional fields." Fifty-five percent of men had college degrees. By contrast, fewer than 5 percent of African Americans in that city shared these attributes. Pioneers were equally distinct in temperament. More than half of Jayne's subjects "anticipated similar treatment as other Negroes who had moved into all-white neighborhoods." Men in two families acted on this expectation by spending their first night on guard in the living room — one with a loaded .38 revolver.[53]

Not surprisingly, pioneering was not a first choice for most families. In a 1962 study of African Americans in Philadelphia, fewer than 15 percent of 1,500 respondents expressed a desire to live in all or mostly white neighborhoods. The majority associated the practice with "danger," "vandalism," "ostracism," or a "lack of ease."[54] One Philadelphia mother told her daughter, "I realize that somebody has to be a pioneer, but I don't want it to be anyone in my family."[55] Thus, a black professional in Syracuse, New York, spoke for many when he claimed, "I don't want to be a pioneer. I don't want to have to lie awake thinking someone may throw a brick through my window or set fire to my house."[56] According to Urban League official Reginald Johnson, "Negroes as well as other people do not want to be told where to live," but pioneers were the type of people who moved to precisely those places where they were told they could not.[57]

By pressing their claims to "full access and equal treatment" in the housing market, black pioneers not only opened avenues for others to follow but forced housing discrimination into the public eye.[58] Moreover, they distinguished themselves by risking violence against their families and their property by moving into neighborhoods where they could reasonably expect to be harassed, if not assaulted. Just as the direct action campaigns of the southern civil rights movement depended on individuals who were willing to be jailed or beaten to advance their rights, the struggle against discrimination in housing relied on black families who put themselves in harm's way to defend their right to buy a home without restriction.

Like attacks on southern civil rights workers, too, racist assaults against pioneers galvanized black communities to demand equal opportunity in housing, politicizing the search for "good houses in good locations," and transforming individual choices about where to live into acts of racial protest.[59]

Prior to *Shelley*, this association was often inevitable, since restrictive covenants remade otherwise routine housing transactions into explicit acts of civil
disobedience, forcing black home seekers to break the law in order to occupy
a home of their choosing. Even afterward, the persisting "curtain of prejudice"
made it difficult to ignore the link between the choice of a home and the
struggle for equality.[60]

When the Wilbur Gary family of Richmond, California, bought an $8,700
house in the all-white Rollingwood subdivision in 1952, the resulting out-
burst solidified the local black community. Several hundred whites milled
about the home, lobbing bricks and burning a cross on the lawn. In response,
the local NAACP organized round-the-clock protection for the family. Pick-
ets, made up of African Americans and a number of progressive whites, paraded before the home with the American flag, reading from the Constitution.
The message for North Richmond political activist Margaret Sparks was the
need for racial unity regardless of social difference. "Communists, Uncle
Toms, preachers and everybody had to pull together. Where you were born
wasn't the issue, but where you could go was the problem."[61]

Pioneers themselves were quick to make the connection between their
personal aspirations and this larger struggle. Clarence Wilson, a Brooklyn cosmetics entrepreneur, advanced this point after vandals torched his new home
in Copaigue, Long Island, in 1953. "This doesn't only concern me," he said.
"It concerns the rights of any citizen to live peacefully in any neighborhood
he desires." Choosing a home in a white suburb represented to Wilson part
of "my fight for human rights."[62] Even the entertainer Nat "King" Cole, often
criticized for his conservative personal politics, appealed to the language of
civil rights when white neighbors tried to block his purchase of a fourteen-
room "ivy-covered English Tudor style home" in the Hancock Park section
of Los Angeles near Beverly Hills, California, in 1948. "I am an American citizen," Cole exclaimed, "and I feel that I am entitled to the same rights as any
other citizen. My wife and I like our home very much, and we intend to stay
there the same as any other American citizen would."[63]

Not all pioneers expressed the bonds between individual and civic action
so clearly, but similar statements were common enough in the postwar decades to highlight a correspondence between housing choice and civil rights.
A sampling of black families who moved into predominantly white neighborhoods in suburban Westchester County, New York, disclosed that although
most had purchased their homes "*not* primarily for race-improvement reasons," the broader implications of breaking the suburban color line were never

far from the surface. Respondents regarded their decisions as representing "progress" or as having "racial importance as well as meeting . . . personal needs." One respondent claimed that by purchasing his home in an all-white neighborhood, he had "fought prejudice with money." Reflecting the same connection between personal and collective protest, two-thirds of the pioneer couples in Dorothy Jayne's study had been members of the NAACP before they moved to white neighborhoods.[64] For these buyers, like any, the decision to purchase a home reflected a calculus of desires including affordability, size, convenience to work, family and schools, neighborhood amenities, investment potential, and social status; but in the postwar period, purchasing across the color line or in suburbs generally had political implications, which linked the class-making efforts of upwardly mobile African American families to a larger project of racial and spatial advancement.

The Black Press

Through coverage of housing discrimination and African American efforts to overcome it, the nation's black media also encouraged readers to make the link between housing choice and civil rights. From the first gathering of anti-covenant activists in 1945, press leaders cooperated closely with civil rights organizations in publicizing and mobilizing grassroots support for open housing.[65] Across the country, editorials and investigative reporting exposed policies of redlining, restrictive covenants, and discrimination by Realtors, banks, and developers. Headlines broadcast the latest outrages against black families, offering a forum for the victims of discrimination to express themselves. In so doing, the press held up for public view articulate models of black assertiveness in the housing market, and they advanced an image of black success that equated equality with crossing the color line.[66] Press coverage of discrimination against prominent blacks such as Ethel Waters, Hattie McDaniel, Percy Julian, Jackie Robinson, Larry Doby, Lena Horne, Nat Cole, Sidney Poitier, Floyd Patterson, and Willie Mays revealed the restrictions facing all African Americans and helped to galvanize black support for open housing.[67] If African Americans recognized and debated class distinctions among themselves, such incidents illustrated that even the most successful blacks shared the burden of race and reinforced a sense of racial similarity among African Americans regardless of class, region, or ethnic background. For middle-class blacks themselves, such incidents shaped an understanding of middle-class identity that was rooted in racial struggle and collective advancement.

Black Real Estate Brokers

A third salient for activism in the housing market issued from blacks in the real estate industry. Throughout the early twentieth century, African American real estate brokers, contractors, and financial institutions played critical roles in expanding "opportunity for Negroes and other racial minorities to obtain good housing in decent neighborhoods."[68] They continued these roles after the war, promoting a vision of private business interest in service to the black struggle for freedom. In the late 1940s, black builders, real estate brokers, and financial institutions established national trade organizations to promote and coordinate black efforts in the field of housing. Members of the brokers' organization, the National Association of Real Estate Brokers, called themselves "Realtists" to distinguish them from "Realtors," whose organization had historically excluded blacks. Underlining the relationship between their business and the civil rights struggle, they adopted the motto "Democracy in Housing."[69]

Realtists pursued this goal primarily by working to open up white neighborhoods to African Americans. Speakers at early Realtist conferences emphasized this point, urging fellow brokers to blanket prospective neighborhoods with calling cards and mailings, to "ring doorbells," to read the obituaries and sheriffs' sale announcements, and to make "personal contacts" in "changing" neighborhoods. As one of the founders of the organization put it, "Selling white houses to blacks . . . that was apple pie for us."[70] It was also a source of special pride in Realtists' efforts to expand the African American housing market. Brokers' advertisements emphasized their role in breaking the color barrier or opening up "new frontiers."[71] Queens, New York, real estate agent William Urquhart played on the concept of pioneering by encouraging readers to "drive your covered wagon" to his office.[72] Brokers not only called attention to their work as a service to all blacks, but they enticed buyers to share in the cause, implying that their purchase of such housing constituted a blow to racism. Of course, Realtists and other black real estate brokers sought to profit from their work, and their advertising revealed the malleability of civil rights rhetoric for private gain. But for most, the approach involved no contradiction. Brokers recalled with pride their efforts to expand the supply of housing available to black families. Pasadena real estate broker Theodore Bartlett recollected that "selling to blacks into totally white neighborhoods" in Pasadena and nearby suburbs "was something I had a lot to do with, and I've always been proud of it."[73] In another instance, the obituary of Evanston, Illinois, real estate agent William Gill suggested the pride he must have felt about selling housing across the color line. In a list of his life's accomplishments, Gill's family emphasized that "it was through his efforts that many areas were opened to Negroes."[74] Thus, for black brokers, like many middle-class African Americans, race progress was a class responsibility. They worked hand in hand with black home seekers, supporting their aspirations and reinforcing the belief that housing was an arena of struggle in which all African Americans had a stake.

Government and Suburbanization

In his 1955 study of discrimination in housing, *Forbidden Neighbors*, urban planner Charles Abrams compared federal housing policies unfavorably to the jim crow system of the South. In his view, federal housing efforts had amounted to a program of "separate for whites and nothing for blacks."[75] Subsequent scholarship has generally supported Abrams's conclusions, highlighting federal culpability in expanding segregation and transforming private real estate practices such as redlining and racist property appraisal into national policy.[76] This portrait is accurate to a degree, but it rests ultimately on an image of suburbia in which African Americans were in fact excluded as well as an analysis of the federal housing bureaucracy that fails to encompass the whole of its activities. Explaining the expansion of black suburbanization, rather than its absence, requires a more complex picture of federal action. Ironically, programs that did so much to shore up racial exclusivity in white suburbia were instrumental in assisting a large proportion of black families who actually moved to the suburbs.[77]

Limited federal support for black suburbanization was not an aberration. As historian Thomas Sugrue argues, the New Deal state encapsulated competing and often contradictory visions of racial democracy. While the mass of white voters expected government to "protect the privileges associated with property ownership and race," African Americans struggled to advance their own vision of liberalism, which emphasized not only economic opportunity but racial equality, pressing their claims through collective and individual action.[78] At best, federal housing agencies represented deeply racist mediators between white and black interest groups at the state and local levels. From their inception in the 1930s through the early 1950s, federal housing programs either required or encouraged racial segregation, but struggles at the local level were crucial to determining the nature of black participation. State action usually reinforced racial segregation, but it did so sometimes by excluding and sometimes by including African Americans.

Wartime Housing

The most important federal influence on African American suburbanization during the 1940s was the Emergency Defense Housing program established under the Lanham Act of 1940. Created to provide shelter for war workers in areas of heavy defense production, the war housing program harbored more than a million American families by 1945, among which more than 90,000 were African American. With the inclusion of black veterans in the program after the war, this total rose to more than 150,000 black families by 1950. Coupled with federally subsidized public housing for low-income black families, the emergency war housing program was the largest source of new housing for African Americans in cities and suburbs during the 1940s.[79]

While affecting American cities in a variety of ways, the war housing program also augmented African American communities in the suburbs. Unlike depression-era public housing, which was designed as a complement to slum clearance, the Lanham Act required that new dwellings be built on vacant land. Consequently, many of the projects built under the program were located in suburbs or the outer reaches of a central city. The legislation also mandated the construction of a proportionate number of housing units for white and nonwhite war workers. Although many communities evaded this provision, federal officials in most areas tried to satisfy the law by building separate projects for black war workers. Further, as federal housing official Booker T. McGraw explained, because of "strong local and neighborhood opposition" to racial integration among whites, most emergency housing projects for African Americans were built in areas where blacks were "previously . . . established."[80] Thus, a disproportionate number of war housing units were built near existing black neighborhoods outside the urban core, reinforcing prewar black residence on the suburban fringe and laying a foundation for new migration after the war.

In cities such as Detroit, Pittsburgh, Cleveland, Cincinnati, Oakland, and Philadelphia, war housing had precisely this effect.[81] Federal officials in Detroit built Lanham housing adjacent to black communities in the suburbs of Ecorse, River Rouge, Inkster, and Royal Oak Township, as well as adjacent to the outlying Conant Gardens neighborhood in the city. By the end of the war, close to 10,000 African Americans lived in suburban war housing near the Motor City, representing almost a third of black population growth in area suburbs during the 1940s.[82] In Cleveland, officials built temporary war housing for nearly 500 black families in the Miles Heights neighborhood, which had been a largely black suburb until its annexation by the city in 1932.[83] The largest concentration of emergency war housing in the country was constructed in San Francisco's East Bay region, where more than 30,000 African Americans lived in suburban war housing projects by 1945. By the early 1950s, as many as 80 percent of African Americans in the East Bay suburbs of Berkeley, Richmond, Alameda, and Vallejo were living in housing projects constructed under the auspices of the Lanham Act.[84]

Despite criticism during the 1940s for haphazard planning, flimsy construction, and sterile architecture, these hastily built projects served as a shelter and point of entry for tens of thousands of black migrants during a pivotal chapter in their lives. In the East Bay, thousands of black suburbanites, mostly southern migrants who had come west for jobs in the local shipyards, endured substandard conditions in war housing projects for as long as a decade. Nonetheless, many looked back favorably on their years in the projects, where shared spaces and experiences fostered a "sense of community."[85] Lovie McIntosh, a migrant from Arkansas, recalled creating a circle of associations that began with the woman next door:

> I got acquainted with her and soon picked up other friends. I gather friends real easy. So we got to know people, and it was really nice. They were all people who had migrated. Some was from Texas, and some was from Mississippi, but there was several families from Arkansas, which was really nice. And I got involved with the church right up the street, and began to do PTA work too.[86]

In Cleveland, similarly, African Americans found much to praise in the Seville Homes, a 500-unit Lanham project constructed by the Cleveland Housing Authority on the southeastern edge of the city. *Call and Post* housing reporter Simeon Booker Jr. described the development as a "model G.I. village . . . nestled among the rolling hills of the suburbs." The wife of one veteran, who had been doubled-up in an older neighborhood before moving to the project, claimed, "I wouldn't want a better place to live."[87]

Even though most of the temporary projects were demolished in the 1950s, thousands of migrants had built social and institutional networks that they refused to abandon. In Richmond and Berkeley, California, African

Fig. 5.6   *Richmond — Housing for Shipyard Workers.* Dorothea Lange, 1944.
Seated on a pile of building materials in front of her temporary home in North
Richmond, California, this woman was one of many black southerners who moved
to San Francisco's East Bay for wartime jobs. Housing shortages in areas of intensive
war production spawned makeshift communities across the United States. North
Richmond's small prewar black community served as a beachhead for suburban
expansion in the 1940s. (Copyright the Dorothea Lange Collection, Oakland
Museum of California, City of Oakland. Gift of Paul S. Taylor)

Americans resisted the strenuous efforts of white officials to force them out,
and they succeeded by hook or by crook to stay even as the projects came
down.[88] A large number saved money to make down payments on homes
of their own. After the war, families expanded into adjacent white neighborhoods, while some moved to unplanned subdivisions in North Richmond,
where the thrifty built homes of their own. Others purchased new homes in a
handful of tracts built for African Americans. During the 1950s, the number
of black home owners in Berkeley and Richmond increased by almost 4,000;
by 1970 the latter suburb had a black majority.[89]

Lanham housing in other cities, too, drove a wedge of opportunity for
subsequent suburbanites. Developers in Detroit built tract homes for blacks
on former defense housing sites in River Rouge, Ecorse, Inkster, and Royal
Oak Township. In Cleveland, the Seville Homes made way for FHA-approved
two-bedroom ranch homes.[90] Even in smaller cities, such as Muskegon,

Michigan, and Wilmington, Delaware, wartime housing projects became focal points for postwar suburbanization. In these and other suburban areas, emergency war housing solidified prewar patterns of African American residence and established a foundation for accelerated suburbanization after the war.[91]

Federal Support for Privately Developed Housing

Even more important than war housing to the landscape of postwar suburbia were federal programs designed to support private housing construction and home ownership. The primary agencies responsible for stimulating new home building, the Federal Housing Administration and the Veterans Administration, reflected racial ambiguities apparent throughout the New Deal state. Both were racist institutions that disproportionately served the interests of white home buyers and the white real estate industry.[92] Nonetheless, they were also public agencies, subject to political and legal pressure from groups demanding that the benefits of an expanded federal state be distributed equally. By the late 1940s, direct pressure from civil rights organizations as well as legal precedents and evolving state legislation led these agencies to modify their practices, enhancing the ability of African American families to purchase and rent new housing. Although both agencies refused until the 1960s to promote fair-housing practices in the private market, by the early 1950s both had made a rhetorical commitment to open housing and had devoted limited resources to "[increase] the supply of adequate housing for minority groups."[93] Federal support remained grossly unequal, but even agency critics acknowledged a "radical change" in FHA policy and conduct. Future Housing and Urban Development secretary Robert Weaver and fair-housing activist Hortense Gabel acknowledged in 1953, "The Federal Housing Administration . . . has finally recognized the need for more private, non-white housing."[94]

A modest indicator of change in the FHA was its appointment in 1947 of five "race relations advisors" to "provide assistance to local communities and the building industry in stepping up the production of housing for minority groups."[95] The advisors—all African American men—were assigned to each of the FHA's five regional offices, and they reported to division chief Frank Horne, who had served as an advisor on race matters within the Housing and Home Finance Agency since 1938. Working from inside the agency and through contacts in the black finance and real estate industries, this group recruited and offered technical assistance to prospective developers, facilitated contact between builders and financial institutions, made routine field inspections to identify suitable locations for "minority housing," and gathered and disseminated data to overcome resistance to such housing within the white-dominated housing industry.[96] In addition, race relations advisors lobbied within FHA regional offices for the approval of projects designed to increase the supply of housing available to African Americans and other nonwhites. Horne and his team had greatest success in promoting "Negro housing" in the South, but FHA advisors also were influential in securing agency assistance for tens of thousands of new dwellings in other parts of the country.[97] In addition, the race relations service played a crucial part outside the South in garnering FHA support for truly nonsegregated housing.[98] Despite subsequent depictions, there were African American civic leaders in the mid-fifties who believed that "the national housing program has the best record of any agency for equality of treatment, and this must be attributed in large measure . . . to the wise actions in providing for race relations advisors in the program."[99]

FHA publications and correspondence indicate the breadth of agency involvement in new home building for African Americans. In 1951, for example, agency records reveal that race relations staff were deeply involved with black housing struggles nationwide. Advisors met with builders from Atlanta, Birmingham, Miami, Dallas, West Palm Beach, Washington, Philadelphia, Orlando, and Long Island. Staff assisted the McKissack Brothers of Nashville in securing FHA insurance for their College Hill development; in Atlanta regional advisor Albert Thompson convinced the Atlanta Life Insurance Company, a black firm, to purchase FHA-insured mortgages from black home buyers in the Elliston Heights subdivision near Memphis. Advisors inspected potential development sites during field trips to Tacoma, Oakland, Birmingham, and Miami, and they kept tabs on housing controversies in Dallas, Baltimore, New Orleans, Biloxi, Tampa, and Savannah, as well as suburbs of Chicago, Detroit, and Philadelphia, lobbying local and federal officials to prevent discrimination in federally supported housing.[100] A 1951 article in the FHA quarterly, *Insured Mortgage Portfolio*, depicted nearly two dozen FHA-assisted projects for African Americans that had been completed in cities and suburbs across the United States. Projects ranged from an eighteen-unit garden apartment building in Montclair, New Jersey, to single-family housing tracts in South Bend, San Bernadino, and South Los Angeles, plus numerous projects across the South.[101] Reflecting the comparatively small number of middle-income black households, most of these subdivisions were not large—ranging from ten to two hundred houses. Homes themselves were usually modest in size and price, but they boasted standard suburban planning and architecture and the latest conveniences, such as forced-air heating and new electric appliances. Indeed, there was little in the initial residential landscape to distinguish these subdivisions from the thousands being built at that time for whites of the same income level.[102]

Despite obvious discrimination, the enormous volume of FHA/VA activities meant that even token federal investments translated into a substantial number of housing units. Contemporary estimates suggested that less than 2 percent of FHA-insured mortgages and 3 percent of VA-guaranteed loans during this period went to the 11 percent of Americans who were "nonwhite."[103] Taken together, however, these agencies insured or guaranteed more than 10 million private home mortgages between 1945 and 1960. Adding FHA-insured rental and cooperative housing projects, the two agencies may have subsidized the purchase and rental of as many as 300,000 new homes by nonwhite families between 1945 and 1960. Because most of these were built after 1950, FHA/VA-assisted housing may have accounted for as much as 40 percent of the new housing occupied by African Americans in the metropolitan United States during the decade.[104]

All told, the race relations staff played a key role in the construction of thousands of new housing units open to blacks and other minorities, and they nudged the FHA away from the exclusionary stance it had adopted since 1934. FHA policy continued to reflect contradictions inherent within the New Deal state as well as the ambivalence that many African Americans felt toward it. Federal housing programs disproportionately assisted whites and reinforced white racism in the housing market; they also helped several hundred thousand African American families purchase or rent new homes. Frustrating as was the resistance to change within the federal bureaucracy, African Americans remained cautiously optimistic about the potential for achieving racial equality through an expanded federal state, and they worked within its bounds to reach this goal.

Conclusion

The postwar period was a period of transition in African American suburbanization. During the depression, suburban black communities had consolidated in population, but as World War II rekindled the black exodus from the rural South, suburbs once again attracted African Americans in growing numbers. Rising incomes and the birth of a new black middle class, vigorous civil

Fig. 5.7　During the late 1940s and early 1950s, the Federal Housing Administration publicly promoted its efforts to "mak[e] better housing available to racial
minorities" and to dispel the idea that "the Negro is a poor credit risk and slum
dweller by preference." This photographic collage illustrated the diversity of
the new FHA-financed "Negro housing." (*Insured Mortgage Portfolio* 16
[winter 1951])

rights activity, and marginal increases in federal assistance facilitated a growing black migration to the outer reaches of the metropolitan United States.

At the same time, massive white suburbanization and the spread of hostile suburban municipalities produced a style of racial exclusion that was far more comprehensive than had prevailed in prewar suburbia. By 1960 planning and land-use regulation had largely curtailed older pathways of working-class suburbanization. For a time, streams of working- and middle-class suburbanization coincided, but by 1955 the middle class had gained numerical superiority, a pattern that would survive for the rest of the century.

Despite these changes, the making of race and place remained fused in the process of black suburbanization. Discrimination remained a fundamental stumbling block, maintaining high levels of residential segregation and reinforcing a racial basis for political behavior. Where upwardly mobile families made strides in the suburbs, moreover, they usually followed well-established paths. Just as working-class African Americans before the war had built new homes on an older foundation, the homes and communities of prewar suburbanites offered a wedge of opportunity for a new generation of more affluent families seeking their own suburban dreams after the war.

Looking ahead, it was also clear that structural changes in the suburban housing market and the rise of middle-class suburbanization coincided with a changing palette of black suburban dreams. Despite spatial continuity with older settlements, new suburbanites affirmed their class position not only through achievements in income, occupation, and education, but also in how they chose to live. Growing numbers expressed residential preferences that they shared with a broad spectrum of middle-class Americans. The dream of improved life in the suburbs, reflecting both the history and contemporary circumstances of the new suburbanites, remained a potent force, and they sought to give it life in spite of white efforts to stop them. Thus, the history of black suburbanization offers a window into the interwoven process of race and class formation at midcentury.

Chapter 6

"The House I Live In"

Race, Class, and Suburban Dreams in the Postwar Period

Ten-room house, at least 60 years of age, badly in need of repair and redecoration. House is cold in winter and hot in summer. Conveniently located near smoky factories, noisy railroad yards and receives frequent fragrance from nearby stockyards. The neighborhood is highly deteriorated and is well supplied with all the factors that encourage crime and delinquency. Heavy truck traffic in area. No nearby playgrounds. Firetrap school house within walking distance. Best thing available for nice Negro family at exorbitant rent.

— Mock advertisement for African American housing, NAACP (1948)[1]

IF INCREASING suburbanization reflected growth in black incomes, accelerated civil rights activism, and limited intervention by the federal government, progress rested fundamentally on the individual effort of black families to find better places to live. These efforts bent to economic constraints and the burden of racial discrimination, but they also reflected preferences that the new suburbanites brought to the market. Some of these — premiums on home ownership, open space, and family-based communities — were values that African Americans had long cherished. Others were more novel developments that coincided with changes in the socioeconomic composition of suburban migration. Just as the values of early suburbanites had been situated in the historical experience of a particular class of southern migrants before World War II, African Americans' aspirations for housing and neighborhoods changed as suburbanizing families moved further from this experience.

African Americans' decisions about where to live also represented part of an ongoing dialogue about race and class in the mid-twentieth-century United States. As households situated themselves spatially in the metropolis, they also did so socially. Thus, for many households, suburbanization was a conscious class-making act. As upwardly mobile blacks achieved middle-class incomes, occupations, and education, they also expressed a sense of class through aesthetic preferences, patterns of consumption, and choices of a place to live. Like millions of other Americans, new suburbanites sought to own modern homes in recognizably middle-class neighborhoods. Their suburban dreams emphasized leisure-time pursuits, opportunities for children, proximity to jobs and services, and architecturally uniform residential landscapes. Suburbanization became a means for middle-class households to express and reinforce their newly won social position.

Nonetheless, shifts in suburban ideology did not connote a lessening of racial distinctions or a "whitening" of the middle class. As racial outsiders in a predominantly white society, African Americans could not be "ordinary" suburbanites even if they wanted. Their distinctive public experience indelibly shaped the meaning of private space, such as homes and neighborhoods, and it nurtured a distinctive politics related to housing. By achieving widespread suburban living patterns, African Americans asserted their equality and consciously minimized the social distance that whites sought to maintain as a privilege of race. In so doing, they challenged and subverted a central element of the dominant suburban ethos, which was white supremacy.[2]

Suburbanization further reinforced racial distinctions by contributing to an "intraracial discourse" on class among African Americans themselves.[3] Despite growth in incomes and a marginal decline in barriers to social mobility, black families approached migration to the suburbs as members of African American communities and as people embedded in the larger context of black life in the United States. Even as middle-class families adopted residential tastes and standards that were popular among middle-class whites, class remained a social distinction that African Americans drew largely in relation to other blacks. Indeed, the recognition and enactment of social differences such as class, color, ethnicity, gender, region, and other aspects of social identity were an important part of the experience of being black. In other words, class was not something separate from racial identity, but rather was integral to it. As an emerging element of middle-class status, therefore, suburbanization tended to strengthen migrants' identities as black people even as it reinforced patterns of stratification among African Americans themselves.

Images of Home

The clearest evidence of continuity between pre- and postwar suburban values was the persisting appeal of home ownership among African Americans of every social class. Attitude surveys uncovered a widespread inclination among African Americans to own homes of their own, and for many it included the wish to buy in the suburbs. A nationwide survey of black veterans in 1947 disclosed that between one-third and one-half of veterans in cities such as Philadelphia, Detroit, Indianapolis, Atlanta, Houston, and Baton Rouge hoped to buy or build a home of their own within the next twelve months.[4] A 1948 study of 600 "middle-income Negro families" in New York City revealed that three-quarters "would like to move to suburban areas and nine-tenths of them preferred to buy their own homes."[5] Approaching the question from a different angle, researchers in Philadelphia asked some 1,500 African Americans in 1960 how they would spend a "windfall" of $5,000. More than half reported that they would use the money to buy a new house or pay off an existing mortgage.[6]

Evidence of African Americans' tenacious "demand for home ownership" was apparent in everyday behavior, as well.[7] Supported by gains in income and civil liberties, as well as marginal governmental assistance, rates of nonfarm home ownership among African Americans climbed from 24 to 39 percent between 1940 and 1960. In the most populous suburban areas, however, the proportion of owners rose from 32 to 51 percent. Home ownership, which had long been a goal among African Americans, remained a fundamental aspiration among black suburbanites after the war.[8]

What home ownership meant to these people, however, remained a complex matter. Many suburbanites still viewed home ownership as the basis for economic security through thrift and domestic production. Prewar patterns of suburban life endured in a range of working-class suburbs. Suburbanites relished their gardens and fruit trees, and many insisted on keeping livestock. In places like Chagrin Falls Park, the war did little to change the disposition of residents like Clydie Smith, who fondly remembered gardens, lush with "pinto beans and collards and black-eyed peas and cabbage and beets and squash and peppers" as well as the sow, called "Sookie," that her father kept.[9]

Across the continent in Pasadena, city officials fought a running battle with black householders who kept chickens and ducks in violation of a local ordinance.[10] In Mount Vernon, David Doles, who had prospered as a laundry owner in Harlem before moving to the suburbs, extolled self-provisioning as part of an ethic of thrift that included other productive uses of property as well. Recalling how "we used to eat off our place down home" in Virginia, Doles boasted that he planted "more fruit right here in my place in the back yard than some people with a great big place."[11]

This rustic suburban vision was also evident in black popular culture. In her 1959 drama, *A Raisin in the Sun*, playwright Lorraine Hansberry used this ethic to symbolize both the endurance and violation of African Americans' hopes for a better life in the urban North. The character Mama, a southerner living in a Chicago tenement, dreams of buying "a little place" with "a patch of dirt" in the backyard. She explains, "[I] always wanted me a garden like I used to see sometimes at the back of the houses down home." The sun-starved plant on her windowsill serves as a visual reminder of this deferred dream.[12] In literature as well as real life, the echoes of rural and working-class upbringings reverberated in the choices that migrants made. For as long as they lived, lifeways and mentalities such as these would shape the environment of hundreds of suburban communities.

Many postwar suburbanites also used their homes as a source of income and as an anchor for continued migration by renting rooms to recent migrants and sharing space with kin. Older suburbs in particular witnessed intensified multifamily occupancy during the period. In Evanston, for instance, scores of home owners converted houses to include rental units. In the streets off Emerson Avenue on the west side, the number of owners and renters rose simultaneously despite little new construction, indicating that African Americans were buying and converting their own homes to multifamily use. Similar practices affected neighborhoods in East Orange, New Jersey; New Rochelle, New York; and Pasadena and Berkeley, California, where black home owners capitalized on postwar migration by becoming landlords.[13] Though some residents expressed a more restrictive view of domestic space, charging that "overcrowding" would lead to "possible neighborhood deterioration," old settlers offered a foothold for migrants in established communities, while newcomers afforded rental incomes that supported home ownership and upward mobility for a rising class of black landlords.[14]

Advertisements in the black press indicate that this vision of economic independence through productive use of property remained a marketable option in urban communities through at least the late forties As the war ended, realty companies in Detroit, New York, Chicago, and other cities dusted off old subdivisions and began selling low-cost building lots much as they had before the war. The *Chicago Defender* advertised home sites for as little as "$10 down" in suburbs such as Robbins, Phoenix, East Chicago Heights, and Maywood as well as in predominantly black subdivisions within the city such as Morgan Park and Lilydale. New York's *Amsterdam News* pitched building lots in Westbury, Hempstead, Amityville, Hauppauge, and other suburbs where African Americans had lived since the nineteenth century.[15] A 1947 advertisement for "Farm Homesites" in Farmingdale, Long Island, for instance, depicted a small house and outbuildings surrounded by tilled fields and fruit trees, while the text stressed links to the urban economy, highlighting "easy commuting, close to large airplane factory, plenty of employment."[16] Like advertisements published during the Great Migration, these appealed to a working-class, southern aesthetic, describing semi-rural landscapes, open space, and low-cost property ownership plus "the opportunity to grow your own food" within proximity to established communities and urban jobs.[17]

Owner building and other informal construction practices also persisted in blue-collar subdivisions. In Chagrin Falls Park, Clydie Smith, William Hagler, and George Adams built homes after the war.[18] So, too, did families in suburbs such as Inkster, Michigan; the American Addition near Columbus, Ohio; and North Richmond, California, where lot owners went "to the lumberyard and bought what they could without access to mortgage loans, and . . . put up what they called their home."[19] Advertisements for do-it-yourself house kits, Quonset buildings, and other nontraditional shelters, such as the prefabricated "Port-o-Cottage, the house you have been waiting for," were common fare in the black press through the late 1940s.[20] As this evidence indicates, home ownership remained a productive enterprise rooted in the black working-class experience. To the extent that middle-class status was fleeting or uncertain, these practices remained attractive, representing continuity in African American values and lifeways in the postwar suburbs.

In contrast to the thrift-oriented ethos that prevailed in older suburban areas, an increasing number of new suburbanites articulated preferences for housing that reflected norms prevalent across the wider American middle class. In a study of black professionals and technical employees in upstate New York, Eunice and George Grier concluded that "little if anything . . . distinguishes the requirements of these Negro home seekers from criteria one would expect to find among their middle-class white counterparts." They sought "adequate play space for children, good schools, safety and quiet, good property maintenance, and congenial neighbors of roughly equivalent in-

Fig. 6.1 Advertisements for building lots on Long Island, New York. Like their counterparts during the Great Migration, real estate agents in the 1940s marketed subdivisions that promised urban African Americans a vision of rustic self-sufficiency in a borderland between rural and urban life. Mass suburbanization and the proliferation of suburban land-use regulations sharply curtailed this avenue to suburbia. (*Amsterdam News*, May 24, 1947)

come and educational background." Not surprisingly, most were "looking for a house of post World War II vintage in a suburban area."[21] Dorothy Jayne encountered similar attitudes among pioneer families in suburban Philadelphia. Two-thirds of her respondents hoped to buy a single-family home in a "desirable" suburban neighborhood—a third were looking for ranch or split-level models. They described their ideal neighborhoods as "quiet, clean, with well-kept properties," convenient to shopping with good schools and services and an abundance of "fresh air and green grass." Many indicated, too, that they were willing to pay more to attain these amenities.[22]

Among the attractions of suburban life that many middle-class African Americans shared with their white counterparts was an emphasis on a materially abundant family life in a residential setting removed from the "grind" of paid labor.[23] A glimpse of the ideal lifestyle circulating among middle-class blacks after the war can be seen in the pages of *Ebony* magazine, which appeared on newsstands in 1945 and targeted readers in the aspiring black bourgeoisie. During its first few years, *Ebony* ran regular features publicizing the housing and domestic lifestyles of the nation's black elite. Reporters fawned over "big impressive home[s]," "sumptuous" furnishings, stylish house parties, and the financial success and style that these implied. Many stories featured families who lived in elegant central city apartments, reflecting the continued concentration of black elites in neighborhoods such as Harlem's "Sugar Hill," but an equal number highlighted the owners of detached single-family homes in suburban or suburban-style neighborhoods.[24]

An *Ebony* feature on the Addisleigh Park neighborhood of St. Alban's, Queens, New York, reveals the spatial and social environment that many middle-class African Americans idealized in the postwar decades. With its two-story Tudor and colonial revival houses, green lawns, and canopy of mature trees, the place merited its description as a "swank suburban neighborhood" or a "suburban Sugar Hill" even though it was located inside the municipal limits of New York City.[25]

Reflecting the importance of landscape as a status marker, the writer highlighted residents' richly appointed housing and abundant greenery. The essay featured more than twenty photographs of tree-shaded homes belonging to such celebrities as Ella Fitzgerald, Roy Campanella, Billie Holiday, Jackie Robinson, and Count Basie, underscoring the affluent surroundings and amenities that they enjoyed. "Many home owners have two cars," including "more Cadillacs per block . . . than any other like community in the country," the reporter enthused. Meanwhile, captions listed the dollar value of almost every home pictured, suggesting none too subtly the connection between home ownership, wealth, and taste.

If few *Ebony* readers could afford such luxuries, the article took pains to emphasize Addisleigh Park's down-to-earth social life, which the writer described as "swank without snobbery." According to the reporter, Mercer Ellington mowed his own yard and preferred to "romp with his children on the front lawn," while Illinois Jacquet spent his leisure time in "bull sessions with famous neighbors." When Count Basie wasn't getting his "kicks" playing the organ in his living room, he could be found engaged in "marathon poker games . . . famed . . . for their high stakes and salty talk."

Though residents were household names in black America, the writer pictured Addisleigh Park as a "typical . . . suburban community, with its civic association, women's clubs, Boy Scout troops and Saturday night pinochle games . . . lavish lawn parties and hearty cocktail sessions in pine-walled rumpus rooms."[26] Thus, *Ebony* portrayed a vision of suburban life that many middle-class African Americans could appreciate and to which they might aspire. In its emphasis on comfort and an expressive, consumption-oriented social life, the magazine impressed upon, and no doubt reinforced among its

Jackie Robinson of Brooklyn Dodgers bought $30,000 home on 177th Street. He always stays here when Dodgers are playing home games.

Cootie Williams, noted bandleader, lives in $35,000 ivy-covered Linden Boulevard home. Most of St. Alban's residents do shopping in Manhattan, but buy groceries locally.

ST. ALBAN'S

N.Y. community is home for more celebrities than any other U.S. residential area

THE MOST exclusive Negro residential section in America is located in St. Alban's, Long Island, where more glamour, wealth, talent and achievement are concentrated into a 50-block area than any other comparable community in America. Just barely 30 minutes by train from the heart of Manhattan, this suburban Sugar Hill presents the upper bracket of Negro life at its best.

The swank suburban community of St. Alban's has developed in the past five years—changing from a very staid all-white area housing retired millionaires, bank executives and Wall Street officials into a veritable Who's Who of Negro celebrities. Although the nation's most elite Negro community, St. Alban's is strangely unsnobbish. Its social life is informal and bright, never stuffy. Its inhabitants live a placid, self-contained existence and maintain no local Social Register or community Blue Book.

Actually the quiet, spacious, elegantly-upholstered section of St. Alban's where Negroes live is called Addisleigh Park and is only a part of St. Alban's. Addisleigh Park's Negro population are migrants from apartments in crowded Harlem or brownstone flats in sprawling Brooklyn. Most of its home own-

Carol Brice, famed singer, and her husband, public relations man Neil Scott, have a $27,500 home on 113th Road. Here she fondles their dog on lawn.

Carl Bustic, well-known bandleader, lives in expansive $40,000 home on Murdock Avenue. He and fellow musicians often get together at social affairs in rumpus rooms.

Fig. 6.2 Through its coverage of housing issues, *Ebony* reflected as well as promoted a consumer-oriented vision of suburban living among the nation's growing black middle class. (*Ebony,* September 1951)

readers, a distinctly middle- or upper-middle-class vision of suburban life. In a suburbanizing nation, *Ebony* signaled, middle-class African Americans were gaining equality as citizens through equality in their tastes and acquisitions as consumers, not least of which was their consumption of housing.[27]

Advertisements for new tract homes aimed at black home buyers appealed to a cluster of similar values, further suggesting the strength of this vision among the new black middle class as well as the pressures for conformity that shaped it. A 1947 ad for the Hempstead Park subdivision in West Hempstead, Long Island, was typical. It pictured a modest saltbox-style home in a background of trees, while the text extolled the virtues of the house and neighborhood. For just $9,900, no cash down, black veterans and their families could own "4 ½ spacious, sun-filled rooms" with "large picture windows," on a "large landscaped plot" just a "short walk" from schools, shopping, and Hempstead Lake State Park. With the exception of the ad's placement in a black newspaper, there was nothing to distinguish it from hundreds of advertisements aimed at white veterans. Hempstead Park's amenities—emphasizing children, leisure, home ownership, and a picturesque residential setting—fit squarely within the mass suburban ethos of the period.[28]

Ten years later, an advertisement for three subdivisions in the San Fernando Valley, north of Los Angeles, appealed to the same suburban imagery. The ad in the black-owned *Crown City Press* of Pasadena featured a sleek garage-dominant ranch house framed by tall trees and the written text: "Give your family the pleasure of living in Pacoima's Quality Circle." A map indicated "the most desirable San Fernando Valley location," marking such features as Hansen Dam recreation area, the San Gabriel Mountains, a school, a public park and pool, as well as the highway to downtown Los Angeles. In addition to situating these developments in a recreation-filled landscape that had already become synonymous with middle-class suburban living, the ad emphasized the "exquisitely modern" but cozy amenities of the houses themselves, including "sliding glass walls," "large, cheerful kitchens," and "brick fireplaces," plus a choice of nine "exciting exteriors."[29] Like advertisements for thousands of white subdivisions after World War II, these ads could not have evoked a more distant imagery from the chicken coops, "secondhanded lumber," and upstairs renters that characterized working-class suburban life at the time.[30] They marketed modern, affordable comfort in an environment oriented toward nuclear families and leisure just a short commute from the central city, a suburban dream firmly anchored in the postwar mainstream.

As these examples indicate, another important feature of postwar black suburbanization was an emphasis on the suburbs as a "better place for children" to live.[31] In the early years of the baby boom, children gained prominence in suburban advertising for African Americans much as they did in ads aimed at middle-class whites. "Here is the safety of suburban living for your children," boasted the developer of Ronek Park, a 1,000-home subdivision in North Amityville, New York. "Yes, here, the entire family can enjoy the pleas-

Fig. 6.3   Advertisement for suburban housing near Los Angeles. By the 1950s, mass-produced suburban imagery predominated in the real estate pages of the nation's black press. Like *Ebony*'s reportage, ads for new homes emphasized a vision of suburbia that had wide appeal in the nation's middle class. (*Pasadena Crown City Press*, February 7, 1957)

ures and advantages of a wonderful new community offering everything you ever dreamed of." Another broker, who specialized in "high-class neighborhoods" of Westchester County, encouraged readers of New York's *Amsterdam News* to "bring up your children in this suburban paradise."[32] Developers increasingly incorporated images of children in their advertisements, which also reflected a shift in the class composition of black suburban migration after the war. Though prewar ads often mentioned schools and parks in a list of local facilities, subdividers rarely mentioned children directly—certainly less often than they referred to chickens or vegetable gardens.

Even ads for homes in unplanned suburbs such as Robbins, Illinois, which had attracted working-class blacks since World War I, were not exempt from the national celebration of child rearing that succeeded the war. A 1946 campaign for "homesites" in the Lincoln Manor subdivision depicted children playing in the front yard of a new home while a woman sat on the front steps watching and perhaps waiting for a breadwinning father to return up the front walk. Blending elements of old and new, the ad portrayed a square brick-faced bungalow typical of Chicago's southwest suburbs, plus a large garden plot— tilled for row crops, no less—at the back of the lot.[33] The image of a stay-at-home mother belied economic reality for millions of African American families, but through such advertisements, suburban developers reinforced a vision of middle-class domesticity even in suburbs that had long been home to the black working class.

Suburbanites themselves were also more likely to mention children as the basis for residential choice, often doing so in class-specific ways. Discussing his search for housing, a black professional from upstate New York reported, "Locality would take precedence over price for me because I have a family to bring up and want them to grow up in an area which will aid in their development." Another described his preferred place of residence as "an area where the schools provide opportunities to give my children a good education, and where they could skate, bike ride, and keep pets."[34] The musician Milt Hinton explained that he and his wife moved to the leafy environs of Addisleigh Park from an apartment in Manhattan because they were expecting a baby and "we wanted a nice, clean place to raise a child."[35] In contrast to the emphasis that working-class suburbanites had placed on extended families, nuclear families and children loomed large for the middle class, and suburbs appeared the ideal place to raise them.[36]

The centrality of children in middle-class ideology emerged in discussions of other preferences as well. For African Americans who valued racial integration as the antithesis of segregation, children were an important justification. Celebrity couples such as Jackie and Rachel Robinson and Sidney and Juanita Poitier justified their decisions to look for housing in mostly white neighborhoods in just such terms. "We feel if our children have an opportunity to know people of all races and creeds at a very early age, their opportunities in life will be greater," Jackie Robinson explained.[37] For the Poitiers, it was the lack of such opportunities in Los Angeles that caused them to rethink their move to that city in 1960. After having difficulty finding a house in West Los Angeles, Mr. Poitier stated, "Our children are established in a multi-racial community in Mount Vernon [New York]. They attend multi-racial schools. The difference in color is no longer a curiosity to our children. We don't want to barter that kind of atmosphere for something that is hostile."[38] Likewise, Winston Richie, a dentist who moved to Shaker Heights, Ohio, in 1956, explained that he wanted his children to learn that they "could compete with all people at all levels if they are prepared themselves. Living in an all-black community," he argued, "makes this lesson a bit harder to learn, or at best, it comes later in life."[39] For parents such as these, selecting suburban neighborhoods rested heavily on the opportunity they perceived for their children to grow up as equal citizens.

Race, Class, and Suburbanization

If many new suburbanites aspired to goals that they shared with middle-class whites, they also approached homes and neighborhoods as people with a distinct history and experiences that distinguished them from whites. "Being middle class," sociologist Mary Patillo-McCoy notes, "did not annul the fact of being black."[40] Discrimination blocked African Americans' most ordinary aspirations, forging out of individual choices a politics of housing linked to the quest for racial equality. Suburbanization underlined racial cohesion in a practical sense, too, by forcing house hunters to rely on black social and institutional networks, especially if they sought housing beyond established black areas.

Direct confrontations with racism also shaped the experience and understanding of suburban life. For thousands of families, the search for housing was a struggle that left economic as well as emotional scars. Legal activist Loren Miller explained:

Those who cannot buy in the open market in a free-enterprise economy are subject to obvious disadvantages. The special market to which they are forced to resort tends to become and remain a seller's market. Supply is limited. In the ordinary situation that supply will consist of those items that cannot be sold or will not bring satisfactory prices for one reason or another in the open market. The disadvantaged buyer is in no position to reject shoddy merchandise or haggle over prices. He must take what he can get and pay what he is asked.[41]

The struggle for housing could be emotionally trying as well. Black home seekers described their experiences in the housing market as "difficult," "degrading," "nerve-racking," or "like knocking your head against a wall."[42] After numerous unsuccessful attempts to find a home in upstate New York, a black engineer admitted to researchers that "in all my life I have never felt so completely shut out." A doctor's wife in San Francisco suggested that repeated rejection in the housing market had left her feeling "like a leper and a criminal." A psychologist recalled the search for housing with equal poignancy: "Having worked my way up to a responsible position, I had gained a certain amount of self-respect. Then I moved to this town and had to find housing, and once again found myself viewed as something less than human. This problem is more than economic—there's a great deal more involved." A black physician concluded: "Any kind of move for a Negro family today is expensive in terms of dollars and ruinous in terms of mental happiness."[43]

Jim and Ann Braithewaite's experience in suburban Philadelphia illustrates the emotional repercussions that many couples felt in trying to move to the suburbs. Repeated encounters with racism put a strain on their marriage and family, affecting how they viewed themselves and the people around them. When discrimination "happens to *you* it hurts more," Mr. Braithewaite explained. He had difficulty sleeping. His mind wandered at work. Resentments welled up inside. "I just kept thinking about it," he said. "I was tired twenty-four hours of the day." Moreover, he felt bitter, alienated, and prone to "explosion," all of which "made for a very unhappy family life."[44]

In addition, the experience led him to focus his anger outward, questioning his job with a Cold War defense contractor and even his "allegiance to society." He asked himself, "Why am I defending this kind of people—people who have so great a desire for personal satisfaction that they place this above all other convictions they may have—religious, national, and sociological?" A year after their move, the Braithewaites' three children were adapting well to their new schools, and they counted white friends among their circle of playmates, yet the injury lingered. "What does it cost me to be a Negro?" Braithewaite asked rhetorically.[45] For upwardly mobile African Americans, such questions perhaps never seemed so real nor the answers so disheartening as during the search for suburban homes.

The legacy of discrimination also affected suburbanites' perceptions of homes and neighborhoods. African American suburbanites were more likely than whites to express ambivalence about their present home. Many families moved where they did because it was the only place available. More than half of families in Dorothy Jayne's study "had no choice" in the home they selected, and a number expressed dissatisfaction with their neighborhoods,

ranging from the proximity of taverns or busy thoroughfares to poor transportation and shopping, distance from schools, and subsequent changes in the
racial and socioeconomic character of the neighborhood. In several instances,
the family's arrival touched off panic selling by whites. "It's like the black
plague," said one couple, "everyone wants to escape." Others felt isolated or
intensely scrutinized like "goldfish in a bowl." One woman reported sadly, "I
don't want to be intimate with my neighbors, but I had hoped they would be
friendly." Another lamented that the neighbors "are killing us with silence."[46]

For black pioneers, especially, the desire for equal amenities and opportunities for children often ran at cross purposes with their desires for safety and
a sense of belonging. For those who moved to mostly white areas, moving day
was often the prelude to hostility, vandalism, and even violence. The William
Myers family, which broke the color bar in Levittown, Pennsylvania, endured
two months of organized harassment. Whites paraded in cars at all hours, the
phone rang constantly, and a white group rented an adjoining house from
which a loudspeaker blared songs such as "Dixie" and "Old Black Joe"
throughout the day. With the help of a group of supportive white neighbors,
the family was able to hang on. Nonetheless, the Myerses longed for black
company. "They used to say about Levittown, 'You never have to live in Levittown and look at a black face,'" Mr. Myers said. "I'd like to look out and see a
black face."[47] Even under the best circumstances, many pioneers found it difficult to "feel completely comfortable" or to escape the gnawing awareness that
"there are people within a quarter mile who don't want me here." If suburbanization reflected the fruition of black economic success and civil rights activism, it was an uncertain and often painful harvest.[48]

As these examples suggest, the meaning and experience of suburbanization was bound up in African Americans' experience as racial outsiders in
white-dominated space and society. In a world where public places were routinely hostile and whites behaved as though the greater part of metropolitan
territory belonged to them, private spaces such as homes and neighborhoods
became places of refuge from and sites of resistance to the wider white world.

In many suburbs, black pioneers sought to create racial communities that
transcended place by maintaining and reinforcing contacts with other African
Americans. Suburban pioneers often worshiped, shopped, and purchased services like hairstyling in black neighborhoods "back in the city" or in nearby
suburbs. They maintained ties with black peers through active involvement in
sororities, fraternities, and other social or civic organizations, and they made
special efforts to find black peers for their children. One family in southern
New Jersey recounted the miles they and other parents logged in order to

maintain a black peer group for their teenaged children via "the biggest car pool you ever saw."[49]

In addition to reaching outward for social contacts, African Americans also turned inward toward their homes to create safe, private places that shielded them from the worst abuses of public space. Though many pioneers were "joiners" by nature, participating in community activities such as parent-teacher and neighborhood associations, most nurtured what sociologists St. Clair Drake and Horace Cayton described as "home-centered" social lives based on family, relatives, and close friends.[50] A family who designed their own house "planned this living room with the idea of entertaining church groups here." One suburbanite remarked archly that he hadn't moved to Westchester County to "eat and drink" with his white neighbors. Families entertained "professional groups, church groups, wives' clubs, bridge clubs," as well as "children's and international groups."[51]

The largest number of postwar suburbanites avoided the hazards of racial isolation altogether by settling in neighborhoods where a significant number of blacks already lived. Racial discrimination and fears of "having a cross burned on my lawn" acted as weighty constraints on choice, but African Americans also made decisions that magnified racial concentration, as a respondent told researchers in Philadelphia, because they simply "[felt] more at home" with other black people.[52] Actress Ruby Dee gave voice to these concerns, recalling why she and her husband, actor Ossie Davis, selected an "already well integrated" neighborhood of New Rochelle, New York, when they moved from a smaller house in nearby Mount Vernon. Though a white acquaintance urged them to strike a blow for open housing by buying in one of the suburb's all-white areas, they declined. Dee explained:

> I want my children to feel safe. I want to feel safe. I'm away so much, I want to be friends with my neighbors. I don't want to be tolerated, on my best behavior, always seeking my neighbor's approval. I want to be able to knock on a door, assured that my neighbor would more likely welcome any one of the family. Or if I should need help. . . . I admire the pioneers who risk so much in the process of integration, but I cannot break that ice. . . . Thanks, but no thanks. We just don't choose to struggle on this front.[53]

Surveys suggest that the Dee-Davis family was in good company. In the late 1950s, anywhere from 45 to 65 percent of African American home seekers expressed a preference for neighborhoods that were at least one-half black.[54] For the majority of African Americans who indicated preferences for interracial living, racial isolation was apparently something they hoped to avoid. Most upwardly mobile African Americans — black people with the greatest latitude of personal choice — simply preferred areas where an appreciable number of black families already lived.

Suburban racial congregation also reflected the conduits of information and association available to African American families. Like most Americans, blacks trusted their social networks — friends, neighbors, relatives, church members, coworkers, and other associates — for information and assistance in finding places to live.[55] Because of their exclusion from conventional real estate channels, however, the legacy of past segregation reinforced the concentration of home seekers in just a handful of suburban areas. One study of middle-class families in Philadelphia, for example, revealed that 80 percent of respondents had "no Negro friends who lived in predominantly white areas outside the city limits."[56] In such circumstances, media reports of white resistance and stories of racial hostility passed through the grapevine gained weight in black perceptions of suburban opportunity. Lacking firsthand knowledge or positive experiences with white suburban areas, many families preferred to avoid the unknown.

Emphasis on homes and neighborhoods as safe spaces was not unique to African Americans, of course. As historian Elaine Tyler May demonstrates, many postwar parents perceived suburban homes as "a secure private nest removed from the dangers of the outside world," a "warm hearth" in the midst of a cold war.[57] But for African Americans, who experienced not only the international anxieties of the era but the palpable dangers of U.S. racism, the vision of home as a refuge had special resonance. As sociologist Bart Landry points out, because middle-class blacks were "denied ready access to the recreational and cultural facilities in the community," they "developed a lifestyle centered around home and clubs. The home grew in importance not only as a comfortable, secure place that shielded them from the stings of white society but was also the center of their social life."[58]

Black-oriented publications reinforced this connection, celebrating hospitality and conviviality focused on black homes and neighborhoods. *Ebony* "home" columns dwelled on spaces of domestic entertainment such as "pine-walled rumpus rooms," "informal redwood den[s]," "spacious" patios "fac[ing] a big swimming pool," "expensive oak wood" bars "with matching chairs, phonograph radio combination and two large sofas," "lavish lawn parties," and "expensively equipped kitchen[s]."[59] To be sure, tasteful entertaining was a staple of home-oriented magazines targeted at whites, but this emphasis had special resonance among African Americans, who were excluded from or faced harassment in public spaces frequented by middle-class whites. In the postwar era, *Ebony* portrayed an idealized domestic life, reflecting the exceptional value that middle-class blacks placed on their ability to entertain well at home. *Ebony*'s article on St. Alban's evoked a similar image of the neighborhood as a "self-contained" "refuge" and "happy haven," applauding it as a place where residents found "comfort, relaxation, and breathing space." Early residents had overcome white attempts to restrict the area, the essay pointed out, but by the 1950s the neighborhood was a site not of racial activism but "placid privacy" where celebrities "come home to rest."[60] Just as many working-class African Americans had used their homes as shelter from the insecurities of wage labor under industrial capitalism, members of the rising middle class valued their homes and neighborhoods as places of shelter from the racial hostility they experienced in public life. Whether they created spatially separate black enclaves or dispersed racial communities centered on private homes, they sought safe black spaces in the suburbs.

In these ways, race marked the process of suburbanization, even as growing numbers of African Americans entered the middle class. These markers were not primarily governmental nor imprints of the state—though these played a role—but were rooted in localized struggles over space between black families and communities and the white people around them. By the same token, African Americans' attempts to attain and control suburban residences contributed to a continuing conversation about class in black communities. Given the pervasiveness of race in postwar society, however, even the process of class stratification tended to reinforce a sense of racial solidarity among African Americans.

"A Better Class of People"

Since the nineteenth century, class was an important feature of African American social life, but within the racialized society of the United States, class stratification in black communities rested significantly on distinctions that African Americans drew "relative to other blacks."[61] Based in part on objective characteristics such as occupation, income, and wealth, which situate people within the wider political economy, class distinctions also reflect values and behavior related to work, education, leisure, consumption, and place of residence. For African Americans, who were barred from the achievement of stable occupational and income markers that were essential to class stand-

ing among whites, class distinctions traditionally relied on patterns of behavior—what historian Willard Gatewood describes as "performance"—that
people developed as a means of identifying their peers and distinguishing
themselves from others.[62] Even as a larger cohort of African Americans at-
tained economic positions comparable to middle-class whites in the postwar
period, class remained a distinction that African Americans drew largely in
reference to other blacks.

Of course, class was a spatial as well as a social distinction. For the urban black middle class, in particular, geographic separation from poor and
working-class blacks was an important emblem of class status as were the
physical characteristics of the homes and neighborhoods they occupied.
Writing in the 1940s, St. Clair Drake and Horace Cayton argued that socioeconomic divisions within black communities produced a process of "sift-
ing and sorting" by neighborhood.[63] More recently, Mary Patillo-McCoy
concluded that "like other groups, African Americans . . . always tried to
translate upward class mobility into geographic mobility."[64] In this view, class
was not merely a measure of what one did for a living or how one behaved, but
also how and where one chose to live. In the postwar period, suburbanization
represented a continuation of this process across the city limits.

The comments of middle-class suburbanites reveal that concerns about
class and distance from poorer blacks were thoroughly intertwined with other
residential preferences. In various contexts, middle-class blacks drew implicit
contrasts between the types of neighborhoods to which they aspired and
those in which they had been "bottled up" with other African Americans
before the war. As the housing activists George and Eunice Grier reported,
middle-class blacks sought the "freedom to choose an environment in ac-
cord with middle-class standards, instead of housing restricted to the overcrowded, run-down neighborhoods generally available to Negroes." However, the contrasts that families drew focused as often on the social as the
physical environment. "I would be very satisfied with an all-Negro neighborhood if it were a decent neighborhood," one black professional told the
Griers. "I do not see why I, because I am a Negro, should be forced to live in
a neighborhood where I have nothing in common with others around me."[65]
A black attorney in San Francisco expressed a similar recognition of class
difference when he commented that the "thing that struck me when I moved
out of the ghetto was that for the first time I was friendly with my immediate
neighbors. They have the same interests that we do."[66] Reinforcing this im-
pression, leading black real estate brokers in Westchester County, New York,
reported screening clients on the basis of their "social and cultural qualifi-

cations" in order to protect the "character" of suburban neighborhoods and ensure that their customers were a "credit . . . to the race." Referring to people he called "Negro trash," one broker exclaimed, "I wouldn't damage a neighborhood with people who don't know how to live in it. I put them in their place."[67]

The same emphasis on class separation was evident in suburbanites' descriptions of their ideal neighborhood. Middle-class respondents said that they preferred environments "where the neighborhood would be congenial and stimulating—a middle-middle neighborhood," "an area where the general income level was equal to my own," "an area which will aid in [children's] training and development . . . where people are interested in the surroundings they live in," or simply "a quiet, well-kept middle-class neighborhood."[68] Correspondingly, middle-class references to "respectable," "clean," "quiet," "well-kept," or "decent" neighborhoods betrayed an obvious class-consciousness if not antagonism toward working-class and poor blacks. The musician Nat "King" Cole made the point as clearly as anyone. When white neighbors opposed his purchase of a house in 1948, on the grounds that "we don't want any undesirable people moving into the neighborhood," Cole shot back: "Neither do I. If I see anybody undesirable coming in, I'll be the first to complain."[69]

Several studies of upwardly mobile African Americans in metropolitan Philadelphia during the 1950s revealed that the desire to live among a "higher" or "better class of people" played a role in families' choice of neighborhoods. Dorothy Jayne's study of black pioneers found that over half had initiated their search for new housing when "a poorer class moved in[to]" the neighborhoods where they were living. Class concerns also surfaced in respondents' observations about their new neighborhoods. One couple expressed disdain for their "small-time snobbish" white neighbors, lamenting that they had "underbought." Another, recalling harassment by whites, pointed to their class status vis-à-vis other African Americans as well as their new neighbors. They were "annoyed," they said, because "we're not trash . . . our status is so much above theirs."[70] By implication, it was not their citizenship nor humanity that earned them the right to move where they pleased, but their membership in a particular social class, a status they had achieved and learned to express through everyday behavior. Having drawn boundaries between themselves and other blacks, moreover, they resented their neighbors' inability or unwillingness to recognize the distinction. Another couple declared their "philosophy" as the ability of "decent folks to be able to live decently without regard to religion or race."[71] In the view of these pioneers, class made a difference not only in who was "decent" and who was not but in the rights that each group should enjoy.

By emphasizing their rights as citizens and their membership in a particular socioeconomic class, middle-class black suburbanites articulated a vision of racial equality that largely ignored or evaded inequalities based on socioeconomic class. Political scientist Preston Smith points out that most approached the problem of race with a class bias, defending a brand of "racial democracy" in which "affluent blacks should have access to the same housing as affluent whites. Likewise working-class and poor blacks would have the same quality of housing as working-class and poor whites." Hence, open-housing advocates such as Carl Fuqua, the executive secretary of the Chicago NAACP, could argue that "the goal is to let a man live where he wants to live, if he can assume the proper responsibilities." In Smith's view, "embracing racial democracy meant black civic elites accepted class privileges and the distribution of social goods according to conventional political economy." This adequately summarized their vision of space as well.[72]

African Americans' expressed preferences for racially mixed neighborhoods also reflected concerns rooted in class as much as race. Quite unlike the majority of white suburbanites, many middle-class African Americans said they were willing to live in racially integrated settings.[73] For most, integrated neighborhoods were a means to an end: better schools and services, proximity to work, and other environmental factors. As George and Eunice Grier noted, "Racial composition was not in itself an essential criterion, however, most felt that areas generally open to Negroes . . . did not meet their standards of a 'good neighborhood.'"[74] For these families, living in integrated neighborhoods was not only a means to a higher living standard but also an assertion of their right to share equally in the benefits of suburban location. Just as well, some "Negro professionals insist[ed] on looking outside 'Negro areas'" as a means of distinguishing themselves from poorer blacks. The San Francisco Council for Civic Unity spoke for many when it asserted that "individual people of Negro . . . or other non-white ancestry may feel more at home with people not of their own race but of their socio-economic level." For many middle-class African Americans, the desire to live in integrated settings was as much a means of achieving social distance from the black working class as securing social intimacy with middle-class whites.[75]

By the 1950s, a new generation of middle-class blacks began to push their way into the suburbs. Their efforts, prefaced by the struggles of working-class suburbanites and strenuously resisted by whites, reinforced the salience of both race and class in postwar life. By transgressing racial boundaries, they redefined the racial ownership of suburban space and also extended the geographic continuity of black residential areas. On the cusp of the civil rights movement, too, suburban pioneers carved out distinctive race and class politics, resisting segregation and imputed inequality as well as negotiating class distinctions within African American communities. If they sought, by enjoying the privileges of middle-class life, to close the social distance that whites had established, they also took steps to distinguish themselves from less fortunate blacks, using space as an important measure of difference.

Considering the whole landscape of African American suburbanization in the postwar period, however, necessitates special attention to the South, where the dynamics of racial power produced a distinctive pattern of suburban settlement and political action. Facing entrenched white supremacy, but also trusting in inherited means of collective advancement, black southerners negotiated with white political and civic leaders for separate suburban space. Building on historic patterns of black residence outside the urban core, they used the threat that black migration and pioneering posed to the racial status quo to bargain for territory where African Americans could develop suburban neighborhoods of their own.

Chapter 7

Separate Suburbanization in the South, 1940–1960

"I GREW UP believing I lived in a near-perfect world," journalist Sam Fulwood begins his memoir of "life in the black middle class."

> God in Heaven was perfection, and I had the closest thing on Earth, in Charlotte, North Carolina. I lived with my father, mother and brother on a quarter-acre lot in a single-story, five-room redbrick house in a subdivision called McCrorey Heights. A community of 130 homes, McCrorey Heights was a place where preachers, schoolteachers, principals, college professors, doctors, dentists, lawyers, police officers and homemakers lived comfortably. . . . In the spring, my neighborhood could have been the suburban setting for a Hollywood movie. Dogwood trees opened their buds, unfurling a blazing display of pink and white, while sweet and sticky sap oozed from pines and huge emerald hands sprouted from oak trees. . . . This was a world where all the girls had Barbie dolls, the boys G.I. Joes, and every kid owned roller skates and bicycles. We played oblivious to the powerful forces of race and class from which our families shielded us.[1]

Fulwood's parents were not alone among middle-class African Americans who sought to raise their children in the comfort and security of new suburban neighborhoods after World War II, but in the South this quest took a distinctive form. In contrast to the urban and suburban North, where the bulk of black community growth unfolded in an atomized fashion through racial transition in existing neighborhoods and scattered construction in a handful of older suburbs, African American communities in the urban South grew in large measure through the construction of new housing on the metropolitan fringe. By 1960 black subdivisions like McCrorey Heights — Washington Shores in Orlando, Pontchartrain Park in New Orleans, Richmond Heights and Bunche Park near Miami, Crestwood Forest in Atlanta, Carverdale in Oklahoma City, and many others — housed a large proportion of the region's black middle class.[2] Some of these neighborhoods were inside the city limits; some were outside. Others, still, changed status as central cities across the region annexed suburban territory after the war. Regardless of their relation to the city limits, these neighborhoods epitomized a suburban strategy of black community growth that was a distinguishing feature of postwar urban history in the region. Until the late 1950s, when the demolition of city neighborhoods for urban redevelopment and highway building overwhelmed the process, new construction at the urban fringe was the predominant means by which black communities expanded in the urban South.

"Ozzie and Harriet enclaves" like McCrorey Heights were only the most commodious examples of new housing built for African Americans.[3] Reflecting the comparatively low incomes of blacks in the region — and the conservative input of white authorities — apartments and public housing units were integral to the decentralization of black communities after the war. Despite the stereotype that single-family houses were a defining feature of suburban development, multifamily housing was an essential element of black suburbanization in the postwar South. Taking advantage of a variety of new housing developments, African Americans participated to a greater extent in the decentralization of southern cities than in any other region of the country.

Perhaps the most profound difference between black suburbanization in the South and other parts of the United States was the process of planning and political negotiation that underlay it. In various southern cities, white and black civic leaders collaborated to solve the postwar housing crisis by building new homes in sanctioned "Negro expansion areas" at the edge of town.[4] For whites, the object was less to provide better housing than to preserve racial segregation and avoid the turmoil that resulted when African Americans moved into white areas. By contrast, African Americans sought primarily to build better black neighborhoods. Their willingness to compromise on the question of segregation reflected a tradition of racial advancement rooted in strong black communities and a deep ambivalence about residential integration, as well as a pragmatic appraisal of what was possible within the existing racial system. For black contractors, real estate brokers, and civic elites across the South, defeating "segregation" did not necessarily imply integrating with whites. Rather, it meant overcoming the inferior conditions and second-class citizenship that discrimination imposed. In housing, they wanted equality—by which they meant new housing, expanded home ownership, and a residential landscape common to middle-class suburbs nationwide—and they believed they could achieve it on a racially separate basis.[5]

The compromise of separate suburbanization masked not only sharp differences in the aims of black and white communities but also their power. White insistence on racial segregation, reinforced by the threat of violence, remained an inflexible constraint on all African American planning. Nonetheless, black civic leaders saw separate community building as a means of racial improvement as well as an immediate remedy for the "frightful" conditions in which most blacks lived in the urban South.[6] Given this reality, they made it their first priority to expand and improve the supply of available housing. Just as well, some perceived the construction of up-to-date neighborhoods as an assertion of equality and, thus, a direct challenge to white supremacy in which separation was a badge of inequality. As Atlanta housing activist Robert Thompson put it, the construction of even small numbers of "luxury" homes was important "if for no other reason than to assist in changing the white man's image of the Negro relative to the Negro's desire to live decently in suburbia."[7] For this reason, southern black community leaders saw no contradiction in building self-contained African American communities at the same time that they attacked segregated schools and public accommodations. In the South, at least, the struggle to acquire and develop land for new housing was one piece in a quilt of black protest, a fabric stitched in black communities and reliant on a solidarity nurtured in separate black spaces. Ironically, the apparent compromise with segregation facilitated the construction of the finest African American residential neighborhoods in the United States, and it opened greater opportunities for black southerners to buy homes in new suburban and suburban-style neighborhoods than in any other region of the country.

As Sam Fulwood points out, however, new houses and neighborhoods symbolized much more than shelter from the natural elements. They were also places of refuge from social pressures bearing down on and welling up from within African American communities in the midcentury South. Separate community building promised respite from the evident dangers of white racism as well as advancement in a profoundly inequitable society. It was a means for African Americans to create spaces of self-expression, independence, and belonging as black people. By the same token, suburban homes represented a means for upwardly mobile families to distinguish themselves from the masses of poor and working-class blacks. The purchase of modern homes in comprehensively planned subdivisions not only removed them spatially from the black poor and working class, but it marked the social and economic gulf between them through the physical landscapes in which they lived. As in the North and West, members of the black middle class secured the greatest benefits from the process. Separate suburbanization bound African Americans to one another through a common struggle for better housing within a social context that distributed or withheld resources on the basis of race, even as it divided them on the basis of their success in attaining them.

Through an analysis of separate suburbanization in two cities, Atlanta and Dallas, this chapter adds to the growing literature on race and city building in the South. Since the mid-1990s, a number of scholars have explored the evolution of southern cities in the postwar period, placing special emphasis on the magnification of racial separation in space that coincided with the decline of segregation in law.[8] Following historian Arnold Hirsch, who tracked the rise of an expansive and sharply segregated "second ghetto" in postwar Chicago, they have emphasized the role of white planners, politicians, and neighborhood activists, highlighting especially the deleterious impact of federal policy at the local level.[9] In a study of Miami, historian Raymond Mohl explicitly adapted Hirsch's second-ghetto model to a southern case. With the exception of William Wilson, who examined the origins of a black subdivision in Dallas, however, Mohl and others have paid only limited attention to the construction of new housing for African Americans, especially during the decade and a half after World War II. This is all the more striking since new construction accommodated the better part of black community expansion in the urban South during this period. Before the late 1950s, when the demolition of core city neighborhoods for urban renewal and freeway construction projects forced tens of thousands of black families to seek housing in older white neighborhoods, and in turn heightened the similarities between southern and non-southern cities, black community building in much of the urban South shared as much with the process of suburbanization as with "ghettoization"— the block-by-block turnover of existing neighborhoods that characterized black community expansion in cities of the Northeast and Midwest. Although many of these new neighborhoods were eventually annexed by a central city, the process of decentralization through new construction was very much a part of the postwar suburban trend.

Atlanta and Dallas are ideal locations for study. No other city boasted black achievements in housing as great as Atlanta. The city became a model for "Negro housing" efforts across the South. Through travel, correspondence, and leadership of trade organizations, as well as through cooperation with federal officials, black Atlantians influenced home building throughout the region. By contrast, Dallas followed a pattern that was more common among cities with smaller, less economically and politically established black communities. Whites in the "Big D" exercised predominant influence over the style, quantity, and location of new African American housing. Nonetheless, Dallas's black leadership lobbied for influence, using the implicit threat of racial chaos in city neighborhoods as a means of igniting white action. Both cities reveal the limits on black agency in the jim crow South, as well as the varied efforts and expectations of African Americans to participate in the process of suburbanization after World War II.

African American Community Building in the Metropolitan South

The roots of separate suburbanization in the South lie in the peculiar political, economic, and historical circumstances of the region. As a whole, the South underwent rapid social and economic change during the 1940s and 1950s marked by the collapse of the plantation economy, industrial and commercial expansion in key cities, massive rural-to-urban migration, and the first stirrings of the civil rights revolution. Huge numbers of African Americans fled the rural South for urban and suburban areas where they yearned for new opportunities. Between 1940 and 1970, over 4 million people boarded trains and buses bound for cities of the Northeast, Midwest, and West Coast, but the number of African Americans in the urban South also increased sharply, rising from 37 percent to 58 percent of all black southerners between 1940 and 1960.[10]

The exodus from southern agriculture and the hurried industrialization of the region sparked by World War II translated into economic gain for black southerners. Black incomes nearly tripled during the 1940s; by 1949 nearly one in five African Americans in the urban South earned more than $3,000, compared to one in two hundred ten years earlier. Another 20 percent brought home between $2,000 and $3,000 per annum. Millions of southern blacks contended with poverty, but by the 1950s, an observer wrote, "better housing, better clothing, household appliances, and other items making for more pleasant living [were] now in the reach of a sizeable part of the Negro population."[11]

Increases in urban incomes and population sparked a boom in black housing construction. During the 1950s, southern builders completed as many as 220,000 housing units for African Americans, compared to 104,000 in the North and 108,000 in the West. In the South, new housing constituted 57 percent of the housing into which black communities expanded during the decade, compared to 17 percent in the North and 40 percent in the West.[12] In other words, black communities in the urban South grew mainly through the construction of new housing for at least a decade and a half after World War II. This contrasted sharply with the urban North, where African American neighborhoods expanded largely through the turnover of existing homes. Private developers in Atlanta led the way, building more than ten thousand new dwellings between 1945 and 1960, half of them single-family homes.[13] Houston produced nearly as many units in an array of subdivisions southeast of the city. In Memphis and Miami, developers built more than four thousand new homes for black families; even in smaller cities, such as Nashville, Savannah, Oklahoma City, Tampa, and Orlando, private developers erected more than fifteen hundred houses and apartments for black families in the outer reaches of town during the early 1950s.[14] These enterprises did not solve the desperate housing shortage among African Americans in the urban South, but they represented unprecedented efforts to provide more and better housing.

Southern urban history also affected the pace and process of change. Compared to larger cities in the North, the urban South exhibited low population densities, and many cities contained large undeveloped acreages inside the municipal limits. Black populations in most southern cities also grew more slowly during the 1940s and 1950s than in large metropolitan areas outside the region, which meant that builders could accommodate growth with fewer new homes and a slower pace of construction. Finally, since African Americans had owned land and lived in small communities in the urban margins for more than a century, their demands for housing were easier to accommodate than in either the North or West. There was more available land on which to build, and much of it already belonged to African Americans.[15]

As elsewhere, older black communities laid a basis for postwar suburbanization. Charlotte's McCrorey Heights, where Sam Fulwood and his neighbors raced their bikes, was typical. The subdivision, begun in the 1950s, was adjacent to Biddleville, an "old and distinguished street-car suburb for blacks" that itself had developed in the shadow of Johnson C. Smith University, a former freedmen's school established after the Civil War.[16] Throughout the South, similar subdivisions unfolded in the vicinity of historically black colleges. Tennessee A&I in Nashville, Dillard and Southern Universities in New Orleans, North Carolina A&T in Greensboro, Gammon Seminary in Atlanta,

Table 7.1: Expansion of the Nonwhite Housing Stock in U.S. Metropolitan Areas, 1950–1959

Area	Dwelling Units Occupied by Nonwhites, 1959			
	Total	Units Added, 1950–59		
	Total Nonwhite-Occupied Units, 1959	"Transition Units"[a]	New Construction 1950–59	% Constructed 1950–59
United States	4,775,000	1,124,404	674,000	37%
Metro Areas	3,248,000	978,598	434,000	31%
North[b]	1,731,000	654,365	103,917	17%
South	2,445,000	165,565	223,380	57%
West	599,000	158,666	108,000	40%
New York[c]	459,985	165,884	39,460[d]	19%
Chicago	269,628	124,047	17,188	13%
Los Angeles	179,776	81,232	28,151	26%
Philadelphia	172,399	49,859	8,293	14%
Detroit	142,566	71,786	7,613	10%
Cleveland	74,548	35,581	2,957	8%
St. Louis	73,735	23,832	6,505	21%
Pittsburgh	53,738	17,941	1,762	9%
Washington	108,400	34,536	9,010	21%
Baltimore	97,606	29,160	12,256	30%
Atlanta	55,738	5,419	17,188	76%
Dallas	46,682	5,743	18,396	76%

[a] Dwellings occupied by nonwhite households in 1959 that were occupied by white households in 1950.
[b] Census-defined Northeast and North-Central Regions.
[c] New York and New Jersey metropolitan areas combined.
[d] Includes a large percentage of the fifty thousand public housing units built in New York in the 1950s.

Source: Karl E. Taeuber and Alma F. Taeuber, *Negroes in Cities: Residential Segregation and Neighborhood Change* (Chicago, 1965), 193; U.S. Census of Housing: 1960, vol. IV, *Components of Inventory Change,* part 1A–B, *1950–59 Components* (Washington, D.C., 1962), 26–27, 64, 86, 108, 130.

Table 7.2:   African American Population Growth, 1940–1960,
Selected Metropolitan Areas

Metropolitan Area (SMSA)	1940	1950	% Change 1940–50	1960	% Change 1950–60
New York	669,000	1,018,000	56%	1,228,000	21%
Chicago	329,000	587,000	78%	977,000	66%
Philadelphia	222,000	465,000	44%	670,000	44%
Detroit	170,000	357,000	110%	559,000	57%
Cleveland	88,000	152,000	73%	257,000	69%
Los Angeles	75,000	218,000	190%	465,000	113%
Washington	219,000	324,000	47%	468,000	44%
Baltimore	195,000	265,000	35%	373,000	41%
Birmingham	179,000	209,000	16%	220,000	5%
New Orleans	160,000	201,000	· 26%	267,000	33%
Memphis	155,000	180,000	16%	227,000	21%
Atlanta	149,000	166,000	16%	232,000	40%
Houston	104,000	150,000	45%	246,000	64%
Dallas	62,000	83,000	35%	155,000	46%
Miami	50,000	65,000	23%	98,000	34%

Source: U.S. Census of Population: 1940, *Census Tracts* (Washington, D.C., 1943), table 1;
U.S. Census of Population: 1950, *Census Tracts* (Washington, D.C., 1952), table 1;
U.S. Census of Population and Housing: 1960, *Census Tracts* (Washington, D.C., 1962), table P–1.

Bishop College near Dallas, and many others provided footholds for postwar development.[17]

The process that contemporaries referred to as "Negro expansion" reflected southern history not only in the accumulation of spatial patterns but also in ideas, strategies of racial uplift, and modes of racial politics. For African Americans, home building in planned "Negro expansion areas" followed a long tradition of racial politics. During the late nineteenth and early twentieth centuries, urban African Americans devoted much of their collective energies toward improving the neighborhoods where they lived. Despairing of political influence at the city or state levels, African Americans mobilized to improve the quality of life in what historian Earl Lewis calls "the home sphere"—which meant alternately the home, the neighborhood, and the black community at large.[18] Civic leaders negotiated with white officials to attain public expenditures for street paving, water, sewers, parks, schools, and hospitals—all on a segregated basis. Business leaders, too, emphasized the efficacy of self-help as a strategy of racial uplift as well as a practical compromise with racism in the short term, building an infrastructure of businesses and civic institutions to put these ideas into practice. By the late 1940s, even small southern cities, such as Durham, Macon, Montgomery, and Shreveport, had a durable infrastructure of black institutions that supported the drive for postwar home building. These institutions, strengthened by economic and political gains during the 1940s, served as the basis for a tradition of moderate black politics that remained dominant in most southern cities until the generational shift in black activism spurred by the student sit-in movement of 1960. Separate community building after World War II represented a continuation and fruition of this tradition.[19]

For white officials and city planners, too, "Negro expansion" was an easy extension of old habits. Racial planning had a long history in the South, including efforts to enforce racial zoning, to limit city services, and to design roads and other public works as racial boundaries. For whites, the construction of African American housing in designated areas on the outskirts of town was a means to remedy the African American housing crisis without upsetting racial segregation. Moreover, the separate expansion of African American communities promised not merely to maintain residential segregation but to extend it to a greater extent than ever before.[20]

In addition to heeding these precedents, white officials behaved as they did in response to increased pressure from African Americans. Following Supreme Court decisions in the mid-forties, which invalidated the use of the white primary as a means of disfranchising blacks, African American voter registration surged in the urban South. By the mid-1950s, African Americans constituted an important voting block in various cities, a political influence they wielded to win concessions in land and city services.[21] The 1948 *Shelley v. Kraemer* decision, which invalidated race-restrictive covenants, further bolstered African Americans' demands for equal treatment in the housing market. Finally, black families themselves forced "Negro housing" to the top of the public agenda by pioneering in existing white neighborhoods. In cities such as Atlanta, Birmingham, Dallas, and Miami, black pioneers provoked violent outbursts by moving across well-recognized racial boundaries. By the late 1940s, many southern white officials had reached the same conclusion. As a city planner in Atlanta noted, "The city has the choice of trying to handle this problem [of housing African Americans] itself or its consequences."[22]

The *Brown* decision in 1954 only reinforced the disposition of some officials to furnish "separate, all-Negro communities," since segregated neighborhoods produced racially homogenous student populations without the necessity of assigning students on the basis of race.[23] In the context of rising black purchasing power, a severe housing shortage, the changing legal climate, and the willingness of African Americans to challenge jim crow directly in city neighborhoods, white officials across the South supported "Negro expansion areas" as a means of preserving racial segregation over the long run.

Finally, the ability of many southern cities to annex suburban land after World War II proved essential to the process of "Negro expansion." In contrast to most large metropolitan areas in the North, where independent suburbs ringed central cities and blocked their expansion, many southern cities grew geographically by annexing their suburban fringe. Cities as diverse as Tampa, Memphis, Charlotte, Oklahoma City, San Antonio, and Atlanta annexed suburban areas double or triple the size of the old city during the 1940s and 1950s. Dallas and Houston expanded in Texas-sized fashion, each annexing more than two hundred square miles (roughly the area of Chicago) and gaining more than 100,000 residents. A range of smaller cities did the same. As a result, much of postwar residential expansion in the urban South, "suburbanization" in other parts of the country, took place inside the newly drawn limits of a central city.[24]

Annexation met a variety of goals for central city boosters. As in northern urban areas earlier in the century, white officials pursued annexation as a means of increasing their economic and political clout as well as managing growth on the city's doorstep. In the postwar South, however, annexation struggles were also intimately related to the politics of race. In Atlanta, Memphis, and Richmond, annexation of mostly white suburban areas was a means of ensuring white political supremacy even as black populations (and voting rolls) expanded.[25] In the context of the postwar housing shortage, annexation also cleared the way for new construction, which officials hoped would divert black housing demand away from white neighborhoods. Thus, cities including Savannah, Orlando, Memphis, Atlanta, and Dallas annexed suburban territory as an integral part of "Negro expansion" planning for the city's outer rim.[26]

African Americans, too, had reason to support municipal expansion. Annexation shifted land-use authority in the suburban rim from county officials, who tended to be hostile to black population growth, to central city governments, where African Americans had at least a margin of political influence and officials' interests were often more catholic as a result. Additionally, the annexation of suburban expansion areas allowed politically conscious African Americans to achieve residential goals common to U.S. suburbanites without jeopardizing the political or economic influence of central city black communities. Thus, annexation linked the urban political interests of blacks and whites with the suburban residential aspirations of African Americans to produce a distinctive process of black community building and decentralization in the postwar South.[27]

"Negro Expansion" in Atlanta

By the 1940s, Atlanta was the hub of black business and higher education in the Southeast. Businesses along "Sweet Auburn" Avenue included three of the strongest black financial institutions in the South as well as the nation's largest black daily newspaper, the *Atlanta Daily World*.[28] The city was home to four historically black colleges — Clark, Morehouse, Morris Brown, and Spelman — plus the graduate schools of Atlanta University. Employees of these institutions — professors, journalists, librarians, bank tellers, insurance agents, and a varied administrative and clerical staff — were the foundation for a black middle class of unprecedented size, providing a ready and discerning market for new housing. Finally, economic prosperity sparked by the war led to "impressive" changes in black home-buying power. "Fattened as never before with big savings as a result of the war boom," the *Atlanta Daily World* proclaimed, African Americans "sought to buy land and homes."[29]

Despite growing economic means among its middle and upper classes, black Atlanta suffered from patterns of economic deprivation common across the South. Per capita income in 1949 remained less than half that among whites despite a decade of economic growth. One-third of black men and half of black women worked in unskilled or domestic service occupations, and skilled and college-educated blacks faced steady opposition to their employment in the public and private sector.[30]

Conditions in housing starkly reflected African Americans' economic status. Blacks constituted a third of the city's population, yet they occupied just one-fifth of its land area. Ninety percent lived in six aging neighborhoods splayed outward from the central business district. These areas were extensions of historic neighborhoods such as Beaver Slide, Jenningstown, and Summerhill that African Americans had settled on the edge of the city after the Civil War.[31] As Atlanta grew, black families pushed outward from these communities toward the pine-forested edge of town, but by the late 1940s most had been "fenced in" by white neighborhoods.[32] Within these enclaves, African Americans lived in dilapidated bungalows and shotgun houses that

Fig. 7.1 House in Slum Clearance Area, Atlanta. Bill Wilson, ca. 1940s. Crowded and substandard rental housing typified African American neighborhoods across the urban South. In Atlanta and other southern cities, public services usually stopped where black neighborhoods began. (Bill Wilson/*Atlanta Journal-Constitution*)

crowded the unpaved streets. A 1947 survey observed that 72 percent of black-occupied dwellings were substandard, while the vacancy rate for blacks was a microscopic .1 percent. Atlanta may have been the capital of the southern black middle class, but members of every social strata faced a crisis in housing that posed, in the opinion of the Atlanta Urban League, "a direct menace to health, safety, morals and the prosperity of the entire community."[33]

On the fringes of Atlanta's older neighborhoods, a small number of black households lived in a scattering of well-built homes. Early in the century, prominent families had moved into a neighborhood of two-story Victorian houses that had originally been built for whites just east of the Auburn Avenue business district.[34] On the west side of town, near Atlanta University, faculty from the local colleges lived on "Ph.D. row" across from the campus. In the 1910s and 1920s, other families had built homes in small subdivisions west of the university. While these developments offered decent housing for a small number of elite households, they were slight relief compared to the desert of need in the community at large.[35]

Public housing addressed the black shelter crisis more substantially. During the 1930s, Atlanta undertook the South's most aggressive public housing program, building more than three thousand new apartments for African Americans.[36] The projects represented a marked improvement over most of the housing stock available to blacks; however, since federal regulations tied new construction to the demolition of "slums," public projects did nothing to ease the shortage. Moreover, highway construction and the demolition of residences for code violations, business expansion, and various civic projects during the 1930s and 1940s diminished the number of dwellings available to African Americans in Atlanta and its suburbs.[37] As demobilization of the armed services and renewed migration from rural Georgia swelled the city's black population after the war, they created the context for a new round of public and private attention to "Negro housing."

Even before the war's end, black Atlantians had begun laying the foundations for a postwar home-building program. The pioneer in the field was Heman Perry, a magnetic entrepreneur who had arrived from Texas early in the century. During the 1910s, Perry built a small business empire serving the black community, and by the early 1920s, his holdings included pharmacies, laundries, a bank, an insurance company, and a real estate and construction firm.[38]

Early on, Perry had recognized the potential for profit as well as community service by building new housing for black families at the western edge of town. According to one associate, "Perry wanted to get hold of the West Side before Negroes were fenced in by whites."[39] Although most elite blacks lived on the east side at the turn of the century, the cluster of colleges to the west made the area attractive to the middle class. In addition, because the east-side black community was surrounded by white neighborhoods, the west side promised the greatest hope for expansion. During the 1910s and early 1920s, Perry bought several large land parcels west of Ashby Street near Atlanta University, building homes and making mortgage loans to new buyers. In one of the first examples of comprehensive community planning for African Americans in the nation, Perry deeded land to the city for Atlanta's first black high school and city park. Although his financial empire collapsed in the mid-1920s, Perry succeeded in building an African American bungalow suburb on the west side similar to those available to whites across the city. More importantly, Heman Perry's vision of building self-contained black neighbor-

Fig. 7.2   Built in the early 1920s, Heman Perry's Washington Park subdivision became a model for the planned postwar expansion of black Atlanta. To ensure an upscale clientele and to advance the interests of African Americans more widely, Perry donated land across the street for the construction of the city's first black public high school. (Courtesy of Timothy J. Crimmins, Georgia State University, 2002)

hoods on the developing edge of town became the blueprint for black housing efforts for the rest of the century.[40]

Following closely in Perry's footsteps was building contractor Walter H. Aiken, who had worked with the Texan early in his career. A 1914 graduate of Hampton Institute, Aiken devoted much of his life to personal business success and community service through the construction of new homes for African Americans. He served an apprenticeship in the building trades in Philadelphia in the mid-1910s before enlisting in the army and rising to the rank of captain during the First World War. After the armistice, Aiken worked briefly for the YMCA in Washington, D.C., and coached football at Howard University. In 1921 he moved to Atlanta, marrying Lucy Rucker, a member of one of the city's leading black families. The Ruckers owned considerable property in Atlanta, and Aiken joined them in the real estate business. By the late 1920s, "Chief" Aiken was one of the leading home builders in Atlanta. His work on the suburban estate of middleweight boxing champion Tiger

Flowers in 1927 established him as *the* builder of homes for Atlanta's black elite, but he also built moderately priced "economy houses" for middle-income families and pioneered the development of mass-production techniques in home building.[41]

Like many black businessmen of his age, Aiken was a fervent believer in economic success as a means of combating white racism. Like Booker T. Washington, whom he had met while a student at Hampton and whom he was fond of quoting, Aiken propounded a philosophy of self-help for African Americans in conjunction with political pressure and personal advancement. Aiken urged black audiences to "pool their resources" and "guarantee for themselves a democratic way of life." In a 1946 interview he asserted, "I don't mean that we should relax our fight against jim crow, but I think one of the ways of combating it is to force recognition through achievement." Similarly, in an address to black real estate agents in 1950, Aiken advocated accomplishment through self-help. According to the reporter, he "derided certain 'thought trends' of some leaders" who pushed for reliance on court decisions and anti-discrimination legislation to advance the cause of black equality. "We must start showing our independence and equality by producing," he argued.[42] In his approach to racial uplift, then, Aiken exemplified a tradition of conservative black leadership in the South on the eve of the civil rights movement.[43] In addition, he represented a direct link between the program of black uplift through architectural reform that had been popular in many black industrial colleges at the turn of the century and the boom in black home building that followed World War II.[44]

Although he was a proponent of self-help and free enterprise, Aiken was not averse to federal aid for his industry. During the depression, he became one of the first Georgia builders to utilize the new mortgage insurance program of the Federal Housing Administration. During World War II, Aiken used his contacts in the FHA to secure material priorities for the construction of emergency war housing for blacks near Atlanta University. Through that effort he built approximately 250 units of single-family and two-family housing in a subdivision called Fairview Terrace, which was located on the western margins of the city. He also purchased land in the western suburbs beyond the edge of white development as an outlet for future expansion.[45]

After the war, Aiken became widely known as "the largest Negro homebuilder in the country."[46] He was a founding member of the National Builders Association and the National Association of Real Estate Brokers, the major trade associations representing African Americans in real estate. As president of both organizations during the 1940s, he traveled and corresponded widely,

Fig. 7.3   Walter "Chief" Aiken used federal aid to build 250 "economy houses" in his Fairview Terrace subdivision in Atlanta, which he completed during World War II. By the late 1940s, Aiken was recognized as the nation's leading African American home builder. (*Insured Mortgage Portfolio* 18 [fall 1953])

promoting efforts to develop housing by and for African Americans. Building on his early association with the FHA, Aiken also developed especially cordial relations with the agency's race relations office after World War II, which put him at the center of the "Negro housing" movement in the United States.[47]

Aiken also played a lead role in the planning and development of separate "Negro expansion areas" in suburban Atlanta. Despairing of city action to remedy the postwar housing crisis, twenty-five black civic leaders met in Aiken's offices in late 1946, as he put it, to "discuss and work out plans for developing more housing for Negroes."[48] The gathering was a who's who of the black financial and real estate communities in Atlanta, but it also included men such as A. T. Walden, co-chair of the Atlanta Negro Voters League, the city's chief black political organization, and C. A. Scott, a veteran who was soon to assume his father's position as publisher of the *Atlanta Daily World*. At Aiken's suggestion, this Temporary Coordinating Committee on Housing (TCCH) established subcommittees to "investigate further the possibilities of getting out-let areas for Negro expansion" and to establish a private corporation to purchase land and develop housing for African Americans.[49] Aiken was already building a 200-home subdivision outside the city on land that he had purchased during the war, but he and others recognized that solving the housing shortage would require concerted effort within the black community as well as support from whites, so that "both groups fully understand that Negro citizens may live and build additional houses without intimidation and fear."[50]

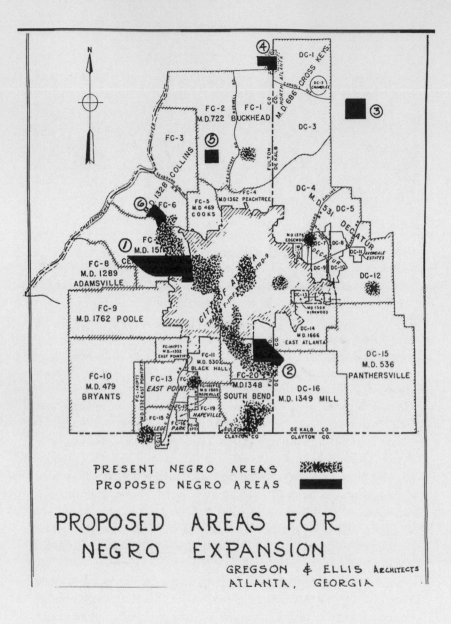

PROPOSED AREAS FOR
NEGRO EXPANSION

GREGSON & ELLIS Architects
ATLANTA, GEORGIA

Fig. 7.4 "Proposed Areas for Negro Expansion." Atlanta Housing Council, 1947. Published by a group of black civic and business leaders, the 1947 plan for "Negro expansion" reflected the effort of African Americans across the urban South to shape postwar development and to share in suburban living on a separate but equal basis. (Atlanta Urban League Papers, box 252, folder 1, Atlanta University Center, Robert W. Woodruff Library)

As a result of these efforts, the TCCH land committee, restyled as the Atlanta Housing Council (AHC), published a report in May 1947 titled "Proposed Areas for Expansions of Negro Housing in Atlanta, Georgia," distributing copies to twenty-six civic and business groups in the city. The report contained plans for six areas in the suburban ring of the city that the committee called "the most logical and appropriate areas for the expansion of Negro housing."[51]

Like "Negro expansion areas" in other southern cities, each site was adjacent to a "present Negro area" in the outer rim of the city. The areas were convenient to employment centers and existing black institutions, and each was sufficiently isolated to minimize white resistance. Several of the proposed sites were geographically secluded from white neighborhoods by railroad tracks, roadways, or industrial strips. Where they were not, the report proposed surrounding them with "green-belts or strip parks." Plans for a "typical housing project for proposed Negro expansion" included with the report featured a "150 feet deep green belt of trees." The plan explained the screens as a means to "protect" residents from "unfavorable surrounding developments," but their existence signaled in no uncertain terms that the city's black leadership was willing to live behind buffers of its own design.[52]

The language of the report revealed the uneasy balance of interests and clashing visions of space that underlay "Negro expansion" across the postwar South. For whites, the report emphasized that "complete self-contained" black neighborhoods would protect the city's white areas from infiltration by African American households, thus reducing "friction between the races." Moreover, the plan's insistence on "generally accepted and recognized" areas "suited to the expansion of Negro housing" signaled the council's willingness to leave residential segregation undisturbed for the time being. For African American readers, the proposal offered a solution to the housing crisis. It emphasized the protection of rights to purchase and occupy land regardless of race as well as access to new housing in "properly planned Negro neighborhoods." Walking uneasily on the distinction between de facto and de jure segregation, the report conceded, "The above areas cannot be legally designated as areas for expansion of Negro housing. However . . . it is hoped that business and civic groups alike will recognize and endorse the above . . . areas as being in fact, if not by law, the proper areas in which Negroes may build and live without racial or economic conflict."[53]

Among white officialdom, responses to the report were cautious but supportive. The Chamber of Commerce requested clarification of boundaries and racial characteristics in the neighborhoods affected by the proposal. Officials from the surrounding counties, where the expansion areas were located, "consented to cooperate" in providing services to several existing African American sections. The local FHA office lent advice and support, and the city press praised the group's "realistic and practical approach" to the problems facing blacks and whites in the city.[54] For its part, the City Planning Commission adopted the concept of "Negro expansion" in its 1952 Metropolitan Plan for the region.[55] Lacking force in law, the Housing Council proposal nonetheless became the de facto master plan for black community building in Atlanta for the next fifteen years.

Essential to white acceptance of the plan were several related, but uncoordinated, actions on the part of African Americans themselves. Most important was the continued "infiltration" of African Americans into white neighborhoods. As black families moved into what blacks trenchantly described as "forbidden areas" of the city, racial friction mounted. Mob gatherings, arson, house bombings, and other incidents raised the specter of a full-scale race riot such as the city had suffered in 1906. In the opinion of Robert Thompson, a social worker with the Atlanta Urban League and the principal author of the AHC report, "The town was about to explode."[56]

One key trouble spot was a neighborhood called Mozley Park, which was located just west of the subdivisions that Heman Perry had developed in the 1920s. The site was attractive to middle-class African Americans because of its proximity to Atlanta University as well as the package of city services, such as paved streets, sewers, and city water, which were still lacking in most black neighborhoods.[57] Home owners on the edges of the neighborhood, finding few white buyers for their property, had begun selling to African Americans in the late 1930s, though intimidation by other whites had prevented blacks from moving in or building in the neighborhood.[58]

Pressures for black expansion intensified after the war. Complicating matters, Walter Aiken began building his Simpson Heights subdivision to the north and west of Mozley Park in 1946. Soon, local whites were sandwiched between growing black neighborhoods. As African Americans encroached on the buffer zone that had separated black and white neighborhoods, a white supremacist group calling itself the "Columbians" became active in the area, promising violence if blacks broke the color line. Against this background, white civic leaders tacitly accepted the AHC proposal and slowly began working with black leaders to find common ground.[59]

Just as important to the expansion program as the threat of violence was blacks' access to the ballot. Following the 1946 Supreme Court decision in *Chapman v. King*, which invalidated the white primary in Georgia, Atlanta blacks — including future members of the TCCH — launched a massive voter registration drive. Between February and May 1946, the number of registered black voters in Atlanta tripled. Almost overnight, blacks constituted a quarter of the local electorate, gaining political influence that they used for the next two decades to secure improved services in black neighborhoods, the hiring of black workers by the city, construction of schools and parks, representation on civic bodies, and access to better housing. Though African Americans remained unequal citizens throughout the long administration of Mayor William Hartsfield (1937–40, 1942–61), by the late 1940s they had become key members of the electoral coalition that kept him in office. Their relationship with the racially pragmatic mayor helped ward off racial violence of the kind that was common in other southern cities, and it won them modest concessions in city services and support for efforts to help themselves, including the campaign to build what banker L. D. Milton called "sound, orderly and well-conceived housing developments for Negroes."[60]

Finally, black Atlantians gained leverage in the housing effort because the concentration of African American real estate and financial institutions in the city allowed them to take initiative without waiting for whites to act. Atlanta's three largest black financial institutions — Mutual Federal Savings and Loan Association, Citizens Trust Bank, and the Atlanta Life Insurance Company — financed a number of early real estate developments as well as individual loans for black pioneers. By 1955 these institutions had investments of more than $14 million in first mortgage loans, mostly to African Americans in the metropolitan area. In the view of Citizens Trust president L. D. Milton, black institutions "shattered the myth" among white lenders that "the Negro is financially irresponsible" and paved the way for larger white institutions to provide capital for a growing program of home building.[61] In addition, the black housing coalition included a phalanx of real estate brokers and building contractors, "a building supply firm, a fire and casualty insurance firm, a mortgage company, a registered architect, and a[n interior] designer."[62] Together, these firms represented an infrastructure for self-help in housing that both underlay and profited from the politics of Negro housing in the city.

Against this backdrop, black civic leaders took concrete steps to build new housing in the areas outlined in the 1947 proposal. Aiken was already building homes in two new subdivisions in the west-side "expansion area number one" at the time of the report. Within months the Housing Council launched additional plans to find and develop vacant land on the west and south sides, an effort they expanded to all six areas by 1950.

To the south and east of the city, black housing leaders focused on building moderately priced apartments to meet the large demand for housing among families earning between $2,000 and $3,000 per year. In South Atlanta, members of the Housing Council recruited Morris Abram—a Rhodes scholar, veteran, and leader in the city's politically progressive Jewish community—to build a "high-class, highly restricted" apartment project on land that had belonged to the AME Church. Initial plans sparked opposition from white groups in South Atlanta, leading the Fulton County Commission to shrink the development from 800 to 450 units, designed to coincide with a 900-unit public housing project on an adjacent site. Completed in 1950, the Highpoint Apartments modeled various features of suburban landscape planning for families with moderate incomes. One- and two-story brick-clad buildings sat back from winding streets in a parklike setting. Grassy areas between and behind each unit offered abundant space for play, gardening, outdoor cooking, and socializing.[63] Moreover, the development opened the door to new and modern housing for black Atlantians who wanted to live outside the urban core but could not afford to buy a home. Although apartments may conflict with the popular image of postwar tract housing, they represented an important element of black suburbanization in Atlanta and other southern cities, where average incomes among African Americans remained comparatively low.

On the west side of Atlanta, African American housing leaders concentrated on building single-family homes for the black middle class. By 1952 they had initiated, in addition to Aiken's developments, half a dozen subdivisions ranging in size from five to two hundred houses. In the area where Heman Perry had pioneered comprehensive neighborhood planning for African American expansion, black Atlantians developed what would become the premier black residential district in the country. By the time Atlanta officials annexed the six expansion areas in 1952 and ratified the concept in that year's metropolitan plan, African Americans and white allies had initiated new construction in four of the six areas proposed in 1947.[64]

Race, Class, and the Politics of Space

In addition to support from local real estate professionals, the housing struggle in Atlanta profited from the full-time commitment of the Atlanta Urban League and especially its housing secretary, Robert A. Thompson. As in other cities, the group sought to improve African Americans' social position through strategic engagement with white civic leaders, especially in employment and recreation. Due in part to Thompson's influence, the Atlanta Urban League developed a distinctly spatial approach to the civil rights struggle. The organization was responsible for calling the initial meeting of housing proponents in Aiken's offices in 1946, and Thompson was a principal author of the expansion proposal that followed. Over the next fifteen years, Robert Thompson and the Urban League staff participated in the development of as many as half of the privately constructed homes for African Americans in the city and its suburbs.

Ambitious and upwardly mobile, Thompson was like many middle-class African Americans who rose to influence in the city's civic life prior to the mass action phase of the civil rights movement. He had moved to Atlanta from Virginia in the 1930s to attend graduate school. He stayed because of the concentration of black talent and the opportunity he saw to make a difference in black life. Like many graduates of black colleges in the South, Thompson believed in self-help as a means of overcoming discrimination, and he devoted much of his adult life to putting this philosophy into practice.[65] Based on his experience with the 1939 Federal Real Property Inventory — a precursor to the first U.S. Census of Housing in 1940 — Thompson was drawn to the field of housing and the possibilities of using residential space as a means of racial advancement. "I had discovered at that time," he said, "that . . . Negroes lived mostly in the city limits of Atlanta. I decided, looking around, . . . I could do something about that . . . find land, and get blacks to do something for themselves."[66] By building new homes on vacant land, Thompson felt, blacks could purchase "a better home at a lower cost" and also reap the benefits of property appreciation and up-to-date services that often evaded them in older neighborhoods. New home building also allowed "a better planning job for suburban living" than in "neighborhoods in which the property values are on the decrease."[67] With these goals in mind, Thompson and the Atlanta Urban League took a hand in the development of thousands of units of new housing for African Americans.

Thompson's most important role with the Urban League in the 1940s and 1950s was to identify vacant land for the development of new housing. Here the impact of black agency on patterns of residential expansion in Atlanta is most clear. In spite of official "sanction and support" for the 1947 expansion plan, black Atlantians faced an uphill battle to secure land and build homes in these areas.[68] Whites' demand for housing in Atlanta's periphery also peaked after the war, and they had significant advantages in income and access to capital. Moreover, white neighborhood organizations throughout the city vehemently opposed the construction of "Negro housing" in their vicinity, even in isolated areas where blacks may have lived for a century. Many of these groups also had greater leverage with white politicians in the city and its surrounding counties.[69] Hence, even where African Americans had an advantage in land ownership, prior settlement, or the support of central city officials, they risked losing their foothold to white developers. To overcome these disadvantages, Thompson directed a series of land-ownership surveys in the six expansion areas in order to identify and facilitate development on African American–owned land and other strategic parcels. Thompson and the Urban League initially surveyed the west and south sides in 1947. Again in 1951 and 1956, they conducted similar surveys to update and expand their data bank as well as to recruit developers to buy land and build homes for African Americans.[70]

For Thompson and other members of Atlanta's black leadership, the greatest threat to their plan was the "encirclement" of black neighborhoods by white communities, particularly on the west side.[71] Although the 1947 expansion plan outlined a circumscribed area for development on the west side, these activists privately envisioned black neighborhoods stretching from the center of the city to the Chattahoochee River, which marked the western border of Fulton County. If whites were able to develop land at the outer edges of the west-side community, they might succeed in blocking future expansion. Hence, for Thompson and other leaders in the struggle for space and housing, expansion in west Atlanta was in essence a race to the county line.[72]

To prevent encirclement, black Atlantians worked to outmaneuver whites, even to the point of manipulating racism for their benefit. In the western suburbs, black housing leaders used tactical land purchases to provide an outlet for future expansion and also to discourage whites from developing additional housing nearby. The publication of the expansion area proposal was itself an attempt to dissuade whites from building new homes in the specified sections. At the same time, African Americans took more concrete action by purchasing suburban land. In 1951, for instance, the Urban League and members of the TCCH launched what they called "Project X" to identify and "quietly acquire" land at the western edge of Fulton County. The plan envisioned "a land ownership analysis of about 2,600 acres which we hope Negroes will buy as 'farm' land. Once this property, outside the city limits, is in Negro hands efforts will then be made to have the land subdivided for Negro homes." Thompson and other participants wagered that the purchase of five hundred acres of this land would be enough to discourage white development and secure the rest for African Americans. To accomplish this task, members of the TCCH corporation committee—chaired by J. W. Whittaker, president of the black-owned Mutual Federal Savings and Loan Association—

formed a corporation for the purpose of buying and developing land. With twenty-three shareholders — most from the Auburn Avenue business community — Western Land Incorporated purchased 177 acres in three parcels by the fall of 1951. Thompson and others contacted private buyers, who eventually bought and developed more.[73]

Recognizing that whites, too, feared being encircled by black neighborhoods, Western Land bought property designed to discourage whites from building on the west side. In 1951 Thompson reported to shareholders that efforts to purchase one strategic parcel had been stalled because the owner was asking too much money. "Hence, the plan is to circumvent and purchase property beyond these tracts in order to reduce the land value and the possibility of such property being used for white occupancy."[74] Reckoning that there would be little market for "pocketed" land among white developers, Thompson advised fellow board members to purchase beyond the holdout and limit his options. In another instance, Thompson recalled: "Dr. J. B. Harris bought fifty-two acres on Peyton Road. The whites, when they found out that blacks owned the land, they like to have died, but they couldn't do a damn thing about it." Next, Thompson said, "we persuaded Ben Chennault to buy 125 acres of land where Southwest Hospital is. The whites in between Peyton Road and the hospital found that they were pocketed, so they ran. They squawked and raised hell, but they couldn't do a damned thing about that. Blacks had bought the land." In retrospect, Thompson described African American community expansion in the western suburbs as a "leapfrog" process. "We jumped over the whites," Thompson said. "As we jumped over, the whites moved further and further out. . . . Got to the point where they couldn't run no damn further. . . . So they went south into Cobb County" and "blacks took over."[75] Building on the dual base of black financial resources and white racial fears, African Americans secured access to land and ultimately housing on the west side.

In addition to promoting the purchase of land, the Urban League provided technical support for the developers of African American housing. The Urban League's most direct involvement was to sponsor construction of the 200-unit Fair Haven subdivision between 1948 and 1950. Working with members of the Chennault family, who had purchased the land during the war, the Urban League enlisted representatives of the white Chamber of Commerce to arrange financing from the white-owned Life Insurance Company of Georgia. They also negotiated with FHA officials for underwriting approval and prepared a subdivision plan in cooperation with Albert Thompson, the regional race relations advisor. Contractors of both races were recruited to prepare the site and build houses, while the Urban League marketed the resulting "beautiful FHA homes" to black home seekers throughout the city.[76]

Fair Haven represented Thompson's and the Urban League's most extensive involvement with any one subdivision, but throughout the 1940s and 1950s, Thompson facilitated the construction of scores of new projects by working as a liaison between local developers, federal officials, county commissioners, zoning and planning boards, and white and black community groups. He compiled statistics on the black housing market and served as a clearinghouse for information within Atlanta's black real estate community. He solicited lending institutions throughout the United States for mortgage financing, and he recruited land buyers and builders to develop new housing. From 1947 to 1960, when he assumed directorship of the Atlanta Urban League, Thompson was the "go to" man for information, statistics, and technical support for black housing in the city.[77]

Through the varied efforts of the Urban League, FHA officials, and members of the real estate industry, African Americans in Atlanta initiated the construction of three dozen single-family housing tracts and perhaps twice as many low-rise duplex and multifamily apartment projects between 1945 and 1960. The majority of these new homes were built on land that had been outside the city until 1952, when Atlanta annexed eighty-two square miles of its suburban hinterland.[78] From a physical standpoint, most of these developments shared the basic features of postwar suburban home building across the country. Developers used mass-production techniques to build modestly priced single-family homes and apartments. Most met FHA or Veterans Administration requirements, and buyers were able to borrow money through a standard long-term mortgage from a bank or savings and loan association. Houses of several designs sat a uniform distance from the street on spacious lots, and the new owners relied on automobiles to commute to work in the center city or surrounding suburbs. In all of these respects, "Negro expansion" in Atlanta mirrored patterns of suburbanization nationwide.

These features were not accidental. Rather, they reflected the specific intentions of the city's black middle class to share fully in the suburbanization process after World War II. Beginning with the 1947 "Negro expansion" plan, black civic leaders proposed that developers build "properly-planned Negro neighborhoods" in a residential environment that middle-class suburbanites across the United States would have recognized and appreciated. The proposal envisioned "self-contained" black neighborhoods developed under "basic model planning conditions," including extensive land-use planning and deed restrictions. Planned features included separate areas for residences and commerce, minimum lot sizes and set backs, "rear yards of clear open space," curvilinear streets, and space for multifamily housing, as well as parks, stores, and schools. Suggested deed restrictions included limits on the location of front fences and hedges and standards for the construction of garages and outbuildings, plus formal review of building plans and prohibitions against occupancy before "sewer, water, and other essential utilities" were connected. The latter two restrictions, in particular, proscribed practices that were common among working-class suburbanites.[79] In contrast to the heterogeneous and haphazard construction of homes in existing black neighborhoods in the city, members of the Atlanta Housing Council envisioned the expansion of the city's African American middle class into tightly controlled residential neighborhoods characteristic of planned suburbs nationwide.

The middle-class suburban vision so evident in the planning process was actualized in the residential landscapes of the city's new black neighborhoods. At one end of the new home market was the Urban League's Fair Haven subdivision, which opened in the western suburbs in 1950. Two-bedroom ranch-style houses sold initially for as little as $6,500. With brick exteriors, ample backyards, and a uniform streetscape of front lawns, concrete steps, and wrought-iron railings, these homes created a residential landscape that would have been immediately familiar to middle-class suburbanites anywhere in the United States. They also presented a marked contrast to the bulk of working-class housing in the city. Most of the first residents were in their late twenties or thirties. They included teachers, social workers, postal employees, and faculty from the local colleges, as well as more than a third who held blue-collar jobs. Two-income households were not uncommon. Physically and socially, Fair Haven was a spatial embodiment of the city's new black middle class.[80]

One feature that challenged the middle-class image of the development was its streets, which remained unpaved when the first residents moved in. To ensure a housing price affordable to the widest market—an acknowledgment of the tenuous economic position of middle-class black families—the developers had completed the tract without paving or curbs. Nonetheless, new residents immediately sought to complete the middle-class landscape of the neighborhood. Within months of moving in, they petitioned the Fulton County Commission to pave the streets and install curbs, storm drains, and streetlights.[81]

Even more pointedly, residents indicated their desire to preserve a particular class character for their neighborhood by defending it against the arrival of lower-income families. In 1952 they petitioned the city to block construction of a 95-unit apartment complex on an adjoining property, complaining

Fig. 7.5   Penelope Street, Fair Haven subdivision (ca. 1952). Sponsored by the
Atlanta Urban League, the Fair Haven subdivision was among the first developments constructed in the suburban expansion areas proposed by the Atlanta Housing Council in 1947. On moving in, residents lobbied the county government to
complete the subdivision's middle-class landscape by paving its streets. (Atlanta
Urban League Papers, box 328, folder 2, Atlanta University Center, Robert W.
Woodruff Library. Photographer: Wray Studio, Atlanta, Georgia)

that the project "would tend to lower property values of the existing home
owners" and raise population density, "a major factor in the development
of a slum."[82] In addition to emphasizing class-oriented concerns, Robert
Thompson, who was a Fair Haven resident, appealed to his neighbors' sense
of racial solidarity, urging them to speak out to stop "white developers . . .
[from] ruining your neighborhood."[83] Much to the chagrin of Fair Haven's
middle class, their protests fell on deaf ears at the city's white zoning board.
As Thompson ruefully reported, "Apartments renting for $39 to $44 per
month were located just across the street from two new homes costing approximately $40,000."[84]

Like other suburbanites, residents also made individual efforts to "insure a
better quality of housing in Fair Haven" by upgrading their own homes.[85] In
the process, they enhanced not only their own property values but the class
status of the neighborhood as a whole. Responding to individual needs,

they added family rooms, extra bedrooms, second stories, and other features. Reflecting what local Realtist T. M. Alexander called the "home-loving" tendency of African Americans across the city, residents also proved remarkably stable in the decades after their arrival.[86] In an era of relatively swift residential turnover, almost 60 percent of residents lived at the same address ten years later. Forty-three percent remained after twenty years, and by 1981, thirty years after the subdivision was completed, a third of Fair Haven's original residents lived in the same homes.[87]

If Fair Haven epitomized the suburban housing available to moderate-income black families, the city also afforded opportunities for its black executive class. At the upper end of Atlanta's housing scale were "luxury" home developments on the far west side, such as Collier Heights Estates, which opened in 1959. Described in its advertisements as "Atlanta's newest and most exclusive subdivision," the development offered four "beautiful" split-level home designs ranging in size from 1,400 to 1,800 square feet for between $17,500 and $18,500. Houses featured "Hot Point built-in ranges," "paneled family rooms," "ample storage space," "sliding glass doors," "spacious rooms throughout," and large lots "to insure privacy." Advertisements depicted each home model on an impeccably manicured front lawn with a wall of shade trees behind, almost beckoning the viewer to abandon the world of the street for the shelter of the backyard. Unlike the well-used lots and makeshift homes of Atlanta's working-class neighborhoods, these images depicted an orderly, ornamental, and thoroughly middle-class vision of domestic space.[88]

Separately, subdivisions such as these offered houses and amenities to satisfy the variety of incomes within Atlanta's black middle class; together, they comprised a well-groomed suburban landscape on the outskirts of the old city. On the west side in particular, separate planning for "Negro expansion" produced a residential district that mirrored middle-class white suburban areas across the region, except for its political status (after 1952) as part of a central city.

In addition to revealing the extent to which middle-class African Americans shared popular residential aspirations, the process of separate suburbanization illuminates ambiguities in the goals and strategies of black protest on the eve of the mass-action phase of the civil rights movement. On the one hand, the quest for new black neighborhoods reflected a political pragmatism molded to the region's racial climate. "For southern blacks in the age of Jim Crow," historian Robin Kelley notes, "politics was not separate from lived experience or the imagined world of what is possible."[89] In postwar Atlanta, as elsewhere, black "pragmatism" developed in a context where violence was

Fig. 7.6 "Big Grand Opening: Collier Heights Estates" (ca. 1959). Handbill advertisement for an executive-class subdivision for African Americans on Atlanta's far west side. After 1952, the city's newly annexed suburban fringe provided space for thousands of African American families to secure the amenities of postwar "suburbia." (Atlanta Urban League Papers, box 249, folder 12, Atlanta University Center, Robert W. Woodruff Library)

a prevailing feature of white power. Even more than the desire to avoid racial disorder that motivated white officials to accommodate "Negro expansion," the experience and historical memory of white terror molded African Americans' expectations and actions. When Walter Aiken laid out his case for planned expansion to a congressional committee in 1947, for instance, he explained that every attempt by African Americans to breach white-imposed

Fig. 7.7   Collier Heights, 1997. Forty years after its construction, Collier Heights Estates remained a highly attractive neighborhood with all the physical attributes of postwar suburbia. Inside the city limits or out, neighborhoods like these allowed southern African Americans to benefit more from the process of urban decentralization than blacks in any other part of the United States. (Photograph by Andrew Wiese, 1997)

boundaries in his twenty-five years of experience had resulted in violence. In fact, "as far back as 1923," he said, night riders had set fire to several houses that he was building. As he understood it, violence was a predictable consequence of expanding into "forbidden areas."[90] History also informed the views of Robert Thompson. Recalling events of the late forties, he explained why the Atlanta Housing Council took the actions it did. "Blacks were moving up against white adjacent areas. Tension. Ku Klux Klan bombing, Columbians, race riot. Atlanta had witnessed a race riot before [in 1906]. We were determined for that not to occur again."[91] Thompson's emphasis on the threat of riot is especially revealing since he did not move to the city until a generation after the 1906 disturbance. Nonetheless, the reality and recollection of white violence marked the outer limits of black decision making. If African Americans challenged white supremacy in politics and the law, they also walked a dangerous line, tailoring their plans for housing in the shadowy light of a torch-lit mob.

In such a setting, Atlanta's black elite harbored no illusions about the

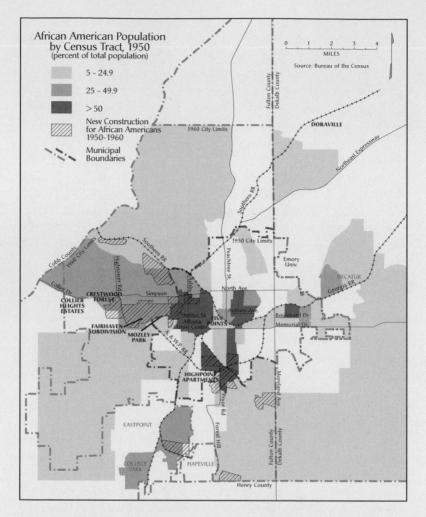

Fig. 7.8   Housing Construction for African Americans in Metropolitan Atlanta, 1950–1960. (Map by Harry D. Johnson)

possibility of building racially integrated housing or neighborhoods. In fact, during the fifteen years after World War II, no one in a position of influence in Atlanta advanced residential integration as a goal; among those planning for Negro expansion, Hylan Lewis and Robert Thompson reported, the subject "hardly ever arose."[92] The effective choice was separate housing or no new housing at all. Given the alarming condition of black housing in Atlanta after the war, most believed that African Americans could not await the fruits of a "sit-down strike" against segregation in order to have more and better homes.[93] Even Forrester Washington, the Atlanta University sociologist who had raised the only dissenting voice against the proposal for "Negro expansion areas" in 1947, conceded that although "the ideal would be not to have any specific Negro communities in Atlanta . . . we cannot afford to wait to improve Negro housing until that goal is achieved."[94] Black housing leaders remained committed to the principle of equal opportunity, or "democracy," in housing, but they built new homes on what was essentially a separate but equal basis.

The record also suggests that Atlanta's black civic leadership saw no necessary contradiction between opposition to racial segregation at large and the construction of separate subdivisions for black families. For Robert Thompson, "the central objective at this time" was "to ensure that Negro residents will not be excluded from Atlanta's suburban growth," whether or not this effort exacerbated patterns of de facto racial segregation.[95] Without direct action on their own behalf, Thompson believed, blacks would be "hemmed in" and confined to old neighborhoods in the central city. As a result, they would be prevented from sharing in the advantages of modern suburban space: well-built, affordable housing and the likelihood of property appreciation, up-to-date services, access to federal mortgage subsidies, and the social benefits of successful neighbors. For its proponents, separate suburbanization was a means of expanding black opportunities rather than limiting them.

Thompson stressed this point in a 1997 interview. "The expansion areas were where the blacks already lived," he asserted. "And what we said, blacks said, to the power structure [was] . . . 'We already live here. Now we need to have access to develop that land we own in the area that we live, to live peaceably.' But that did not preclude our moving out beyond the boundaries."[96] In fact, separate community building served as a means of undermining white residential borders on the west side, which led to the consolidation of the area as a solidly African American section of the city. In the question of integration or segregation, however, African Americans played only one part. As Thompson pointed out, "I'm sure that our doing all this caused the white people to move, but hell, we couldn't control that. All we was going to do is get blacks to be home owners and live in safe, decent housing. If the whites want to deal with that, okay. If they don't, leave. They chose to leave."[97]

Constrained as they were, leaders of the black housing struggle in Atlanta initiated a process of community building designed to expand African American choices and to create black communities in which they could benefit from the process of metropolitan expansion. The business and civic elite that waged the campaign for "Negro expansion" in Atlanta opposed enforced racial segregation and the liabilities it imposed on black families, but they did not reject the positive value of living in black communities nor the potential for empowerment inherent to spatial congregation. Black Atlantians viewed the city's better black neighborhoods, its colleges, and its business district as objects of pride and cultural affirmation. Like African Americans across the South, they worked to enhance these even as they mounted challenges to discrimination in other areas of civic life. Moreover, they recognized that black neighborhoods were the very basis for this undertaking. For the architects of "Negro expansion" in Atlanta, then, desegregation in housing did not imply side-by-side integration of the races but rather an end to discrimination and second-class living conditions in whatever neighborhoods African Americans chose to live.

Although whites held the balance of power in the city and their insistence on racial segregation fixed an absolute limit on what African Americans could achieve and where they could live, black Atlantians made strategic choices that affected postwar decentralization in profound ways. Through planning, political agitation, and private land development, they created suburban landscapes and amenities that were closed to all but a few African Americans in the Northeast and Midwest. Yet they also reinforced white efforts to build a segregated city, and they contributed to increasing residential segregation in Atlanta, even before the full onset of urban renewal in the late 1950s.[98] By building better black neighborhoods, they helped ensure that de facto segregation would persist after legal segregation had passed away. For Atlantians and many other black southerners, increased racial separation over the long run was the price they paid for improved living conditions and access to the fruits of suburban space.[99]

"Negro Housing" in Dallas

The struggle over "Negro expansion" in Dallas had its roots in the social and economic transformation wrought by World War II. Dallas's historically small black population grew by a third during the 1940s from 62,000 to 80,000. With the coming of war, aeronautics firms such as Lockheed, North American Aviation, and Southern Aircraft built giant airplane factories on the periphery of the city, creating thousands of well-paying defense jobs and sparking a surge of regional migration to the city. In the first two years of the war, as many as 25,000 families migrated to Dallas. Though blacks were largely excluded from

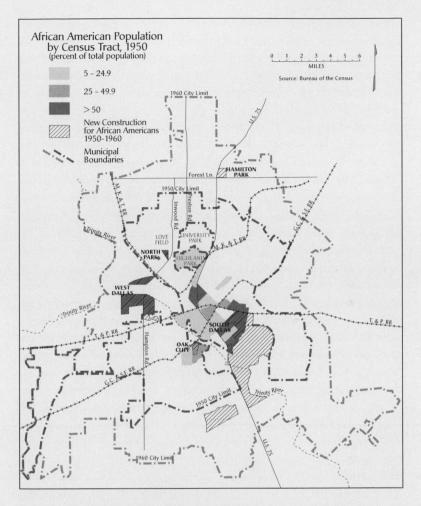

Fig. 7.9   Housing Construction for African Americans in metropolitan Dallas, 1950–1960. (Map by Harry D. Johnson)

aeronautics employment, the subsidiary economic boom attracted thousands of African American men and women as well. One result was a desperate shortage of housing. By 1943 the deficit was so acute that the War Department declared the city a critical labor shortage area and prohibited the development of new industry for lack of any place to house workers.[100]

Among those hardest hit by the housing crunch were African Americans. Dallas's black population grew by as many as 7,000 households during the war, yet the supply of available housing barely increased. Local and federal officials built more than 7,000 units of emergency defense housing in Dallas, but fewer than 200 were designed for African Americans. In addition, the city completed 900 units of low-income public housing for blacks as part of a prewar slum clearance project, but since these were "set down in areas so thickly settled formerly that many housing units were displaced," they did little to ease the overall housing shortage.[101] Consequently, migrants crowded into one-room apartments, camp trailers, garages, boxcars, and even chicken coops, while hundreds of families built makeshift homes in the unregulated periphery of the city. By the late 1940s, African American civic leaders described conditions in the city's black neighborhoods as "unbearable," "wretched," and "appalling."[102] An estimated 22,000 families lived in just 12,500 dwellings, two-thirds of which were substandard. In the opinion of FHA race relations advisor Maceo Smith, "It is harder to find homes for Negroes in Dallas than in any other city in the South."[103]

Contributing to the "vast and desperate need for adequate housing" among African Americans was an unyielding demand for racial segregation among local whites.[104] As urban planner Harland Bartholomew explained in 1944, white neighborhoods surrounded "each of the six major concentrations of Negro population," making "impossible any logical and unhampered expansion of the city's Negro areas."[105] When blacks tried to move out of these enclaves, they met stiff, often violent, resistance. In 1940 white citizens mounted a campaign of terror in South Dallas after African Americans began buying homes in a white neighborhood. Over an eighteen-month period, the neighborhood was the scene of nineteen house bombings. Assailants fired gunshots into black-occupied homes, and stone-throwing mobs intimidated newcomers. Dallas police were unable or unwilling to quell the violence. The city council lent support to the segregationists by passing a racial zoning ordinance that restricted the area to whites and enacting a plan to buy out black home owners. It repealed the zoning ordinance after the NAACP sued in court, but the city proceeded with the racial buyout, creating a strip of parkland designed to mark the line between the black and white neighborhoods. By 1947, a representative of the local NAACP noted, African Americans in Dallas were "hemmed in to narrow . . . insufficient limits, by an iron curtain" of white resistance.[106]

Among the few places where African Americans were able to freely buy and build homes were a number of unregulated working-class communities on the outer rim of the city. The largest and most notorious in the eyes of white officials developed behind the levees of the Trinity River, just outside the city limits in West Dallas. Here, hundreds of Anglo, Chicano, and African American families erected "jerry-built" housing in separate sections linked by un-paved streets and interspersed with garbage heaps and cat-tailed lowlands.[107]

In the view of Dallas's white elite, working-class enclaves such as these were as much a menace to the image of a progressive southern city as violent dis-cord in its racial borderlands. In 1950 a panel of white civic leaders toured the area to get a firsthand look. In one section "typical of several," the group found "fifty persons . . . living in nine shacks, less than three feet apart, all fifty people using one dry toilet, and all using, close by the toilet, one outdoor hydrant for their drinking water, bathing water and laundry water." "Such places," they concluded, "are a disgrace to our community" and a "great dis-credit to our city."[108] By the late 1940s, pressure was building among white city leaders to resolve the black housing crisis; in the end, it was African Amer-ican pressure reflected in disorderly working-class suburbanization and re-newed migration into South Dallas that forced them to act. Much as in Atlanta and other southern cities, they pursued plans to build separate African Amer-ican housing on the outskirts of town.

If African Americans prodded whites to take action, they also helped direct the course they would follow. In a 1947 hearing before a joint committee of Congress held in Dallas, representatives of the city's leading black political, re-ligious, and business organizations framed the issues facing African Ameri-cans, and they proposed a solution that whites would ultimately accept. "In every community in this city," emphasized the Reverend Ernest Estell, "we are hemmed in, and we cannot expand."[109] "Congestion and wretchedness" prevailed in black neighborhoods, the delegation asserted, which led to the "evils of crime, vice, and disease." Moreover, white failure to make room for upwardly mobile black families to buy or build new homes led to neighbor-hood violence, which placed "a black mark on the city of Dallas."[110] Accord-ing to the delegation, the solution lay in "the provision of new areas of the city of Dallas [for] Negroes to live and the erection thereon of low rent and sales housing consonant with the capacity of Dallas Negroes to rent and buy."[111] Hammering the point home, NAACP officer G. F. Porter concluded, "Some-thing must be done to rid us of these conditions, which bind us within this iron gate. They hold us to ourselves and will not let us stretch out and breathe the air that God gave us." That something, he declared, was the construction of new housing in new areas of the city and suburbs.[112]

In addition to airing their case in public, African Americans took concrete steps to ease the postwar housing crisis. Enlisting the support of several white builders, black civic leaders, including Negro Chamber of Commerce secre-tary John Rice and the regional FHA race relations advisor A. Maceo Smith, initiated planning for five separate housing developments for African Americans in the Dallas suburbs between 1947 and 1950.[113] In each case, opposition from neighboring whites (some as far as four miles from the proposed subdivision) chilled the interest of white financial institutions and officials. Blacks met federal resistance as well. Despite Maceo Smith's involvement, the white director of the regional FHA office enforced a personal policy of refusing to underwrite African American housing where there was any "controversy over location."[114] In reality, there was almost no place blacks could build in the suburbs of the jim crow South that was not controversial to whites somewhere. As one Dallas developer noted in frustration after distant opponents and obstructive city officials had blocked his proposal for a black subdivision in 1948, "If you set up a Negro community on an island in the Pacific Ocean, . . . I guess the fish would rise up in protest."[115] Absent the political and economic clout exercised by African Americans in Atlanta, Dallas blacks were forced to rely on the efforts and goodwill of the city's white establishment.

If African Americans were unable to attract sufficient white support to build new housing in the late 1940s, they were nonetheless responsible for forcing the issue of "Negro housing" onto the public agenda. As in Atlanta, the specter of interracial violence in city neighborhoods finally provoked white officials and civic elites to act. As whites began moving to suburban housing after the war, vacancies became available in older neighborhoods such as South Dallas. In February 1950, black pioneers searching for homes breached the decade-old buffer zone in the neighborhood, and a second wave of bombings rocked the area.[116] Recognizing the need either to find additional space for African Americans or face the civic consequences of a racial melee, a coalition of white elites—including the mayor, the city council, and the business-dominated Dallas Citizens Council—began to consider proposals to build new housing in specially designated "Negro expansion areas" in several parts of the city. In spite of official and grassroots resistance among whites, the actions of individual black families became the motive force for breaking the logjam in housing.

Nonetheless, the level of white involvement in Dallas led to significant differences from the process in Atlanta. Among the first proposals to emerge from the city council was a plan for the city to purchase three thousand acres of vacant land in the Trinity River floodplain for the construction of a separate "Negro city of 45,000."[117] After short deliberation, the Negro Chamber of Commerce rejected the overture, citing environmental conditions as well as the social implications of the plan. Not only was the site ringed by levees, but

its location on a river bottom — the traditional location of so much black housing in the South — was especially galling. "It seems that these people still think
that anything is good enough for a Negro," said one woman. "We came out
of the river bottoms. Some of us are still either in them or are so crowded into
slum areas that decent home life is not possible. . . . We women are going to
fight with our leaders to stay out of this place . . . where we'll have to live the
rest of our lives among mosquitoes, frogs, dampness and snakes."[118] Furthermore, the transparent proposal of enforced racial isolation in "a single segregated unit" disturbed black critics.[119] Facing opposition, the council tabled the
proposal. Nonetheless, the underlying assumption of segregated and secluded
new housing would govern subsequent efforts to solve the housing shortage
for Dallas's growing black community.

As the bombings continued in South Dallas in the spring of 1950, white
elites at last mobilized to produce new housing for African Americans. A joint
committee of the Dallas Chamber of Commerce and the Dallas Citizens
Council — the city's most influential political and civic institutions — prepared
a report on "Negro Housing in Dallas County" that encapsulated the issues
facing Dallas and dozens of other southern cities. Echoing the language used
by black leaders in 1947, they reported that "the present Negro residential
districts are 'hemmed in' and cannot possibly be expanded without losses, disturbed and distressed communities, unrest, tension and trouble."[120] This sort
of turmoil, they explained, Dallas must avoid. The report also addressed the
problem of housing for poor and working-class blacks. "At the very time we
are eliminating slums within the city," it exclaimed, the city was "actually
building new slums" in outlying areas such as West Dallas. The proposed remedy was threefold. First, the city should annex areas "with slum-type housing" and "clean them up through enforcement of zoning and platting laws
and other city ordinances." Where this proved unworkable, local legislators
should initiate state legislation to permit county governments to impose
zoning and building regulations to prevent the spread of other owner-built
neighborhoods on the city's doorstep. Third, Dallas should undertake to build
new "Negro housing sections" in "suitable segregated sites." Reinforcing the
aims of African American civic leaders, the report concluded that "it is the
unanimous conviction of the joint committees that it is important to have a
number of Negro residential sections in various parts of the city."[121]

Anticipating white opposition, the committee emphasized the conservative nature of the plan. "The only satisfactory and permanent solution to
this problem," they noted emphatically, "can be realized where there is racial
segregation." Still, they "remind[ed] the people of Dallas that if we do not

provide home sites for Negroes who want to, and can afford to buy or rent suitable and decent homes, the alternative is terrible overcrowding, dissatisfaction, disease, tension resulting from Negroes buying into white neighborhoods, and many other serious consequences." In this context, "white citizens must choose between some inconveniences that may be involved by providing suitable new residential districts for the Negroes in various areas or, what would be a thousand times worse, the bad results that inevitably will follow if we continue our present course of action, or lack of action."[122]

Following the release of the report, momentum for African American housing moved in two directions. First, city officials steamed ahead with a vigorous program of annexation and slum clearance. Between 1950 and the end of 1952, the city annexed fifty-three square miles of adjacent territory, including the river bottoms of West Dallas, and it had outlined the areas destined for the wrecking ball.[123] To rehouse working-class and poor families, they drew up plans for a thousand units of public housing on the edge of South Dallas as well as thirty-five hundred units of low-income housing in West Dallas. By April 1954, a month before the Supreme Court invalidated de jure segregation in the nation's schools, city crews had demolished a substantial portion of the "slums, sloughs and garbage dumps" of West Dallas and replaced them with three segregated housing projects, one each for African Americans, Chicanos, and non-Hispanic whites.[124]

In West Dallas, especially, public housing satisfied several agenda items among Dallas's white elite. In place of an unregulated working-class "shack" district, the West Dallas project substituted new standard housing under centralized management.[125] By replacing the interracial mixture of blue-collar families in makeshift homes with orderly rows of racially segregated public apartments, redevelopment also strengthened the tripartite Texas color line.[126] By design, the 1,450 black families living at Edgar Ward Place, the African American housing project, were physically isolated from white neighborhoods so that even growth from this base would not soon threaten to encroach on white residential areas.[127] Although working-class African Americans sought rustic subsistence through owner building, self-provisioning, and other venerable uses of marginal space, white officials exerted the power of the state to shore up racial segregation and reinforce an ideology of white racial purity by preventing interracial residential mixing in the unregulated margins of the city.

Although public housing is rarely considered a hallmark of suburbanization, it was an integral part of urban decentralization in Dallas and other southern cities. In tandem with private housing construction, officials across the region built public housing on the urban fringe as a means of reducing pressures for racial transition in existing neighborhoods and easing the way for slum clearance and urban renewal downtown.[128] In many cities, the process represented an explicitly suburban strategy for achieving urban redevelopment. Moreover, slum clearance and public housing construction on the outskirts of cities like Dallas reflected the national trend toward increasing regulation and racialization of land use in the suburban rim. Furthermore, to the extent that white planners envisioned a racially segregated metropolitan future, public housing served as a means of securing the racial character of the urban periphery and shaping subsequent development. That these dwellings were built with public funds to house poor people does not alter their importance as a widespread feature of urban decentralization in the region.

The second strategy for solving the black housing crisis coalesced around the construction of single-family homes for the middle class, though in Dallas whites played the dominant role, limiting eventual construction to just a few small areas. Several months after the report on "Negro Housing in Dallas County," members of the Citizens Council and the Chamber of Commerce established the Dallas Interracial Committee, which included members of the white business elite as well as John Rice, Maceo Smith, and a representative from the local NAACP, to work out the details of "Negro expansion" for middle-class families. The group considered locations for more than a year until 1952, when, on Smith's recommendation, it established a nonprofit corporation to purchase and develop a 179-acre subdivision eight miles north of downtown. Drawing on the leadership of influential whites such as oilman Jerome Crossman, banker Karl Hoblitzelle, and home builder Leslie Hill, the group successfully planned and built 730 suburban homes for middle-income black families in a subdivision called Hamilton Park.[129]

In spite of their political and economic clout, the group carefully tailored the Hamilton Park project to minimize white opposition. Hamilton Park's developers chose a site that met conditions common to successful "Negro expansion areas" across the South. First, it was distant from white home owners, several miles beyond the present edge of development in North Dallas. Forest Lane, which ran past the site, was a two-lane ribbon of county asphalt when the Interracial Committee visited in 1952. In addition, black families had owned and farmed land near Hamilton Park since Reconstruction; the committee noted that there was "a Negro school, two Negro churches, and a small Negro shopping area" in the vicinity. The site also recommended itself because it was located in unincorporated territory outside the Dallas city limits where no municipality could zone the site out from under them. Even so, the Interracial Committee sought to allay potential opposition by developing a community with clear physical boundaries. Two creeks and a railroad line bordered the community in a triangular shape to the west and southeast, and planners offered just two outlets from the community onto Forest Lane to the south. The subsequent construction of Interstates 75 and 635 only reinforced these barriers, perpetuating a thoroughly enclosed African American residential community. Like the developments envisioned for "Negro expansion areas" in Atlanta, Hamilton Park was expressly planned as a self-contained black community.[130]

Hamilton Park was also designed to be a middle-class community. The Interracial Committee selected a "high, beautiful and well-situated site" with a view of downtown and a "cool" breeze on hot summer nights.[131] The plat divided the property into large lots with ample space for grass, trees, and other landscaping, and the developer constructed houses ranging in size from two to four bedrooms. Covenants ensured a uniform residential landscape, limiting front fences and hedges, restricting the construction of outbuildings, and prohibiting nonresidential uses of homes. Plans also included a twenty-acre park, a small shopping center, and a neighborhood school. Using their contacts in the city government, Hamilton Park's sponsors secured its annexation by the city and the extension of municipal services, and they received approval for FHA mortgage insurance on the new homes through the recalcitrant regional office. In 1954 the first of 3,000 residents moved into their new suburban community.[132]

For African Americans, the attractions of Hamilton Park were obvious. New housing with a full outfit of municipal services, a uniformly planned residential landscape, home ownership, new schools, a safe environment for children, and a community of like-minded families—Hamilton Park offered Dallas blacks the mainstays of a national suburban dream. Reflecting the limited economic opportunities available to African Americans in Dallas, most of Hamilton Park's initial residents had blue-collar occupations, but they saw themselves rising into the middle class. According to historian William H. Wilson, they shared a set of bedrock values for home ownership, education, "industry, and thrift, bolstered by family and community life." In the context of Dallas's existing black neighborhoods, residents described Hamilton Park as "a step up in life, a little progress," or "something better and different for my kids."[133] For hundreds of African American families, Hamilton Park represented the fruition of a thoroughly American suburban dream with adherents in middle-class suburbs across the nation.

No less than their counterparts in Atlanta's suburbs, Hamilton Park residents sought spatially to enhance their class standing, evincing concerns for the preservation of a middle-class suburban atmosphere, as well as the status, comfort, and property values that it reflected. On evenings and weekends, residents devoted themselves to landscaping and other exterior improvements; so much so that the community drew carloads of onlookers. One resident recalled, "On Saturday evening, and especially on Sundays after church, people would come up our streets and just look at us as if we were something really special. Here you are — you have houses, new houses. Nothing filtered down here." According to another resident, "The idea was ownership and the pride to build up a place which had been labeled as not going to last."[134] Within months of moving in, residents organized groups to satisfy their social, political, educational, civic, and spiritual needs. These included churches, a PTA and Dad's Club, scout troops, and organizations focused on neighborhood improvement. The most influential, the Hamilton Park Civic League, functioned as a property owners association, petitioning government for better services, registering complaints about potholes and traffic signs, and sponsoring awards for the "lawn of the week" and "best Christmas display." During the 1950s, the Civic League also mobilized to improve local amenities, including paving for alleys, street lighting, and shelter and rest room facilities for Willowdell Park. Like many such organizations, too, the group badgered noncompliant home owners to maintain their properties, and it filed suit in several instances to defend the community against the construction of apartments and commercial developments, which they believed would cause the neighborhood to deteriorate. Similar to residents of Atlanta's Fair Haven subdivision and other middle-class suburban areas, Hamilton Park's Civic League fought to block the construction of a local apartment complex on the class-based logic that Hamilton Park was a "single-family area."[135]

If residents saw Hamilton Park as a middle-class community, they very clearly cherished its racial identity as well. As in Atlanta, residents expressed a conspicuous ambivalence about desegregation at the neighborhood level. Throughout the era of *Brown* and the mass-action phase of the civil rights movement, residents actively supported the construction and maintenance of an explicitly segregated school. According to historian William Wilson, residents were "realists who lived in the world as it was." But beyond realism about the limits that racism imposed, their support for separate housing and institutions suggests a deeper conflict between values they held about space and the wider struggle to defeat segregation. Like other southern African Americans, they took pride and comfort in the separate places and institutions that they had developed under jim crow, and many worked to achieve equality within a "separate but equal" formula—even after this strategy had been discredited among intellectuals and civil rights leaders. They sough to abolish the white supremacist vision of the city that reserved the best locations for whites and relegated African Americans to the devalued margins, but they did not abandon the idea of racialized space altogether. They clung instead to a dream of safe, supportive, and empowering black space in which they could reap the fruits of suburban life as people with a shared racial identity. In the case of the local high school, Wilson points out, residents' "focus was on improving the school as it was—not on desegregating it." As a hub of community life, the school was a touchstone for individual as well as collective memories—of academic successes and victorious sports teams, organizational meetings, proms, and hopeful graduations. Together, these anchored a local sense of racial identity. In the end, federal pressure, not local agitation, led to the school's closure in 1969.[136]

By 1960 the process of politically sanctioned "Negro expansion" in Dallas had run its course. Private builders had completed close to twenty-five hundred additional housing units in separate subdivisions and apartment developments in three other peripheral areas proposed by the Joint Committee in 1950, as well as on sites near Love Field in northwest Dallas, south along the Trinity River levee, and adjacent to the projects of West Dallas. The construction of a new campus for historically black Bishop College in the late 1950s opened another door for African American settlement south of the city.[137] Less substantial than the black housing program in Atlanta, or even neighboring Houston, Dallas in the 1950s added approximately sixty-four hundred new housing units for African Americans at the outer edges of town. Of these, twenty-four hundred, or 38 percent, were built in public housing projects.[138]

The politics of "Negro housing" in Dallas provide instructive comparison with the process in the Georgia capital. Fundamental similarities reflected the unequal balance of power among African Americans and whites across the jim crow South and the pattern of racial politics that arose from it. Nonetheless, the historical setting of each city shaped different outcomes. In both cities, African Americans and white civic leaders reached a political compromise over residential segregation in order to facilitate the construction of new housing for African Americans on the metropolitan rim. Because Dallas's smaller black community lacked the political and economic clout of its counterpart in Atlanta, white elites played an even more important role in the planning and construction of new neighborhoods for African Americans in that city. As a result, new housing was limited to a handful of middle-class subdivisions, which were dwarfed in number by low-cost apartments and segregated public housing. Moreover, "Negro expansion" in Dallas was linked from the beginning to a slum clearance program designed to eliminate unregulated working-class communities that had grown up on the outskirts of the city. In Atlanta, by contrast, a self-directed program of black home building offered an alternative model of urban decentralization for more than a decade after the war before being overwhelmed by downtown-driven urban renewal in the late 1950s. In both areas, African American agency—through migration, pioneering in white neighborhoods, and political advocacy—was at the root of white interest in "Negro housing." Through concerted efforts to purchase and develop land beyond the edges of white settlement and to pioneer in white neighborhoods, black Atlantians used whites' racial fears to pressure local officials to give informal sanction to "expansion areas" that would be available for the construction of new African American housing. Without challenging the structure of racial separation itself, blacks initiated the process of planning new neighborhoods and undertook to convert their plans into reality. In Dallas, too, African Americans sought access to new housing in the suburbs, but they were forced to rely on the political and economic muscle of the city's business elite to overcome grassroots resistance among ordinary white suburbanites. Reflecting this balance of power, "Negro expansion" in Dallas produced as many units of public housing as single-family homes, in contrast to Atlanta, where the ratio favored private homes by a margin of more than two to one.

In both cities, separate suburbanization offered middle-class African Americans the opportunity to indulge residential preferences that they shared with other postwar Americans. Developers built new homes with amenities identical to those being offered to millions of white suburbanites at the time, and they advertised suburban living as a domestic retreat from the city, ideal for children, and replete with every modern convenience. Black middle-class home owners stressed many of the same points. They desired homes of their own complete with modern services and amenities. They wanted well-maintained, even ornamental, residential landscapes with open space, grass, trees and, room for gardens. They hoped that their homes would prove to be sound investments as well as good places to raise children, and, like Americans elsewhere, they wanted to live in neighborhoods with people of a similar background and outlook. In the midcentury South, that meant neighborhoods that were black—as well as middle class. Given the shortage of decent housing within black neighborhoods, some families were willing to risk their property, as well as their lives, by moving into white neighborhoods—this would become increasingly true as urban redevelopment demolished existing black housing in the 1960s — but in the postwar years, most families signaled their preference for black communities, and they bent their efforts to this end.

As part of the larger story of African American history, separate suburbanization illustrates the growing assertiveness of black communities on the eve of the civil rights movement, as well as the persistence of traditional strategies of "home sphere" politics and community building throughout the era. African Americans stepped outside their communities to challenge white supremacy, but they also recognized that black communities were the spatial and social precursors to these initiatives. Struggle to achieve desegregation and to improve black communities, rather than being contradictory impulses, were complementary aspects of the same regional movement for black equality and empowerment.

Chapter 8

Something Old, Something New:

Suburbanization in the Civil Rights Era, 1960–1980

Here I come!
Been saving all my life
To get a nice home
For me and my wife.

> *White folks flee —*
> *As soon as you see*
> *My problems*
> *And me!*

Neighborhood's clean,
But the house is old,
Prices are doubled
When I get sold:
Still I buy.

> *White folks fly —*
> *Soon as you spy*
> *My wife*
> *And I!*

—Langston Hughes, "Little Song on Housing"[1]

IN 1967 artist Norman Rockwell briefly focused a national spotlight on black suburbanization with a cover illustration called "New Kids in the Neighborhood" for the weekly magazine *Look*. The cover depicts a tentative encounter between black and white children on the driveway of a suburban home. In the backdrop, movers unload furnishings from a van. A row of single-family

Fig. 8.1 *New Kids in the Neighborhood.* Norman Rockwell, 1967.
Rockwell's 1967 cover for *Look* magazine captured the challenge that African
American civil rights posed to the nation's white suburbs. (Printed by permission
of the Norman Rockwell Family Agency, copyright 1967, The Norman Rockwell
Family Entities; Collection of the Norman Rockwell Museum of Stockbridge,
Massachusetts, Norman Rockwell Art Collection Trust)

houses, tidy landscaping, and a lemon-yellow convertible are visible up the
block. The scene is quintessential Rockwell, with slightly gangly children
clutching pets and baseball gloves in an all-American setting. Its details —
ribboned pigtails, lacy socks, freckles on a tomboy's cheek — evoke a childly
innocence and the tension between young personalities and their parents'
hand. Yet the subject is also jarringly serious. The black children stand with
their backs to their home, outnumbered and facing strangers. They appear
curious, even eager to meet their new neighbors, but it is not clear whether the
next moment will bring gestures of welcome or insult, or worse.

By freezing the moment just so, Rockwell seems to invite his audience to
consider for themselves, "What will happen next?" Clues to his own opinion
seem evident. The children's similarities in age, interest in pets and baseball,
and their shared social class suggest the artist's faith in their capacity to ignore
differences in complexion. Nonetheless, it was the behavior of adults that
shaped the future of suburbia, and for them, race was more than a matter of
skin color. In the United States of 1967, powerful agents did everything they
could to reserve the newest, most spacious, and economically robust sub-

urban areas for whites only. In the era of the civil rights movement, African American suburbanization reflected an ongoing contest over access to metropolitan space and the privileges of race and class that went with it.

Rockwell's sentimental optimism aside, his illustration signaled a provocative truth. During the 1960s and 1970s, the number of black suburbanites more than doubled. Suburbs added 3.5 million African Americans, and for the first time in the century, African Americans moved to suburbs at a faster rate than whites.[2] In selected metropolitan areas, rates of increase were unparalleled. Outside Washington, D.C., the number of black suburbanites quadrupled, surpassing 400,000 people by 1980, when almost half of black households in the metropolitan area lived in the suburbs. Suburban populations also multiplied around cities such as Cleveland, Newark, St. Louis, Miami, Houston, and Los Angeles. Building on a foundation established by earlier suburbanites, millions of African Americans packed their belongings and moved to the suburbs.[3]

Though the scale of black suburbanization after 1960 was unprecedented, the factors responsible for it showed considerable continuity with the past. Growth in the black middle class expanded the market for a wider range of suburban housing. The civil rights movement emboldened African American families to assert their rights with new vigor, and the passage of protective legislation eased the way for larger numbers to move to suburbs. For many middle-class families, a suburban address symbolized not only the dream of "a decent house in a decent neighborhood," but a firm sense of class and race progress.[4] More than ever, a suburban home represented a stride toward freedom.

The surge in black suburbanization also reflected the culmination of two parallel trends affecting metropolitan areas in the 1960s and 1970s. First, economic currents that had stoked an exodus of industrial jobs from the nation's cities since World War II reached a crescendo. Plant closures and layoffs resulted in long-term unemployment, impoverishment, and simmering frustration in urban neighborhoods. As conditions deteriorated for the black poor and working class, a growing number of middle-class families looked to the suburbs. Second, after 1960 African American neighborhoods in many central cities, which had been expanding since the Great Migration, reached the municipal limits. This was especially true of older cities that had failed to grow through annexation after World War II. Fueled by rising incomes, growing population, and deterioration and demolition at the urban core, black neighborhoods "spilled over" into the surrounding suburban ring.[5]

Even as African Americans suburbanized in growing numbers, white opposition remained a barrier to free settlement. Rockwell's depiction of a peace-

Table 8.1: African American Suburban Population, and Percentage of African Americans in the Suburbs, Selected Metropolitan Areas 1960–1980[a]

Metro Area	1960	% Suburban	1970	% Suburban	1980	% Suburban
Washington	94,581	16%	166,033	24%	404,813	47%
Los Angeles	117,093	26%	240,247	31%	398,020	42%
New York[b]	139,694	11%	217,188	12%	318,775	15%
Philadelphia	142,064	21%	190,509	23%	245,527	28%
Chicago[c]	77,517	9%	128,299	10%	230,826	16%
Newark	90,525	40%	148,050	40%	226,042	54%
Atlanta	79,973	30%	148,050	27%	215,915	43%
St. Louis	81,114	27%	124,834	33%	201,470	49%
Miami	72,086	53%	113,510	60%	193,324	69%
San Francisco–Oakland	68,012	30%	109,319	33%	145,467	37%
Detroit	79,738	14%	100,189	13%	131,593	15%
Baltimore	60,406	16%	69,802	14%	125,721	23%
Cleveland	8,099	3%	44,773	14%	94,299	27%

[a] Totals based on 1980 SMSA boundaries.

[b] Metropolitan area includes Rockland, Westchester, Nassau, and Suffolk Counties.

[c] Metropolitan area includes Cook, DuPage, Kane, Lake, McHenry, and Will Counties, Illinois.

Source: U.S. Census of Population and Housing: 1960, *Census Tracts* (Washington, D.C., 1962); U.S. Census of Population and Housing: 1970, *Census Tracts* (Washington, D.C., 1972), table P-1; U.S. Census of Population and Housing: 1980, *Census Tracts,* Final Report PHC(1), (Washington, D.C., 1983), table P-7.

able suburban moving day belied the reality of hostility and sporadic violence that stalked black efforts to move to the suburbs. In the same year that *Look* published "New Kids in the Neighborhood," suburban terrorists tossed pipe bombs into black-owned homes in integrating neighborhoods, police and fair-housing demonstrators clashed in a dozen cities, and hundreds of people were arrested or mobbed during open-housing protests. Rather than uprooting inequality in suburban housing, the passage of fair-housing legislation stoked renewed white resistance.[6] Real estate brokers, lenders, and suburban officials devised new ways to discriminate, and politicians such as California's governor Ronald Reagan led a racist backlash, declaring that laws prohibiting racial discrimination in housing violated a "basic human right."[7] Armed with new tools, resources, and resolve, African Americans elbowed their way into the suburbs, yet whites on the whole met every advance with fierce opposition.

For all these reasons, the 1960s marked a new chapter in a continuing struggle over race and metropolitan space. Black suburbanites won access to better housing, schools, and amenities, yet the period saw little change in the process of cumulative and contested residential expansion that had characterized black suburbanization since the beginning of the century.[8] Whether growth occurred through new construction or racial transition in existing neighborhoods, suburbanization tended to reinforce patterns of spatial segregation. One result was the emergence of what the National Committee Against Discrimination in Housing described as "suburban black belts."[9] "Without heroic effort and more than a bit of luck," *New York Times* reporter Clarence Dean observed in 1961, black suburbanites were "obliged to live in the Negro quarter or on the fringes of it."[10]

Equally apparent was the continuing racialization of suburban areas where black families moved. Although many suburbanites appreciated the comfort and security of mostly black neighborhoods, most of them settled in places that were older and more expensive to maintain than the outlying sections where many white suburbanites were moving. As African Americans arrived, whites often moved away, and the marketability of these areas to others declined. In perceptual and practical terms, new neighborhoods shifted into the domain of the black housing market. Most black suburbanites paid higher property taxes than whites, and they fought ongoing battles with redlining, commercial flight, service reductions, poor school performance, and socioeconomic decline. All told, African American suburbanites achieved real gains in housing, education, and community services, but these were frequently shadowed by compromised expectations and the perpetuation of racial inequality in space.[11] If the migration represented "a harbinger of a new era of black suburbanization," demographer Karl Taeuber wrote in 1975, "it is obvious that the old era will be with us for a long time."[12]

The New Suburbanites

The leading edge of the suburban migration between 1960 and 1980 remained solidly middle class. Working-class and poor families continued moving to the suburbs, but the greatest number of newcomers were "younger, more affluent, and better educated" than existing suburbanites or the average central city resident.[13] Joining the pioneers of the 1950s, this cohort re-made the socioeconomic composition of black suburbia. By the mid-1960s, for the first time suburbanites surpassed city dwellers in income, education, and occupational achievement. In class terms, African American suburbanites evinced national norms, rising in economic status with their distance from the central city.[14]

Suburbanites' improved economic circumstances were apparent in the diversity of places to which they moved. In addition to the varied working-class communities where African Americans had congregated since the Great Migration, the fastest-growing black suburbs of the 1960s and 1970s were diverse in age, size, housing stock, and socioeconomic composition. In Chillum, Maryland, an unincorporated area adjoining Washington, D.C., black families bought tidy brick homes typical of postwar housing in outlying neighborhoods of the city and its suburbs. In East Cleveland, Ohio, thousands bought or rented "artistic" Victorian houses and boxy two-flats with deep front porches that had been built before widespread availability of the automobile.[15] In Opa-locka, Florida, African Americans moved to a neighborhood of whimsical "Arabian" bungalows built during the real estate bubble of the 1920s. By contrast, upwardly mobile blacks in bougainvillea-draped San Diego bought new homes in subdivisions that stretched eastward from the core to the sage-topped margins of the city. Across the South, too, new construction remained an essential part of suburban growth. In Atlanta, Miami, and Washington, D.C., as well as smaller cities such as Charlotte and Shreveport, southern suburbanites purchased brick- and aluminum-clad ranch homes, town houses, and custom-built residences in the developing suburban fringe.[16]

Another attribute of the new suburbanization was a growing migration to suburbs where few African Americans had ever lived, signaling for some the possibilities of racial integration and a radical overhaul of the way Americans lived. Following decades during which growth had been confined largely to suburbs with established black communities, African Americans entered scores of formerly white communities. By 1970 as many as a quarter of black suburbanites lived in areas that were less than 15 percent black.[17] In many cases, this statistic reflected a passing moment in a process of racial turnover, but in other suburbs, integration endured. In Denver and Phoenix, cities with small African American populations, more than half of black suburbanites settled in suburbs that were at least 90 percent white, and by 1980 in Denver, there was no suburban neighborhood in which African Americans comprised more than a quarter of the population.[18] In a select number of suburbs in the

Fig. 8.2   Houses in Chillum, Maryland, near the District of Columbia, 1988.
Inner-ring suburbs were among the main targets of African American suburbanites
after 1960 as whites fled and black households settled in neighborhoods adjacent
to black communities along the city limits. (Photograph by Andrew Wiese)

Northeast and Midwest, too, white suburbanites stirred by a commitment
to racial liberalism and compelled by concern for their property values made
special efforts to retain integration. Teaneck, New Jersey; Oak Park, Illinois;
and Shaker Heights, Ohio, responded to the arrival of African American families by crafting mechanisms to resist resegregation. With mixed success, these
places became leaders in a fleeting movement for managed racial integration.[19]

Despite these new wrinkles, African American suburbanization remained
a geographically conservative process embedded in a stubbornly segregated
housing market. Of the two dozen fastest-growing black suburbs in the
1960s, three-quarters were home or adjacent to an older African American
community.[20] The most striking reflection of this pattern was the emergence
of several dozen new black-majority suburbs. In Los Angeles, journalist Earl
Caldwell observed, "blacks came spilling out of south central L.A. . . . following their white counterparts to suburbia."[21] More than 80,000 settled in
the suburbs of Compton and Inglewood, which boasted street upon street of
modest postwar ranch homes. A continent away, the aging suburb of East
Orange, New Jersey, added 45,000.[22] Other black suburban boomtowns,

Fig. 8.3 Single- and two-family houses in East Cleveland, Ohio, 1988. An early commuter suburb of Cleveland, East Cleveland became one of the fastest-growing black suburbs in the nation during the 1960s. Twenty-three thousand African Americans replaced 21,000 whites in a convulsive cycle of blockbusting, white flight, and resegregation. (Photograph by Andrew Wiese)

Fig. 8.4   Developed during the 1920s, Opa-locka, Florida, was one of several dozen
suburbs that gained a black majority during the 1960s. Its fantasy Arabian style
suggests the diversity of the new black suburbia. (Courtesy of John Archer, 2000)

such as Warrensville Heights, Ohio; Wellston, Missouri; Harvey, Illinois;
East Palo Alto, California; Suitland, Maryland; and Roosevelt, New York,
also witnessed wholesale replacement of whites by African American households. "Places that contained fewer than 100 blacks in 1960," wrote black
studies scholar Harold Connolly, "quite suddenly became the place of residence for several thousand Negroes by 1970. In some instances, as a result of
doubling, tripling, or even more rapidly multiplying black numbers, Negroes
formed a majority of the population in 1970."[23] By 1980 more than a million
people — 18 percent of all black suburbanites — lived in 112 majority-black
suburbs. In a number of larger cities, however, as many as half of black suburbanites lived in mostly black suburbs.[24] More than any other feature, the
emergence of these new black suburbs symbolized the continuing spatial significance of race despite rapid gains in suburbanization and civil rights.

The New Black Middle Class

The most important factor responsible for the surge in suburbanization was
economic. During the 1960s, national economic prosperity fueled impressive

economic gains for black households.[25] For the first time in the century, black families began to close the economic chasm between themselves and the white majority. The median income among black households increased 55 percent for the decade, climbing from 54 to 61 percent of the white median and reaching 72 percent in two-parent households.[26] Economic recession and the erosion of central city manufacturing stalled this trend during the 1970s, but the short burst of economic advancement opened the way for as many as a third of black families to attain a fragile middle-class position.

Concurrent with gains in family income, the number of African Americans holding white-collar jobs grew rapidly. The proportion of white-collar workers jumped from 13 to 25 percent during the 1960s. By 1980 the number of professional and managerial workers had tripled, and the number of black sales and clerical workers, approximately half of whom were women, quintupled. Helping to secure occupational improvements, the number of black college students almost doubled from 522,000 to more than 1 million between 1970 and 1980. Moreover, employees in professional, technical, and managerial occupations experienced the greatest relative gain in earnings compared to whites.[27] The result, in the view of sociologist Bart Landry, was the emergence a "new black middle class," a group distinguished from earlier middle-class cohorts by the racial climate in which formal markers of segregation had begun to fall and by the improved economic circumstances that allowed a greater number of black men and women to attain middle-class standing and pass it on to their children.[28] As in the 1940s and 1950s, many families expressed their sense of status through their desires for better housing, educational opportunities, public services, and neighborhood amenities, all of which had long been associated with the suburbs.

Gains in black family income also reflected expanded economic opportunities for black women, who remained far more likely than white women to hold a paid occupation. Reflecting the fragility of African American economic standing, more than half of African American middle-class families relied on at least two wage-earning adults compared to approximately 30 percent among whites. Paid labor by black women proved essential to the growth of the black middle class.[29]

Prosperity alone did not explain the rise in African Americans' economic fortunes or their migration to suburbia; rather, financial improvement was as much a political as an economic process. Bart Landry points out that it was the "simultaneous occurrence of prosperity *and* civil rights [that] created the necessary conditions for a new black middle class."[30] Specifically, federal civil rights legislation of 1964 and 1965 proscribed discrimination in public accommodations, employment, and voting. Combined with state proscriptions and affirmative programs designed to improve blacks' economic status, federal legislation helped to reduce barriers that had confined all but a few African American workers to low-skilled blue-collar employment since the turn of the century. Legal guarantees did not redraw the map of discrimination nor erase the concentration of black workers in poorly paid job categories, but African Americans were able to seek work on a more equitable basis than ever before.

"The Negro Revolution"

Just as civil rights legislation in employment served as a springboard for black economic progress, the struggle for civil rights in housing combined with direct protest in suburbs themselves to facilitate black suburbanization after 1960.[31] Driven by the mass mobilization for equality that swept the country after the student sit-ins of 1960, African Americans and a smaller number of white sympathizers mounted what the *New York Times* billed as "aggressive" and "militant" protests against discrimination in the suburbs and the housing market at large.[32] According to journalist Milton Bracker, writing in 1962, "Challenges have already jolted communities where a generation ago, the employer-servant relationship between white and Negro seemed as simple as the fact that a house had both a front door and a back door."[33] Activists organized marches, petition drives, sit-ins, school boycotts, and other forms of nonviolent direct action, and they combined these with an assault in the courts and legislative assemblies that eventually overturned the legal underpinnings of suburban racial discrimination. By the early 1960s, black suburbanites themselves indicated, the days of front door/back door were over for good. The nature and permeability of the new color line, however, would remain a matter of lasting dispute.

Heightened "rank and file involvement" in suburban civil rights demonstrations was especially evident in metropolitan New York, where civil rights groups and residents in more than a dozen suburbs challenged housing discrimination, urban renewal planning, police brutality, and "racial imbalance" in the local schools.[34] In Englewood, New Jersey, a group of residents including World War II veterans, younger clergy, and students established the Englewood Movement in 1962, responding to what the group called "frustrations so deep that one almost has to be black to understand it."[35] Long-standing housing bias had confined African Americans to one predominantly black neighborhood near the center of town. By 1960 enrollment at the

Lincoln Elementary School, which served the area, was 98 percent black. The Englewood Movement shook up the suburb's conservative black clergy as well as its white elite by inviting Malcolm X to address a protest rally in August 1962. Spokesman Paul Zuber, a New York attorney who had won a landmark school segregation case in suburban New Rochelle, New York, in 1961, called for a boycott against local merchants, threatening to "turn this town into an Albany, Georgia," the scene of recent protests in the South, if white leaders did not eliminate de facto segregation in the local schools.[36]

In other suburbs, too, the southern uprising presented an opportunity for activists to build momentum for local change. In Evanston, Illinois, 1,000 people marched in July 1963 to protest the murder of Mississippi NAACP leader Medgar Evers. Addressing an interracial crowd of residents and Northwestern University students, the Reverend Maurice Higgenbotham, pastor of Ebenezer Baptist Church, which was Evanston's largest black congregation, condemned not only the tragedy in Mississippi but the "impenetrable wall of gentlemen's agreements" that prevented blacks from living or moving freely in the suburb.[37] In the context of the southern movement, leaders like Higgenbotham encouraged suburbanites to interpret and act on the freedom struggle in local terms.

Among the most dynamic organizations in the suburban civil rights campaign was the Congress of Racial Equality (CORE). Following the explosive Freedom Rides across the South, which the organization sponsored in 1961, CORE president James Farmer called on the group's nonsouthern members to take the struggle for equality home to their own communities.[38] In 1962 northern and western affiliates opened a campaign against housing discrimination called Operation Windowshop in which they encouraged black volunteers to fan out into real estate offices and housing developments to force discrimination into public view.[39] Adopting the more provocative tactics of the southern student movement, members of the Los Angeles branch launched a "thirty-three-day sit-in" in March 1962 at a housing tract in suburban Monterey Park, where the developer had refused to sell a home to a black couple.[40] Demonstrations such as these enhanced both visibility and support for the campaign against housing discrimination. By the time crowds assembled for the March on Washington in August 1963, CORE activists had attacked bias in dozens of suburbs across the country. Near Detroit, for instance, activists sponsored marches in a number of suburbs notorious for antiblack hostility.[41] In Bowie, Maryland, CORE helped orchestrate a test case to uncover federal complicity in suburban discrimination. After the builder William Levitt refused to sell homes at his Belair development to a black economist and a scientist with the Food and Drug Administration, CORE assisted the men and their families in lobbying the Federal Housing Administration to suspend aid to the developer under a new executive order that barred discrimination in publicly assisted housing. When the agency refused to intervene, CORE organized a sit-in at the project to maintain public pressure on both organizations.[42]

The summer's protests reached a climax in Los Angeles, where CORE led a series of highly publicized demonstrations in the suburb of Torrance designed to coincide with debate in the state capital over a controversial state fair-housing bill. During July and August 1963, crowds of up to 1,000 singing, sign-waving demonstrators picketed the "lily white" Southwood Riviera subdivision, demanding that the developer, Don Wilson, sell a $30,000 home to a black professional couple whose application he had refused. In addition, CORE called on the builder to hire black salespeople, advertise in the black press, and "publicly affirm" a policy of nondiscrimination.[43] In response, the all-white Torrance city council enacted an anti-picketing ordinance and ordered police to arrest violators. Subsequent protests produced more than two hundred arrests before CORE withdrew and refocused its attention elsewhere without having achieved a satisfactory settlement.[44] In Sacramento, pressure had paid off in the form of a new state fair-housing law, but in Torrance and other locations, local whites proved dogged adversaries, forcing civil rights proponents to wage long and exhausting struggles for even modest victories. By the early 1960s, however, these campaigns signaled that even all-white suburbs were not exempt from the demand for racial equality that was sweeping the nation.

In conjunction with direct action at the local level, civil rights organizations including CORE maintained pressure on federal and state governments, much as they had since the late 1940s. During the 1960 presidential campaign, candidate John F. Kennedy had promised civil rights supporters that if elected he would wipe out discrimination in all federally assisted housing with "one stroke of the pen."[45] After waiting more than a year for the pen stroke, activists such as James Farmer concluded that "the President's pen must have run dry."[46] Through the newsletters and publications of its affiliate organizations, the National Committee Against Discrimination in Housing coordinated an "Ink for Jack" campaign, flooding the White House with thousands of ballpoint pens. Under growing pressure from the pro–civil rights wing of his party, Kennedy issued Executive Order 11063 in November 1962—safely after midterm congressional elections—instructing federal agencies such as the FHA and Veterans Administration to "take all action necessary and appro-

priate to prevent discrimination" in the sale or rental of federally assisted housing.[47] Although the order covered less than 20 percent of the new housing
stock — principally homes backed by FHA and VA mortgage insurance, public
housing, and housing constructed in urban renewal areas — it represented the
strongest statement of federal support for equal access to housing since the
Reconstruction era.[48] Furthermore, with each incremental step, state action
established the principle that housing discrimination was wrong, and it laid
the groundwork for the enactment of this principle as national law.

More important than executive action, fair-housing proponents lobbied
for the passage of legislation barring discrimination in housing. Building on
municipal victories in the early 1950s, advocates pressed for open-occupancy
legislation at the state level. By 1959 fourteen states — all of them outside the
South — had passed legislation barring discrimination in some segment of
the housing market — usually the small part comprised by public housing
and urban renewal projects.[49] Four states with small minority populations —
Washington, Oregon, Colorado, and Massachusetts — had enacted anti-bias
legislation covering some portion of the private market as well. As grassroots
pressure mounted after 1960, however, civil rights advocates won important
legislative victories in states where large numbers of African Americans lived.
Beginning with New York, where a coalition of labor and liberal groups
based in New York City supplied the legislative muscle needed to overcome
upstate opposition in 1961, Pennsylvania, California, and Connecticut enacted legislation banning discrimination across large segments of the private
housing market. Several states and municipalities also moved to forestall
panic real estate speculation in integrating neighborhoods by enacting bans
against "for sale" signs, uninvited real estate solicitations, and "blockbusting,"
a multifarious activity in which speculators used the threat that blacks had
moved or would move to a neighborhood as a means of persuading white
property owners to sell at a loss.[50]

The legislative campaign for open housing reached its peak with the
passage of the national Civil Rights Act of 1968, better known as the Fair
Housing Act. Momentum for the legislation grew during consecutive summers of urban unrest in the mid-1960s and growing concern among liberals
over the corrosive effects of racial segregation in the nation's cities and suburbs. After several failed attempts, a bipartisan coalition of northern legislators
introduced a bill in Congress "to protect the freedom of individuals to choose
where they wished to live."[51] In the Senate, a fair-housing bill sponsored by
Democrats Walter Mondale of Minnesota and Edward Brooke of Massachusetts — the Senate's only African American member — overcame the threat of a

filibuster by southern Democrats and passed the chamber in March. Opponents in the House promised a more determined struggle; however, the assassination of Martin Luther King Jr. in Memphis on April 4 marked the turning point. In the days of grief and outrage that followed, rioting erupted in 130 cities, including Washington, D.C., where representatives debated the bill with helmeted troops protecting the Capitol and smoke from burning neighborhoods billowing overhead. In less than a week, Congress passed the last major piece of civil rights legislation of the 1960s and sent it to President Johnson, who signed the legislation on April 11, 1968.[52]

The Fair Housing Act prohibited "discrimination based on race, color, religion, sex, and national origin in the sale or rental of housing," including among proscribed activities blockbusting, real estate steering, and redlining.[53] Bowing to pressure from moderate legislators, the bill exempted rental units in owner-occupied housing; nonetheless, it represented the most sweeping statement in support of equality in housing to date.

Two months later, the Supreme Court ratified and expanded the principle with its decision in the case of *Jones v. Mayer*. Responding to a petition from the plaintiffs, a black couple that was refused a home in suburban St. Louis, the Court ruled that a long-dormant Reconstruction-era statute, the Civil Rights Act of 1866, guaranteed that "all citizens shall have the same right . . . to purchase real property." Discrimination in housing, the Court held, represented "a relic of slavery."[54] Even more comprehensive than the Fair Housing Act itself, *Jones* outlawed racial discrimination in housing across 100 percent of the housing market. By the middle of 1968, the legal foundations for racial discrimination in housing, which had sustained residential segregation since the beginning of the century, had been swept away.

While these decisions represented the high-water mark for the fair-housing movement in the United States, the law proved slow to alter established practices in the real estate industry or the separate and unequal housing markets they helped to sustain.[55] Part of the problem stemmed from the Fair Housing Act itself, which, the U.S. Commission on Civil Rights opined, lacked "effective enforcement mechanisms."[56] In order to attract majority support in the Congress, sponsors had designed the statute with few teeth. Thus, while the U.S. Justice Department could bring suit where they became aware of a significant "pattern or practice of housing discrimination," the legislation conveyed no affirmative duty to investigate real estate practices nor did it provide funding to support such an effort. With the inauguration of Richard Nixon in 1969, who rode to victory on a "Southern strategy" of appealing to southern and suburban whites who were disenchanted with the Democrats' support for civil rights, federal enforcement of the housing act was a low priority. Instead, the victims of housing discrimination were forced to bear the costs of investigation and prosecution by bringing suit in federal or state court. "Rather than falling barriers everywhere at once," the urban policy analyst Robert Lake pointed out, "the path to non-discrimination [was] pursued slowly on a case by case basis."[57] Sociologists Douglas Massey and Nancy Denton took an even dimmer view. In their opinion, the act was "intentionally designed so that it would not and could not work."[58]

These appraisals aside, it is clear that fair-housing legislation bolstered black suburbanization by supporting African Americans' own efforts to gain better housing. Like earlier civil rights initiatives, it also reinforced the bond between individual choices and the rights of African Americans at large, imbuing housing mobility with a racial purpose. By redefining the rights of citizens in the housing market, fair-housing legislation encouraged African Americans to assert their right to live "wherever housing is available that they could afford."[59]

Suburbanites themselves were quick to make these connections. For Larman Williams, a school principal in suburban St. Louis, moving to a "lovely house" in a safe suburban neighborhood reflected his belief that he had the right to live "like any other citizen."[60] Other families described moving to the suburbs as a "challenge" to be met or as "a political statement in support of civil rights."[61] Some underscored the political implication of housing choice by using the "threat of a public hearing" or civil complaint as a means of overcoming the resistance of developers or landlords.[62] Irving Winter, an engineer at Brookhaven National Laboratory on Long Island, asserted a clear connection between mobility in housing and the struggle for civil rights in 1965. "If the Negro doesn't take advantage of the laws and opportunities afforded him now," Winter argued, "even the good [areas to live] will be lost to him and the hateful [areas] will never change."[63] In an era marked by the mass movement for black equality, African Americans remained "fiercely determined," said one fair-housing organization, "to have for [their] famil[ies], the cultural, educational, and social advantages available to [their] white counterparts."[64] For families like these, suburbanization was an act of resistance to racial inequality, and the passage of fair-housing legislation reinforced their capacity to assert their rights.

Despite its shortcomings, fair-housing legislation also offered a weapon with which to assail routine practices in the real estate industry. With legal authority provided by the law, nonprofit groups took up the job of government and attacked housing discrimination through routine testing and litigation, a point encapsulated by the slogan "Sue the bastards," adopted by the pro-integration group National Neighbors in the early 1970s.[65] Despite cumbersome enforcement and halfhearted federal support, open-housing laws curtailed the most routine forms of housing discrimination and forced Realtors, builders, and lenders to modify their behavior, if not their opinions. Over the next two decades, many state and municipal governments institutionalized fair-housing enforcement by creating civil rights divisions with the power to investigate, mediate, and litigate complaints of racial bias in housing. One case at a time, fair-housing proponents battled to remake the suburban housing market just as fervently as white suburbanites labored to stop them.

White Resistance

The chief stumbling block to black suburbanization after 1960 was the entrenched resistance of white home owners and real estate professionals, who met each new turn with creative determination. African American suburbanization in the 1960s and 1970s remained an intensive struggle between black families seeking to exercise their rights and white suburbanites intent on defending what they saw as theirs. Given whites' superiority in numbers and resources, they won more often than they lost, yet the outcomes were not ones that most would have planned nor foreseen; instead, black migration to the suburbs followed paths determined through an ongoing confrontation between insistent adversaries.

Despite the groundswell in support of fair housing, white suburbanites and real estate organizations mounted a counterattack meant to preserve the racial status quo. In California, passage of the Rumford Fair Housing Act in 1963 provoked an immediate white backlash. The California Real Estate Association, the state's whites-only organization of real estate brokers, led the drive for a ballot initiative, Proposition 14, to amend the state constitution to protect the "right" of Californians to "sell, lease, or rent" housing to whomever they chose.[66] Backers portrayed the issue as a contest between "property owners' rights" and what they called "forced housing," but in plain language they sought to defend racial discrimination by writing it into the state constitution.[67] In the guise of "safeguard[ing] the rights of the people of California," proponents of "Prop. 14" maintained that the right of white property owners to discriminate on the basis of race represented a greater public good than the right of all citizens to purchase or rent a home where they could afford it. With support from the Catholic Archdiocese of Southern California and conservative groups throughout the state, the Realtors association cultivated a sense of white victimization that foreshadowed the backlash against liberalism that would propel the Republicans to repeated national electoral victories after 1968.[68] In November 1964 California voters supported the initiative by a two-to-one margin. Eventually, the state supreme court nullified "Prop. 14" on the grounds that it violated the state constitution, but real estate representatives in other states, emboldened by its passage, fought to block fair-housing statutes across the country, and white home owners dug in their heels to prevent residential integration of almost any kind.[69]

Opposition at the ballot box was matched if not exceeded by intransigence in the housing market itself. Notwithstanding state and federal rulings, real estate agents, home builders, and lenders demonstrated extraordinary flexibility in obstructing black access to the housing market. As the *New York Times* put it, they simply "found other ways to discriminate against the Negro buyer."[70] Throughout the 1960s, housing tests, in which matched pairs of black and white couples visited real estate offices and compared their treatment for evidence of racial bias, discovered unwavering "anti-Negro bias on the part of builders and real estate brokers."[71] Tests in suburban New York in 1962, a year after passage of the state's landmark fair-housing law, found that black testers sent to forty-two Long Island suburbs "were rebuffed in all areas," while white testers who visited the same offices "encountered no trouble." Tactics meant to impair blacks included "requests for excessive down payments, inability to show the house at that particular time, statements that the house was already sold and suggestions that it would be impossible to find a mortgage."[72]

Home seekers themselves reported similar treatment. One fair-housing survey in suburban Philadelphia in the mid-1960s found that black professional couples encountered "crude" and "consistent" opposition in the housing market "practically independent of [their] financial status."[73] Discriminatory practices ranged from "outright refusal[s] to sell" or show them housing to more "devious tactics" such as the "removal from [the] market of [a] house selected for purchase," "dummy or bogus bills of sale for properties listed . . . erection of sold signs on properties not sold and being sold to white home seekers," and other "tricks . . . like keys not being available at designated times [and] incomplete service in making arrangements to see houses."[74] As a result, the survey reported, even well-educated and affluent black families faced a choice between "sub-adequate housing" in "traditional Negro areas" or "degrading, frustrating, and often unsuccessful searches" for housing in neighborhoods that were otherwise easily available to whites.[75] By the mid-1960s, federal official turned housing activist Frank Horne concluded that "racial restriction in housing . . . stands like a rock, unmoved by the swirling maelstrom of the current civil rights upsurge." Housing discrimination, he said, remained "the last practically unbreached barrier to first-class citizenship."[76]

Despite the passage of federal and state legislation, housing discrimination continued unabated during the 1970s. Instead of open bias, though, African Americans met increasingly subtle and sophisticated resistance.[77] Throughout the 1970s, real estate professionals brushed off black applicants with plausible lies: "The property has been sold"; "The rent is higher"; "The landlord doesn't allow children"; "We can't meet at that time"—only rarely were they told that Negroes were not welcome. Without matched tests, in fact, many home seekers never even realized that they had been victimized. The complexity of buying property, especially, merely facilitated discriminatory intentions. As social scientist Donald Foley pointed out, "Every routine act, every bit of ritual in the sale or rental of a dwelling unit can be performed in a way calculated to make it either difficult or impossible to consummate a deal."[78] Nationwide housing audits in 1979 and 1984 indicated that real estate personnel were well aware of the fact. Overt expressions of racism had declined, but the likelihood that blacks would confront discrimination in any visit to a real estate agent or landlord ranged from 25 to 50 percent.[79] Regardless of region and despite state and federal legislation, African Americans faced persistent discrimination by real estate agents, landlords, lenders, and ordinary suburbanites throughout the 1960s and '70s.

An equally serious obstacle to black suburbanization was exclusion by suburban municipalities themselves. Even as state and federal governments faced growing pressure to countermand racial discrimination in housing, local municipalities wielded extensive power to exclude or even expel nonwhites through apparently nonracial means. "Like country clubs screening new membership applications," social scientist Bernard Frieden wrote, suburban governments restricted access by working-class and poor families.[80] Local land-use regulations were an especially potent tool. As early as 1962, the Regional Plan Association of New York reported that "two-thirds of all vacant land zoned for residence" in the metropolitan area was "zoned for half acre lots or larger."[81] During the 1960s and 1970s, however, so-called "snob zoning" increased. In New Jersey, the quintessential suburban state, more than 150 municipalities "amended their zoning ordinances to increase required minimum lot sizes" between 1960 and 1967.[82] Other areas witnessed similar trends; in the newest and most distant suburban areas, the wealthiest Americans created a vast green landscape open only to people like themselves. From

Chagrin Falls Township and Hunting Valley, Ohio, with their horse farms and five-acre-lot minimums, to the hunt country of Middlesex County, New Jersey, or the eucalyptus groves of Rancho Santa Fe, California, zoning was an invisible rampart that maintained artificially high housing costs, blocked the construction of affordable housing, and limited the access of moderate- and low-income families in perpetuity.

Reflecting the white and increasingly suburban composition of their members, U.S. courts and state legislatures remained largely supportive of municipal efforts to restrict residence on the basis of class. In a series of rulings during the 1970s, the Supreme Court drew a bright line between discrimination based on race and class, rejecting the former and upholding the latter.[83] In zoning, the landmark case emerged from a dispute over the construction of apartments in Arlington Heights, Illinois, a suburb of Chicago. In 1977 the Supreme Court ruled that Arlington Heights' refusal to rezone land for a church-sponsored apartment development was legitimate, despite its potentially discriminatory effects. Only those regulations clearly designed "with racially discriminatory intent," the Court held, violated the Constitution.[84] The case represented a blow to the suburban aspirations of working- and lower-middle-class families, and it provided constitutional support for the stratification of metropolitan areas into enclaves of privilege and poverty. It represented a blow to racial desegregation efforts as well. Because of their economic position, African Americans were disproportionately affected by class-based zoning. In addition, as a federal appeals court warned, legal reliance on racist intent provided ample cover for race bias since "clever men may easily conceal their motivation."[85] By the late 1970s, race had largely evaporated from the rhetoric of exclusion. Instead, suburban racists concealed their intentions in the circumspect language of property values, historic preservation, environmental protection, or slow growth.[86] Hence, while fair-housing advocates fought discrimination one case at a time, white suburbs, with the support of the U.S. judiciary, reinforced exclusion on a wholesale basis, erecting economic barricades that substantially prevented African Americans from moving to hundreds of suburbs.[87]

Despite the veil of racial neutrality, race was rarely far beneath the surface of suburban regulations. In St. Louis County, Missouri, white suburbanites followed a tested recipe. When developers proposed to build a racially integrated apartment complex in Spanish Lake Township in 1970, residents hastily incorporated as the suburb of Black Jack. Within days the new government posted notice of a proposed zoning ordinance prohibiting multifamily housing, enacting it a month later.[88] The developer brought suit under the Fair

Housing Act, and a U.S. Appeals Court ultimately ruled that Black Jack had violated federal law by "exercis[ing] its zoning powers in a racially discriminatory manner."[89] More often, however, local decisions went undisputed, or after 1977 they were resolved in favor of the municipalities. State judges, many of whom had risen through the ranks of suburban government or the politics of white resistance, turned a blind eye to the racist effect of purportedly race-neutral policies. The realities of private enterprise worked against militancy among builders as well. Few construction firms had the resources or resolve to fight officials in one municipality that might jeopardize their ability to build in others. In this context, exclusionary zoning and land-use policy remained an effective barrier to suburbanization by families with low and moderate incomes, as well as the great majority of middle-class African Americans who could not afford the large lots and grandiose homes mandated by law in most outlying suburbs. As in the early postwar years, suburban land-use policies sharply limited the area in every metropolitan region where most African American families could live.

One additional obstacle to black suburbanization was the extralegal opposition of white suburbanites themselves. No less than in earlier decades, institutional and official discrimination was backed by the threat of violence and harassment at the grassroots level. Arson, vandalism, and house bombings remained common enough to deter most black families from venturing into the white unknown.[90] One black suburbanite joked in 1965 that he felt free to buy a house in "any section of Long Island's white suburbia. . . . The problem would be in getting a truck big enough to take it away."[91] Incidents of harassment ranging from broken windows, hate mail, and social ostracism to verbal and physical attacks on children, death threats, and other "unpleasant experiences" greeted racial pioneers throughout the period.[92] Where the deftly crafted barriers designed in suburban council chambers and planning departments proved insufficient, white suburbanites met African Americans' attempts to share in the "American way" with force.[93] Whether their weapon was a zoning map or a firebomb, they refused to surrender the privileges of whiteness without a fight.

Even where such measures failed, whites retained a final option that ensured the future of racial segregation and the stratification of metropolitan space. As African Americans began arriving in the suburbs in large numbers, millions of whites exercised residential choices of their own, moving away or avoiding areas where blacks had settled. Unlike African Americans, who consistently expressed preferences for racially balanced neighborhoods, most whites expressed intolerance for even modest levels of racial integration. Despite two decades of civil rights protest, national opinion surveys in the late 1970s revealed that more than a quarter of whites were unwilling to move to neighborhoods in which as few as 8 percent of residents were black. Half said they would not move to a neighborhood in which one resident in five was African American.[94] As the builder William Levitt had argued in the late 1950s, "the plain fact" was that "most whites prefer[red] not to live in mixed communities."[95] Coupled with sharply circumscribed housing demand among African Americans and routine racial steering by real estate brokers, both reactions—flight and avoidance—almost guaranteed that vacancies left by whites in areas where African Americans were moving would be filled by other blacks.[96]

Moving to the Suburbs

While social scientists have often described recent migration to the suburbs in a language of statistics or social models, suburbanization represented the sum of numberless African American decisions inflected by diverse residential preferences, financial concerns, personal circumstances, and perceptions of opportunity.[97] With a growing body of law on their side, black families pressed their rights to share in the apparent benefits of suburban life. Whether they sought to "break up the new territory" as pioneers, to secure a "safe place for our boys to play," or to find a "quiet residential neighborhood with good schools and good neighbors and the many other things that make for comfortable living," African Americans fought for access to suburban places that had previously been reserved for whites.[98]

At one level, thousands of families moved to suburbs to escape the compounding spatial disadvantages of black neighborhoods in the city, where, one suburbanite summarized, "the schools and public services were poor and . . . in the larger food chains you would find mold hidden under the extra label on the cheese."[99] For Leo and Janice Eaton, who moved to Menomonee Falls, Wisconsin, from Milwaukee in 1971, a combination of factors clinched their decision to leave the city: "The kids were doing all right at school, but we'd seen a lot of things happening, crime started to escalate and everyone had a tendency to want to get away from it, both black and white. We wanted to get away from the hustle-bustle, the unexpected visits."[100] For Larman and Geraldine Williams, who left St. Louis in 1968, crime was also a signal issue. Mr. Williams explained:

Mainly where we were, we were dissatisfied with the facilities, we were dissatisfied with the clientele in and around the block. There was high crime in the area, in the neighborhood and on the block, there were attacks on neighbors. One lady across the street was hit on the head with a hatchet, robbed, murdered. Down the street from me on the left a lady was raped and was found the next morning in the nude. . . . My child was chased from school through an alley by someone, some man who was trying to seduce her. And for all those reasons I just was afraid to come home to find my family maybe dead or my child raped or just afraid.[101]

Under circumstances such as these, and many that were less severe, black families hoped for something better in the suburbs. Suburbanites' residential tastes varied, of course. Hazel Dukes, who was one of thousands of black New Yorkers who moved to Roosevelt, Long Island, in the late 1960s, believed that her neighbors "wanted backyards and front yards, they wanted a garage for themselves, they wanted comfortable spaces. They didn't want apartments, they wanted houses."[102] Some suburbanites envisioned "a green manicured lawn and a modern house with push-button facilities," places that matched their image of success and supported a "lifestyle that justifies a reason for going to work every day"; others aspired to landscapes marked by "highly individual, well-kept old houses, and . . . huge trees."[103]

However they imagined the setting, like their predecessors in the 1950s, most sought to improve their social and economic situation by moving through space. They sought not merely new physical surroundings, but places with spatial advantages that compounded in their favor instead of working against them, advantages like "new schools of the latest construction," well-paid teachers, safe streets, top-notch services, and robust property values.[104] Larman Williams explained, "I wanted to locate in an area where I could get the best facilities for the amount of money that we were paying, and fire services and police protection, where the crime rate was low, like any other citizen would want."[105] Harlem businessman Percy Sutton highlighted similar spatial motives, speaking to the U.S. Commission on Civil Rights in 1971: "Black people, just as white people," he said, "seek to live wherever their job opportunities are, to live . . . where educational opportunities are, so they are seeking to move into the suburbs."[106] Like Sutton, many people thought that they could do better by staying in the city, but a growing number believed that their future was in the suburbs.

A Matter of Dignity

Emblematic of the aspirations and exertions of many new suburbanites was Theodore W. "Ted" Wheeler, who moved with his family to the mostly white Chicago suburb of Oak Park, Illinois, in 1964. A native of Rossville, Georgia, a graduate of the University of Iowa, a veteran of the Korean War, and a member of the 1956 Olympic team, Wheeler's biography exemplifies the kind of personal striving that marked the careers of many members of the new middle class. Wheeler not only had a long acquaintance with white racism but also with predominantly white institutions and their uses—both for good and ill. As one of the first African Americans to compete nationally as a distance runner, Wheeler had been jeered by white crowds at track meets throughout the United States, but he had also had "firsthand positive relations" with white people, starting with a Quaker family that had employed his parents in Georgia when he was a child. Like many suburban pioneers in the 1960s, Wheeler was an integrationist with a firm belief in the power of interracial experiences to produce better citizens and a better society.[107]

Ironically, Wheeler's faith in integration stemmed in part from his own experience in a segregated but multiracial suburb. After leaving the South as a teenager in the late 1940s, he ended up in Evanston, Illinois, which was a move that changed his life. Coming from "a ghetto that was in Lafayette, Georgia, that had a one-room schoolhouse for blacks," Wheeler said, "I came . . . into an ideal place, Evanston. . . . I was there two years and was able to ascertain why people were very successful." Despite Evanston's "restricted housing patterns," Wheeler came into contact with "these incredible people who were diverse," not only blacks but "Jews and rich and poor people," as well as a number of challenging teachers who encouraged him to grow through wide reading and exposure to public affairs. For "a human being who was trying to better himself intellectually and humanly," Wheeler said, the experience was pivotal. Evanston had "an accumulation of people from everywhere, and it gave me a real appreciation for people and how it could change somebody. And that environment changed me and gave me an uplift in the sense of how important growth was through people." Further, Wheeler remarked, although he "didn't identify with dollars or income or how big the house was," he said he "recognized where class was going, what it was going to get you, good education and such and maybe an income."

If his brief experience in Evanston hinted at the potential of a multiracial society as well as the socioeconomic and educational advantages available in select suburbs, Wheeler had left the South with an insatiable desire to be free and an electric sense of personal dignity that was rooted in a proud family and a series of dangerous confrontations that his father had provoked by resisting the protocols of jim crow life. "If you're a black person in the South," Wheeler said, "the answers that you get to live on are so perverse that you have to figure out what your own rules are in the sense of what fairness is, and ignore the social laws." As a child, Wheeler recounted, "I'd seen my father challenged many times, and he set an example of, you know, you die or else. Maintain your dignity. . . . So that was probably one of the motivating factors that I had experienced as I grew up. And I had my grandfather, my father's father, who was a slave, and the interesting thing is that [his dignity] was in that his sons would not have to be slaves. And my father's dignity was in that no one would tell us where or how much liberty and respect we should have." Taken together, Wheeler's "passion for dignity" and his desire to achieve personal "balance" through interaction with "a cross section of people" put him on a road that many African American families eventually took to the suburbs.

By the early 1960s, Wheeler had been to college and Korea and the Melbourne Olympics. He was married with two children, working as the first black white-collar employee for a major pharmaceutical firm and living in an apartment in Chicago. Looking ahead, the Wheelers began contemplating their children's future and the possibility of making a life in the suburbs. In 1961 they moved from Chicago to "black suburbia," a duplex in a predominantly black neighborhood in the western suburb of Maywood, where many black families had originally moved for steel industry jobs after World War I. Since the 1950s, Maywood had also attracted a trickle of white-collar blacks. As the community grew, whites fled the adjacent neighborhoods, opening up to families like the Wheelers, modest but well-built housing, elm-shaded streets, and the hope of improved public services and schools.

"When we moved to Maywood," Wheeler said, "we were looking for the better schools, . . . we wanted a safer neighborhood, and we . . . thought that a black neighborhood in suburbia would be ideal for us." "In Chicago we were looking at the ACT scores, and they were dismal. We got to Maywood, and we were there for several years, and although the youngsters, Ted and Mary, were not going to school yet . . . the school was not outstanding. The same problems that existed to some extent, not as bad, as in Chicago, existed in Maywood."[108]

Thus, in 1964 the Wheelers began planning a second and more challenging move. "At that time Ted [II] was five years old and started kindergarten in Maywood, and we wanted to have better schools, and more, a guarantee of a good education." "We did our research on paper and looked at areas. . . .

We looked at the houses, price of houses, and the neighborhoods and the incomes of people and the circumstances of opportunity to move there." The Wheelers also made a survey of local high schools to determine which "were producing students with the most ability to go on to college." Through this process, they narrowed their search to a handful of northern and western suburbs, but they were also shopping for places with particular "cultural benefits," as Wheeler described them. "We were looking for a neighborhood, an area where we had a cross section of people and cultures from the very high to the very low. The milkman and the policeman and the fireman all living in the community," an area where the schools were top-notch but not necessarily "orientated in its education to people who were making 'bucks,'" a neighborhood where Wheeler felt his children might learn the same kinds of lessons, "in the sense of their dignity," that he had learned through his own upbringing.[109]

In the end, the Wheelers confined their search to Oak Park, a "snug, secure and confident" suburb of tree-lined streets, with a strong tradition of civic participation and some of the best public schools in Illinois.[110] In Wheeler's view, Oak Park "had a cross section of America, which is I think, a very rich experience for any youngster, no matter what color he was. And I . . . didn't find any other neighborhoods that were close to that, whether it was Hyde Park in Chicago or Evanston or New Trier, Highland Park, or Elmhurst. So I found Oak Park to be a bastion of all the ingredients of America."[111]

One ingredient that *was* missing was a black community. Nonetheless, Oak Park was "across the street" from Chicago on its eastern border, and the Wheelers had "good friends two, three miles away" on the black West Side, where they and their children could "see and identify with black people." In that sense, Oak Park offered the opportunity for the family "to be in both worlds." Just as well, they hoped that Oak Park itself would provide "a healthy cultural environment for black people" and that it might soon attract other black residents.

"Percy Julian moved there in 1949," Wheeler explained, referring to the black research scientist whose family had broken the color line in Oak Park:

And he'd already fought a battle and [had] the back of his house burned off. . . . Then we had another friend of ours, who lived in Maywood, a neighbor of ours, . . . an interracial couple . . . [who] moved to Oak Park with their three black children, and there was an organization developing in Oak Park to integrate. So they had a strong political group, a strong Democrat group. The Democratic Party was strong in the western suburbs, not so much in Oak Park, but they had a strong group that was organizing with regard to open housing.[112]

Recognizing the likelihood of resistance as well as the possibility that there was a "built-in support group" in town, Wheeler explained his bottom line: "We had a passion for dignity and dignity for our children, and that passion for dignity meant that you would do the very best for your children." Part of that dignity also "comes about with not being told where to live, but living where you decided you wanted to live." Whether or not their neighbors would want or welcome them, Wheeler said, "my son was going to be in school, in the first grade that year, and that's where I wanted him to be, and I couldn't deviate from that focus." Lastly, Wheeler measured the risk against his own experience. Oak Park, with its saddle shoes and tennis apparel, was a long way from rural Georgia. If there was trouble, he figured he could "handle" it.

Even for skilled and ambitious families like the Wheelers, moving to a place like Oak Park in 1964 was easier planned than accomplished. For decades, local Realtors had jealously guarded the real estate market against purchases by undesirable persons, so defined by their religious or ethnic heritage or the color of their skin. Oak Park Realtors maintained a separate multiple-listing service with brokers in the neighboring suburb of River Forest, which gave the board tight control over most local sales.[113] Unable to use this network of brokers, the Wheelers planned "a surprise attack" with the help of white friends they had met in the interracial milieu of track and field.

"We had to circumvent the whole process," Wheeler recounted. "We decided to get, just like doing a play, the actors who were going to fulfill our steps, in the sense of purchasing the house: someone who was ideal looking with the features and with the cultural affectations to be accepted and to buy a house [in Oak Park]. So we got a five foot six blond with blue eyes" and "the most suburban-looking white dude you ever saw," a graduate student who Wheeler knew from the University of Chicago track club.[114]

Wheeler explained the plan:

I said [to them], "Well, we can't buy a house. You can buy a house. And I trust you with the eight or ten thousand–dollar down payment. And you'll own the house, and then you're gonna, when the banks get ready to deal with it, you'll sign it back over to me, and we'll go from there." . . . And we met each of them individually and told them that that was a role that they would play and gave them the script, and then they came down and met each other, and then they would take off and go to the real estate place.

To complete the performance, Wheeler said, smiling at the recollection, "they went about visiting real estate places in Oak Park, in a convertible ['red with white side walls,' Wheeler allowed on another occasion] with golf clubs in the back seat."

They looked like, you know, the couple that they would want to move there. . . . They weren't married, but of course they gave all the cosmetics of a good marriage, and [they were] a good-looking couple with enough money to have a big down payment to put down on the house. So, they proceeded to show them houses. . . .

We gave them our price range and where we wanted to live, and then they started pursuing, looking at houses and had no trouble. And then when they decided to look at the house that . . . they thought we would most like, they brought it to our attention, went over with us, and we gave our approval. And they went back to the Realtor and gave the initial money to . . . start the work running.

The ploy succeeded. By the end of August, the Wheelers' "third party" had purchased a three-bedroom turn-of-the-century house on Grove Street, just a few blocks from the grade school where their son would begin classes in the fall.[115] Even with the purchase behind them, however, the Wheelers' struggle had just begun.

Moving day we moved in. . . . It was like a disease. We moved in, had movers come in, rented a moving truck and friends came with us. And the neighborhood was in a state of shock. You'd think that the plague had showed up. It was all over the community. People were standing, white folks were standing around. There were some who stayed inside, but their kids would sneak out . . . and were just looking at us like . . . it was a bad dream.

Well, the next day . . . people wrote us notes that [said] why did we want to do this to their children. You know. And we had them say, well, they'd just moved from Chicago to get away from *us*. And here *we* are. And that they had lost money in Chicago and now they were gonna lose money here because we had moved in and ruined their property values.

During the first week, notes appeared under the door and the phone rang with threats. One night "the fire company showed up . . . because there was a threat to burn the house."

A week after moving in, the Wheelers awoke in the middle of the night with the glint of flames reflecting in their bedroom window. In the front yard was a flaming cross "about ten-foot high," framed by an eerie stillness. If any of the neighbors were awakened, none left their houses, either to extend a hand or to acknowledge their hostility. Instead, they watched in the darkness and waited to see what the Wheelers would do next.

"I got up the next morning very early," Wheeler remembered, "after putting out the fire that night, and reconstructed the cross with writing on the cross. I put on the cross in huge letters, 'Struggling is not segregated,' you know, and I put a picture of a black guy and a white guy in Vietnam." "It happened to be a Saturday night, and I made sure that everybody in the neighborhood was able to see their cross on Sunday."

From inside the house, the Wheelers

proceeded to watch the show, because people were going to come from all over. Finally the police chief showed up and came in and said to me, "That cross really looks bad. We need to get it out of there." And I said, "I don't think so." He said, "You know what we're going to do, Ted," he said. "We're gonna take our station wagon and come back," and they had a big white sheet on top of this station wagon, "and take the cross and lay it in there and take it down to the FBI, and then we're gonna go through all the garbage in the neighborhood and find out who did this." And I said, "Everybody in the neighborhood knows who did it." I said, "This cross is mine, today. You can have it Monday."

After the departure of the police, white people continued to mill about in the neighborhood. Cars with gawking passengers cruised slowly by. Neighbors came and went from church glancing furtively at the charred cross and burned grass on their neighbors' lawn. Later that morning, while Wheeler was painting an upstairs bedroom and his children were looking out the window, several white youths ran onto the lawn, "grabbed the cross and took off." Wheeler recalled, "I was in pretty good shape in those days. . . . In two or three steps I was on top of them . . . and apprehended them." The incident led to a scuffle in the street as Wheeler tried to hang on to the struggling teens. Somebody called the police. "[I] had not done anything obtuse," Wheeler said, "but the police came quickly" and sorted things out. Clearly relishing the irony, he said, "They had stolen my cross, and the police wanted to know if I wanted to prosecute them." Eventually, the police defused the situation by removing the youths in a squad car.

After this incident, the neighborhood remained cold but generally quiet, though "it went for over a year where we had physical, emotional confrontations with people." The Wheelers' children, especially, bore the brunt of verbal abuse, which also engaged Wheeler in a number of ugly incidents with white adults. For the most part, however, neighbors kept their distance. Unlike whites in many suburban neighborhoods, they also stayed put.

The Wheelers' saga might have ended there in a lasting standoff, but Oak Park whites as a whole responded to the arrival of the Wheelers and subsequent black families in a distinctive fashion. As Wheeler had known before, there was a small group of white activists in the community who were advocating the adoption of a local open-housing law and who openly sought to make Oak Park a racially integrated community.[116] In April 1964 they had published a statement in several west suburban newspapers declaring: "We want residence in our villages to be open to anyone interested in sharing our benefits and responsibilities, regardless of race, color, creed or national origin."[117] Some of these people had ridden buses to the March on Washington in 1963, and they came home committed to bringing civil rights with them in the form of racial integration. Word of the Wheelers' arrival reached members of this group overnight, and the next day half a dozen white people came to the Wheelers' door to "meet us and show their support and to do anything that they could to help us." Also, Wheeler remembered, "they wanted us to be part of their group."[118]

Over the next several years, the group evolved into a Citizens Committee for Human Rights. They lobbied the city government for an open-housing ordinance and attempted to change the dual-housing market that funneled most whites and African Americans to racially segregated neighborhoods. Members also recruited white home owners who were willing to sell across the color line. They tested local real estate firms for discriminatory practices, and they staged public demonstrations to call attention to discrimination at the local level. In 1964 members picketed the offices of the suburb's largest real estate agency for twenty-five straight weeks. They organized house tours to interest African Americans in buying in the community, and black members like the Wheelers shared their experiences with other African Americans, encouraging them to make Oak Park their home. In May 1968, a month after passage of the national Fair Housing Act, the group succeeded in convincing

Fig. 8.5   Ted Wheeler stands near the spot where neighbors burned a cross on his lawn in 1964. Raised in rural Georgia, Wheeler moved to suburban Oak Park, Illinois, prepared to "handle" whatever might happen. (Courtesy of Ted Wheeler and Sheila Creth, 2003)

the Oak Park city council to enact a local fair-housing ordinance, empowering the city to investigate and prosecute individuals suspected of discrimination.[119]

Oak Park's commitment to integration also extended to the way the suburb responded to racial change. During the 1960s and early 1970s, the adjoining Chicago neighborhood of Austin underwent swift and painful racial turnover accelerated by blockbusting and white flight. After 1970 a number of black families began moving across the Chicago border to southeast Oak Park, leading to fear and uncertainty among whites in the neighborhood. The appearance of agents from real estate firms well known for blockbusting in Chicago stoked concern that "what happened in Austin" might be repeated in Oak Park.[120] To prevent this possibility, the suburb became a leader in the movement for managed racial integration. The city created a housing referral service, which sought to combat traditional racial steering and retarget black demand for housing away from just one section of town by marketing housing to African Americans throughout the suburb.[121] It enacted a ban on "for sale" signs to dampen the perception that white residents were fleeing, and it stepped up enforcement against unwanted real estate solicitation, racial steering, and discriminatory lending, which were already apparent in southeast Oak Park.[122] Among its more controversial moves, the suburb acknowledged and responded openly to white racial fears. The housing office organized house tours to encourage whites as well as blacks to consider Oak Park, the police beefed up patrols to dampen white misperceptions that crime had increased since blacks began settling in larger numbers, and the city adopted a program of "home equity insurance," promising to pay insured residents if the market value of their homes declined. Through the 1990s, the city had never had to pay a claim. Confounding the skeptics, Oak Park remained racially integrated over time, welcoming a growing number of African American residents without precipitating the abandonment of the city and its institutions by whites. Oak Park was no racial utopia — tensions and misunderstandings along the color line flared on many occasions — nonetheless, over thirty years, it remained one of a handful of U.S. suburbs to sustain a relatively integrated housing market. By 2000 the community was 78 percent white and 22 percent black in a total population of 52,000 people.[123]

The Wheelers' move and subsequent events in Oak Park highlight several important features of black suburbanization in the 1960s. Like other suburbanites, the Wheelers' decision to move to Oak Park reflected a personal assessment of what would be best for their family. They sought to guarantee their children's access to the best education possible. They wanted to live in a community where they could interact with a wide spectrum of people without isolating themselves from the social and cultural opportunities of Chicago's wider black community. Like millions of Americans, they wanted to own a home, though their personal preferences were idiosyncratic. Altogether, their choices illuminate a wider set of social, spatial, and political orientations that underlay the collective migration of African Americans to suburbs after 1960.

In the first place, the Wheelers' insistence on securing superior educational and social opportunities for their children was characteristic of middle-class suburbanites. Beyond producing well-rounded individuals, a strong education represented the best available means for families to assure their children's future economic security as well as their social position. Suburban schools paved the way to a college diploma, which was the ticket to clean, comfortable, and dignified work with a steady income. For black men and women who had struggled up from a world of one-room schoolhouses, overalls, and dust caps, "yes, sir" and "yes, ma'am," lifting their children above the hardship of their history was a fundamental ambition. In that sense, suburbanites' emphasis on providing "better schools" or "a better life for their children" reflected not only the natural desire of parents to protect their offspring but a spatial strategy among a rising middle class to reproduce itself into the next generation.[124]

The family's move also underscores the link between suburbanization and politics, most importantly, the civil rights struggle that Wheeler simply called "the movement." Like thousands of their peers, the Wheelers drew inspiration from the racial contest engulfing the country. Wheeler highlighted this connection in the way he told the story, locating his family's move to Oak Park within a precise chronology of the movement, including the cataclysmic demonstrations in Birmingham in the spring of 1963, the March on Washington that summer, and passage of the Civil Rights Act in 1964. "Without that direct and indirect intellectual support that came from the movement," Wheeler believed, he would not have risked moving to Oak Park.[125]

At the same time, the Wheelers' choice of a place to live was itself a contribution to the struggle. Their move represented a conscious engagement with the politics of race and housing that shaped the color line in metropolitan America. To buy a suburban home and send their children to the type of schools that white executive families took for granted, they were forced to conduct an elaborate charade and then withstand the psychological assault of their neighbors. In fact, racism almost ensured that their decision would be perceived as a challenge to white privilege, regardless of their motives. Wheeler acknowledged that his move to Oak Park represented a deliberate political choice, even if it was only "an underriding factor" in the family's decision. By "living where you decided you wanted to live," the family indicated publicly that they would not accept second-class schools, housing, or other facilities, that they would not be governed by "social rules" written by whites. To the best of their ability, they would write their own rules.

Looking back, Wheeler admitted, "There's always been a stupid drive in me to think that if I had an opportunity to change things, then other people would be able to do the same thing, and perhaps things would move forward." In buying a house in Oak Park, he explained, "I was stupid enough to think that the world needed to be changed and I could have some indirect effect with what I would do." "In that sense," Wheeler conceded, "my movement to Oak Park was not just Oak Park." Rather, it was one act in the collective outpouring that was the civil rights movement.[126]

The Wheelers' social and political engagements also illustrate the importance of space in the postwar struggle for freedom. The family recognized implicitly that location was linked to inequality, that some areas, all of them reserved for whites, routinely produced the kinds of social success that they envisioned for their children. Like other middle-class families, they wanted access to these advantages. Thus, it is not surprising that the Wheelers believed that the ability to move freely was essential to their struggle for equality. Finally, having surmounted Oak Park's exclusionary real estate market, Wheeler deftly undermined his neighbors' conception of racial ownership over the area. Recognizing the value of symbols, he took possession of and defended the charred cross on his lawn, indicating to all who cared to look that his yard was his. The neighborhood belonged to him, too, and it was white territory no longer.

Although he was more outspoken than many, Wheeler's commitment to racial integration reveals further connections between suburban space and the politics of race and class in the mid-1960s. As common as the Wheelers' residential aspirations were among middle-class Americans, their decision to select a home in a white neighborhood in a nearly all-white suburb implied a revolutionary vision of the future. Like other pioneers, their insistence on nonsegregated living challenged the whole structure of segregated institutions and second-class living standards that bound race to space and reinforced white supremacy in metropolitan America. In Wheeler's opinion, integration was a valuable social goal in itself; living with and learning from "a cross section of white and black people" was a means to individual and collective growth. His aim, then, was not just to undermine the regime of white spatial privilege but to deracialize space altogether. Through his own actions, he sought to model a society in which white and black people were free to live where they pleased and actually chose to live in racially integrated settings.

Even for suburbanites like Wheeler, of course, integration was not strictly an end in itself but was a means to other goals they held dear, be they better housing and public facilities, good schools, property appreciation, or safe streets. Wheeler, himself, acknowledged such concerns in his emphasis on college acceptance rates and finding an area that would help his children develop their dignity. Suburban pioneer Jackie Robinson, too, stressed similar views in 1959:

> People of all races and creeds in the immediate future are going to vie for opportunities according to abilities, and we feel if our children have an opportunity to know people of all races and creeds at a very early age, their opportunities later in life will be greater, and that also of the white individuals. If they get the opportunity of knowing and understanding people of all races and creeds, they won't have the problem later in life of having to learn to understand while they are vying for jobs, which would make it much more difficult for the Negro as well as the white person.[127]

In this view, integrated neighborhoods represented a training ground for competition in a multiracial society. Not only would integration allow enterprising African Americans to enjoy the same public facilities and advantages as white people of their class, but, like access to suburban education, it would prepare their children to succeed in a society dominated by white people. For suburbanites such as these, integration conjoined practical personal aims with a long-term vision of society in which no place was reserved to one race or another.

Suburbanization by "Spillover"

Lest the Wheelers' "success" story is taken to represent the history of all African American suburbanites during these decades, it is important to point out that the suburban record during the 1960s and 1970s was decidedly more ambiguous. In the face of rising black incomes and nationwide civil rights protections, whites waged a persistent counterstruggle to defend the prerogatives of racially defined space. As a result, the majority of black suburbanites in these decades moved to a small number of older inner-ring suburbs where they found many of the same fiscal and social problems that they had faced in the adjoining city. These included inferior municipal services, low-performing schools, high property taxes, and elevated crime rates.[128] A resident of the

Runyon Heights section of Yonkers, New York, encapsulated a national complaint when he charged that he and his neighbors paid "Scarsdale taxes and receiv[ed] ghetto services."[129] Redlining, declining services, and deteriorated schools, factors that reinforced racial stratification in the nation's central cities, trailed African Americans even as they streamed to the suburbs.

In many areas, the largest proportion of black suburbanization involved the spatial expansion of black central city neighborhoods into adjacent suburbs, a process that observers called "spillover." Fueled by growing incomes, continued migration from the South, and the demolition of housing closer to the core, black neighborhoods expanded outward. Meanwhile, millions of whites, better able to take advantage of low-interest mortgage programs, inexpensive land, and low-cost housing in the suburbs, abandoned central city communities. By the 1960s, the outer edge of many black neighborhoods had reached the city limits, and growing numbers of families began moving to the adjoining suburbs.

Inner-ring suburbanization was especially pronounced in metropolitan areas with geographically small central cities and large black populations, places like Newark, St. Louis, and Washington, D.C., where expanding African American neighborhoods reached the city limits sooner than elsewhere. In St. Louis thousands of black families left the city's West End during the 1960s for adjacent suburbs such as Wellston, Northwoods, Pine Lawn, and University City.[130] More than 40,000 African Americans left Newark for the adjacent suburb of East Orange. Near Washington, the black population of Prince George's County, Maryland, mushroomed from 30,000 in 1960 to almost 250,000 by 1980 as the area gained cachet as a place of residence for the city's black middle class. In these years, several fingers of African American settlement at the eastern and southeastern edges of the city fused into a single majority-black region stretching from the city line to the Interstate 495 Beltway, five miles beyond.[131]

Because of its connection to the expansion of black urban neighborhoods, inner-ring suburbanization provoked critical reception among social scientists and others who equated the process with "ghettoization"—racial transition, resegregation, and economic decline—in the central city. In the view of black studies scholar Harold Connolly, the burst in new suburbanization was "fundamentally attributable to the physical expansion of inner-city ghettos into contiguous areas." In St. Louis, an observer wrote, the "significant black movement into the suburbs . . . has not been because of racial integration but because the ghetto has reached the county line and moved across it."[132] Geographer Harold Rose concurred in 1976: "Black suburbanization as it is now occurring," he wrote, represented "the spatial extension of the ghettoization process with all that implies regarding the quality of life dimensions for its residents."[133]

There were good reasons to be skeptical of black suburbanization "spilling over" from the central city through racial transition. Unlike the nonracial filtering of housing from one group of people to another, racial turnover left deep scars in the urban fabric, contributing to the stratification of urban places on the basis of race.[134] In many white neighborhoods, the appearance of black families ignited violence or panic selling by white residents. Transition was frequently accelerated by the activities of real estate speculators known as "blockbusters," who specialized in manipulating racial fear for a profit. To stir up listings, blockbusters approached white home owners in borderland neighborhoods, warning that African Americans were buying in the area and that property values would soon fall. If the owner agreed to sell immediately, the agent promised them a fair price. Once the first home had sold, however, agents stoked panic and shaved prices on the remaining homes.[135] Agents blanketed target neighborhoods with sales cards, doorbell solicitations, and phone calls that played on white racial fears with "all the familiar scare threats."[136] "We were told you get the listings any way you can," admitted one blockbuster.

> It's pretty easy to do; I just scare the hell out of them. And that's what we did. We were not only making money, we were having fun doing what we were doing. We all liked selling real estate — if you want to call what we were doing selling real estate. And it got to a point that in order to have fun while we were working, we would try to outdo each other with the most outlandish threats that people would believe and chuckle at the end of the day. . . . I had fun at it. I'd go down the street with a [black] buyer and ask, Which house do you want? He'd pick one, and I'd ring the door bell and say, these people want to buy your house. If the lady said no, I'd say the reason they're so interested is that their cousins, aunts, mother, whatever, it's a family of twelve, are moving in across the street, and they want to be near them. Most of the time, that worked. If that didn't work, you'd say their kid just got out of jail for housebreaking, or rape, or something that would work.[137]

In the most exploitative instances, blockbusting companies bought houses below their market value and resold them to black clients at markups ranging from 30 to 100 percent of the original sales price. For whites who sold to the speculators, the prophecy of declining values came true. Frightened of losing their equity and their financial security, many home owners sold at a loss, often feeling lucky to have gotten out before their houses became "worthless." Meanwhile, African Americans paid more than the original market value for homes because they had few alternatives. The speculators put the difference in their pockets.[138]

To compound matters, many banks refused to lend in changing neighborhoods, which forced buyers to turn to dubious sources — often the speculators themselves — for a home loan.[139] One blockbuster explained, "I make my money — quite a lot of it incidentally — in three ways: (1) by beating down the prices I pay the white owners by stimulating their fear of what is to come; (2) by selling to the eager Negroes at inflated prices; and (3) by financing these purchases at what amounts to a very high rate of interest."[140] In many places, the dominant mode of financing in changing neighborhoods was the contract deed, under which the seller retained title to the property until the terms of the contract had been met. In some racially changing neighborhoods of Chicago, a startling 85 percent of sales to black home buyers between 1940 and 1960 were made through contract deeds.[141] Like borrowing from a loan shark, however, buying on contract was risky business. Usually, buyers paid monthly installments until the purchase price, plus interest, had been paid in full. A missed payment could mean eviction and forfeiture of all previous payments. Under the pressure of high interest rates and other fees, thousands of black families lost their homes and savings through this means.

Additionally, land contracts depressed the incentive of both seller and buyer to maintain the property, and steep terms often left purchasers so financially strapped that they were unable to make necessary repairs, let alone improvements to the property. Absentee slumlords also bought in changing markets, subdividing older units and charging high rents to poorer families who sought to escape crowding and deteriorated conditions in neighborhoods where the process had already run its course. In some cases, too, newcomers took in lodgers to help make their payments. Population densities rose, city services were overburdened, housing deteriorated, and, all the while, incomes and tax revenues declined. As surely as day became night, historian Arnold Hirsch writes, the exploitative real estate practices that facilitated racial transition "'fast [made] slums" out of residential areas.[142]

In addition to producing neighborhoods that conferred multiple disadvantages on their residents, change of this kind reinforced a racial understanding of urban space. Hirsch points out, "As racial succession progressed, the conditions produced by real estate speculation and exploitation began to yield visible proof to those who believed that black 'invasion' meant slum creation."[143] For whites who had witnessed or been victimized by the process, the lessons seemed clear: Black people must be confined to neighborhoods of their own. As whites moved on to the suburbs, they did everything they could to prevent blacks from following.

The question of race and property values has sparked debate since at least the 1910s. As late as the 1950s, real estate brokers, builders, bankers, and federal officials openly promoted the view that African Americans and other minorities destabilized real estate prices, and they advocated racial segregation to secure property values in white neighborhoods. In the late 1950s, however, empirical studies showed that there was no demonstrable connection between racial transition and property value decline. Luigi Laurenti, who authored the most influential study, found that in the short run, property values actually increased during racial transition. Popular wisdom and everyday real estate practice paid little heed. Partly for this reason, the long-run impact of racial transition was more difficult to map than the initial transfer of housing from white to black families. In the long run, most studies suggest, racial transition in the context of a dual real estate market and limited incomes among African Americans tended toward varying degrees of socioeconomic decline—though not necessarily falling real estate prices.[144]

The experience of the Adel Allen family of Kirkwood, Missouri, highlights the difficulties that many African Americans faced in racially changing neighborhoods, whether they were in central cities or suburbs. The Allens moved from Wichita, Kansas, in 1962 when Mr. Allen took a job as an aerospace engineer with McDonnell Aircraft Company in suburban St. Louis. They "ended up in Kirkwood," a nineteenth-century railroad suburb west of the city, Allen said, "because I wasn't allowed to live any place else, mainly." After fruitless house hunting in the northwest suburbs near McDonnell, they found a house in a "lower income white" area adjacent to "the Negro section of Kirkwood," an old black suburb called Meacham Park. The house they bought was less expensive than they could afford and less spacious than they were accustomed to, but compared to the "third floor apartments in the inner city" that they had been shown elsewhere, it was an improvement. The neighborhood also left something to be desired. "The character of some of the people that were in the neighborhood was questionable," Allen judged. "[T]hey had bad conduct, they weren't good neighbors. Some of them were litterers and I wouldn't allow my kids to play with some of their kids." Subsequent events did little to restore the Allens' confidence.[145]

Whites began to leave almost immediately. "Some of the neighbors that lived there told us that they welcome black people and told us that they are glad that we came and all that," Allen recalled, "but the next day we saw the signs going up 'For Sale' all around us." One by one, black families replaced them so that by 1970 the neighborhood had shifted from "approximately thirty white families and one black" to the inverse. "The only [white] people that are left," Allen noted, "are the ones that are too poor to leave."[146]

Though the Allens believed that the quality of the neighborhood improved as African Americans moved in, racial turnover brought new problems. In the eight years following their move, services had "almost gone completely to pot." The city of Kirkwood, which remained more than 90 percent white, greeted racial change on its southern border coldly. As the neighborhood became increasingly black, the city scaled back services and improvements. Allen catalogued the deficiencies:

> I can't recall seeing the streets being cleaned the last year. We now have the most inadequate lighting in the city. You can tell when you are in our area by the inadequate lighting. . . . [W]e have the people from the other sections of town that now leave their cars parked on our streets when they want to abandon them. . . . I reported three this morning. . . . Other sections of the city I believe are being forced to take sidewalks, for example. We are begging for sidewalks. Other portions of the city are being forced to get curbs. We can't even get them to come out and look at the curbs. . . . It takes a determined effort to get the dog catcher to come over, or the mosquito control group to come over and spray. We have to have chain phone calls, for example, to get the things that already belong to us.[147]

"In other words," Allen concluded, "what they are making now is a ghetto in the process."[148]

As the Allens found in Kirkwood, accelerated racial transition and concerted municipal neglect in the suburbs reproduced patterns of racial segregation and neighborhood deterioration characteristic of central city areas. Private real estate brokers also contributed to the process. Working from the assumption that resegregation was inevitable once the first black family arrived, white brokers steered whites away and redirected black clients to the area.[149] Black brokers, too, participated in the resegregation process since they relied for a living on commissions in the relatively few neighborhoods open to African Americans. As new areas became available — or they opened them themselves — they redoubled their efforts to get listings for their black clients.[150] A neighborhood might be home to just a few black families, but in the dynamic of the segmented real estate market, it had shifted to the black segment. As one suburban editorialist remarked, "Buildings still look good, but the only thing changed is people's minds."[151] With whites being channeled away, vacancies in "changing" neighborhoods almost inevitably were filled by other African Americans. In urban and suburban neighborhoods alike, the period between the arrival of the first black family and the departure of the last whites was seldom very long.[152]

East Cleveland, Ohio

A final example, African American suburbanization in Cleveland, illuminates the process and the effects of high-speed racial transition in the suburbs. For a variety of reasons, large-scale black suburbanization came late to northeast Ohio. In 1960 just 6,455 blacks lived in Cleveland's suburbs amidst some 900,000 whites.[153] Nonetheless, at the eastern reaches of the city, African American majorities in neighborhoods such as Glenville, Lee-Harvard, and Buckeye began looking eastward for housing opportunities in the suburbs that overlooked the city. A few black families had ascended the escarpment that marked the city limits, settling in Shaker Heights during the 1950s, but nothing prepared these cities for the changes to come. During the 1960s, 32,000 African Americans moved across the city line to four adjacent suburbs—East Cleveland, Cleveland Heights, Shaker Heights, and Warrensville Heights—all of which experienced some form of accelerated racial change.[154]

The process was most explosive in East Cleveland, an aging suburb of 38,000 situated astride Euclid Avenue, the faded main street of the Forest City. East Cleveland had seen its heyday before the Great Depression. By 1960 the once-"select" commuter suburb was home to an aging population of lower-middle-class and blue-collar whites. John D. Rockefeller's Forest Hill estate had long since been subdivided, and East Cleveland's three-story Queen Anne homes, two-deckers, and "ornate apartment buildings" had begun to show wear.[155] As residents aged, they ceased to be replaced by younger white families, and grown children moved away, often to newer suburbs farther east, such as Mayfield and Euclid. Like many suburbs of its vintage, East Cleveland lost population during the 1950s. Meanwhile, the adjacent Cleveland neighborhood of Glenville became in effect an all-black community.

In 1960 East Cleveland remained 98 percent white, and most of the suburb's 800 black residents lived within a few blocks of the Glenville border.

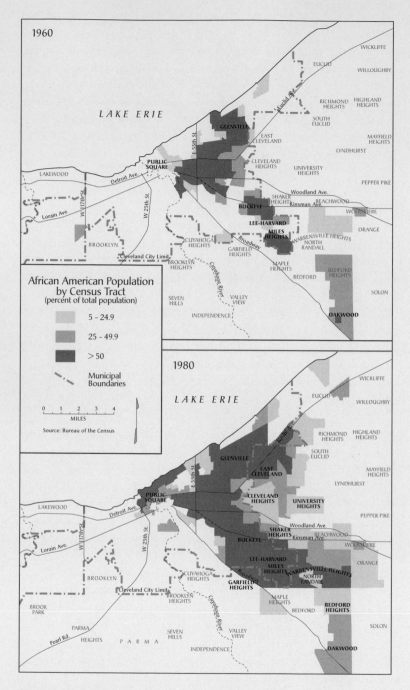

Fig. 8.6   Black Suburbanization in Cleveland, Ohio, 1960 and 1980.
(Map by Harry D. Johnson)

Fig. 8.7 Architecturally distinguished homes built for whites at the turn of the last century attracted upwardly mobile African Americans from Cleveland to the suburb of East Cleveland in the 1960s and 1970s. (Photograph by Andrew Wiese, 1988)

Over the next ten years, however, nearly 23,000 black Clevelanders settled in the suburb, succeeding the exodus of 21,000 whites, and the suburb became almost 60 percent black.[156] Racial transition in East Cleveland began in the neighborhoods on East Cleveland's boundary with Glenville as real estate companies promoted change one or two blocks at a time. "As housing became available, black families began to move in," a consultant to the city wrote. "The process was quickly accelerated by panic, capitalized upon by the activities of blockbusters. From 1963–1967, block after block underwent rapid transition."[157] In a wavelike fashion, rates of housing turnover peaked in one neighborhood before appearing on adjacent streets, where the process repeated. "It seems like I went to bed one winter night, woke upon a spring day and everybody had moved out," said Mae Stewart, a mother of school-aged children who moved to East Cleveland from the city in 1960. "The white flight was really something." Real estate agents "would call some of the neighbors and say, '[T]he neighborhood is changing. Maybe you'd better sell and get out.'"[158] By 1967 thousands had followed this advice. In the two northernmost sections of the suburb, African Americans formed 80 and 60 percent of the population. Meanwhile, two neighborhoods that were farther from the city remained 88 and 91 percent white.

Nonetheless, racial transition swept steadily through the suburb. The eruption of rioting in Glenville in July 1968, including a prolonged gun battle between police and black nationalists, marked the last straw for many local whites. In the next ten years, most of the remaining white families left the suburb, and more than 8,000 black Clevelanders replaced them.[159] By 1980 every neighborhood in the city had a black majority, African Americans comprised 86 percent of the population, the schools had long since resegregated, and the small number of remaining whites resided mostly in the exclusive Forest Hill section, which was secluded from the rest of town by Forest Hill Park.[160]

Although the occupational status of the new suburbanites tended to be lower than that of outgoing whites, the newcomers were considerably better off than most black Clevelanders. Seventy-two percent of new black households contained two parents, which in most cases meant two incomes. Their rate of employment was significantly higher than black Clevelanders as a whole, and they boasted a record of job stability equal to that of East Cleveland whites. When asked, the largest share of black newcomers explained that "home ownership" was their primary reason for relocating. Indeed, 40 percent bought homes in East Cleveland, compared to just 12 percent who had owned a home before moving.[161] In almost every respect, the first wave of black suburbanites to East Cleveland represented a cross section of the city's new, if precariously situated, black middle class.

In spite of the newcomers' economic advantage over most black Clevelanders, the socioeconomic consequences of resegregation in the suburb mirrored patterns in the city. As in urban neighborhoods such as Hough and Glenville, where aspiring black families had once replaced departing whites, blockbusters and unscrupulous landlords taxed the newcomers' financial resources. Some East Cleveland property owners maximized their investments by converting older homes into rooming houses through the cheapest possible means. Area banks redlined the area, and the local commercial district suffered as the customer base changed and owners fled with their businesses. Butchers, neighborhood drugstores, restaurants, and small specialty shops closed their doors. As a result, the municipal tax base plummeted (20 percent between 1967 and 1970, alone) and the city was forced to curtail services. Meanwhile, the younger and poorer families who moved into newly subdivided homes placed heavier service demands on the city—particularly its schools—while contributing less to the local tax coffers.[162] During the 1970s, as the economy slipped into recession and manufacturing employment collapsed across the rustbelt, home foreclosures and abandonment gripped those East Cleveland neighborhoods closest to the city, and the suburb's population

Fig. 8.8   By the 1980s, East Cleveland neighborhoods nearest to the Cleveland border suffered from disinvestment and abandonment similar to neighborhoods inside the city. (Photograph by Andrew Wiese, 1988)

dipped by 2,000 residents. Home owners began to sell out, and by the early 1970s, the suburb's first black city manager conceded that East Cleveland was "an inner-city suburb with all the problems of the central city."[163]

Despite these challenges, East Cleveland remained a predominantly working- and lower-middle-class black suburb with pockets of poverty as well as a core of professionals. The suburb offered a variety of neighborhoods and housing options that were superior to those in most sections of black Cleveland. Nonetheless, between 1970 and 1980, the median income of the suburb slipped and the local poverty rate doubled, climbing to 22 percent.[164] Home ownership dropped below one-third as absentee landlords subdivided existing properties, and the suburb entered a self-reinforcing cycle of fiscal decline. As African Americans' options expanded elsewhere, many middle-class families moved away, and bad publicity discouraged others from replacing them. Financial stagnation and curtailed services placed an increasing burden on those who stayed behind. Thus, perceptions of East Cleveland as a deteriorating black area — a representation of space to which most Clevelanders subscribed — contributed to the community's problems. A Realtor in neighboring Cleveland Heights explained: "It's a rough area. If they put a listing out, it lasts a long time. People know about the crime, the poverty level, all the subsidized housing that's over there, the water department, the police department. People tend to stay away from East Cleveland, if they can."[165] Under the weight of growing socioeconomic burdens, compounded by official malfeasance, the state took receivership of the suburb's finances in the late 1980s. By the 1990s, East Cleveland was among the poorest cities in Ohio, school performance ranked at the bottom of the metropolitan area, yet, journalist Erick Trickey pointed out, "residents [paid] some of the highest taxes in Cuyahoga County."[166]

In East Cleveland, economic shifts affecting urban areas throughout the country combined with a history of racial inequality in the region to produce rapid racial and socioeconomic change. The suburb's demise was extreme, but its general trajectory traced a path followed by dozens of inner suburbs in the 1960s and 1970s.[167]

Pushed forward by gains in income and legal rights as well as the persistent efforts of black families to attain better places to live, African American suburbanization expanded during the 1960s and 1970s. Led by the growing black middle class, the new suburbanites sought residential amenities and advantages on par with those available to middle-class whites. Moreover, in the context of the national civil rights struggle, many of them saw their individual housing choices in explicitly political terms. In the face of relentless white resistance, they understood that social concepts such as upward mobility and equality entailed a struggle on the physical terrain of the city, a contest involving both the construction and representation of space.

Nonetheless, for the new suburbanites, gains via suburbanization measured poorly against those of whites. Disinvestment through redlining and commercial flight, higher taxes, socioeconomic decline, and crime pursued even middle-class African American families to the suburbs. On average, black suburbanites received less for their money than suburban whites, and due to the age and service burden in many communities, they paid higher taxes for the privilege. Despite unprecedented legal progress in civil rights, movement to the suburbs did little to undermine the racialized character of metropolitan areas. As a result, African Americans were much less able to convert class mobility into the same spatial benefits as their white counterparts. As the 1970s closed, race remained a structural feature of metropolitan life: embedded in the physical landscape, marked in social and residential patterns, expressed in policy and perception, and reflected in the fiscal conditions under which blacks lived.

Chapter 9

The Next Great Migration

*African American Suburbanization in the
1980s and 1990s*

DURING THE last two decades of the twentieth century, as many African Americans moved to the suburbs as in the preceding seventy years. The black suburban population leaped from a record 6.1 million to just under 12 million, and suburbanites expanded in proportion from one-quarter to one-third of the black population.[1] The magnitude of change was evident in metropolitan areas across the country. In Chicago, the land of promise for three generations of black southerners, the African American population fell during the 1980s for the first time in the twentieth century while the suburbs added more than 100,000 blacks.[2] The black suburban population of Washington, D.C., grew by half a million, while Atlanta added more than 700,000. In both areas there were nearly a million black suburbanites at the turn of the century. Suburbanization also became less concentrated than before. By 2000 there were fifty-seven metropolitan areas with at least 50,000 black suburbanites, compared to thirty-three in 1980.[3] In size, speed, and significance, movement to the suburbs was the next Great Migration.

The new suburbanites were a diverse group with social, political, and cultural affiliations as deep and wide as the black nation itself. The leading edge, however, remained firmly middle class, as it had been since the 1950s. Suburbanites were economically comfortable in national terms but privileged by comparison with other blacks. By 1990 black suburbanites earned 55 percent more than African Americans in central cities, averaging $32,000 per year, which was slightly below the national median of $35,000.[4] In a variety of areas — Atlanta, Washington, Chicago, and Hartford among them — black

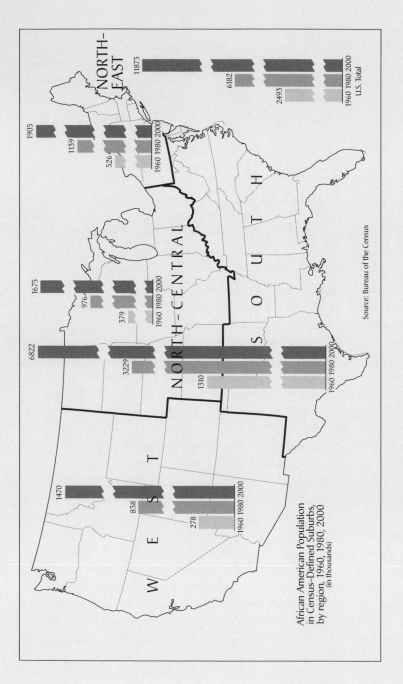

NORTH-
EAST

11873

6182

2493

1960 1980 2000
U.S. Total

1905

1139

526

1960 1980 2000

1675

976

379

1960 1980 2000

6822

3229

1310

1960 1980 2000

1470

838

278

1960 1980 2000

NORTH-CENTRAL

WEST

SOUTH

African American Population
in Census-Defined Suburbs,
by region, 1960, 1980, 2000
(in thousands)

Source: Bureau of the Census

Fig. 9.1   Suburban African Americans by Region, 1960, 1980, and 2000. (Map by Harry D. Johnson)

suburbanites boasted higher levels of income and education on average than suburban whites.[5] In the words of Joel Garreau, one of the first journalists to approach the subject in national terms, suburbia witnessed the emergence of a "large, churchgoing, home-owning, childrearing, back-yard barbecuing, traffic-jam-cursing black middle class remarkable only for the very ordinariness with which its members go about their classically American suburban affairs."[6]

Black suburbanites attracted new attention in the housing market as well. Near Atlanta and other cities, black and white developers catered to affluent African American home buyers. In Dekalb and Clayton County, Georgia, southeast of Atlanta, journalists reported that "raw subdivisions [sold] off half-finished homes to black professionals as merrily as giant dealerships selling off new cars."[7] In the Stone Mountain area, birthplace of the modern Ku Klux Klan, "pine forest and pasture land [gave] way" to "a subdivision world of cul-de-sacs and manicured lawns" designed "for black families seeking homes above $200,000."[8] Near Washington, D.C., Prince George's County, Maryland, became the first majority-black suburban county as "upscale, well-educated African Americans" relocated to deluxe building tracts and sprawling subdivisions. By 1990, the *Washington Post* pointed out, "blacks with college degrees . . . outnumber[ed] college-educated whites" in the county, and "more blacks than whites live in households with incomes in excess of $50,000."[9] At the end of the century, the *Post* reported, Washington's "black intelligentsia and business leaders and, indeed, the rock-ribbed middle class of teachers, federal workers and salespeople, [were] grounded firmly in the suburbs instead of the city."[10]

To many observers, the explosion in black suburbanization symbolized just how far the United States had come since the civil rights movement. To journalist Garreau, the expansion of middle-class black suburbia represented "one of the biggest changes in black affairs in American history," signaling the declining significance of race and the supremacy of class in American life. "The third of African Americans that is fairly described as suburban middle class," he wrote, "is becoming statistically indistinguishable from whites of the same class, not only in income and education, but in consumer behavior and attitudes toward government." They were, he said, "succeeding by the standards of the majority white culture in mainstream America."[11] Historian Lawrence DeGraaf added that the "dispersal" of black suburbanites to fast-growing and formerly white suburbs, the largest part of the migration in some areas, was an "unheralded triumph" that signaled greater residential choice and wider geographic mobility for African Americans than ever before.[12] By the 1990s, economic hardship and spatial segregation—key pillars of racial inequality, but also black identity in the twentieth century—were beginning to weaken, leading some to question whether suburbanization might herald the denouement of "African American culture" altogether.[13]

Despite shifts in the relationships between race, class, and space, there was little evidence that African Americans' racial or class identities were on the wane in suburbia. Race and class remained complicated, shifting, and context dependent, but important structural features underlay individual experiences and perceptions, providing a basis for collective attachments as well as antagonisms. Racial subordination, while diminishing, retained its central place in American life. Regardless of their social class, African Americans faced discrimination in the markets for jobs, housing, and capital, as well as in everyday life. They earned less money than whites, held fewer assets, and were less likely to own their own homes.[14]

African Americans remained spatially differentiated as well. Despite growing access to newer, more economically dynamic suburban areas, most black suburbanites in 1990 lived in older inner-ring suburbs, which exhibited a variety of fiscal shortcomings, such as high taxes, mediocre services, low-performing schools, commercial disinvestment, and anemic rates of property appreciation.[15] Likewise, the geographical link between older and newer suburban communities endured. The tendency of whites to shun integrated neighborhoods and most blacks' disposition to avoid untested white areas meant that the majority of black suburbanites lived in racially segregated neighborhoods. Moreover, it meant that most areas of new growth were contiguous to old ones. Rather than upsetting the familiar stratification of metropolitan areas into white and black spaces, the suburban explosion expanded it over a greater area. These factors—material distinctions that gave substance to racial difference—remained salient features of contemporary American life.[16]

If structural conditions reinforced the significance of race, black suburbanites also evaluated and gave them meaning in relation to a larger set of social relations, interests, and memories that helped to reproduce a sense of themselves in race and class terms. Their suburban dreams—visions of real and imagined space—reflected a balancing act perched on overlapping interests as well as perceptions of race and class. Thousands of middle-class households expressed preferences for "nice suburban African American communit[ies]," isolated from the social problems associated with working-class neighborhoods but also sheltered from the everyday slights and feelings of cultural alienation that many experienced in predominantly white areas.[17] By the same token, the growing number of families who moved to mostly white suburbs made special efforts to fortify their ties to black communities and institutions. Larger and more economically secure than ever before — but also less secure than middle-class whites — the black middle class sought through a variety of means to fashion spaces of its own in the suburbs, places that reflected the concerns of a group integrally defined by both race and class.

Restructuring Class and Space

Perhaps the greatest paradox of late-twentieth-century African American history was the concurrent magnification of privation and privilege: grinding economic misfortune for the poor and working class coupled with the rise of a well-educated, home-owning middle class. Epitomizing the paradox in space were the warring symbols of urban crisis and suburban accomplishment.

Underlying the incongruity were economic changes affecting cities and towns across the United States. During the 1970s and 1980s, the nation experienced convulsive economic restructuring, a collapse in manufacturing employment, and the transition to a service economy marked by job growth in health, education, government, retailing, personal services, and professional fields such as finance, insurance, real estate, law, and business consulting.[18]

One result was a steady polarization of income and wealth. In contrast to the large number of middle-income jobs in basic manufacturing — often unionized, assembly-line positions requiring little formal education or training — the new "service economy" manifested a distinctive financial and geographic profile. Compensation in the service sector tended toward the financial extremes: high salaries for well-educated managerial and professional employees and a growing pool of low-waged, often "pink collar" occupations, with comparatively little in between.[19] For a quarter century after 1970, four of five U.S. households suffered declines in real income. Only the very highest income brackets saw gains, reaping most of the windfall from restructured growth. The greatest losses, meanwhile, befell the poorest Americans.[20]

Economic restructuring led to a polarization of places as well. Cities and regions dependent on manufacturing foundered, producing a "rustbelt" of declining cities stretching from New England through the Great Lakes. As business and property tax receipts slipped, cities faced fiscal calamity; they cut back services, delayed infrastructural maintenance, shut libraries and museums, and curtailed trash collection. Polarization was manifest within metropolitan areas as well. In city and suburban manufacturing districts and the residential areas dependent on them, deindustrialization produced a landscape of broken windows and abandoned homes, potholed streets, peeling paint, and widespread evidence of social despair. At the same time, central business districts and outlying parts of the same metropolitan areas witnessed a boom in office construction, retail expansion, and upscale housing development, precipitated by the growth in high-paying white-collar work.[21] Like shuttered factories and toxic brown fields in metropolitan manufacturing belts, the glass and steel skyscrapers rising in central business districts and edge city office parks were physical emblems of the new economy.

For African Americans, restructuring resulted in a world of extremes. Migration since World War I had concentrated in precisely the cities and suburbs that suffered most during the seventies and eighties. The hollowing of the manufacturing economy and the departure of industrial jobs from central locations led to skyrocketing unemployment, falling property values, and failing schools in black neighborhoods. Rates of poverty climbed, ensnaring a third of African Americans by the mid-1980s. Furthermore, the spatial segregation of African Americans from other groups tended to concentrate levels of poverty in the neighborhoods where blacks lived. Thus, in many neighborhoods, poverty rates hovered closer to 50 percent.[22] In the Midwest, which was especially hard hit, black unemployment averaged more than 20 percent, and among black teens and young adults, rates of unemployment often topped 40 percent.[23] Crime rates rose and local means of social control weakened in many neighborhoods, leading residents to mold their daily lives to evade the menace of the streets. The built environment, too, hardened, with windowless walls, razor wire, and wrought-iron security bars manifesting this sense of insecurity.

Paradoxically, the 1970s and 1980s also witnessed the rise of a "new black middle class," rooted in comfortable outer city and suburban neighborhoods. Supported by gains in civil rights, college-educated African Americans moved upward in step with their white peers. By 1998 more than a third of black households earned more than the national median of $35,000, and 12 percent earned more than $50,000, a jump from just 4 percent in 1980.[24]

"Black and poor," once a seemingly inexorable bonding of race and class that had marked black life throughout the century, began to disentangle.[25] In its place were a more polarized class structure and a more uncertain relationship between race and economic position. For those families who climbed the economic ladder in the 1960s and 1970s, prospects were encouraging. Children of these "early strivers" came of age in a world of new racial freedoms that allowed their prospects to rise and fall more closely with whites of the same class.[26] As their earning potential peaked as they reached their forties and fifties, the black middle class boomed. Meanwhile, poor and working-class households found themselves in bleak economic straits that were compounded by the geographic disadvantages of poor schools, services, and health care; inadequate access to financial institutions; and high rates of crime in the neighborhoods where they lived.

Observing these changes in the late 1970s, sociologist William J. Wilson concluded that class was supplanting race as the key determinant of blacks' life chances. What Wilson saw as the increasing significance of class, however, did not necessarily signal the decline of race in the United States. Class and race were not related as inverse proportions of African American identity. If some members of the black suburban middle class were "becoming indistinguishable statistically from whites of the same class," as Joel Garreau put it, racial distinctions in housing, wealth, access to capital, and public treatment remained fundamental features of African American life.[27]

More important, race had always been something more than statistics could measure. It was not only a marker of imposed inequality but a perception of "linked fate" in a racist society, a matter of affiliations and connections, a sense of shared history and distinction from others. Just as important, for most blacks in the twentieth century, these impressions were closely bound up with the separate spaces that they shared.[28] As friends, family, fellow congregants, and neighbors of people who were struggling to survive, middle-class African Americans were, in the words of political scientist Jennifer Hochschild, "entwined with other blacks both because they choose to be and because they cannot escape."[29]

"The Good Life"

Black suburbanization at the end of the century, as in the past, reflected the collective weight of decisions made by many individuals, measuring their aspirations against their options in a specific historical context. Like other American home seekers, black suburbanites brought a myriad of experiences, needs, and desires to the housing market. Their residential choices expressed concerns with the price of housing, journey to work, proximity to friends and social attachments, and the quality of schools and neighborhood amenities, as well as preferences related to landscape and the built environment.

Suburbanites' position and perceptions as members of the black middle class also shaped their choices in subtle and not so subtle ways. As members of a disproportionately urbanized group, most black suburbanites shared the experience of living in a fiscally troubled central city. In the context of urban decline, they placed especially high priority on personal security and superior public services. As people with rising incomes and aspirations, whose economic status was still far from secure, the new suburbanites sought residential locations that would complement if not strengthen their social position. As black people, however, they still found themselves chafing against what Ted Wheeler had described as "social rules" written by whites. Like many of their predecessors, thousands sought residential environments where they could train their children for economic success without sacrificing a sense of cultural identity or fellowship with other black people. They maintained connections to black institutions and peers, and many sought a sense of shelter and sustenance that they believed was only available among black neighbors. As the century came to a close, "living where you decided you wanted to live" remained a personal and political decision closely connected with the making of race and class.[30]

For African Americans who had attended college, secured well-paying jobs, and struggled for a place in the middle class, suburban homes represented an attempt to reap the spatial advantages that their economic status could buy. Many new suburbanites saw residential space as a means to protect their hard-won gains. They sought value for money, the latest accoutrements of residential comfort, and sound public schools, as well as distance from the problems associated with poor and working-class communities.[31] Nate Parker, a self-described "law-abiding, tax-paying African American suburbanite" who moved to Chicago's western suburbs as part of a corporate relocation, said he selected his neighborhood "for the reasons [other] people choose this suburb: good schools for our children, a short commute to work and safe, clean streets."[32] Gwen Snow, an Atlanta real estate agent and suburban home owner, concurred. "Black people want quality just like anybody." When they attain the means to move up, she said, "they want to upgrade."[33] In the opinion of Ronald Walters, a Chicago-area real estate agent, his suburban clients were simply "looking for more affluent living." They sought new homes, often with very specific residential amenities in mind: "the Jacuzzis in the bedroom, the acreage in the backyards."[34] Like middle- and upper-middle-class families before them, demographer William Frey, pointed out, African Americans "translated their moves up the socioeconomic ladder into a suburban lifestyle."[35]

Other suburbanites, too, expressed aspirations that were widely held among middle-class Americans. Tony Massengale, an organizer for a non-profit housing agency in Los Angeles, explained that he and his wife decided to move to Pasadena, after a decade of living in surrounding communities in and outside the city, because of its combination of good schools, solid economic base, and "strong city service lineup." In addition, they favored a number of classically suburban attractions. "What I like about it," he said, "is that there's just a lot of the old nostalgic stuff that I used to think of as a nice place to live: a lot of trees, green yards and picket fences, a bunch of parks."[36] For other suburbanites, the enticements were as varied as they were commonplace: "contemporary homes," a "one-acre woodsy lot," the "slower pace," "green grass, the trees, the fresh air," or just "peace and quiet."[37] In these aspirations, black suburbanites mirrored the residential appetites of millions of middle-class white households, who had long sought to marry the benefits of "country living" with the latest urban services and amenities.

Like middle-class parents since the 1920s, recent suburbanites also stressed the importance of education as a factor in moving to the suburbs. If they fled city schools that they saw as "intolerable," they also expressed hope that suburban districts could provide a sound, affordable education that would increase their chance of passing their class position along to their children and grandchildren.[38] William Wheeler, who had lived in suburban Glencoe almost since arriving from Georgia in the 1940s, resettled in Northbrook, Illinois, with his daughter and her children because he was "determined my grandkids would go to school here. . . . Before I even bought this house, I talked to the superintendent of the schools for this area, and I already heard it was very expensive to go to school in this area without having property. If you had property, it was automatic. So, . . . we looked for a house."[39] Stephanie Giglio, who moved from southwest Chicago to the western suburbs, explained: "We decided it was time to move. The schools are not that great, they're turning quickly predominantly black. Not that that's bad—I don't know how to say it—but they weren't the right type, middle-income and concerned about property and schools."[40]

As Giglio's comments indicate, middle-class families were often explicit about their desire to put distance between themselves and poorer neighbors, or at least to surround themselves with people of the same class. Suburbanites said they hoped to be "near people who share many of the same goals that we do" or to live "in a community with a large number of black professionals."[41] "When you get right down to it," said Doug Bechtel, a demographer at the University of Georgia, "these social class things run very deep. You want to live in a nice, safe neighborhood, and have a nice car," goals that many people believed were more easily accomplished in a suburb.[42] In the opinion of Vincent Lane, head of the Chicago Housing Authority, "Suburbanization isn't about race now. It's about class. Nobody wants to be around poor people, because of all the problems that go along with poor people: poor schools, unsafe streets, gangs."[43]

As much as the new suburbanites sought to stake out comfortably middle-class lives, comments such as these indicate that the sensibilities they brought to the marketplace reflected the overlapping influences of race as well as class in their lives. In the first place, African Americans' frame of reference usually included residential experience in a central city or, before that, a depressed rural area. In contrast to whites, who were most likely to have moved from one suburb to another, African Americans who moved to suburbs in the 1980s and 1990s frequently asserted their hopes in the form of a contrast between the suburbs they imagined and the city they knew. Sometimes that contrast was implicit; as Black Entertainment Network entrepreneur Robert Johnson argued, suburbanites sought "better schools, better homes, better quality of life."[44] Just as often, suburbanites pointed to explicit differences, such as "intolerable" schools, "poor city services," high crime rates, or the "clutter and confusion and politics of city life" as their reasons for moving to suburbs.[45] Pat Lottier, the publisher of a black business periodical who made her home in Atlanta's northern suburbs, revealed the historically structured type of comparisons that many black families made before moving to the suburbs.

> My husband and I . . . felt the need from the very beginning to live away from the inner city. We wanted to move away from everything the inner city has. We wanted our kids to have the very best, and the best was outside of any major city. Safety. Amenities. The best shopping centers. A house with an acre or more. The freedom to leave your house and check on one door and not all the doors and not all the windows. The best schools — being able to go into the school and say I need to see the teacher and someone saying, "Yes, Mrs. Lottier, sit down." Inner city doesn't give you that. And unfortunately I don't think it ever will.[46]

Despite Lottier's emphasis on what she saw as differences between "inner" cities and suburbs, her comparison, in fact, juxtaposed wealthy suburban areas with the disadvantaged urban neighborhoods where most African Americans, and especially the poor, lived.

In the context of racially polarized urban restructuring, many suburbanites, like Lottier, compared cities and suburbs on the basis of the services, amenities, and other advantages that their investment would buy. The "city" represented a kind of racialized space that they sought to escape. According to Clarence Simmons, a Chicagoan who moved to suburban Grayslake, Illinois, in the mid-1990s, the explanation for increased suburbanization was simple: "Blacks see the money going to the suburbs and not their neighborhoods."[47] Dierdre Clayton and her husband cited similar reasons for moving from Chicago's South Shore neighborhood to Flossmoor, a fast-growing suburb with a large black middle class. "In a southern suburb you get more land," Clayton said, "and I don't have to pay the taxes of the city and still send [my children] to a private school. We're talking about the value of a dollar when we're talking about the suburbs."[48] Gwen Snow, who moved from Washington, D.C., to a predominantly black subdivision in suburban Atlanta, seconded the thought: "You get more bedrooms for your money and newer schools in the suburbs." "Who wouldn't want that, instead of lead paint?"[49] Reflecting on the race-structured circumstances that African Americans faced in central cities as well as the interests they shared as members of the middle class, thousands of upwardly mobile families moved to suburbs.

Perhaps the most compelling factor underlying the middle-class exodus was a concern for personal safety. Here, too, class and race factors entwined. Numerous suburbanites identified urban crime as a chief motivation for moving to the suburbs. During the late 1980s and early 1990s, central city crime rates reached appalling heights. Washington, Detroit, Houston, Los Angeles, St. Louis, Baltimore, and other cities traded dubious distinction as the nation's murder capital.[50] African American neighborhoods and young African Americans in particular felt the worst of the onslaught. By the late 1980s, young black men were ten times as likely to be the victims of a violent crime than young whites, and homicide surpassed automobile accidents as the leading cause of death among black teens and young adults. In Washington, D.C., where the annual murder tally peaked at 489 in 1990, one in four hundred black teens died in a homicide.[51] Poor communities suffered most, but many middle-class urbanites, people who had deep community roots and whose participation in local affairs contributed to the quality of city life, also felt threatened. Where long-standing residents found themselves unable to exert effective social control over their neighborhoods, where they felt their physical security and that of their children at risk, many began considering the suburbs.[52]

A survey of 3,000 people who left Chicago in 1992 revealed that the "desire for a safer place to live" was a leading reason for their move. Black and white Chicagoans, the study reported, felt "pushed out" by "crime . . . poor schools, the noise, the congestion. And also by the sense that there is nothing that anyone—not themselves or city officials—can do to make city life better."⁵³ African Americans often found themselves closer to the front lines than whites. Larznell Harper Sr., who left the predominantly black Woodlawn district for suburban Broadview, was one of many black Chicagoans whose commitment to urban living was shaken by violence: "Crime was rising," he explained. "Our cars were stolen three times in four months. But the biggest factor was a rape of a 12-year-old girl behind our alley." "I felt that, even though you can never guarantee your child's safety this was way too close to home. It was just the final straw."⁵⁴

In other cities, black suburbanites justified their decisions similarly. Michael and Verna Frazier saw themselves as committed Washingtonians, but a nighttime break-in marked the turning point. "I heard them and they heard me," Mr. Frazier said, "and so they left, but our physical safety had been jeopardized. That did it for us." The Fraziers moved across the city limits to Temple Hills, Maryland.⁵⁵ John Curtis and his wife moved from New York City to Montclair, New Jersey, in the mid-1990s for related reasons. Curtis explained:

> When we lived in Brooklyn and [my son] was on his bike or just outside, I could never let him get beyond my line of sight. I got tired of worrying about him every moment. . . . I know there are some people back in Brooklyn, some of the brothers, who might say I sold out or turned my back on the neighborhood. That's all right. I know I did the right thing, and I've never looked back . . . not even once. . . . I did what I had to for my family. I wanted to live someplace where I felt my son would be safe.⁵⁶

Teresa Tigg underscored the same point, leaving Buffalo's east side for historically white Tonawanda, New York, in the late 1980s because of "a terrible drug problem and crime problem in the surrounding community."

> The kids would go to the store, and people selling drugs would approach them. . . . [T]he weekend after I left, a person was shot in my yard. . . . I just want my kids to be safe. That's not to say there's no

crime in the suburbs. But I can send my kids to the store and be confident they won't be approached by anyone. Some of my friends (in
Buffalo) have lost kids to crime, and that's more than I could take.[57]

As violence convulsed urban neighborhoods in the 1980s and 1990s, thousands of African Americans moved to suburbs out of concern for their families' safety.

Although race and class concerns mixed in the way suburbanites explained
their residential decisions, some factors clearly distinguished African Americans from other suburbanites on the basis of race alone. The most important
of these was discrimination in housing. Notwithstanding black migration to a
larger number of suburban areas than ever before, discrimination remained a
prevailing feature of U.S. real estate markets. In 1992–93 alone, local, state,
and federal housing agencies received more than ten thousand fair-housing-
related complaints. A national study by the federal Department of Housing
and Urban Development in 1991 discovered that "more than half of blacks
buying or renting homes suffer some kind of discrimination."[58] In the Chicago area, housing tests involving economically matched pairs of black and
white testers revealed evidence of discrimination in a third of contacts with
landlords or real estate agents.[59] Much the same story unfolded in the home
finance market. National surveys of mortgage lending in 1989 revealed that
blacks were "twice as likely as whites at comparable income levels to be denied
mortgages."[60] In eighty-five out of a hundred metropolitan areas surveyed,
high-income blacks were rejected for mortgage loans more often than low-
income whites. These findings reflected not only direct anti-black bias on the
part of lenders but the web of racial disadvantage that African Americans
faced. Discrimination in employment, as well as poor schools, high taxes, and
lower rates of property appreciation in neighborhoods where most blacks
lived, limited their incomes and undermined their ability to accumulate
wealth, creating ostensibly objective bases for rejection. Difficulty borrowing
money merely reinforced the cycle, limiting the range of houses and neighborhoods that families could afford and weakening their ability to leverage
their current economic assets to build wealth.

In addition to constraining African Americans' freedom in the housing
market, discrimination reinforced a racialization of metropolitan space by
shaping blacks' perceptions about the places they were free to live and the
choices they were likely to make. Dogged bias made many African Americans
leery about moving just anywhere. "Unpleasant experiences," as St. Louisan

Adel Allen had described them, perceptions of "gentlemanly quotas," and incidents of vandalism or violence led many people to confine their housing choices to known options: places where friends, family, or an appreciable number of other blacks already lived.[61] In metropolitan Chicago, for example, a 1993 survey found that between half and three-quarters of blacks "expect[ed] problems" in moving to mostly white communities.[62] "Even as far as we've come," said suburbanite Barbara Sutton, "there is still a fear of going into some areas."[63] Teresa Travis, who reassessed her decision to move to suburban Alsip after a local developer blocked her purchase of a home, explained, "You don't want to move to a suburb where you have to worry about whether you were waited on second because you are black."[64] "Differences in treatment," according to fair-housing advocate James Shannon, no longer posed the insurmountable difficulties that they had in the immediate postwar period, but they exerted an important influence on black residential choices, causing many families to think twice before venturing too far from the beaten path.[65]

The combination of discrimination, perception, and blacks' lower overall economic position fortified existing patterns of concentrated settlement, segregation, and inequality among suburbs, despite obvious social changes following the civil rights movement.[66] Thus, in 1990 more than 40 percent of black suburbanites in metropolitan Chicago lived in just fourteen suburbs, all of them in the general vicinity of neighborhoods that had been occupied by black families since the Great Migration. Even "when wealthier African Americans moved to predominantly white suburbs," the *Chicago Tribune* reported in 1995, "most picked those close to majority black communities."[67] Further, analysis of the 1990 census revealed that the "typical African American in the Cook County suburbs," which were home to two-thirds of area black suburbanites, lived on a block that was less than 10 percent white.[68] On Long Island, New York, too, historic patterns of racial separation proved resistant to change. In 1990 two-thirds of neighborhoods in Nassau and Suffolk Counties were less than 1 percent black; half had no black residents at all.[69] While the number of racially homogenous suburbs declined in the 1980s and 1990s, raising the possibility that children of the next generation might never know a "lily-white" suburb, patterns of suburban racial segregation diminished only marginally.[70] Despite hopes that black suburbanization represented, in the words of magazine publisher Hermene Hartman, "a new emerging trend where race is not as important as income," everyday life in the nation's metropolitan areas reflected persistent racial stratification, which contributed to the continuing significance of race.[71]

Fig. 9.2   Afternoon in black suburbia: Prince George's County, Maryland.
By the 1990s, black suburbanization was big business for construction firms in
Washington, Chicago, Atlanta, and other metropolitan areas. (Photograph by
Andrew Wiese, 2001)

"Black Xanadu"[72]

On a weekday afternoon in late October, the ebb and flow of suburban life
pulse along Lottsford Road in central Prince George's County, Maryland,
outside Washington, D.C. Thickening traffic signals the waning of the workday. Yellow school buses trundle along new asphalt. Children step off in knots.
Two boys race after one another flashing smiles. Girls in braids roll brightly
colored backpacks up the street, clutching class projects on pink and blue
poster board. One child trails behind, dragging his coat on the sidewalk in the
Indian summer sun as though the weight of the world rested on his shoulders.
Nearby, billboard advertisements for new subdivisions beckon with the promise of "carefree living."

   At Woodmore, which the *New York Times* described as "a predominantly
black gated community . . . with private security, town houses, sprawling estates and a golf course," pickup trucks exit the brick gateposts, discharging
Latino landscaping crews and white tradesmen onto Woodmore Road.[73]
Traffic backs up in the direction of Washington as working moms in late-

Fig. 9.3 Woodmore South, October 2001. Five-bedroom colonial-style homes on half-acre lots were but the most conspicuous features of the new landscape of black power in central Prince George's County. (Photograph by Andrew Wiese, 2001)

model SUVs with vanity plates signal left, transporting children from school. Commuters speeding eastward provide a veritable auto show of models in the over-$40,000 range: Jaguars, Range Rovers, BMWs, and Lexus sedans, outward emblems of affluence that made the area a showplace for the black upper middle class.[74] By 1990, with African Americans constituting 52 percent of the population, Prince George's County was the first majority-black, majority-affluent county in the United States.[75]

With its "big houses, sleek cars and decidedly upscale and consciously black residents," the new Prince George's County juxtaposes unsettlingly — as suburban sprawl always does — with the remnants of the county's rural past.[76] Yet the contrast is amplified by the shift in social power that has accompanied the transformation in landscape. In Upper Marlboro, the county seat, the cavernous buildings of the Marlboro Tobacco Market and the Planters Tobacco Warehouse bespeak not only the region's agricultural roots but its jim crow traditions: sharecropping, segregated schools, political exclusion, and police brutality. Just down the road is the neat county administration center, designed in the style of a suburban office park and presided over since 1994 by an African American chief executive.[77]

Fig. 9.4   Mailboxes at the historically black Duckettsville settlement juxtapose awkwardly with the design of neighboring subdivisions. As in many parts of the Southeast, recent suburbanization near Washington added a new layer of black settlement to a landscape that African Americans had shaped for centuries. (Photograph by Andrew Wiese, 2001)

Like other parts of the upper South, souvenirs of Prince George's black history are evident as well: a clutch of battered mailboxes on the Duckettown Road, the weathered buildings of Mount Nebo and Union Bethel churches, the old Fletchertown Colored School near Bowie, or the former Lakeland High School in College Park (now a Korean American church).[78] Augmenting these remains are landscapes laid down in more than a century of suburbanization: black municipalities such as North Brentwood, built by Union army veterans and their descendants; Glenarden, a trolley-car suburb first subdivided in the 1910s along the Washington, Baltimore, and Annapolis Electric Railroad; and Fairmount Heights, whose founding residents included federal workers, schoolteachers, laborers, and professionals such as architect William Sidney Pittman and his wife, Portia, the daughter of Booker T. Washington.[79]

Prince George's transformation from "white, agricultural and segregated" to the "best-educated and most affluent black community in the nation" illustrates the confluence of history and geography that gave rise to spectacular increases in black suburbanization after 1960.[80] Adjacent to a central city with a growing black population and a booming middle class, located in the line of black geographic expansion, and boasting an African American history of its own, Prince George's was ripe for black suburbanization after 1960. Blacks were just 12 percent of the county's population in 1950, but during the next decade, black migration and block-by-block expansion in the eastern half of Washington, D.C., consolidated three formerly separate African American neighborhoods into a single majority-black region reaching the Prince George's border. Soon, middle-class families began moving to white neighborhoods across the city limits. On the northeastern edge of the District, several thousand African Americans moved to the neighborhoods of Takoma Park and Chillum after 1960. Similar numbers settled across the southeastern city limits in suburbs such as Oxon Hill and Hillcrest Heights. The third and largest salient emerged at the eastern corner of the capital in the rolling country between Fairmount Heights, North Brentwood, and Glenarden.[81] As black families moved in, whites moved out. "They'd speak to you," recalled a woman who moved to tidy Peppermill Village in the midsixties, "but evidently they didn't want to live by you."[82] The result was a swift process of racial turnover much like the one that had transformed northeast Washington in the 1940s and 1950s. By the early seventies, African Americans were on their way to a majority in neat residential suburbs all along the city line.[83]

The pace of suburbanization accelerated after 1970. Expanding from this base, "blacks with money . . . mov[ed] farther and farther out in the county."[84] Whites continued to flee. Hastening the process, a 1972 lawsuit by the local NAACP led to court-ordered busing to desegregate county schools, and consistent legal pressure led the county police force, which had no black officers before 1969, to hire and eventually promote African Americans.[85] African American families replaced whites in neighborhoods throughout central Prince George's County. In addition, developers built apartments, condominiums, and single-family homes, attracting black Washingtonians with a range of incomes.[86] As they did, the area between the District of Columbia and the Interstate 495 Beltway gained a black majority. Finally, during the 1980s and 1990s, concurrent with rising crime and fiscal decline inside the capital, the black population of the county mushroomed and the number of whites began to decline.[87] Blacks held a slim majority of 51 percent in 1990. Four years later, black voters converted their numbers into political power, electing the county's first African American executive officer, Mitchellville lawyer Wayne K. Curry.[88]

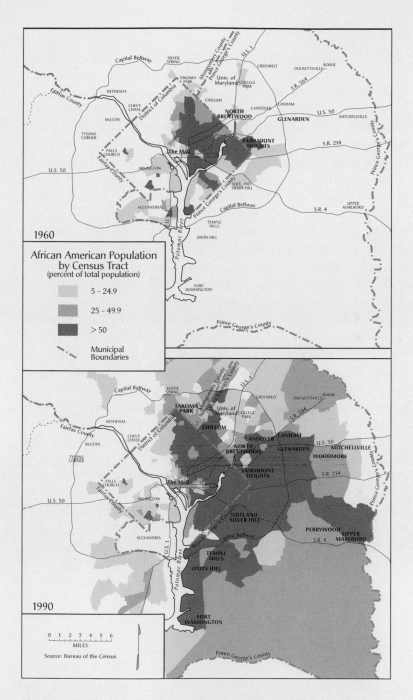

Fig. 9.5   Black Suburbanization in Washington, D.C., and Prince George's County, Maryland, 1960 and 1990. (Map by Harry D. Johnson)

If middle-class blacks in the 1960s moved to the county "in search of a slice of suburbia," as one native put it, by the 1990s Prince Georgians' suburban dreams encompassed a greater vision of suburban space that included remaking the county, socially, politically, and symbolically, as black and middle-class territory.[89] Like earlier suburban dreams, this one embraced not only aesthetic preferences but images of race and class empowerment. Going beyond the defensive aspects of shared space and the individualistic efforts of families to use location to secure their economic well-being, residents envisioned a place where middle-class blacks would exercise political and economic power equal or superior to that of whites. It was not control in the context of a racially marginalized "ghetto" that they sought, but rather an economically robust suburban area. They aimed to create a place that was synonymous with the new black middle class. In a nation of racially stratified places, they sought to redefine the meaning of black-occupied space.[90]

Prince George's prevailing residential ideology was apparent in dozens of new subdivisions that sprang up in the 1990s. Among the most prominent of these was Perrywood, a glistening new community of more than a thousand single-family homes and town houses not far from the mostly black golf-course communities of Woodmore and Lake Arbor. The development featured two-story, four-bedroom homes from the mid-$200,000s, plus paved bicycle and jogging paths, a swimming pool, basketball and tennis courts, man-made duck ponds, and a winding layout of streets named for waterfowl: Black Swan Drive, Widgeon Court, and so on. Affluent and predominantly black, Perrywood was a quintessential end-of-the-century suburban development for families with incomes between $50,000 and $100,000.

While its class emblems were obvious, the development also reflected attempts to reinforce a racial identity for its majority. A model home for sale by the Patriot Homes Company revealed just one means to this end. Standing among other recently completed models on Whistling Duck Drive, the four-bedroom, 2,600-square-foot house sold for approximately $260,000 in the fall of 2001.[91] Inside, the company's marketing staff assembled the material elements of a lifestyle meant to attract upscale black families. In the light-filled kitchen, four martini glasses filled with acrylic gin and olives rested on a Corian countertop as though the host and hostess had stepped momentarily into the backyard with their guests. Contemporary jazz filtered into the room from ceiling-mounted speakers. The decor in the adjoining family room resembled a Pottery Barn store with an African American accent—leather armchairs, early American prints, and a potted calla lily, plus African masks on the wall and an ebony rhinoceros over the fireplace. The first-floor "library" evoked a composite class, race, and gender identity for the man of the house. High-end electronic gadgets — a CD-DVD player, flat-screen computer monitor, and the like — indicated expensive professional and leisure-time pursuits. On the walls, framed art posters depicted Cuban cigars, an advertisement for the Montreux Jazz Festival, Miles Davis cradling a trumpet, and a gathering of midcentury civil rights leaders on the stoop of a Harlem brownstone, suggesting a man with cultural and political commitments to race. Upstairs, the household tableau continued with children's bedrooms furnished alternately in football paraphernalia and country French pastels. In the master bedroom, class privilege reached its peak with his and her walk-in closets, cathedral ceilings, a king-size bed, and a master bathroom the size of a Manhattan studio apartment, replete with a sunken Jacuzzi tub, tile floors, and dual vanity sinks.

Although Patriot Homes built identical models across the metropolitan area, at Perrywood they took special steps to make African Americans feel at home. Signifiers of class *and* race appealed to black professionals, evoking the home's ideal household and implying a complementary population in the neighborhood beyond. Their marketing choices, from the smartly dressed black sales agent — European sedan parked out front — to the not so subtle decor, give every indication that people with similar values and social positions will live next door: they will be home-owning, child-rearing, well-educated, heterosexual, nuclear families, who are also sociable, cosmopolitan, affluent, and proud of the nation's black heritage. If they are not African Americans, they are likely to be comfortable with racial difference and a community of black neighbors. There is little chance of moving next door to Archie Bunker here.

Though the ideal manifest in the Perrywood model home was the work of a white-owned development company, the proliferation of similar subdivisions and marketing techniques throughout the country indicates that the image is not unappealing to middle-class African American home buyers. Journalist Sam Fulwood offers additional support for the point, describing his own first encounter with lifestyle marketing of this sort — in an Atlanta suburb — as a deeply satisfying experience. The "subtle, subliminal persuasions aimed at racial pride and feelings of estrangement from white neighborhoods" hit home for Fulwood, who had grown up in a middle-class black subdivision near Charlotte and who had been unimpressed with the cool reception he and his wife had received in comparable developments aimed at whites.[92] When the Fulwoods relocated to Washington in the early 1990s, they knew just what they were looking for: "a sense of racial community and isolation from the white mainstream."[93] They wanted "open, honest and friendly black folks" as their neighbors, people like the ones they knew in the middle-class communities where they had been raised. They wanted a neighborhood that would be quiet, dependable, and "affirming" for their daughter as well as for themselves. Economically capable of choosing a home in any number of neighborhoods in the city or its suburbs, they selected a mostly black, upscale subdivision in Fort Washington, Maryland, because, Fulwood wrote, "we wanted comfort on our own terms."[94]

By the 1980s, it was clear that the Fulwoods were in good company. For scores of new Prince Georgians, the "critical mass of middle-class blacks" was a chief attraction.[95] Barron Harvey, an accounting professor at Howard University who moved to Prince George's County from a predominantly white suburban area in Virginia, explained, "We always wanted to be in a community with a large number of black professionals and to feel part of that community. . . . We always wanted to make sure our child had many African American children to play with, not just one or two."[96] The Harveys' Prince George's neighborhood promised to fulfill these desires. "Two doors down from us is a black cardiologist. There's a dentist on the block, a couple of lawyers, an airline pilot, a college professor, an entrepreneur," Harvey said. "My daughter needs to be exposed to that."[97] Like the Harveys, Frank and Kathryn Weaver sought a mostly black middle-class community so that their daughter would develop "a sense of pride in her identity as a black person" as well as the ability to compete with people of all kinds.[98] For economically comfortable families, one measure of growing residential choice was the freedom to dream of suburban life without having to give up either their economic interests or racial comfort.

According to columnist Betty Winston Baye, many families chose to settle in neighborhoods with "a significant black presence" not only so that their children could "know and socialize with black people who bust the negative stereotypes," but, like the Fulwoods, because they wanted to re-create "the supportive environments in which many . . . grew up," what she referred to as "buppie cocoons."[99] David Ball, a contract administrator in Washington who settled in Fort Washington in the late 1980s, explained: "I really wasn't interested in moving into an all-white neighborhood and being the only black pioneer down there. I don't want to come home and always have my guard up. After I work eight hours or more a day, I don't want to come home and work another eight."[100] Jan Summers, a psychologist and Prince George's resident, gave the same explanation. "I didn't want to be a novelty," she said. "I wanted a neighborhood where the kids would run toward me rather than away from me."[101]

In contrast to earlier pioneers like Ted Wheeler who, in an intensely segregated world, believed that predominantly white suburbs could provide a kind of social balance as well as the quality schools and services that upper-middle-class white communities delivered as a matter of course, many of Prince George's professional blacks sought to ensure a different kind of spatial and social balance — one they felt that they were in jeopardy of losing through integration. Working in white-dominated job settings, under pressure to ignore, contest, reeducate, or simply endure white attitudes, many took refuge in black middle- and upper-middle-class neighborhoods.[102] Moreover, for their children, they hoped that growing up among accomplished black neighbors would give them a strong foundation from which to compete in "the mainstream culture."[103]

Intertwined with social and economic aspirations such as these, new Prince Georgians also expressed a political vision reflecting the sentiments of many African Americans in the post–civil rights era. As the county edged toward a black majority, it gained significance as a locus for black achievement and empowerment of the sort that many residents had once ascribed to Washington and other predominantly black cities. In this, they built on a tradition of spatial nationalism with roots stretching into the self-help ideology of Booker T. Washington — whose adherents had established local suburbs like Fairmount Heights and Lincoln — through midcentury black business and real estate associations and their supporters in the federal race relations departments to the black power movement, the Black Panthers and the Nation of Islam. In their 1967 manifesto, *Black Power*, for example, Stokely Carmichael and Charles Hamilton had argued against integration as a means of overcoming the spatial disadvantages imposed on black neighborhoods. "What must be abolished is not the black community," they wrote, "but the dependent colonial status that has been inflicted upon it."[104] In cities like Washington, D.C., there were thousands of people who agreed. District of Columbia city planner James Gibson explained, "We had a larger black middle class than many cities, and for a long time it didn't move. Initially it didn't move because of segregation in the suburbs. But even after desegregation, there was an identification with this black government and a desire to see this experiment work. It was when that vision defaulted that the exodus stepped up."[105] Lucenia Dunn, who moved from the city to Woodmore in 1989, concurred, "We were first proud of the Chocolate City, and it's hard to unloosen that level of loyalty to the concept of having a successful African American–owned and –operated and –run city. It grieves us that it's in trouble." As the city suffered financial and social hardship, however, Prince George's County became, according to journalists Steven Holmes and Karen DeWitt, "the capital of transplanted dreams."[106]

Prince George's resurgent territorial nationalism was especially apparent among its leading civic figures. In the opinion of the Reverend Grainger Browning, whose Ebenezer AME church grew to more than 8,000 members after relocating to the Fort Washington area from Georgetown in 1983, Prince George's County represented "the next phase of the civil rights movement." "Many persons in the county have been the beneficiaries of the '60s. We now have some economic ability to make changes, so we can own businesses and be in corporate, academic and political leadership, and really have the opportunity to become a model of black-white relations and black political empowerment."[107] County executive Wayne Curry agreed, "For black people, we are talking about the last frontier — political and economic power."[108] "We're the only example in the history of America," he said, "of a major jurisdiction that's gone from being virtually all-white to majority-black where income and education have gone up and not down."[109] Though Curry overlooked numerous lesser examples where African Americans had enhanced the socioeconomic status of neighborhoods, his statements highlight the fervency of Prince George's new image as a mecca for the black middle class, or in his words, the "jewel in the crown of the American post–civil rights era."[110]

This vision of Prince George's County as a symbol for black empowerment and a concrete place in which to achieve it was not restricted to the county's political elite. A countywide survey in 1994 revealed that 75 percent of black residents said they were "proud" to live in the county — among households making more than $50,000 annually the proportion was even higher. A third believed that the county was "a special place."[111] Many residents saw the county not only as a comfortable "buppie cocoon," but as a place where, as one resident stated, African Americans can "control our own destiny."[112] With "so many well-educated blacks from across the country," said Clayton Powell Jr., a lawyer who grew up in North Brentwood and came home after graduating from Harvard Law School, "Prince George's is becoming a switching point for that black power elite, giving us a first crack at leadership right here in our community. More so than the District because there is no question of home rule. Once we get control, it will be ours."[113] Said Glenn Dale lawyer Ronald Handy, "I think we have an opportunity to really develop a prosperous, diverse county with a high quality of life for a large majority of the people."[114] In light of these statements, it was clear that county executive Curry spoke for many people when he said that he dreamed of Prince George's County as "a place where we can define ourselves and not be defined by the stereotypical dictates of others."[115]

Nevertheless, as much as middle-class Prince Georgians sought to define their community on their own terms, they were not insulated from the larger forces shaping race, class, and space in the metropolitan region. Through the 1990s, residents confronted social and economic challenges that they shared with black suburban areas across the country and that distinguished them from their white neighbors. Their efforts to solve these puzzles reflected the tenuous balancing act of maintaining middle-class black communities in a racially stratified society.

One persisting "sore spot" was the shortage of commercial and recreational facilities to match the rising status of the county's black population.[116] Although household incomes grew faster in Prince George's County during the 1990s than in neighboring counties, the area's commercial strips, from College Park to Mitchellville, offered little more than bargain retailing, fast-food franchises, and middle-of-the-road chains. Rising socioeconomic status and a booming black middle class, notwithstanding, white-owned retailers remained hesitant to invest money in the county. In 1994 four-fifths of residents reported that "the absence of high-end retail stores is a big problem," and many residents complained that they had "to drive to Montgomery County or Virginia to have a good meal."[117] Clyde W., who moved to the area for a post at the University of Maryland, put the matter in a nutshell: "I went to the drive-thru at Wendy's, and everyone was in a Jaguar or a BMW. I knew something was wrong."[118] The dearth of "classier dining, shopping and socializing options"—amenities of the sort that upper-middle-class white suburbanites took for granted—was a common complaint.[119]

More significant than the distance to Nordstrom or "Bloomies," however, large parts of the county inside the Beltway displayed serious signs of commercial flight and disinvestment. One study found that a lack of banks and other financial institutions made it "difficult for many people to open bank accounts or apply for credit to purchase homes."[120] Despite significant economic achievements, residents felt, in the words of Wayne Curry, a "quiet, slow burn" over the "cultural lag" that distinguished them from adjacent suburban areas.[121]

Even more troubling was persistently low performance in the county's public school system. Gauged by standardized test scores—an admittedly incomplete measure of school quality—Prince George's schools, the nineteenth-largest district in the United States, stumbled in the 1990s, dropping to second lowest among the state's twenty-four districts by the end of the decade. Only in Baltimore, a district with substantially lower incomes, were scores lower.[122]

Prince George's difficulties stemmed in part from the political legacy of racial turnover. In 1978, when the greater part of the county electorate was still white — but the schools were on their way to a black majority — voters imposed a property-tax limit that set the stage for perpetual underfunding, a financial time bomb set to go off as blacks took control of the county schools.[123] The district posted improvements throughout the 1980s, but as the county grew in the 1990s, per pupil spending fell below the state average, teacher salaries lagged, and enrollments outstripped the district's ability to hire new teachers or build needed schools. In 1998 more than fifty local schools reported "serious" crowding, 10,000 of the district's 125,000 students attended school in temporary trailers, and 15 percent of its teachers lacked state certification — compared to just 1.5 percent in neighboring Montgomery County.[124]

Compounding the district's fiscal limitations were disputes over management. Tension between board members and parents from inside and outside the Beltway and "political bickering" between the school board and its superintendent in the late 1990s merely heightened the difficulty of resolving the property-tax shortfall.[125] Witnessing what some residents viewed as a "circus" in Upper Marlboro, citizens questioned whether district administrators could be trusted to spend the money already allocated to them.[126] Finally, in 2002, under pressure from black lawmakers who feared that wealthy African American families would desert the schools without immediate action to improve them, the state legislature voted to replace the elected (and mostly black) school board with an appointed body, allocating new state aid to support the reforms.[127]

Fragile schools posed an acute challenge to the interests of middle-class residents and their vision of territorial empowerment. Images of the county as "an enclave of black prosperity" relied implicitly on the strength of the local schools, which were a cornerstone of suburban economic advantage throughout the nation. Without strong schools, residents' hope of creating a place that would enhance both their class and race interests threatened to come undone. U.S. congressman Albert Wynn of Mitchellville summarized many of his constituents' worst fears pointing squarely to their concern with racialized space. Without decisive action to secure school quality and solve other problems, he said, the county risked becoming "a ghetto — big cars, big houses, poor schools, high crime and no economic development."[128]

Prince George's growing pains were not uncommon in rapidly developing suburban areas, but they also mirrored fiscal and social conditions that the county shared with other increasingly black suburban areas, matters of racial distinction that challenged residents' efforts to secure middle-class privileges in well-integrated or predominantly black jurisdictions. The new suburbanites were younger and more likely to have children than the white households that preceded them, and they placed greater demands on district resources. The shortage of commercial and industrial enterprises in the county exacerbated the district's funding difficulties, situating the burden of educational financing squarely on the shoulders of local home owners. Of particular salience, however, was the growing number of working-class and poor black families who placed demands on the county that many suburban districts did not share.[129] By 1995, 40 percent of students in Prince George's County schools received subsidized meals, a benefit restricted to families with poverty-level incomes. The figure had climbed to 45 percent by 2000.[130] Growing poverty in suburbs closest to the city required the district to allocate its limited funds for specialized reading programs, expanded Head Start classes and after-school tutoring targeted at poor children. It also amplified a host of social problems common to low-income communities, including high rates of student turnover, sporadic parent involvement, peer pressures to resist high achievement, and a segment of children who came to school hungry, emotionally upset, or disrespectful of authority.[131] Segregation by class as well as race meant that students from poorer families, and the extra challenges they brought with them, were concentrated in a select number of schools.[132]

Sharing a school district with working-class and poor families, Prince George's middle class epitomized the position of upwardly mobile African Americans in cities and suburbs across the United States; they were physically and socially separate from the black working class, but not by much.[133] In some neighborhoods close to Washington, run-down apartments, vacant lots, and battered single-family houses betrayed the concentration of poverty and other social problems: as Peppermill Village native Kevin Merida put it, "Too many police sirens at night, too many bars on windows, too many hoodlums hanging out on street corners."[134] During the late eighties and early nineties, inner Beltway suburbs like Capitol Heights, Lanham, Landover, and Kentlands became corridors for drug trafficking and violence that included execution-style murders, drive-by shootings, serial rapes, and other crimes.[135] In Glenarden the city manager pioneered the concept of "midnight basketball" in 1986 after watching local violence peak during the hours between 10 P.M. and 2 A.M.[136] As working poor families left even more troubled neighborhoods in the city and existing county residents struggled with fluctuations in a changing economy, rates of poverty in the county climbed in step with its affluence.[137] By the 1990s, Prince George's County was home to two black suburban populations divided on the basis of class.

The Continuing Significance of Class

Sensitivity to class among middle- and upper-middle-class Prince Georgians, therefore, reflected not distance but proximity to the black working class and the very real dangers of downward economic mobility that this implied. Prince George's black middle class struggled not only to distinguish itself from surrounding white suburbanites, but to insulate itself from the troubles engulfing poorer sections of the county, neighborhoods that some residents readily described as "the ghetto."[138]

The brick gateposts and guardhouse at the entrance to Woodmore were an extreme physical manifestation of class divisions in the county—marking not just difference but exclusion—but class concerns infused many other areas of county life. The election of county executive Wayne K. Curry in 1994, which was hailed as a "historic step" in racial terms, did little to change the pattern of elite-oriented politics that had long governed in Upper Marlboro.[139] Among his campaign issues, according to *New York Times* reporters Steven Holmes and Karen DeWitt, Curry argued that developers were building too many "high density, low-income housing units in the county." After taking office, he threatened to deny water and sewer connections to several developments "unless the builders made the houses larger and more expensive."[140] Curry and other county power brokers also backed a successful plan to end two decades of court-ordered busing in 1996, which had the effect, observers noted, of enhancing class segregation by blocking the transfer of students from inner suburbs to schools outside the Beltway. In the opinion of Marcy Canavan, a white school board member, the message was "very clear that some [people] don't want ghetto kids in their school buildings."[141] Relations between the school board and superintendent Iris Metts, too, soured in the late nineties, when, among other things, she backed a plan to funnel money from affluent areas outside the Beltway to struggling schools closer to the District. "Even as people in Prince George's seek a better life," Holmes and DeWitt wrote, "they often seem concerned about not becoming too much of a haven for Washington's poor."[142]

Encapsulating the class anxieties of the county's black strivers was a 1996 incident that attracted national media attention. That summer the Perrywood home owners' association voted to employ off-duty police officers to patrol their local basketball courts, preventing uninvited visitors from playing or congregating there. The controversy arose after the Perrywood courts became a popular place for black teenagers from the neighborhood and surrounding communities—including the city—to play ball and hang out. Complaining that the nightly company of teens with cars, bikes, and stereos represented an "eyesore" and warning that "we have already experienced violence and property damage," the association hired the police to escort outsiders from the neighborhood.[143]

The decision illuminated the complicated bonds of race and class that underlay African American life in the county. Some residents objected on racial grounds to the use of police, long a symbol of white power, to control young black men. Others protested the message it conveyed about themselves—setting up distinctions they wished to diminish or deny despite their decision to live in a neighborhood where residents' above-average incomes were guaranteed by the price of their homes.

Disturbed by "the idea of black people asking police to keep other black people from their neighborhood" and the "negative message" it sent to young black men, a number of Perrywood residents disputed the plan. "I thought our kids shouldn't have to grow up feeling that they're a security threat just because they're black," said twenty-nine-year-old record producer Robert Lewis. Moreover, he added, "I don't think I'm better than any other blacks."[144] Anthony Jaby, the local neighborhood watch chairman, disagreed, portraying the decision as a blow for local control, even freedom. "The police are here to make everybody feel better, safer," he said. "The security seems harsh because it seems that we are trying to patrol our own people, but in reality, we're just asking to live in an environment where you can feel free." Other residents readily admitted socioeconomic interests and anxieties, a matter of "us" and "them" defined by the ability to afford a home in the neighborhood. "People who don't live here might not care about things the way we do," said Ed Connor. "Seeing all the new houses going up, largely unprotected, someone might be tempted." Resident James Newborn tried to minimize the imputed class distinctions, claiming, "We're just strong working people who want something nice." Nonetheless, he acknowledged, "people have a tendency to stick together because they want to maintain their property values, their homes—class issues." Fourteen-year-old Bryan Davis, a resident of neighboring Lake Arbor, drew his own conclusions: "White neighborhood or black neighborhood—it doesn't matter. People start to act the same whatever color they are. If they see somebody suspicious, it really doesn't matter where they are. They just want to protect what's theirs."[145]

In the view of columnist Susan Saulny, Prince George's "black middle class [sought to] do what the white middle class has long done: carve out residential space for themselves."[146] Moreover, in the privately controlled grounds of Prince George's new subdivisions, they gained access to means of local control that many, as former Washingtonians, had found lacking in the streets and playgrounds of their old neighborhoods. Even as members of a group that was especially sensitive to the dangers of crime and downward social mobility, however, there were limits to the distance many middle-class blacks were willing or able to put between themselves and less fortunate families. Notwithstanding gates and security guards at a few local subdivisions, black Prince Georgians rarely approached exclusivity with the ferocity or self-righteousness of their white peers.

Despite the "widening gap between haves and have-nots," families in the affluent eastern and southern portions of the county remained politically, socially, and spatially linked to their counterparts inside the Beltway. Middle-class families were no less likely to be the victims of police harassment and public discrimination. Most, too, acknowledged the reality of racial inequities, which reinforced a perception of linked fate with other blacks.[147] Many shared closer social connections still; they were fellow church members, friends, childhood associates, former neighbors, and kin to people who were, as one suburbanite put it, "just not making it."[148] As in other suburban areas, Prince George's middle class was likely to live nearby, competing for but also sharing public services and political representation. Because of their proximity, middle-class families were likely, in sociologist Mary Patillo-McCoy's words, to "contend with the crime, dilapidated housing and social dislocation that gravitates in their direction."[149] As much as some families sought to distance themselves from working-class communities, affluent blacks remained socially, politically, and geographically connected to other African Americans.

A "Third Way"

As the twentieth century came to an end, the challenge of suburbanization for middle-class blacks remained strikingly similar to that they had faced since World War II: to achieve the spatial advantages of suburban life without sacrificing either economic interest or racial identity. While wider ideological currents had shifted, tracing a drift from explicit integrationism to more varied expressions of nationalism, suburbanites' individual spatial struggles turned on very similar issues. Freer than ever before to select a home on the basis of their preferences and their pocketbooks, African Americans sought to create suburban spaces that supported both their economic interests and racial sensibilities in ways that fitted them as individuals.

Despite the economic success of black professionals in places like Prince

George's County, the national picture of black suburbanization in the 1980s
and 1990s indicated the difficulties that African Americans faced in achieving
these goals. Thirty-odd years after the civil rights movement, the majority of
black suburbanites lived in communities that were simply not equal to the
suburbs where most whites lived. As a group, they were still concentrated in a
comparatively few suburbs, which exhibited dispiriting fiscal profiles, including higher-than-average rates of taxation and public debt, lower median incomes and home values, slower property appreciation, and financially challenged public schools. In 1990 residents of suburbs where even 15 percent of
the population or more were members of a minority group paid property taxes
that were on average 65 percent higher than those paid by residents of suburbs
that were greater than 85 percent Anglo and white.[150] A study by political
scientist Andrew Beveridge discovered that black suburbanites in eighteen of
thirty-one major metropolitan areas paid higher taxes than suburban whites.
In some suburbs, the difference could be measured in thousands of dollars per
year, money that families might have spent on home improvements, investments, college tuition, or medical expenses, not to mention everyday items
like food and clothing.[151] "If one of the routes . . . to middle-class status has
been to move to the suburbs and live a comfortable suburban lifestyle," Beveridge concluded, "trying to achieve that is going to cost more for blacks."[152]

Not only did suburban life tend to cost blacks more; it often delivered less.
Given the fiscal circumstances of the suburbs in which most of them lived,
black suburbanites were less able than whites to accumulate wealth or to guarantee their children access to a high-quality education, two key factors in the
ability of parents to bequeath their status to their children. In short, African
Americans were significantly less able than whites to translate economic
achievement into spatial privilege. As Mary Patillo-McCoy stresses in her
study of a middle-class black neighborhood in Chicago, the distinctive circumstances of the black middle class emerged from the fact that they were *"not
equal* to the white middle class."[153] Despite numerous examples of individual
success, suburbanization only marginally altered these conditions by the year
2000. By and large, black suburbanites remained separate from and unequal
to whites.[154] The old racial stratification of metropolitan space haunted them
still.

Recognizing the spatial disadvantages of the older suburbs where most
black suburbanites lived, a growing number of African American households
in the 1980s and 1990s pursued an alternate course. Like pioneers in the
1950s and 1960s, they moved to suburbs that matched their socioeconomic
means but were also largely absent of other blacks.[155] In these places too,

however, pressures of race unavoidably shaped the way they led their lives. Suburbanites reported experiencing "subtle and sometimes not so subtle white racial resentment," unwanted scrutiny, or "unpleasant incidents" that often left them feeling unwelcome, alienated, or culturally isolated.[156] In response, they made exceptional efforts to stay connected to black communities and institutions, to make sure their children did not "lose a sense of themselves," despite the difficulties of time and distance that this might pose.[157] Thus, in the opinion of sociologist Joe Feagin, blacks "pa[id] a price" almost wherever they chose to live.[158]

Whether they sought homes in welcoming "buppie cocoons" or migrated individually to suburbs where few other blacks lived, the new suburbanites faced challenges to their position and perceptions as black and middle-class people. In this context, their struggles to control, use, and profit from residential space remained as salient as ever. Reflecting on her own experience as well her perspective as an academic, American studies scholar Shelley Parks, a resident of suburban Howard County, Maryland, encapsulated the black suburban dream and dilemma at the turn of the century. Facing what she saw as two equally unpalatable options—economic marginalization or racial assimilation—families like hers, she said, were "trying to find a third way," a way to be thoroughly middle class, thoroughly African American, and comfortable in the best neighborhoods they could afford without sacrificing a sense of themselves as black people. Moreover, she added, "we're . . . making it up as we go along."[159]

Conclusion

If Parks keenly summarized the experience she shared with thousands of recent black suburbanites, she also, unintentionally, pointed to a begging separation between the past and present in perceptions of African American suburbanization. In some ways, the new suburbanites *were* "making it up" as they went. Many of them exercised greater ability to choose from among a wider range of suburban options than ever before. Nonetheless, there were considerable historical precedents. If suburbanites felt that they were exploring uncharted territory, it was partly because, until very recently, African Americans had been written out of the nation's suburban history.

Contemporary debates surrounding the migration of African Americans to suburban areas suffer from this same omission. Lacking a sense of history, popular as well as scholarly dialogue has tended to marginalize, if not demonize, the third of African Americans who live in suburbs. By moving to territory presumed to belong to whites, black suburbanites faced attack from critics who questioned their racial identities and sympathies. "When many blacks make it to the middle class," concluded a black radio entrepreneur in Washington, D.C., "they move to the suburbs and just maintain their black skin. They take on a white mentality."[160] Recent films and literature have rendered unflattering pictures of black suburbanites. Spike Lee's film *Crooklyn*, for example, depicts the protagonist's suburban relatives as shallow, deceptive, and preoccupied with their possessions. Their home is a distorted pink fantasy world absent the love that pervades the well-used Brooklyn brownstone where most of the story is set.[161] Gloria Naylor presents an even harsher appraisal of black mobility in her 1985 novel, *Linden Hills*, which portrays life in a black middle-class suburb as an allegory for Dante's descent into Hell.[162] "It's clear," points out historian Henry L. Taylor Jr., that "there is a very powerful sentiment inside our community [that] feel[s] very negative about our people moving into the suburbs."[163]

Academic scholarship, too, has often reinforced these perceptions. In his influential book *The Truly Disadvantaged*, sociologist William J. Wilson asserts that "the exodus of middle- and working-class families from many ghetto neighborhoods removes an important 'social buffer' that could deflect the full impact of . . . increasing joblessness."[164] More recently, historian Thomas Sugrue strengthened this position, noting that in Detroit the struggle of upwardly mobile African Americans for better housing "set into motion a process that over the long run would leave inner-city neighborhoods increasingly bereft of institutions, businesses, and diversity."[165]

Glancing reflections such as these have lent weight to a popular juxtaposition between recent suburbanization and a purportedly harmonious and unified "golden age" of black community under jim crow. As columnist Tony Brown argued, "The black middle class has removed itself in the name of integration from its own people and taken all the social, financial and human capital with them."[166] The result has been to freeze popular debates over contemporary black suburbanization into empty stereotypes and misconceptions about the history of black people in cities and suburbs, meanwhile ignoring the compounding disadvantages of segregation and racialized space that propelled out-migration in the first place. The criticism that suburbanites have forsaken "the black community," for instance, only makes sense if we conceive of suburbs as essentially white territory without a black history of their own. It also overlooks the fact that for most African American suburbanites, the move from city to suburbs was a relocation from one black community to another and the pathways that many middle-class families followed to the suburbs were forged by working-class households earlier in the century. Lastly, this critique overlooks the long history of suburban discrimination and the defiant civil rights struggle that it provoked. If nothing else, revealing the diversity of African American suburbs and suburbanites over time undermines the stereotype of suburbs as privileged enclaves of the social elite that are somehow separate from the "real" history of African Americans.

To the contrary, analysis of this history demonstrates that suburbanites were never far from the main currents of African American life. Their struggles for quiet streets, open spaces, and places of their own — whether defined as homes, institutions, neighborhoods, municipalities, or even extraterritorial communities — were not simply a recent phenomenon, the inevitable flip side to urban crisis or the fruits of a misguided integrationism. Rather, black suburbanization was a migration shaped variably over time by jobs, family ties, and social networks, as well as values for housing, strategies of wealth accumulation, and desires to use and control space that African Americans nourished and remade throughout the century.

Lastly, if suburbs were an important setting for the study of African American history throughout the twentieth century, by the outset of the twenty-first century they had become fundamental to it. Home to more than half of the nation's population, more than a third of African Americans, and large numbers of Latinos and Asian Americans, suburbia was the context in which much of the struggle over class, color, and power in the twenty-first century would take place.

Race, Class, and Space

In addition to reclaiming suburbs as an important arena of African American life in the twentieth century, the history of African American suburbanization illustrates the centrality of space and spatial struggles in African American life. Historians' attention to race and space has undergone a pendulum swing in recent decades. Most early analyses traced their roots to the model of urban ecology advanced by sociologists at the University of Chicago in the 1920s. Examining neighborhood patterns in the city where they lived, members of the Chicago school established a fundamental connection between residential location and social hierarchy.[167] Affluent families lived in well-appointed suburbs on the city's rim, while recent immigrants, African Americans, and members of other racial minorities congregated in crowded ghettoes near the core. As individuals moved up in social standing, the urban ecologists held, they moved outward through the metropolis. Thus, spatial and social mobility were two sides of the same coin.

From a contemporary perspective, problems with the model are obvious. First, the urban ecologists believed that individuals, like organisms in a biotic community, resided in the spatial niche for which they were best suited. The result was a view that social inequality was a natural part of the social order rather than the result of conflict and imposition. Although they allowed for individuals to move within the system, the ecologists assumed that every group would follow the same path to "assimilation," a goal they measured in reference to a distinctive group: native-born, upper-middle-class white suburbanites. Despite these shortcomings, the model's simplicity, its conservative social outlook, and its pseudoscientific rhetoric gave it extraordinary staying power, especially in sociology, where it remains, in more sophisticated form, a functioning paradigm.[168]

Urban ecology exercised a fundamental influence on the literature of African American urban life as well. From the 1930s through the 1970s, many scholars disputed features associated with the Chicago school, in particular the view that segregation or African American residence in the worst urban housing was "natural," but, in general, they pursued a subject matter grounded in the ecologists' questions and concerns.[169] Urban ecology's interest in spatial and social position, especially, provided the basis for scholarly emphasis on segregation as the defining paradigm for the study of black urban life.

Beginning in the 1970s and 1980s, a new generation of scholars began to challenge what historian Joe W. Trotter Jr. called the "ghetto synthesis," histories that emphasized racial and spatial separation and the "critical role of white racial hostility and prejudice in the development of Afro-American communities." These studies, Trotter charged, promoted a perspective in which "the main explanatory factor in African American life [was] the nature of black-white interaction, usually in its most hostile, caste-like variety."[170] Instead, Trotter and others sought to investigate African Americans' experiences not as exceptions at the margin of an urban history defined by whites, but as inseparable parts of the whole. In particular, they explored African American migration and blacks' transition from agricultural to urban industrial labor, processes that affected African Americans as well as other groups in different periods and places.[171] Through the metaphors of migration and class formation, a new generation of scholars not only situated African Americans within a larger social and economic history of the modern world, but they emphasized the centrality of their subjects' pre-industrial and pre-urban experiences, focusing, as Kimberley Phillips puts it, on "the continuing meaning of southern black culture" in a variety of contexts.[172] Equally important, these scholars paid increased attention to intraracial distinctions such as class and gender that were consequential aspects of urban African American life. While these correctives have contributed immeasurably to the understanding of African American history, these scholars tended to treat space as little more than the physical setting in which these other processes unfolded.

Since the 1990s, however, a number of scholars have called for renewed attention to the role of space in African American life. Earl Lewis's 1991 study of Norfolk, Virginia, was one of the first inquiries to move in this direction. In a context where white power was unrivaled and workplace solidarities dispersed, Lewis found, African Americans focused a considerable portion of their political efforts on improving the neighborhoods where they lived, what he labeled "the home sphere."[173] Pursuing the line of argument further, in 1995 Lewis called for historians to pay greater attention to "place"—space imbued with individual and collective meaning—as an essential locale (if not condition) for the construction of memory and identity.[174] Drawing on the work of Henri Lefebvre, Manuel Castells, and David Harvey, scholars studying other places and periods have begun to explore the spatial practices, representations, and perceptions that were integral to African American life.[175]

Calling for renewed attention to space is not an invitation to revive the old models of ghettoization or race relations as the primary means of approaching African American urban history. Instead, it is a reminder, as Castells points out, that space is "one of society's fundamental material dimensions," subject to manipulation, replete with meaning, the embodiment of social structure and a terrain of human action.[176] Black spatial practices and perceptions, thus, were not simply reactions to white agency, but rather responses to the physical environment shaped by circumstances of history, power, and culture. For much of the century, African Americans approached and sought to shape space from a cultural context rooted in the black South, where the ability to move freely and to control one's physical surroundings—symbolized in the quest for land ownership—were essential to the meaning of freedom. Within southern black communities, too, domestic spaces became important markers of class and community standing, tokens by which African Americans communicated to one another the social values and distinctions they held dear. Carrying these dispositions with them as they moved to urban and suburban areas, African Americans worked to situate themselves in a hostile world. Restricted in the labor market, black households often relied on domestic spaces to meet economic needs. In the context of migration, they constructed homes and neighborhoods where they could build and re-assemble families and define individual and collective worth in their own terms. In the face of white racism, expressed through extraordinary efforts to limit their freedom to occupy, use, or even move through space, they battled to defend and expand the territory available to them. Against this backdrop, African Americans' spatial struggles took on a central place in the freedom movement, their strategies for economic and political empowerment, and contests over racial and class identities.

At the broadest level, this book argues for the centrality of space in the making of race and class in the twentieth century. Among the most obvious features of black suburbanization was the spatial persistence of race over time and, related to that, the consistent struggle over the meaning and advantages that adhered to the places black people lived. From the early twentieth century, black migration to suburbs was geographically cumulative, and de facto segregation characterized suburbs of all kinds. By the same token, spatial location was closely related to African Americans' economic interests and class position. Through most of the century, socio-spatial practices such as school segregation, redlining, exclusive and expulsive zoning, slum clearance, political gerrymandering, and white avoidance compounded race and class inequality, aligning local interests on the basis of imposed racial disadvantage and limiting the empowering potential of black-occupied space. The "black tax" of segregation made it difficult for African Americans to achieve the same advantages of suburban location as most white suburbanites. The alternative, pioneering in predominantly white areas, reinforced race in its own way, exposing black families to social pressures and acts of racial prejudice that buttressed a racialized view of society. Moving beyond the perfunctory assertion that race still "matters," the book illustrates that in suburbs it did so in large part because of persistent inequality deployed in space and tenacious efforts to overcome it on the same terrain.

Looking to the future, it seems clear that the patterns of suburbanization past will cast a long shadow. By the beginning of this new century, the southern men and women who built suburban communities amidst the Great Migration have all but passed and gone. So, too, have many of the builders, planners, and pioneers who forged a way for blacks in postwar suburbia. Even members of the generation who broke down the doors of jim crow and made a movement that changed the nation have gone elegantly gray. Yet the legacy of their commitment to create better places to live for themselves and their families remains evident: in the shape of suburban churches, expanded to accommodate a tide of migrants; in street names and subdivision titles; in family homes occupied by third-generation suburbanites; in the shrinking number of all-white suburbs and the terrain of black residences stretching from core to periphery in many cities; in politics as well as in the law.

Not least among these legacies is the persistence of racial inequality in space. Thus, as African Americans move to suburbs in greater numbers than ever before, they build on a foundation with deeper footings than many recognize and face challenges that link their efforts to those of suburbanites throughout the twentieth century. As Nobel laureate Toni Morrison has remarked, a central issue facing African Americans in the modern United States is how to overcome racism without losing or denying racial identity, how to build "a race-specific yet non-racist home" from the building materials of a race-troubled society.[177] For black suburbanites, this challenge was always more than figurative. In making places of their own in the margins of the city, they negotiated not only the hurdles of building homes and communities, but lines of color, class, and power embedded in the world around them. The same was no less true in the new century than in the last.

Notes

Introduction

1. "I'm Gonna Move to the Outskirts of Town," words and music by William Weldon, special lyrics by Andy Razaf, quoted in Barry Singer, *Black and Blue: The Life and Lyrics of Andy Razaf* (New York, 1992), 305.

2. In 1960 the U.S. Census counted 2.5 million African Americans in suburban areas (arrived at by subtracting the central city population from the metropolitan population). The 2000 census shows 11.9 million African Americans in census-defined suburban areas. U.S. Census of Population: 1960, vol. III, *Selected Area Reports,* part 1D, *Standard Metropolitan Statistical Areas* (Washington, D.C., 1963), 2; U.S. Census of Population: 2000, data for U.S. metropolitan areas posted on the website of the Lewis Mumford Center at the State University of New York at Albany, http://mumford1.dyndns.org/cen2000/data.html.

3. "Ethnic Diversity Grows, with Little Neighborhood Integration," http://mumford1.dyndns.org/cen2000/data.html (April 3, 2001).

4. Eric R. Wolf, *Europe and the People without History* (Berkeley, 1982).

5. For a sample of this literature, see Reynolds Farley, "The Changing Distribution of Negroes within Metropolitan Areas: The Emergence of Black Suburbs," *American Journal of Sociology* 75 (January 1970): 333–51; Harold X. Connolly, "Black Movement into the Suburbs: Suburbs Doubling Their Black Populations during the 1960's," *Urban Affairs Quarterly* 9 (September 1973): 91–111; Harold M. Rose, *Black Suburbanization: Access to Improved Quality of Life or Maintenance of the Status Quo?* (Cambridge, 1976); Thomas Clark, *Blacks in Suburbs: A National Perspective* (New Brunswick, N.J., 1979); John R. Logan and Mark Schneider, "Racial Segregation and Racial Change in American Suburbs, 1970–1980," *American*

Journal of Sociology 89 (1984): 874–88; Joel Garreau, "The Emerging Cities; Blacks: Success in the Suburbs," *Washington Post Reprints* (November 29–December 1, 1987); William P. O'Hare and William H. Frey, "Booming, Suburban, and Black," *American Demographics* 14 (September 1992): 30–38; and Thomas J. Phelan and Mark Schneider, "Race, Ethnicity, and Class in American Suburbs," *Urban Affairs Review* 31 (May 1996): 659–81.

6. An important exception is Joe R. Feagin, "A House Is Not a Home: White Racism and U.S. Housing Practices," in *Residential Apartheid: The American Legacy,* ed. Robert D. Bullard, J. Eugene Grigsby, and Charles Lee (Los Angeles, 1994), 17–48. See also Elizabeth Huttman, "A Research Note on Dreams and Aspirations of Black Families," *Journal of Comparative Family Studies* 22 (summer 1991): 147–58.

7. William Julius Wilson, *The Truly Disadvantaged: The Inner City, the Underclass, and Public Policy* (Chicago, 1987).

8. Bruce B. Williams, *Black Workers in an Industrial Suburb* (New Brunswick, N.J., 1987); Ann Morris and Henrietta Ambrose, *North Webster: A Photographic History of a Black Community* (Bloomington, Ind., 1993); Henry L. Taylor Jr., "City Building, Public Policy, the Rise of the Industrial City, and Black Ghetto-Slum Formation in Cincinnati, 1850–1940," in *Race and the City: Work, Community, and Protest in Cincinnati, 1820–1970,* ed. Henry L. Taylor Jr. (Urbana, Ill., 1993); Andrew Wiese, "Places of Our Own: Suburban Black Towns before 1960," *Journal of Urban History* 19 (May 1993): 30–54; Andrew Wiese, "The Other Suburbanites: African American Suburbanization in the North before 1950," *Journal of American History* 85 (March 1999): 1495–524; William H. Wilson, *Hamilton Park: A Planned Black Community in Dallas* (Baltimore, 1998); Shirley Ann Wilson Moore, *To Place Our Deeds: The African American Community in Richmond, California, 1910–1963* (Berkeley, 2000); Bruce D. Haynes, *Red Lines, Black Spaces: The Politics of Race and Space in a Black Middle-Class Suburb* (New Haven, 2001). The first synthetic work is Leslie Wilson, "Dark Spaces: An Account of Afro-American Suburbanization" (Ph.D. diss., City University of New York, 1991). Other dissertations include Henry L. Taylor Jr., "The Building of a Black Industrial Suburb: The Lincoln Heights, Ohio, Story" (Ph.D. diss., State University of New York at Buffalo, 1979); Earl Ray Hutchison, "Black Suburbanization: A History of Social Change in a Working Class Suburb" (Ph.D. diss., University of Chicago, 1984); Harold O. Lindsey, "From Fields to Fords, Feds to Franchise: African American Empowerment in Inkster, Michigan" (Ph.D. diss., University of Michigan, 1993); and Andrew Wiese, "Struggle for the Suburban Dream: African American Suburbanization since 1916" (Ph.D. diss., Columbia University, 1993).

9. Exceptions are Taylor, who situates African American suburbanization as part of a larger metropolitan and city building process, and Leslie Wilson.

10. See Dana F. White, "The Black Sides of Atlanta: A Geography of Expansion and Containment, 1870–1970," *Atlanta Historical Journal* 26 (summer/fall 1982): 199–225.

11. Sam Bass Warner Jr., *Streetcar Suburbs: The Process of Growth in Boston, 1870–1900* (Cambridge, 1962). Examples include Dolores Hayden, *Redesigning the American Dream: The Future of Housing, Work, and Family Life* (New York, 1984); Henry Binford, *The First Suburbs* (Chicago, 1985); Michael Ebner, *Creating Chicago's North Shore: A Suburban History* (Chicago, 1988); Kenneth T. Jackson, *Crabgrass Frontier: The Suburbanization of the United States* (New York, 1985); Robert Fishman, *Bourgeois Utopias: The Rise and Fall of Suburbia* (New York, 1987); John Stilgoe, *Borderland: Origins of the American Suburb, 1820–1939* (New Haven, 1988); and Margaret Marsh, *Suburban Lives* (New Brunswick, N.J., 1990).

12. Recent exceptions are Richard Harris, *Unplanned Suburbs: Toronto's American Tragedy, 1900 to 1950* (Baltimore, 1996); Wilson, *Hamilton Park;* Rosalyn Baxandall and Elizabeth Ewen, *Picture Windows: How the Suburbs Happened* (New York, 2000), 171–209; and Becky M. Nicolaides, *My Blue Heaven: Life and Politics in the Working-Class Suburbs of Los Angeles, 1920–1965* (Chicago, 2002).

13. Jackson, *Crabgrass Frontier,* 6.

14. Fishman, *Bourgeois Utopias,* 4.

15. In 2002 the *Los Angeles Times* argued that Orange County, California, was becoming less "suburban" and more "urban" because of growing racial diversity. "Once-Sleepy Tustin a Trendsetter? Census Bureau Report Proves It," *Los Angeles Times,* June 9, 2002, B1.

16. The U.S. Census Bureau defined suburbs in 1940 as the "thickly settled" districts adjacent to a central city or cities of 50,000 or more. The census established metropolitan limits using the boundaries of adjacent counties where fewer than 25 percent of the population worked in agriculture. Suburban population represented the metropolitan area population minus the central city. By this definition, there were 468,000 African Americans in northern suburbs and 32,000 in suburbs in the West in 1940 (compared to 208,000 and 7,000 in 1910). Southern "suburbs" tallied 982,000 African Americans in 1940. Because of the number of black farmers in the metropolitan South, this figure is surely an overestimate. Nonetheless, the number of African American residents of non–farm housing in census-defined metropolitan areas of the South probably exceeded 600,000 in 1940. U.S. Census of Population: 1960, vol. III, part 1D, 2–5.

17. Connolly, "Black Movement into the Suburbs."

18. Farley, "The Changing Distribution of Negroes," 333–51.

19. Richard Harris, "Working-Class Home Ownership in the American Metropolis," *Journal of Urban History* 17 (November 1990): 46–69; Richard Harris, "Self-Building in the Urban Housing Market," *Economic Geography* 67 (January 1991): 1–21; Harris, *Unplanned Suburbs.*

20. Robin D. G. Kelley, "'We Are Not What We Seem': Rethinking Black Working-Class Opposition in the Jim Crow South," *Journal of American History* 80 (June 1993): 75–112; Earl Lewis, "Connecting Memory, Self, and the Power of Place in African American Urban History," *Journal of Urban History* 21 (March 1995): 347–71; Steven Gregory, *Black Corona: Race and the Politics of Place in an Urban Community* (Princeton, 1998).

21. Scholars who have examined the meanings or uses of domestic space among African Americans include James Borchert, *Alley Life in Washington: Family, Community, Religion, and Folklife in the City, 1850–1970* (Urbana, Ill., 1980), 100–42; John Michael Vlach, *Back of the Big House: The Architecture of Plantation Slavery* (Chapel Hill, N.C., 1993); and Lewis, "Connecting Memory, Self, and the Power of Place." On meanings and uses of public space, see Elsa Barkley Brown and Gregg Kimball, "Mapping the Terrain of Black Richmond," *Journal of Urban History* 21 (March 1995): 296–346.

22. Hollis Towns, "The New Black Power," *Atlanta Journal-Constitution*, July 14, 1997, E1.

23. Gregory, *Black Corona*, 11.

24. Following anthropologist Rachel Tolen, I understand class to imply "a relation between rich and poor generated in the context of social and material production and experienced both symbolically and materially in the everyday world." That is to say, class has a material basis, reflecting the position of individuals and families in relation to a wider socioeconomic structure. This position produces certain "orientations and dispositions" as well as distinct and perhaps irreconcilable interests. In addition, class encompasses a social, referential aspect. Class distinctions emerge in everyday relations among differently situated groups of people, mediated through behavior, language, and imagery. Rachel Tolen, "Transfers of Knowledge and Privileged Spheres of Practice: Servants and Employers in a Madras Railway Colony," in *Home and Hegemony: Domestic Service and Identity Politics in South and Southeast Asia,* ed. Kathleen M. Adams and Sara Dickey (Ann Arbor, 2000), 66; Pierre Bourdieu, *Distinction: A Social Critique of the Judgement of Taste,* trans. Richard Nice (Cambridge, 1984).

Scholars of race, such as Michael Omi and Howard Winant, argue that race is "a concept which signifies and symbolizes social conflicts and interests by referring to different types of human bodies." Michael Omi and Howard Winant, *Racial*

Formation in the United States from the 1960s to the 1990s, 2nd ed. (New York, 1994), 55. Steven Gregory and Roger Sanjek describe race as "a framework of ranked categories segmenting the human population." Unlike social distinctions such as class and gender, scholars emphasize the absence of any material or biological precursors for racial distinctions, emphasizing instead the role of fluid and contested social power. Steven Gregory and Roger Sanjek, eds., *Race* (New Brunswick, N.J., 1994), 1; also see Barbara J. Fields, "Ideology and Race in American History," in *Region, Race, and Reconstruction: Essays in Honor of C. Vann Woodward,* ed. J. Morgan Kousser and James M. McPherson (New York, 1982), 143–75.

25. On the role of space in the production of identity, see Manuel Castells, *The City and the Grassroots: A Cross-Cultural Theory of Urban Social Movements* (Los Angeles, 1983), xix, 311–12; Lewis, "Connecting Memory, Self, and the Power of Place"; Robert Self, "'To Plan Our Liberation': Black Power and the Politics of Place in Oakland, California, 1965–1977," *Journal of Urban History* 26 (September 2000), 759–92; Mary Patillo-McCoy, *Black Picket Fences: Privilege and Peril among the Black Middle Class* (Chicago, 1999); Thomas J. Sugrue, *The Origins of the Urban Crisis: Race and Inequality in Postwar Detroit* (Princeton, 1996); and Gregory, *Black Corona,* 109–78.

26. Dirks, Eley, and Ortner point out that this fluidity often flies in the face of individuals' lived experience. The role of space helps to explain this apparent paradox, underlying a perception of fixed social difference that may reinforce racial and class solidarities. Nicholas Dirks, Geoff Eley, and Sherry Ortner, eds., *Culture/Power/History: A Reader in Contemporary Social Theory* (Princeton, 1994), 32, cited in Gregory, *Black Corona,* 12.

27. On place stratification, see John R. Logan, "Growth, Politics, and the Stratification of Places," *American Journal of Sociology* 84 (1978): 404–15; and Mark Schneider and John Logan, "Suburban Racial Segregation and Black Access to Local Public Resources," *Social Science Quarterly* 63 (1982): 762–70.

28. Steven Gregory points out that African American neighborhoods encouraged residents to see themselves as black people because racialized threats to their local interests required them to "[fight] back as a black community." Gregory, *Black Corona,* 11.

29. For articulations of this idea, see Farah Jasmine Griffin, *"Who Set You Flowin'?": The African-American Migration Narrative* (New York, 1995); David J. Dent, *In Search of Black America: Discovering the African American Dream* (New York, 2000), 14–25; and Lewis, "Connecting Memory, Self, and the Power of Place."

30. Nate Parker, letter to the editor, *Chicago Tribune,* May 3, 1994, 18.

31. Joe R. Feagin and Melvin P. Sikes, *Living with Racism: The Black Middle-Class Experience* (Boston, 1994).

Chapter One

1. Carey McWilliams, *Southern California: An Island on the Land* (1946; reprint, Salt Lake City, 1983), 237–38.

2. Photographs of the Farm Security Administration are available on the Library of Congress's American Memory website, http://lcweb2.loc.gov/ammem/fsahtml/fahome.html. For a survey, see James Curtis, *Mind's Eye, Mind's Truth: FSA Photography Reconsidered* (Philadelphia, 1989).

3. Harlan Paul Douglass, *The Suburban Trend* (New York, 1925), 74, 94–98, 106–8, 121. The Piedmont refers to the foothill country southeast of the Appalachian Mountains.

4. Quoted in Richard Harris and Robert Lewis, "Constructing a Fault(y) Zone: Misrepresentations of American Cities and Suburbs, 1900–1950," *Annals of the Association of American Geographers* 88 (1998): 625–28.

5. Richard Harris, "Working-Class Home Ownership in the American Metropolis," *Journal of Urban History* 17 (November 1990): 46–69; Richard Harris, "Self-Building in the Urban Housing Market," *Economic Geography* 67 (January 1991): 1–21; Richard Harris, "The Unplanned Blue-Collar Suburb in Its Heyday, 1900–1940," in *Geographical Snapshots of North America*, ed. Donald G. Janelle (New York, 1992), 94–98; Richard Harris, *Unplanned Suburbs: Toronto's American Tragedy, 1900 to 1950* (Baltimore, 1996).

6. Todd Gardner, "The Slow Wave: The Changing Residential Status of Cities and Suburbs in the United States, 1850–1940," *Journal of Urban History* 27 (March 2001): 293.

7. Richard Harris, "Chicago's Other Suburbs," *Geographical Review* 84 (1996): 394–410.

8. Metropolitan districts included central cities plus adjacent counties in which fewer than 25 percent of the population worked in agriculture. By this definition, there were 982,000 African Americans in southern suburbs (compared to 903,000 in 1910); 468,000 in the North; and 32,000 in the West (compared to 208,000 and 7,000 in 1910). Altogether 5.8 million African Americans lived in metropolitan areas. U.S. Census of Population: 1960, *Selected Area Reports: Standard Metropolitan Statistical Areas,* Final Report PC(3)-1D (Washington, D.C., 1963), 2–6.

9. Area Descriptions, D-12, D-13, D-25, *Security Map of New Orleans, Louisiana, 1939,* box 88, Home Owners Loan Corporation [HOLC] Papers, Record Group 195 (National Archives, Washington, D.C.).

10. Carter G. Woodson, *Rural Negro* (Washington, D.C., 1930), 119.

11. Daniel M. Johnson and Rex R. Campbell, *Black Migration in America: A Social Demographic History* (Durham, N.C., 1981); T. J. Woofter, *Negro Problems in*

Cities (Garden City, N.Y., 1928), 28; African Americans by percent of population in 1920: New Orleans, 26 percent; Nashville, 30 percent; Atlanta, 31 percent; Charlotte, 32 percent; Durham, 35 percent; Memphis, 38 percent; Birmingham and Mobile, 39 percent; Houston, 40 percent; Montgomery, 46 percent; Savannah, 47 percent. U.S. Census of Population: 1920, vol. II, *General Report and Analytical Tables* (Washington, D.C., 1922).

12. Richard Wade, *Slavery in the City: The South, 1820–1860* (New York, 1964); Zane Miller, "Urban Blacks in the South: 1865–1920: The Richmond, Savannah, New Orleans, Louisville and Birmingham Experience," in *The New Urban History: Quantitative Explorations by American Historians,* ed. Leo F. Schnore (Princeton, 1975), 184–204.

13. John Kellogg, "Negro Urban Clusters in the Post Bellum South," *Geographical Review* 67 (July 1971): 287–303; Karl E. Taeuber and Alma F. Taeuber, *Negroes in Cities: Residential Segregation and Neighborhood Change* (Chicago, 1965), 191–92; "Piney woods," in Joint Committee on Housing, *Study and Investigation of Housing, Hearings before the Joint Committee on Housing,* 80th Congress, proceedings at Houston, Tex., October 30, 1947 (Washington, D.C., 1948), 1629.

14. Charles Louis Knight, "Negro Housing in Certain Virginia Cities," *Phelps-Stokes Fellowship Papers* 8 (1927): 57.

15. Thomas W. Hanchett, *Sorting Out the New South City: Race, Class, and Urban Development in Charlotte, 1875–1975* (Chapel Hill, N.C., 1998), 134–36.

16. Charles S. Johnson, *Patterns of Negro Segregation* (New York, 1943), 9.

17. Kellogg, "Negro Urban Clusters," 287–303; John Kellogg, "The Formation of Black Residential Areas in Lexington, Kentucky, 1865–1885," *Journal of Southern History* 4 (February 1982): 21–52; Howard Sumka, "Racial Segregation in Small North Carolina Cities," *Southeastern Geographer* 17 (1977): 59–75; Hanchett, *Sorting Out the New South City,* 43, 118.

18. Hanchett, *Sorting Out the New South City,* 3–8.

19. Woodson, *Rural Negro,* 120.

20. Henry Aaron with Lonnie Wheeler, *I Had a Hammer* (New York, 1991), 8.

21. Woodson, *Rural Negro,* 120.

22. Aaron, *I Had a Hammer,* 9.

23. Ronald Bayor, *Race and the Shaping of Twentieth-Century Atlanta* (Chapel Hill, N.C., 1996), 129; Kellogg, "Negro Urban Clusters"; Rudolf Heberle, "Social Consequences of the Industrialization of Southern Cities," *Social Forces* 27 (1948–49), 35; "Fulton County and Negro Housing," *Atlanta Daily World,* February 1, 1950.

24. Reynolds Farley, "The Changing Distribution of Negroes within Metropolitan Areas: The Emergence of Black Suburbs," *American Journal of Sociology* 75

(January 1970): 346. Only 10 percent of African Americans lived outside the South in 1900. Johnson and Campbell, *Black Migration in America,* 73.

25. Harold M. Rose, "The All-Negro Town: Its Evolution and Function," *Geographical Review* 55 (July 1965): 362–81.

26. Arnold Rampersad, *Jackie Robinson: A Biography* (New York, 1997), 19; U.S. Census of Population: 1960, *Selected Area Reports,* 5, 95, 249, 253.

27. U.S. Census of Population: 1960, *Selected Area Reports,* 3.

28. Lynda R. Day, *Making a Way to Freedom: A History of African Americans on Long Island* (Interlaken, N.Y., 1998); Grania Bolton Marcus, *A Forgotten People: Discovering the Black Experience in Suffolk County* (Setauket, N.Y., 1988); Ira De A. Reid and William Robert Valentine, *The Negro in New Jersey: A Report of a Survey by the Interracial Committee of the New Jersey Conference of Social Work* (New York, 1932), 15–17. A similar pattern prevailed in Missouri and eastern Kansas. Nell Irvin Painter, *Exodusters: Black Migration to Kansas after Reconstruction* (New York, 1976).

29. Armstrong Association of Philadelphia, *A Study of Living Conditions among Colored People in Towns in the Outer Part of Philadelphia and in Other Suburbs Both in Pennsylvania and New Jersey* (Philadelphia, 1915), 54.

30. Ibid., 21, 23, 30, 53.

31. Leonard Blumberg and Michael Lalli, "Little Ghettoes: A Study of Negroes in the Suburbs," *Phylon* 27 (summer 1966): 125.

32. U.S. Census of Population: 1910, vol. II, *Reports by States, Illinois* (Washington, D.C., 1912).

33. U.S. Census of Population: 1940, vol. II, *Characteristics of the Population,* part 2, *Reports by States* (Washington, D.C., 1943), 613–16, 640, 653; ibid., part 3, 870–74, 912; U.S. Census of Population: 1960, *Selected Area Reports,* 88.

34. Quote in Area Description, D-2 (South Atlanta), *Residential Security Map of Atlanta, Georgia,* box 91, HOLC. See also Area Descriptions, D-10 (Edgewood), D-23 (Rockdale Park), ibid.; Area Description, D-7 (North Montgomery), *Security Map of Montgomery, Alabama,* 1937, box 97, HOLC; Area Descriptions, D-25 (St. Bernard's Parish), D-26 (Algiers, Louisiana), D-32 (Harvey, Louisiana), *Residential Security Map of New Orleans, Louisiana,* box 88, HOLC.

35. Robert Thompson, Hylan Lewis, and Davis McEntire, "Atlanta and Birmingham: A Comparative Study of Negro Housing," in *Studies in Housing and Minority Groups,* ed. Nathan Glazer and Davis McEntire (Berkeley, 1960), 53.

36. Glenn T. Eskew, *But for Birmingham: The Local and National Movements in the Civil Rights Struggle* (Chapel Hill, N.C., 1997), 8–10; Graham Taylor, *Satellite Cities: A Study of Industrial Suburbs* (New York, 1915), 251; Thompson, Lewis, and McEntire, "Atlanta and Birmingham," 53, 58. Bessemer's black population

reached 11,700 in 1930. U.S. Census of Population: 1930, vol. III, *Characteristics of the Population,* part 1, *Reports by State* (Washington, D.C., 1932), 109.

37. Woofter, *Negro Problems in Cities,* 140, 168. On planning for African Americans in an industrial suburb, see Dean Sinclair, "'A Community in Itself': The Forgotten Garden City of North Charleston, South Carolina," 1998 Meeting of the American Association of Geographers, Southwest Division.

38. Richard Harris and Robert Lewis, "The Geography of North American Cities and Suburbs, 1900–1950," *Journal of Urban History* 27 (March 2001): 265–70; Robert Lewis, *Manufacturing Montreal, 1850–1920* (Baltimore, 2000).

39. Taylor, *Satellite Cities,* 1.

40. Ibid., 6, 165.

41. Ibid., 165.

42. Area Descriptions, D-13 (Rankin), D-14 (Braddock), *Security Map of Pittsburgh,* box 94, HOLC; Area Descriptions, D-11 (East St. Louis), C-4 (East St. Louis), *Security Map of Metropolitan St. Louis, Mo.,* 1940, box 65, HOLC.

43. Federal Writers Project, *Pennsylvania: A Guide to the Keystone State* (Philadelphia, 1940), 608–11; Quoted in *Negro Housing: Report of the Committee on Negro Housing,* prepared for the cmte. by Charles S. Johnson, ed. John M. Gries and James Ford (Washington, D.C., 1932), 128.

44. Federal Writers Project, *Pennsylvania,* 608–11; Peter Gottlieb, *Making Their Own Way: Southern Blacks' Migration to Pittsburgh, 1916–1930* (Urbana, Ill., 1987), 69–77.

45. U.S. Census of Housing: 1940, vol. II, *General Characteristics,* part 2, *Reports by States* (Washington, D.C., 1943), 34, 246, 793–94, 818, 943; ibid., part 3, 623; ibid., part 4, 185; Mark Kolodny, "The Industrialization of Joliet: Steel and Its Dependencies, 1870–1920," in *Time and Place in Joliet: Essays on the Geographic Evolution of the City,* ed. Michael P. Conzen (Chicago, 1988), 37–45; Federal Writers Project, *Illinois: A Descriptive and Historical Guide* (Chicago, 1939), 156–57, 410–12, 515; Area Description, D-12 (Highland Park, Michigan), *Security Map of Detroit, Michigan,* 1939, box 22, HOLC.

46. Robert Fishman, *Bourgeois Utopias: The Rise and Fall of Suburbia* (New York, 1987), 147.

47. "Camera Caravan Visits Ecorse," *Detroit Free Press,* May 18, 1941.

48. Kenneth T. Jackson, *Crabgrass Frontier: The Suburbanization of the United States* (New York, 1985), 99–102.

49. Edward L. Thorndike, *Your City* (1939; reprint, New York, 1976), 22–33. Thorndike ranked 301 American cities based on thirty-seven "goodness of life" factors, including levels of health, education, wealth, and public spending. Nine of the top ten municipalities were suburbs, five of which (Pasadena and Berkeley,

California; Montclair, New Jersey; Evanston, Illinois; and White Plains, New York) had substantial black communities.

50. Howard H. Harlan, "Zion Town — A Study in Human Ecology," *Phelps-Stokes Fellowship Papers* 13 (1935): 6–7. See also Johnson, *Patterns of Negro Segregation,* 10; Woofter, *Negro Problems in Cities,* 106.

51. Harold X. Connolly, "Black Movement into the Suburbs: Suburbs Doubling Their Black Populations during the 1960's," *Urban Affairs Quarterly* 9 (September 1973), 93. See also Douglass, *The Suburban Trend,* 98.

52. Black populations of Westchester suburbs, 1930: Mount Vernon (3,608), Newburg (894), New Rochelle (4,644), Ossining (1,107), Peekskill (582), Port Chester (873), White Plains (2,150), and Yonkers (3,332). U.S. Census of Population: 1930, vol. III, *Reports by States,* part 2 (Washington, D.C., 1932), 283, 288–92.

53. Because domestic servants enhanced rather than detracted from elites' status, whites in some suburbs openly built and financed African American housing nearby. See Judith Rollins, *Between Women: Domestics and Their Employers* (Philadelphia, 1985), 155–203. Andrew Wiese, "Black Housing, White Finance: African American Housing and Home Ownership in Evanston, Illinois, before 1940," *Journal of Social History* 33 (winter 1999): 429–60.

54. Area Descriptions, D-9 (Mount Vernon), D-8 (Tuckahoe), D-5 (Yonkers), D-12 (New Rochelle), *Security Map of Lower Westchester County, N.Y.,* 1940, box 57, HOLC; see also Area Descriptions, D-4 (Yonkers), and D-10 (North Pelham), ibid.

55. *Negro Housing,* ed. Gries and Ford, 13, 98.

56. Woofter, *Negro Problems in Cities,* 106.

57. Andrew Wiese, "The Other Suburbanites: African American Suburbanization in the North before 1950," *Journal of American History* 85 (March 1999): 1501.

58. Quoted in *Negro Housing,* ed. Gries and Ford, 89–90.

59. For patterns among blue-collar whites, see Harris, *Unplanned Suburbs;* and Becky M. Nicolaides, *My Blue Heaven: Life and Politics in the Working-Class Suburbs of Los Angeles, 1920–1965* (Chicago, 2002).

60. For examples, see Susan G. Pearl, *Fairmount Heights, Maryland: A History from Its Beginnings (1900) to Incorporation (1935)* (Upper Marlboro, Md., July 1991); T. J. Calloway, "Lincoln, [Maryland,]" *Crisis* 10 (March 1915): 240–42; Woofter, *Negro Problems in Cities,* 106, 140; J. M. Ragland, "Negro Housing in Louisville," *Southern Workman* 58 (January 1929): 22–28; Timothy J. Crimmins, "Bungalow Suburbs: East and West," *Atlanta Historical Journal* 26 (summer–fall

1982): 83–94; and "Morgan Park Homes," *Baltimore Afro-American,* August 15, 1925, 19.

61. Christopher Silver and John Moeser, *The Separate City: Black Communities in the Urban South, 1940–1968* (Lexington, Ky., 1995), 9.

62. Knight, "Negro Housing in Certain Virginia Cities," 50, 121–23.

63. Hanchett, *Sorting Out the New South City,* 142.

64. Mamie Garvin Fields with Karen Fields, *Lemon Swamp and Other Places: A Carolina Memoir* (New York, 1983), 163, cited in Hanchett, *Sorting Out the New South City,* 138.

65. Fields, *Lemon Swamp,* 163.

66. Hanchett, *Sorting Out the New South City,* 134–42; on community building in the Smithfield neighborhood in Birmingham, see Lynne B. Feldman, *A Sense of Place: Birmingham's Black Middle-Class Community, 1890–1930* (Tuscaloosa, Ala., 1999), 24–40, 59–68.

67. Ernest Burgess, "The Growth of the City: An Introduction to a Research Project," in *The City,* ed. Robert E. Park, Ernest W. Burgess, and Roderick D. McKenzie (1925; reprint, Chicago, 1967), 48. Even as metropolitan regions have become multi-nucleated and peripheries have overwhelmed the core in economic, demographic, and political terms, the geographic center and the direction of sprawl have remained largely intact, as have many of the forces underlying the process.

Chapter Two

1. August Meier and Elliot Rudwick, *Black Detroit and the Rise of the UAW* (New York, 1979), 5.

2. Laura Scantleberry, interview by Marion Forstall, April 3, 1980, "Voices and Profiles of New Rochelle's Rich, Color-Full History" (New Rochelle Public Library, New Rochelle, N.Y.) [NRPL], 50.

3. Quoted in Arnold Rampersad, *Jackie Robinson: A Biography* (New York, 1997), 16.

4. David Faulkner, *Great Time Coming: The Life of Jackie Robinson from Baseball to Birmingham* (New York, 1995), 18; Jackie Robinson, *Baseball Has Done It,* ed. Charles Dexter (New York, 1964), 28–29.

5. Quoted in Rampersad, *Jackie Robinson,* 18.

6. Sharon Robinson, *Stealing Home: An Intimate Family Portrait by the Daughter of Jackie Robinson* (New York, 1996), 33.

7. Rampersad, *Jackie Robinson,* 19.

8. Quoted in Maury Allen, *Jackie Robinson: A Life Remembered* (New York, 1987), 17.

9. Robinson, *Baseball Has Done It,* 28.

10. Outside the South, the black suburban population grew by 285,000 between 1910–40, compared to a total increase of 1,839,000 in metropolitan areas. Estimates for the South are problematic because suburban growth coincided with losses resulting from the out-migration of agricultural workers from metropolitan counties. U.S. Census of Population: 1960, vol. III, *Selected Area Reports,* part 1D, *Standard Metropolitan Statistical Areas* (Washington, D.C., 1963), 3–5.

11. David Kenneth Bruner, "A General Survey of the Negro Population of Evanston" (senior thesis, Northwestern University, 1924), 45.

12. For hometowns, see obituaries, *New Rochelle Standard Star,* January–July 1975; *Pasadena Star News,* January 1970. Gretchen Lemke-Santangelo, *Abiding Courage: African American Migrant Women and the East Bay Community* (Chapel Hill, N.C., 1996), 4; James R. Grossman, *Land of Hope: Chicago, Black Southerners, and the Great Migration* (Chicago, 1989), 5–6.

13. Daniel M. Johnson and Rex R. Campbell, *Black Migration in America: A Social Demographic History* (Durham, 1981), 58, 63, 68–69. For migration west, see Nell Irvin Painter, *Exodusters: Black Migration to Kansas after Reconstruction* (New York, 1976); and Kenneth Hamilton, *Black Towns and Profit: Promotion and Development in the Trans-Appalachian West, 1877–1915* (Urbana, Ill., 1991).

14. W. T. B. Williams, "The Negro Exodus from the South," *in Black Workers: A Documentary History from Colonial Times to the Present,* ed. Philip Foner and Ronald Lewis (Philadelphia, 1989), 314.

15. Ibid., 312.

16. On the Great Migration, see Joe William Trotter Jr., ed., *The Great Migration in Historical Perspective: New Dimensions of Race, Class, and Gender* (Bloomington, Ind., 1991); Grossman, *Land of Hope;* and Kimberly L. Phillips, *Alabama-North: African-American Migrants, Community, and Working-Class Activism in Cleveland, 1915–45* (Urbana, Ill., 1999).

17. Detroit Mayor's Interracial Committee, *The Negro in Detroit,* vol. 2, *Population* (Detroit, 1926).

18. Sam Butler, interview by Carol Butler, July 6, 1971 (Evanston Historical Society, Evanston, Ill.) [EHS].

19. William A. Wheeler, interview by author, June 16, 1989.

20. Ibid.

21. Cora and Anna Watson, interview by S. F. Patton, May 24, 1974, A/11, EHS.

22. Samples of obituaries from Evanston, Illinois; New Rochelle, New York;

and Pasadena, California, revealed that as many as a third of black decedents who had migrated to these suburbs before 1940 had cogenerational kin living in the suburb at the time of their death. *Evanston Review,* Obituaries, 1950–1990; *New Rochelle Standard Star,* January–July 1975; *Pasadena Star News,* January–November 1970. On the roles of kinship in migration, see Peter Gottlieb, *Making Their Own Way: Southern Blacks' Migration to Pittsburgh, 1916–1930* (Urbana, Ill., 1987), 39–59; and Phillips, *AlabamaNorth,* 127–60.

23. John L. Gaskin, interview by Marion Forstall, April 14, 1980, "Voices and Profiles," NRPL, 21.

24. Mrs. J. Wright, interview by Pasadena Black History Project, 1984 (Pasadena Historical Society, Pasadena, Calif.) [PHS].

25. The Court invalidated zoning by race in the case of *Buchanan v. Warley,* 245 U.S. 60 (1917). On continued efforts to employ race zoning, including a proposed "legal way of race segregation," see National Housing Association, "Race Issues and Zoning," *Housing* 19 (1930): 312–15.

26. LeeAnn Bishop Lands, "The Real Estate Industry and 'Negro Invasion' in Atlanta, 1900 to 1920," Meeting of the Society for American City and Regional Planning History, 2001; *Los Angeles Investment Company v. Gary,* 181 Cal. 680 (1919).

27. Charles Abrams, *Forbidden Neighbors: A Study of Prejudice in Housing* (New York, 1955), 154–62; "The Realtors Code of Ethics," *National Real Estate Journal* 40 (April 20, 1939): 64; Kenneth T. Jackson, *Crabgrass Frontier: The Suburbanization of the United States* (New York, 1985), 198.

28. Henri Lefebvre, *The Production of Space,* trans. Donald Nicholson-Smith (1974; reprint, Malden, Mass, 1984), 36–46.

29. Marc A. Weiss, *The Rise of the Community Builders: The American Real Estate Industry and Urban Land Planning* (New York, 1987), 17–52.

30. B. L. Jenks, "Restrictions for a High Grade Subdivision," *Home Building and Subdividing: Proceedings and Reports of the Home Builders and Subdividers Division, National Association of Real Estate Boards* (Chicago, 1925), 139–51. On race-restrictive covenants, see Clement E. Vose, *Caucasians Only: The Supreme Court, the NAACP, and the Restrictive Covenant Cases* (Berkeley, 1959); and Wendy Plotkin, "Deeds of Mistrust: Race, Housing, and Restrictive Covenants in Chicago, 1900–1953" (Ph.D. diss., University of Illinois at Chicago, 1999).

31. *Negro Housing: Report of the Committee on Negro Housing,* prepared for the cmte. by Charles S. Johnson, ed. John M. Gries and James Ford (Washington, D.C., 1932), 46–47; National Association for the Advancement of Colored People, *A Year's Defense of the Negro American's Citizenship Rights: 19th Annual Report for 1928* (New York, 1929).

32. Abrams, *Forbidden Neighbors,* 99–100; Graham Taylor, *Satellite Cities: A Study of Industrial Suburbs* (New York, 1915), 51.

33. James Crimi, "The Social Status of the Negro in Pasadena, California" (M.A. thesis, University of Southern California, 1941), 72–75; City of Pasadena, "Ethnic History Research Project: Pasadena, California" (March 1995) (Pasadena Public Library, Pasadena, Calif.) [PPL].

34. Ralph Guzman, "The Hand of Esau: Words Change, Practices Remain in Racial Covenants," *Frontier* 7 (June 1956): 13.

35. "Editorial," *Home Gardens Press,* January 29, 1926, quoted in Becky M. Nicolaides, *My Blue Heaven: Life and Politics in the Working-Class Suburbs of Los Angeles, 1920–1965* (Chicago, 2002), 161.

36. Lawrence DeGraaf, "City of Black Angels: Emergence of the Los Angeles Ghetto, 1890–1930," *Pacific Historical Review* 39 (August 1970): 348–49.

37. Ibid., 348–49.

38. Frances Minor, *A History of River Rouge, Michigan* (Monroe, Mich., 1978); Downriver Chamber of Commerce, *Downriver: A Graphic View of Commerce and Industry* (Trenton, Mich., 1959); Burton Historical Collection (Detroit Public Library, Detroit, Michigan) [BHC].

39. Allan Nevins and Frank Hill, *Ford,* vol. II, *Expansion and Challenge, 1915–1933* (New York, 1976).

40. Minor, *History of River Rouge,* 94; "Ecorse Is a Suburb with an Historic Background," *Detroit News,* July 4, 1926, part 11, 1; "Glimpses of City of River Rouge," *Detroit News,* September 19, 1926, part 11, 1; "Development of the World's Greatest Industrial Center," *Pipp's Magazine,* n.d. 1926, 32+, Local History Catalogue, BHC.

41. "Ecorse Is a Suburb with an Historic Background."

42. "Camera Caravan Visits Ecorse," *Detroit Free Press,* May 18, 1941; "Suburb Plans Handsome Educational Structure," *Detroit Free Press,* February 15, 1920, part 4, 15.

43. "Glimpses of the City of River Rouge."

44. U.S. Census of Population: 1930, vol. III, *Reports by States,* part 1 (Washington, D.C., 1932), 1147, 1149.

45. "Statement of a Wyandotte Resident," September 1957, Local History Scrapbooks, "Negroes," (Bacon Memorial Library, Wyandotte, Mich.) [BML].

46. Bill Smedley, "The Life of Negroes in the Automobile Industry," *Black Worker* 6 (August–September 1936): 11, in Foner and Lewis, eds., *Black Workers,* 386. Also, "Why No Negroes Live in Dearborn," *Michigan Chronicle,* April 7, 1956.

47. "Forty Negroes Turned Back on Wednesday," *Wyandotte Daily News,* n.d. 1937, Local History Scrapbooks, BML.

48. Ibid.; "White Bandits Rob Colored Folks," *Wyandotte News Herald,* September 20, 1923, ibid.; "Lynching Prevented as Deputies Guard Negro in Courtroom," *Wyandotte Daily News,* November 1, 1937, ibid.; U.S. Census of Population: 1940, vol. II, *Characteristics of the Population,* part 3, *Reports by States* (Washington, D.C., 1943), 875.

49. On the development of the "informal" real estate market, see Olivier Zunz, *The Changing Face of Inequality: Urbanization, Industrial Development, and Immigrants in Detroit, 1880–1920* (Chicago, 1982).

50. Index Map, City of River Rouge, Wayne County Tax Assessor's Office (Wayne County Administrative Building, Detroit, Mich.); R. L. Polk Company, *Detroit City Directory, 1915* (Detroit, 1915); R. L. Polk Company, *Detroit City Directory, 1920–1921* (Detroit, 1920).

51. Minor, *A History of River Rouge,* 85; U.S. Census of the Population: 1920, *Census Schedules,* Wayne County, Michigan, River Rouge Village, Enumeration Districts [E.D.] 678–82.

52. River Rouge passed its first zoning ordinance in 1948. Ecorse had no municipal land-use regulations until 1941. Office of the City Clerk, River Rouge, Mich., phone conversation with author, January 20, 1993. On land-use planning and working-class suburbanization, see Richard Harris, *Unplanned Suburbs: Toronto's American Tragedy, 1900 to 1950* (Baltimore, 1996), 155–60.

53. Herman Feldman, *Racial Factors in American Industry* (New York, 1931), 43–44.

54. *Census Schedules, 1920,* River Rouge; U.S. Census of Population: 1920, vol. IV, *Occupations,* (Washington, D.C., 1923), 367.

55. Meier and Rudwick, *Black Detroit,* 6.

56. Detroit Mayor's Interracial Committee, *The Negro in Detroit,* vol. 5, *Housing* (Detroit, 1926), 15–16.

57. U.S. Census of Population: 1930, vol. III, part 1, 1147, 1149.

58. "Two Churches Razed by Fire," no citation, April 9, 1927, "E & M" clippings scrapbook, "River Rouge," BHC.

59. Minor, *A History of River Rouge,* 85–88; W. C. Batchelor, "A Survey of the Leisure Time Services and Facilities under Government Auspices in Metropolitan Detroit" (M.A. thesis, Ohio State University, 1948).

60. "River Rouge Seems to Like Standing Still," *Detroit Free Press,* May 8, 1973; "Fifty Years of Peace, and Then . . . ," *Detroit News,* May 4, 1970.

61. For activities in the 1940s, see "Downriver Highlights," *Michigan*

Chronicle, 1944–1950; "20th Anniversary and Homecoming Celebration: John Wesley Methodist Church, 1946–1966," (River Rouge Public Library, River Rouge, Mich.); R. L. Polk Company, *Wyandotte and River Rouge City Directory, 1938* (Detroit, 1937).

62. "Historical Commentary on the River Rouge–Ecorse Community Organization," 1944, file 8, box 55, United Community Services Collection (Wayne State University Archives, Detroit, Mich.); William W., interview by author, June 13, 1991.

63. Polk, *Wyandotte and River Rouge City Directory, 1938*.

64. *Census Schedules, 1920,* Cook County, Illinois, E.D. 194–96 (Maywood), E.D. 215–19 (Harvey), E.D. 221 (Phoenix); Erie County, New York, E.D. 306–11 (Lackawanna); Allegheny County, Pennsylvania, E.D. 132–42 (Homestead).

65. The suburbs were Aurora, Chicago Heights, Harvey, Maywood, and Phoenix, Illinois; East Chicago, Indiana; River Rouge and Hamtramck, Michigan; Chester, Coatesville, and Homestead, Pennsylvania; and Lackawanna, New York. U.S. Census of Population: 1920, vol. III, *Composition and Characteristics of the Population by States* (Washington, D.C., 1922), 261–66, 297, 488–92, 644, 866–70; *Census Schedules: 1920*.

66. Donald Adams Clarke, "Men on Relief in Lackawanna, New York, 1934–35: Social Pathology in a Satellite City," *University of Buffalo Studies* XIV (August 1937): 77.

67. Ibid., 74; John A. Fitch, "Lackawanna — Swamp, Mill, and Town," *Survey* 27 (October 1911): 929–45; William Sheurman, "The Politics of Protest: The Great Steel Strike of 1919–20 in Lackawanna, New York," *International Review of Social History* 31 (1986): 121–46.

68. Clarke, "Men on Relief," 76; *Census Schedules: 1920,* Lackawanna.

69. John A. Fitch, *The Steelworkers* (1911; reprint, New York, 1969), 10; Henry M. McKiven Jr., *Iron and Steel: Class, Race, and Community in Birmingham, Alabama, 1875–1920* (Chapel Hill, N.C., 1995), 41. On race stratification in the Lackawanna mills, see Kelly L. Patterson, "From a Different Place: The Residential and Occupational Experience of Blacks in a Steel-Making Suburb, Lackawanna, New York, 1925" (M.S. thesis, University of Buffalo, 1995), 33–48.

70. *Census Schedules, 1920,* Lackawanna.

71. Margaret F. Byington, *Homestead: The Households of a Mill Town* (1910; reprint, Pittsburgh, 1974), 107; *Census Schedules, 1920,* Lackawanna; ibid., Homestead; Gottlieb, *Making Their Own Way,* 70–71.

72. Women as a proportion of the black workforce in 1940, suburbs: Chicago Heights, IL, 25 percent; Harvey, IL, 24 percent; Maywood, IL, 34 percent;

Waukegan, IL, 26 percent; Ecorse, MI, 14 percent; Hamtramck, MI, 20 percent; Highland Park, MI, 26 percent; River Rouge, MI, 18 percent; Linden, NJ, 23 percent; Rahway, NJ, 31 percent; Lackawanna, NY, 11 percent; Elyria, OH, 28 percent; Coatesville, PA, 28 percent; Homestead, PA, 15 percent; McKees Rocks, PA, 18 percent. Women as a proportion of workforce, cities: Buffalo, 25 percent; Chicago, 34 percent; Cleveland, 31 percent; Detroit, 26 percent; Newark, 36 percent; New York, 45 percent; Pittsburgh, 27 percent. U.S. Census of Population: 1940, vol. II, part 3, 630–36, 643; part 4, 349, 639, 892–97, 928; part 5, 13, 131, 160, 678; part 6, 185–90.

73. *Census Schedules, 1920,* Homestead.

74. Quoted in Grossman, *Land of Hope,* 36.

75. Gottlieb, *Making Their Own Way,* 111.

76. Byington, *Homestead,* 107.

77. Gottlieb, *Making Their Own Way,* 129.

78. Dennis C. Dickerson, *Out of the Crucible: Black Steelworkers in Western Pennsylvania, 1875–1980* (Albany, 1986), 72–76.

79. Gottlieb, *Making Their Own Way,* 129; Clarke, "Men on Relief," 77, 79; Fitch, "Lackawanna," 937.

80. Quoted in Grossman, *Land of Hope,* 37.

81. Clarke, "Men on Relief," 74–79; Gottlieb, *Making Their Own Way,* 129.

82. Alabama Writers Project, *Alabama: A Guide to the Deep South* (New York, 1941), 311.

83. Federal Writers Project, *Illinois: A Descriptive and Historical Guide* (Chicago, 1939), 490.

84. Mount Vernon Chamber of Commerce, *Mount Vernon: The City of Homes* (Mount Vernon Public Library, Mount Vernon, N.Y.) [MVPL], 1911.

85. Dolores Hayden, *The Grand Domestic Revolution: A History of Feminist Designs for American Homes, Neighborhoods and Cities* (Cambridge, 1981), 1–27.

86. Edward L. Thorndike, *Your City* (1939; reprint, New York, 1976).

87. For instance, Dwight and Elizabeth Morrow of Englewood, New Jersey, employed seven servants in 1920: a butler and governess from England, Swedish and Finnish housemaids, a white nurse from Massachusetts, and a black couple from Virginia, employed as "hired man" and cook. *Census Schedules: 1920,* Bergen County, New Jersey, Englewood city, E.D. 22–27.

88. The thirty-three suburbs were East Orange, Englewood, Hackensack, Montclair, Orange, Plainfield, and South Orange, New Jersey; Evanston and Winnetka, Illinois; Freeport, Garden City, Glen Cove, Hempstead, Mamaroneck, Mount Vernon, New Rochelle, Port Chester, Rockville Centre, Scarsdale, White

Plains, and Yonkers, New York; University City and Webster Groves, Missouri; Berkeley, Beverly Hills, Palo Alto, Pasadena, and Santa Monica, California; Darby Borough, Haverford Township, and Lower Merion Township, Pennsylvania; and Cleveland Heights and Shaker Heights, Ohio. U.S. Census of Population: 1940, vol. II, part 1, 614–19, part 2, 631–35; part 4, 225, 892–98; part 5, 130–36, 678–82; part 6, 186–90. The preponderance of service workers was greatest in the most exclusive suburbs, where almost 100 percent of servants lived-in. Domestics in Scarsdale, New York, and Winnetka, Illinois, were almost 30 percent of the working population. Ibid., part 2, 635; part 5, 135.

89. Wilfred Lewin, "A Study of the Negro Population of Mount Vernon," typescript (1935), MVPL.

90. Bruner, "A General Survey," 55. The suburbs under consideration here are those in which most domestic workers lived in households of their own.

91. Women were more than 40 percent of the 1920 black workforce in Orange, East Orange, Montclair, and Plainfield, New Jersey; New Rochelle and Mount Vernon, New York; Evanston, Illinois; and Pasadena, California. U.S. Census of Population: 1920, vol. IV, 365, 369–71.

92. Bruner, "A General Survey," 40.

93. Employed women in domestic service suburbs, 1940 (as a portion of black females over fourteen): Evanston, IL, 56 percent; Mount Vernon, NY, 65 percent; New Rochelle, NY, 62 percent; White Plains, NY, 60 percent; Montclair, NJ, 62 percent; East Orange, NJ, 54 percent; Englewood, NJ, 50 percent; Webster Groves, MO, 54 percent; Pasadena, CA, 41 percent. Rates of female employment in central cities usually ranged from one-third to one-half: Chicago, 36 percent; Cleveland, 33 percent; St. Louis, 37 percent; Newark, 40 percent; Los Angeles, 42 percent; New York, 51 percent. U.S. Census of Population: 1940, vol. II, part 1, 617; part 2, 631, 643; part 3, 445; part 4, 893–96; part 5, 132–35, 160.

94. Scantleberry, interview, 50; Alice Bugg, interview by Nettie Simons, Pasadena Oral History Project, PPL, 4.

95. New York State, *Report of the New York State Temporary Commission on the Condition of the Urban Colored Population* (Albany, 1938), 16–19. Factory work as a proportion of male employment: Coconut Grove, FL, 0 percent; Evanston, IL, 10 percent; Glencoe, IL, 7 percent; Englewood, NJ, 19 percent; Freeport, NY, 4 percent; Mount Vernon, NY, 14 percent. *Census Schedules, 1920,* Pasadena, California, E.D. 504–35; Coconut Grove, Florida, E.D. 36; Evanston, Illinois, E.D., 74–84; Englewood, New Jersey, E.D. 22–27; Montclair, New Jersey, E.D. 74–90; Mount Vernon, New York, E.D. 76, 77, 83–87; Freeport, New York, E.D. 13.

96. Lewin, "A Study of the Negro Population," part VI.

97. Safety in the streets of affluent suburbs was counterbalanced by the threat

of workplace sexual harassment and assault that domestic servants faced in every locale.

98. On gender and migration, see Darlene Clark Hine, "Black Migration to the Urban Midwest: The Gender Dimension, 1915–1945," in *The Great Migration in Historical Perspective,* ed. Trotter, 127–46.

99. Willie Rayne Carrington, interview by Marion Forstall, April 1980, "Voices and Profiles," NRPL.

100. Caldonia Martin, interview by Angela Jackson, n.d.1974?, EHS; also Kevin Barry Leonard, "Paternalism and the Rise of a Black Community in Evanston, Illinois" (M.A. thesis, Northwestern University, 1982), 28.

101. Clydie Smith, interview by author, July 1986.

102. Claudia Robinson, interview by Elizabeth Langley, December 6, 1979, "Black History in Mount Vernon, New York," MVPL.

103. "Iroquois League Aids YMCA," *Evanston Review,* August 1968, clipping file, Evanston-Iroquois League, EHS; Evanston Interracial Council, *The Interracial Council: The Cooperative Way in Race Relations* (Evanston, 1937), 3–4, Evanston Public Library [EPL]; Mrs. John J. Spencer, interview by Wayne Watson, interview notes, n.d. 1974?, EHS.

104. Cora Watson, "The Iroquois League, Inc. 38th Anniversary Tea," April 24, 1955, handwritten remarks, EHS.

105. Melvin Scribner Smith, interview by N. Lawler and T. Welliver, April 27, 1983, transcript, EHS.

106. Pearl Shorey, "Black Families in Mount Vernon," typescript, MVPL.

107. Mack Robinson, interview, Pasadena Black History Project, September 4, 1984, PHS.

108. Bertha Sturdivant, interview by Elizabeth Langley, October 15, 1979, typescript, "Black History in Mount Vernon, New York," MVPL; Mary Ann Courtney, interview by Elizabeth Langley, October 26, 1979, ibid.; Doris Lewis, interview by Elizabeth Langley, May 17, 1979, ibid.; Ann Howard, interview by Pearl Shorey, n.d., "Black Families in Mount Vernon," MVPL. Black women in Evanston also established a Community Day Nursery in the early 1920s. Evanston Interracial Council, *The Interracial Council,* 3–4.

109. John Smith, interview by Marion Forstall, April 14, 1980, "Voices and Profiles," NRPL, 54.

110. Robinson, *Baseball Has Done It,* 29.

111. On gendered recruitment and "apprenticeship" among migrants, see Elizabeth Clark-Lewis, *Living In, Living Out: African American Domestics in Washington, D.C., 1910–1940* (Washington, D.C., 1994), 98.

112. Spencer, interview.

113. Shorey, "Black Families in Mount Vernon"; Sturdivant, interview; also see "'Mother Corry'—Worked Continuously for Freedom Baptist Church for 69 Years," *Pasadena Star-News,* January 17, 1970, 18.

114. New York State, *Report of the New York State Temporary Commission,* 13.

115. Bugg, interview, 4.

116. Quoted in Crimi, "The Social Status of the Negro in Pasadena, California," 36–37; Ruby McKnight Williams, interview by Pasadena Black History Project, 1984, PHS. For similar conditions in New Rochelle, see Chester Jones, interview by Marion Forstall, "Voices and Profiles," NRPL.

117. New York State, *Report of the New York State Temporary Commission,* 14.

118. On school segregation, see Alice Orton Rood, "Negroes in School District 75: An Analysis of Data Collected in 1925" (M.A. thesis, University of Chicago, 1926), 22; Robert LaFrankie, "The Englewood, New Jersey School Conflict: A Case Study of Decision Making and Racial Segregation, 1930–1963" (Ph.D. diss., Columbia University, 1967); Bruce D. Haynes, *Red Lines, Black Spaces: The Politics of Race and Space in a Black Middle-Class Suburb* (New Haven, 2001), 85–86, 101–5; "End Segregation in [Asbury Park] N.J. School," *Chicago Defender,* April 20, 1946, 2; and *Taylor v. Board of Education of New Rochelle,* 191 F. Supp. 181 (S.D.N.Y. 1961).

119. By the 1940s, nearly a quarter of the Negro YMCAs and YWCAs in the United States were located in affluent suburbs, including Montclair, Englewood, Orange, Plainfield, and Summit, New Jersey. *Negro Yearbook: A Review of Events Affecting Negro Life, 1941–1946,* ed. Jessie P. Guzman (Atlanta, 1947). Also see Ira De A. Reid and William Robert Valentine, *The Negro in New Jersey: A Report of a Survey by the Interracial Committee of the New Jersey Conference of Social Work* (New York, 1932), 49–52, 65–67.

120. Renaissance School, Class of 2000, *You Can't Give Up: The Power of the Struggle: Reflective Analysis of School Desegregation by America's Youth* (Montclair, N.J., 2000), 4.

121. Robinson, *Baseball Has Done It,* 29.

122. Quoted in Allen, *Jackie Robinson,* 19.

123. Michael Ebner, *Creating Chicago's North Shore: A Suburban History* (Chicago, 1988); Frances E. Willard, *A Classic Town: The Story of Evanston, by "an Old Timer"* (Chicago, 1892).

124. U.S. Census of Population: 1910, vol. II, *General Characteristics* (Washington, D.C., 1912). For chain migration from Greenwood and Abbeville Counties, South Carolina, see Bruner, "A General Survey," 44–45. Evanston black population, 1940: 6,026; U.S. Census of Population: 1940, vol. II, part 2, 614.

125. Estimate based on three-quarters of employed black women and one-

quarter of employed black men. U.S. Census of Population: 1940, vol. II, part 2, 631–32, 636.

126. In 1920, 54 percent of black women in Evanston worked for wages, 81 percent in services. Fifty-six percent were in the labor force in 1940. U.S. Census of Population: 1920, vol. IV, 370; *Census Schedules, 1920,* Evanston; U.S. Census of Population: 1940, vol. II, part 2, 631–36.

127. William Phipps, interview by Lawrence Schiller, May 1, 1974, EHS.

128. Eight percent of black men worked in professional or proprietary occupations, 6 percent were clerical workers, and 19 percent held skilled jobs. *Census Schedules, 1920,* Evanston.

129. Dorothy Jones, Geneva Lee, Beulah and James Avery, interview by N. Lawler, T. Welliver, and D. Owusu-Ansah, May 4, 1983, transcript, EHS.

130. Jones, interview.

131. Leonard, "Paternalism and the Rise of a Black Community," 30–33; Bruner, "A General Survey," 31.

132. Geraldine Cooper, Beulah Avery, and Ruby Alexander, interview by David Owusu-Ansah, May 4, 1983, EHS.

133. Rood, "Negroes in School District 75," 22.

134. Bruner, "A General Survey," 25.

135. Ibid., 18, 23, and map V; Sanborn Map Company, *Fire Insurance Map of Evanston, Illinois* (Chicago, 1895, 1920, 1946); *Census Schedules, 1920,* Evanston; *Bumstead's Evanston City and North Shore Directory, 1920–1921* (Evanston, 1920); *R. L. Polk's Evanston City and North Shore Directory, 1931* (Chicago, 1931).

136. Andrew Wiese, "Black Housing, White Finance: African American Housing and Home Ownership in Evanston, Illinois, before 1940," *Journal of Social History* 33 (winter 1999): 429–60.

137. Builders erected more than fourteen hundred homes in northwest Evanston during the 1920s and 1930s, none of which were available to African Americans. U.S. Census of Housing: 1940, vol. I, *Block Statistics, Evanston, Illinois* (Washington, D.C., 1942), 5–12.

138. *Baker v. Engstrom,* Superior Court of Cook County, case number 578255 (1933). My thanks to Wendy Plotkin for sharing this material.

139. Ibid.

140. For similar trends in suburban New York, see Ellen J. Skinner, "The War against the Housing of the Minority Poor: White Plains, New York," in *Contested Terrain: Power, Politics, and Participation in Suburbia,* ed. Marc L. Silver and Martin Melkonian (Westport, Conn., 1995), 243–54; New York State, *Report of the New York State Temporary Commission,* 51.

141. Bruner, "A General Survey," map V; Evanston Plan Committee, "Evan-

ston Use Map," (Evanston, 1921), EPL; Evanston Small Parks and Playground Association, "Plan of Evanston," (Evanston, 1917), EPL, 59.

142. On the demolition of "little colored communit[ies]" around town, see Robert White, interview by Glenna Johnson and Thandie Mvusi, May 4, 1974, EHS; Jones, Lee, and the Averys, interview. Melvin Smith, interview; U.S. Census of Housing: 1940, vol. 1, *Block Statistics, Evanston, Illinois;* U.S. Census of Housing: 1950, vol. V., *Block Statistics,* part 61, *Evanston, Illinois* (Washington, D.C., 1951), 3–12.

143. Bruner, "A General Survey," 43.

144. Ibid.; Karl E. Taeuber and Alma F. Taeuber, *Negroes in Cities: Residential Segregation and Neighborhood Change* (Chicago, 1965), 59.

145. Theodore "Ted" Wheeler, interview by author, October 1992.

Chapter Three

1. "Own Your Own Home," *New York Age,* February 26, 1927, 3.

2. "Notice! To the Tenant," *Baltimore Afro-American,* May 21, 1927, 19.

3. Quoted in "Negroes Fight for Better Life in Chagrin Park Shantytown," *Cleveland Plain Dealer,* February 2, 1959, 1.

4. Marvel Daines, *Be It Ever So Tumbled: The Story of a Suburban Slum* (Detroit, 1940); Greg Stricharchuk, "The Secret Chagrin Falls," *Cleveland Magazine* (February 1981): 49–51, 122–27; "Action Will Clean Up Dirty Chagrin Falls 'Pig Pen' Park Allotment," *Cleveland Call and Post,* December 20, 1947, 12A.

5. Leonard Blumberg and Michael Lalli, "Little Ghettoes: A Study of Negroes in the Suburbs," *Phylon* 27 (summer 1966): 117–31; Harold M. Rose, "The All-Negro Town: Its Evolution and Function," *Geographical Review* 55 (July 1965); Harold M. Rose, *Black Suburbanization: Access to Improved Quality of Life or Maintenance of the Status Quo?* (Cambridge, 1976), 9, 249.

6. Important exceptions are James Borchert, *Alley Life in Washington: Family, Community, Religion, and Folklife in the City, 1850–1970* (Urbana, Ill., 1980); and John Michael Vlach, *Back of the Big House: The Architecture of Plantation Slavery* (Chapel Hill, N.C., 1993). See also Barbara Burlinson Mooney, "The Comfortable Tasty Framed Cottage: An African American Architectural Iconography," *Journal of the Society of Architectural Historians* 61 (March 2002): 48–67; and Earl Lewis, "Connecting Memory, Self, and the Power of Place in African American Urban History," *Journal of Urban History* 21 (March 1995): 347–71.

7. For example, see Joe William Trotter Jr., *Black Milwaukee: The Making of an Industrial Proletariat, 1915–45* (Urbana, Ill., 1985); James R. Grossman, *Land of Hope: Chicago, Black Southerners, and the Great Migration* (Chicago, 1989); and

Farah Jasmine Griffin, *"Who Set You Flowin'?": The African-American Migration Narrative* (New York, 1995).

8. Stephan Thernstrom, *Poverty and Progress: Social Mobility in a Nineteenth Century City,* (Cambridge, 1964); Richard Harris, "Self-Building in the Urban Housing Market," *Economic Geography* 67 (January 1991): 1–21.

9. Olivier Zunz, *The Changing Face of Inequality: Urbanization, Industrial Development, and Immigrants in Detroit, 1880–1920* (Chicago, 1982), 152–60; Roger Simon, "Housing and Services in an Immigrant Neighborhood: Milwaukee's 14th Ward," *Journal of Urban History* 2 (1976): 435–58.

10. Insofar as this vision led families to believe that they could make better lives at the edge of town than in its center, it was a suburban dream.

11. Judge Manuel Rocker, interview by author, July 1986; *Geauga County Torrens Record Docket,* no. 1, Geauga County Recorder's Office, Chardon, Ohio.

12. "For This We Waited," *Jewish World,* June 14, 1921, trans. Phillip Horowitz; "New Allotment Is Started," *Chagrin Falls Exponent,* June 23, 1921.

13. *Geauga County Torrens Docket,* no. 1.

14. In part, professionalization and planning represented attempts to stamp out this market. H. Morton Bodfish, "The Free Lot Subdivider: His Method of Operation and the Available Methods of Control," *Journal of Land and Public Utility Economics* 5 (1929): 187–98; Mark A. Weiss, *The Rise of the Community Builders: The American Real Estate Industry and Urban Land Planning* (New York, 1987), 17–52. On low-cost or "informal" real estate markets, see Zunz, *The Changing Face of Inequality,* 161–70; Simon, "Housing and Services"; Harris, "Self-Building in the Urban Housing Market"; and Richard Harris, "Working-Class Home Ownership in the American Metropolis," *Journal of Urban History* 17 (November 1990): 46–69. On African American participation, see Henry L. Taylor Jr., "The Building of a Black Industrial Suburb: The Lincoln Heights, Ohio, Story" (Ph.D. diss., State University of New York at Buffalo, 1979).

15. Ads appeared for subdivisions in Amityville, Deer Park, Yonkers, Croton, and Jamaica (Queens), New York; and New Brunswick, Asbury Park, Hackensack, Plainfield, Westwood, Coytesville, Reevytown, Potter's Station, Rahway, and Fanwood, New Jersey. *New York Age,* April 16, 1921; July 30, 1921; *Amsterdam News,* November 29, 1922.

16. *Chicago Defender,* February 24, 1923; January 17, 1920. The *Gazette* advertised lots in Oakwood and Miles Heights as well as Oberlin, Ohio; Douglass Park, near Washington; and Egg Harbor, New Jersey. *Cleveland Gazette,* April 5, 1924; March 26, 1921. "High Ridge Park, the Land of Promise," *Baltimore Afro-American,* August 15, 1925; "Oakdale Park . . . Florida's Greatest Colored Addition," *Pittsburgh Courier,* March 13, 1926; "$1 a Week Pays for a Crestas Lot"; *Pittsburgh Courier,* May 7, 1927. See also Leslie Wilson, "Dark Spaces: An Account

of Afro-American Suburbanization" (Ph.D. diss., City University of New York, 1991), 76–79.

17. "Be Loyal, Join Hands with Your Own People," *Amsterdam News,* October 17, 1923; "$5 per Month Buys You a Lot Near Hackensack," *Amsterdam News,* November 29, 1922; "Enough Ground to Build Your Home and Raise Chickens and Vegetables. Plenty of Employment for All [near New Brunswick, New Jersey]," *Amsterdam News,* March 21, 1923.

18. Black subdivisions bore titles such as Booker Terrace, Booker Heights (Amityville, New York); Douglass Park, Lincoln (Prince George's County, Maryland); Lincoln Heights (Cincinnati, Cleveland, and Columbus); Lincoln Park (Watts, California); Lincoln Estates (Amityville, New York); and Linconia (Bucks County, Pennsylvania). Street names like Douglass, Booker, and Lincoln also attest to the intended market. "Great Opportunity for Colored People to Own a Home [in Jamaica (Queens), N.Y.]," *Chicago Defender,* July 7, 1917.

19. For real estate prices, see the *Cleveland Gazette,* 1921–27; Essie Kirklen, interview by author, July 16, 1986; William Hagler, interview by author, August 11, 1986; *Geauga County Common Pleas Court Appearance and Execution Docket,* nos. 1–7, 1929–41 (Common Pleas Court of Geauga County, Chardon, Ohio).

20. Using deed records, membership rosters, and other local sources, I compiled a list of 150 heads of households who lived in Chagrin Falls Park before 1950. Using Cleveland city directories, I verified a last place of residence in Cleveland for 93 household heads, occupations for 73, and housing tenure for 66. Compared to 45 percent of black men in Cleveland in 1930, 53 percent of men who moved to Chagrin Falls held unskilled jobs before their move. Nine percent worked in domestic or personal service, compared to 16 percent in Cleveland. Andrew Wiese, *A Place of Our Own: The Chagrin Falls Park from 1921–1950* (Chagrin Falls, Ohio, 1986), appendix. Kenneth Kusmer, *A Ghetto Takes Shape: Black Cleveland, 1870–1930* (Champaign, Ill., 1976). Thirteen of fifteen early residents interviewed for the project were born in the South, as were their spouses and extended families. By all reports, southerners were the great majority.

21. Clara Adams, interview by author, July 29, 1986.

22. Essie Kirklen, interview by author, August 15, 1986; Shepherd Beck, interview by author, August 18, 1986; Lula Hitchcock, interview by author, July 31, 1986.

23. Kirklen, interview, July 16, 1986.

24. Ruby Hall, interview by author, July 7, 1986.

25. Detroit Mayor's Interracial Committee, *The Negro in Detroit,* vol. 5, *Housing* (Detroit, 1926).

26. The 1930 and 1940 totals are for Bainbridge Township. The 1950 total is estimated from the rural nonfarm black population of Geauga County (757). U.S. Census of Population: 1930, vol. III, *General Characteristics of the Population,* part 2 (Washington, D.C., 1932), 521; U.S. Census of Population: 1940, vol. II, *Characteristics of the Population,* part 5 (Washington, D.C., 1943), 628; U.S. Census of Population: 1950, vol. II, *Characteristics of the Population,* part 35 (Washington, D.C., 1952), 183. Home-ownership total represents blacks in Geauga County. Rural nonfarm ownership, the category that comprised the Park, was 73 percent. U.S. Census of Housing: 1940, vol. II, *General Characteristics,* part 4 (Washington, D.C., 1943), 609, 613.

27. Mary E. Crawford, "Bainbridge School Investigation," March 15, 1946, Papers of the NAACP, Cleveland Branch (Western Reserve Historical Society, Cleveland, Ohio); "Memo re *Lois Wilson v. Chagrin Board of Education-Geauga County,*" August 2, 1945, ibid.; "Park School Origins," n.d. (Kenston School Board, Bainbridge, Ohio); Raymond J. Walsh, "Exclusionary Housing Practices in Bainbridge Township, Geauga County, Ohio" (Chagrin Falls Park, Ohio, 1972), author's possession. Rustic conditions characterized many black suburbs through the 1960s. Harold M. Rose, "The All Black Town: Suburban Prototype or Rural Slum?" *Urban Affairs Annual Reviews* 6 (1972): 397–431; Reynolds Farley, "The Changing Distribution of Negroes within Metropolitan Areas: The Emergence of Black Suburbs," *American Journal of Sociology* 75 (1970): 340.

28. Rose, "The All-Black Town," 398–99.

29. Becky M. Nicolaides, *My Blue Heaven: Life and Politics in the Working-Class Suburbs of Los Angeles, 1920–1965* (Chicago, 2002), 135–56.

30. David Kenneth Bruner, "A General Survey of the Negro Population of Evanston," (senior thesis, Northwestern University, 1924), 26, 36; Building Permits, Evanston, Illinois (Evanston Historical Society, Evanston, Ill.); Building Permits, Pasadena, California (City Administration Building, Pasadena, Calif.).

31. Blumberg and Lalli, "Little Ghettoes," 125.

32. Ruby Hall, interview by author, July 20, 1986.

33. Hitchcock, interview; Fannie Detwyler, interview by author, August 19, 1986; Clydie Smith, interview by author, July 29, 1986; Estella Jackson, interview by author, August 18, 1986.

34. Lumpkin divorce, case 8934, November 19, 1937 (Geauga County Common Pleas Court, Chardon, Ohio).

35. Kirklen, interview, July 16, 1986.

36. Ruby and Stephen Hall, interview by author, August 22, 1986.

37. Hitchcock, interview; the Halls, interview; Essie Kirklen, interview by author, August 11, 1986.

38. Nicolaides, *My Blue Heaven*, 51.

39. U.S. Census of Population: 1940, vol. II, part 5, 593.

40. Beck, interview.

41. Chagrin Falls Park Community Center, "Residents' Roster" (Chagrin Falls Park, Ohio, 1983), author's possession.

42. Alma Walker, interview by author, August 12, 1986; Hitchcock, interview; Detwyler, interview.

43. Margaret Marsh, *Suburban Lives* (New Brunswick, N.J., 1990), 99–112; David Contosta, *Suburb in the City: Chestnut Hill, Philadelphia, 1850–1990* (Columbus, 1992), 175–81; Richard Harris, *Unplanned Suburbs: Toronto's American Tragedy, 1900 to 1950* (Baltimore, 1996), 123–30; Nicolaides, *My Blue Heaven*, 103–4.

44. Geauga County Negro Republican Club, "Minutes" (Chagrin Falls, Ohio, May 1, 1940–April 25, 1941), author's possession.

45. "Minutes of Special Meeting," November 6, 1946, Bainbridge Township Board of Commissioners (Bainbridge, Ohio).

46. "Education Committee Minutes," April 3, 1946, Cleveland NAACP Papers.

47. Essie Kirklen, "The History of the Origin of the Church of God," typescript, n.d., author's possession.

48. Adams, interview; Ruby Hall, interview, July 20, 1986.

49. Sam Bass Warner Jr., *The Private City: Philadelphia in Three Periods of Its Growth* (Philadelphia, 1968), 120, 131, 157; Kenneth T. Jackson, *Crabgrass Frontier: The Suburbanization of the United States* (New York, 1985), 45–72; John Bodnar, Roger Simon, and Michael Weber, *Lives of Their Own: Blacks, Italians, and Poles in Pittsburgh, 1900–1930* (Urbana, Ill., 1982), 153–80.

50. Eric Foner, *Reconstruction: America's Unfinished Revolution, 1863–1877* (New York, 1988), 104–6, 374–77; Leon Litwak, *Been in the Storm So Long: The Aftermath of Slavery* (New York, 1979), 398–407; Theodore Rosengarten, *All God's Dangers: The Life of Nate Shaw* (New York, 1974), 236–37, 537–38.

51. "Own Your Own Home," 3.

52. Grossman, *Land of Hope,* 36; Peter Gottlieb, *Making Their Own Way: Southern Blacks' Migration to Pittsburgh, 1916–1930* (Urbana, Ill., 1987), 76, 183, 209–10; Carol Stack, *Call to Home: African Americans Reclaim the Rural South* (New York, 1996), 17–44.

53. *Baltimore Afro-American,* May 23, 1925; May 21, 1927.

54. "If You Are Interested," *Baltimore Afro-American,* June 18, 1927.

55. Detwyler, interview.

56. Nonwhite home ownership, 1940 (city vs. suburban ring): Chicago, 7 percent vs. 25 percent; Kansas City, 15:49; St. Louis, 7:43; Los Angeles, 24:34; De-

troit, 15:49; Newark, 3:17 (Essex County); Philadelphia, 10:28; Pittsburgh, 13:19. For 1930, city and suburban rates tended to range 2–7 percentage points higher. U.S. Census of Housing: 1940, vol. II, *General Characteristics* (Washington, D.C., 1943).

57. Harris, *Unplanned Suburbs,* 109–35; Nicolaides, *My Blue Heaven,* 26–35.

58. Margaret F. Byington, *Homestead: The Households of a Mill Town* (1910; reprint, Pittsburgh, 1974), 46–49; Alice Bugg, Pasadena Oral History Project (Pasadena, 1984). "Keeping fowls or rabbits" in Pasadena persisted into the 1950s. E.g., letter to owner of 523 Pepper Street, April 4, 1952, Building Permit Files, 1922–85, Department of Planning and Permitting (Pasadena, Calif.).

59. Gretchen Lemke-Santangelo, *Abiding Courage: African American Migrant Women and the East Bay Community* (Chapel Hill, N.C., 1996), 139–41. For domestic production in other suburbs, see Wilson, "Dark Spaces," 349; Mary Ann Courtney, interview by Elizabeth Langley, October 26, 1979 (Mount Vernon Public Library, Mount Vernon, N.Y.); Armstrong Association of Philadelphia, *A Study of the Living Conditions among Colored People in Towns in the Outer Part of Philadelphia and in Other Suburbs Both in Pennsylvania and New Jersey* (Philadelphia, 1915), 11–12, 22, 30, 32, 35, 51, 54; Taylor, "Building of a Black Industrial Suburb"; Grace E. Richmond, "Housing Conditions in the Outlying Districts of Columbus" (M.A. thesis, Ohio State University, 1926), 11–12, 18, 37; and Ann Morris and Henrietta Ambrose, *North Webster: A Photographic History of a Black Community* (Bloomington, Ind., 1993), 9, 17.

60. Courtney, interview. See also "'Money in Your Backyard,'" *Pittsburgh Courier,* August 20, 1927.

61. Jackson, interview; Kirklen, interview, July 16, 1986; Adams, interview.

62. "Negroes Fight for Better Life in Chagrin Park Shantytown," 1.

63. Andrew Wiese, "Black Housing, White Finance: African American Housing and Home Ownership in Evanston, Illinois, before 1940," *Journal of Social History* 33 (winter 1999): 446. Albert G. Hinman, "An Inventory of Housing in a Suburban City," *Journal of Land and Public Utility Economics* 7, no. 2 (May 1931): 169–80. U.S. Census of Housing: 1940, vol. I, *Block Statistics,* Evanston, Illinois (Washington, D.C., 1942), 5–12.

64. Trotter, *Black Milwaukee.* On domestic production among white workers, see Lizabeth Cohen, *Making a New Deal: Industrial Workers in Chicago, 1919–1939* (New York, 1990), 11. On the South, see Jack Temple Kirby, *Rural Worlds Lost: The American South, 1920–1960* (Baton Rouge, 1987), 115–33, 298–300.

65. Mayor's Interracial Committee, *The Negro in Detroit,* 58–59.

66. Cohen, *Making a New Deal,* 147–57.

67. On the importance of migrants' southern heritage in building north-

ern communities, see Gottlieb, *Making Their Own Way,* 49–52; Kimberley L. Phillips, "'But It Is a Fine Place to Make Money': Migration and African American Families in Cleveland, 1915–1929," *Journal of Social History* 30 (winter 1996): 393–413.

68. Kirklen, interview August 15, 1986; Detwyler, interview; Beck, interview; Mr. and Mrs. Noah Pounds, interview by author, July 1986; Walker, interview; *Geauga County Torrens Record Docket,* no. 1.

69. Henry MacMiller and his sister, Josephine Young, settled with their spouses in the late 1920s. Josephine's brother-in-law, Eugene Young, and his wife also settled in the Park in the early 1930s. In 1936 Mr. MacMiller's adult daughter, Ruby Hall, moved to Chagrin Falls with her husband. The Halls, interview.

70. On nuclear family ideology in white suburbs, see Marsh, *Suburban Lives,* 67–89, 173–79; and Barbara Kelly, *Expanding the American Dream: Building and Rebuilding Levittown* (Albany, 1993), 106–10. Samples from the 1920 census in eleven suburbs (Freeport and Mount Vernon, New York; Englewood and Montclair, New Jersey; Evanston, Glencoe, Harvey, Robbins, and Maywood, Illinois; River Rouge, Michigan; and Pasadena, California) revealed that 15 to 25 percent of black households included extended family. Many others lived under separate roofs. U.S. Census of Population: 1920, *Census Schedules,* Freeport, New York, Enumeration Districts [E.D.] 13–15; Mount Vernon, New York, E.D. 76–87; Montclair, New Jersey, E.D. 74–90; Englewood, New Jersey, E.D. 22–27; Evanston, Illinois, E.D. 68–89; Glencoe Village, Illinois, E.D. 119; Harvey, Illinois, E.D. 215–19; Robbins Village, Illinois, E.D. 25; Maywood, Illinois, E.D. 194–95; River Rouge, Michigan, E.D. 679; Pasadena, California, E.D. 504–35.

71. The Halls, interview.

72. Adams, interview.

73. Quoted in "Negroes Fight for Better Life in Chagrin Park Shantytown."

74. Sam Bass Warner Jr., *Streetcar Suburbs: The Process of Growth in Boston, 1870–1900* (Cambridge, 1962), 29–31; Jackson, *Crabgrass Frontier* 103–37.

75. Detwyler, interview.

76. Quoted in "Negroes Fight for Better Life in Chagrin Park Shantytown."

77. Stephen Hall, interview by author, August 22, 1986.

78. Beck, interview.

79. Quoted in Wilson, "Dark Spaces."

80. Alice P., interview by author, March 5, 1992.

81. Cora Watson, interview by S. F. Patton, May 24, 1974 (Evanston Historical Society, Evanston, Ill.); Morris and Ambrose, *North Webster,* 17; Wilfred Lewin, "A Study of the Negro Population of Mount Vernon," typescript (1935), MVPL.

82. Kirklen, interview, August 11, 1986.

83. George J. Sanchez, *Becoming Mexican American: Ethnicity, Culture, and Identity in Chicano Los Angeles, 1910–1945* (New York, 1993), 198–201; Simon, "Housing and Services," 447–50; Zunz, *The Changing Face of Inequality,* 170–74; Richard Harris and Matt Sendbuehler, "The Making of a Working-Class Suburb in Hamilton's East End, 1900–1945," *Journal of Urban History* 20 (August 1994): 486–511.

84. On planning efforts to restrict black suburbanization after the war, see Henry L. Taylor Jr., "City Building, Public Policy, the Rise of the Industrial City, and Black Ghetto-Slum Formation in Cincinnati, 1850–1940," in *Race and the City: Work, Community, and Protest in Cincinnati, 1820–1970,* ed. Henry L. Taylor Jr. (Urbana, Ill., 1993), 176.

85. The black population of Bainbridge Township reached 892 in 1960. It had slipped to 507 by 1990, but not all African Americans in the township lived in Chagrin Falls Park. U.S. Census of Population: 1960, vol. I, *General Population Characteristics,* part 37 (Washington, D.C., 1961), 135; U.S. Census of Population: 1990, vol. I, *General Population Characteristics,* part 37 (Washington, D.C., 1982), 572; "Building a Proud Future," *Chagrin Valley News-Herald,* April 19, 1998, A8.

Chapter Four

1. Quoted in Bob Williams, "Arrest Negro Homebuilder, Charge Violation of New Building Code in Woodmere, Village of Pioneers," *Cleveland Call and Post,* August 10, 1946, 1A, 9A; "Suburbanites Fight Bigotry," ibid., April 13, 1946, 1A, 9A.

2. "Building Hopes of Woodmere Now Await Criminal Court Decision," *Cleveland Call and Post,* November 29, 1947, 1A; "Local Court Upholds Solon Building Barriers," *Cleveland Call and Post,* January 14, 1950, 1.

3. U.S. Census of Population: 1960, vol. III, *Selected Area Reports,* part 1D, *Standard Metropolitan Statistical Areas* (Washington, D.C., 1963), 2.

4. "Suburbanites Fight Bigotry," 1A, 9A.

5. "Mrs. V.," phone conversation with author, Woodmere, Ohio, 1992.

6. "Suburbanites Fight Bigotry," 9A.

7. Bob Williams, "Woodmere Villagers Take Fight over Building Code into Courts," *Cleveland Call and Post,* September 27, 1947, 1A, 14B; Williams, "Arrest Negro Homebuilder," 9A.

8. "Housing Tips," *Cleveland Call and Post,* June 3, 1950, 6C. "Local Court

Upholds Solon Building Barriers," 1. In nearby Maple Heights, Ohio, whites initiated a "strong effort . . . to decrease the colored occupancy of this area" in the 1930s. Area Description, D-8, September 6, 1939, *Security Map of Cuyahoga County, Ohio,* box 87, Home Owners Loan Corporation [HOLC] Papers, Record Group 195 (National Archives, Washington, D.C.).

9. For circumstances in other cities, see "Homesite Seizure Voted Over Creve Coeur Mayor's Veto," *St. Louis Globe Democrat,* October 28, 1956, 4A; "Construction Permit Denied Rouge Doctor," *Wyandotte [Michigan] Herald,* July 14, 1949; Morton M. Hunt, "The Battle of Abingdon Township," *Commentary* (March 1950): 234. Also, Henry L. Taylor Jr., "City Building, Public Policy, the Rise of the Industrial City, and Black Ghetto-Slum Formation in Cincinnati, 1850–1940," in *Race and the City: Work, Community, and Protest in Cincinnati, 1820–1970,* ed. Henry L. Taylor Jr. (Urbana, Ill., 1993).

10. Thomas Holt, "Marking: Race, Race-making, and the Writing of History," *American Historical Review* 100 (February 1995): 1–20.

11. California State Advisory Committee to the U.S. Commission on Civil Rights, *The 50 States Report: From the State Advisory Committees to the Commission on Civil Rights* (Washington, D.C., 1961), 45.

12. Kenneth T. Jackson, *Crabgrass Frontier: The Suburbanization of the United States* (New York, 1985), 198.

13. Luigi Laurenti, *Property Values and Race* (Berkeley, 1959). See Donald Phares, "Socioeconomic Transition and Housing Values: A Comparative Analysis of Urban Neighborhoods," *Urban Affairs Annual Reviews* (1974): 183–208.

14. On white fears of integration, see Arnold Hirsch, *Making the Second Ghetto: Race and Housing in Chicago, 1940–1960* (New York, 1983), 186–205; Thomas J. Sugrue, *The Origins of the Urban Crisis: Race and Inequality in Postwar Detroit* (Princeton, 1996), 209–18; Stephen Grant Meyer, *As Long as They Don't Move Next Door: Segregation and Racial Conflict in American Neighborhoods* (Lanham, Md., 2000), 77, 110.

15. Lizabeth Cohen, "Citizens and Consumers in the Century of Mass Consumption," in *Perspectives on Modern America: Making Sense of the Twentieth Century,* ed. Harvard Sitkoff (New York, 2001), 145–61. Also see Becky M. Nicolaides, *My Blue Heaven: Life and Politics in the Working-Class Suburbs of Los Angeles, 1920–1965* (Chicago, 2002).

16. George Lipsitz, "The Possessive Investment in Whiteness: Racialized Social Democracy and the 'White' Problem in American Studies," *American Quarterly* 47 (September 1995): 223.

17. Sugrue, *Origins of the Urban Crisis,* 9, 211–18; Charles Abrams, *Forbidden Neighbors: A Study of Prejudice in Housing* (New York, 1955).

18. Jackson, *Crabgrass Frontier*, 241.

19. U.S. Commission on Civil Rights, *Housing: 1961 Commission on Civil Rights Report* (Washington, D.C., 1961), 140; Sugrue, *Origins of the Urban Crisis*, 218–29; Ewen McKenzie, *Privatopia: Homeowners Associations and the Rise of Residential Private Government* (New Haven, 1994).

20. U.S. Commission on Civil Rights, *Hearings before the U.S. Commission on Civil Rights: Housing, Hearings Held in New York, New York, February 2–3, 1959* (Washington, D.C., 1959), 269.

21. Booker T. McGraw, "Wartime Employment, Migration, and Housing of Negroes in the United States," *Midwest Journal* 1 (summer 1949): 100; Hirsch, *Making the Second Ghetto*, 40; Sugrue, *Origins of the Urban Crisis*, 231–58.

22. "Racists Again Set Fire to Negro's Long Island Home," *New York Post*, November 23, 1953; "Police Guard Home of Long Island Negro after Threat to Burn It," ibid., May 8, 1956; "Sale to Negro Feared, Long Island Home Bombed," ibid., June 19, 1956; for other violent incidents, see Abrams, *Forbidden Neighbors;* and James Hecht, *Because It Is Right: Integration in Housing* (Boston, 1970), 198–201.

23. *Shelley v. Kraemer*, 334 U.S. 1 (1948); Clement E. Vose, *Caucasians Only: The Supreme Court, the NAACP, and the Restrictive Covenant Cases* (Berkeley, 1959).

24. Quoted in William Brown Jr., "Access to Housing: The Role of the Real Estate Industry," in *Black America: Geographical Perspectives,* ed. Robert Ernst and Lawrence Hugg (Garden City, N.Y., 1976), 160.

25. U.S. Census of Housing: 1960, vol. 1, *States and Small Areas,* part 1, *U.S. Summary* (Washington, D.C., 1963), xxvii.

26. Eunice Grier and George Grier, *Privately Developed Interracial Housing: An Analysis of Experience* (Berkeley, 1960), 117; Joseph Ray, "Racial Policy to Govern Administration of HHFA Programs," August 13, 1954, box 961, HHFA Papers.

27. Abrams, *Forbidden Neighbors,* 229; U.S. Commission on Civil Rights, *Housing: 1961,* 59.

28. Jon Teaford, *Post-Suburbia: Government and Politics in the Edge Cities* (Baltimore, 1997), 57–60.

29. Michael N. Danielson, *The Politics of Exclusion* (New York, 1976), 27.

30. For extremes of municipal support for racial exclusion, see Hirsch, *Making the Second Ghetto,* 53–54, 62; Abrams, *Forbidden Neighbors,* 91–100; David L. Good, *Orvie: The Dictator of Dearborn: The Rise and Reign of Orville L. Hubbard* (Detroit, 1989); and Phillip J. Cooper, *Hard Judicial Choices: Federal District Court Judges and State and Local Officials* (New York, 1989), 53–59.

31. Morris Milgram, *Good Neighborhood: The Challenge of Open Housing* (New

York, 1977), 78. See also Grier and Grier, *Privately Developed Interracial Housing,* 78–94.

32. Davis McEntire, *Residence and Race: Final and Comprehensive Report to the Commission on Race and Housing* (Berkeley, 1960), 202–3.

33. George Snowden, "Address to Mortgage Bankers of America," September 29, 1954, box 745, HHFA Papers.

34. Danielson, *The Politics of Exclusion,* 61. For zoning against mobile homes, see *Vickers v. Township Committee of Gloucester Township,* 68 N.J. Super. 263, 172 A. 2d 218 (1961); *Lionshead Lake, Inc., v. Township of Wayne,* 10 N.J. 165 (1952); and *Renker v. Village of Brooklyn,* 139 Ohio St. 484; against apartments, see *Fanale v. Borough of Hasbrouck Heights,* 26 N.J. 320 (1958). For the restriction of home and lot sizes, see *Flower Hill Building Corp. v. Village of Flower Hill,* 100 N.Y.S. 2d 903; and *Fischer v. Township of Bedminster,* 5 N.J. 534 (1950).

35. William Braden, "Negro Suburbia: A Report on the Progress and the Problems," *Chicago Sun-Times,* November 15, 1962, 30–31; Bruce Haynes, *Red Lines, Black Spaces: The Politics of Race and Space in a Black Middle-Class Suburb* (New Haven, 2001), 109–11; William H. Wilson, *Hamilton Park: A Planned Black Community in Dallas* (Baltimore, 1998) 92–107.

36. Danielson, *The Politics of Exclusion,* 29–33; U.S. Commission on Civil Rights, *Hearings before the U.S. Commission on Civil Rights: Hearings Held in St. Louis, Missouri, January 14–17, 1970* (Washington, D.C., 1970), 348–49; ibid., *Hearings Held in Detroit, Michigan, December 14–15, 1960* (Washington, D.C., 1961), 58–59, 115. For building lots at increasing distance from the city, see "Attention Home Seekers: Live in Michigan, Work in Chicago," *Chicago Defender,* May 25, 1946, 2.

37. U.S. Commission on Civil Rights, *Hearings before the U.S. Commission on Civil Rights: Hearings Held in Washington, D.C., April 12–13, 1962* (Washington, D.C., 1962), 44.

38. Abrams, *Forbidden Neighbors,* 211–12; Yale Rabin, "The Effects of Development Controls on Housing Opportunities for Black Households in Baltimore County, Maryland," U.S. Commission on Civil Rights, *Hearing before the U.S. Commission on Civil Rights: Hearing Held in Baltimore, Maryland, August 17–19, 1970* (Washington, D.C., 1970), 698–730; Yale Rabin, "Expulsive Zoning: The Inequitable Legacy of *Euclid,*" in *Zoning and the American Dream: Promises Still to Keep,* ed. Charles M. Haar and Jerold S. Kayden (Washington, D.C., 1981), 103–6.

39. The Bethel AME Church in North Amityville (est. 1815) and the AME Zion Church in Westbury (est. 1834) were among twenty-nine African American churches on Long Island established before 1900. Lynda R. Day, *Making a Way to Freedom: A History of African Americans on Long Island* (Interlaken, N.Y., 1998);

Bette S. Weidman and Linda B. Martin, "Spinney Hill: The Hidden Community," *Long Island Forum* 43 (March 1980): 48–55; Walter G. Clerk, *North Amityville: A History* (Amityville Public Library, Amityville, N.Y., 1976).

40. During the Great Migration, black subdivisions were established in Hempstead, New Cassel, Manhasset, Roosevelt, North Amityville, Wyandanch, and Yaphank. See *Amsterdam News,* August 22, 1928; May 8, 1929; also Subdivision Registration Files (Town Assessor, Town of Babylon, Lindenhurst, N.Y.).

41. U.S. Census of Population: 1940, vol. II, *Characteristics of the Population,* part 5 (Washington, D.C., 1943), 88, 95; U.S. Census of Population: 1960, vol. I, *General Population Characteristics,* part 34 (Washington, D.C., 1962), 137, 141.

42. "Clean up" in Jack Ehrlich and Francis Wood, "Long Island's Ugly Ducklings," part 5, *New York Newsday,* September 20, 1957, 10C. On slum-clearance debates in several Long Island towns, see the five-part series "Long Island's Ugly Ducklings," ibid., September 16–20, 1957, 10–11C.

43. "Negro Tenants Petition Harriman on Evictions," *Daily Worker,* September 9, 1955; "Glen Cove Negro Tenants of Unsafe Homes Fight Evictions," ibid., September 20, 1955, Clippings Scrapbook, "Housing, New York State" (Schomburg Center for Research in Black Culture, New York, N.Y.).

44. Ehrlich and Wood, "Long Island's Ugly Ducklings," part 5, 10C.

45. Key legislation in New York was the State Public Housing Act of 1946 and the National Housing Act of 1949. New York State Division of Housing, *Housing Responsibilities: Annual Report of the Commissioner of Housing* (Albany, 1956); Nassau County Planning Department, *Aspects: An Analysis of Social, Economic and Housing Characteristics of Nassau County, New York,* part 6 (Mineola, N.Y., 1962), 10.

46. Sanborn Fire Insurance Company, "Map of Freeport, N.Y.," 1905, 1910 (New York, 1905, 1910).

47. Quoted in Madeline Ryttenberg, "State's Worst Slum Shames Freeport," *New York Newsday,* March 25, 1949; see also "Clergy Takes a Lead in Fight to End Slums: Freeport Board Acts to Seek Law Setting Up Housing Authority," ibid., February 11, 1941, Clippings File, "Housing" (Freeport Public Library, Freeport, N.Y.). U.S. Census of Population: 1940, vol. II, part 5, 111; U.S. Census of Population: 1950, vol. II, *Characteristics of the Population,* part 32 (Washington, D.C., 1952), 92.

48. "Fate of Slum Clearance to Be Decided Tuesday: Favorable Vote Urged by Village Fathers at Housing Referendum," *New York Newsday,* August 28, 1951, Clippings File, "Housing" (Freeport Public Library, Freeport, N.Y.).

49. Madeline Ryttenberg, "Freeport Slums a Monument to Voters' 'No,'" *New York Newsday,* March 28, 1949, Clippings File, "Housing" (Freeport Public Library, Freeport, N.Y.).

50. "AVC Demands End to Slums in Freeport," *New York Newsday,* January 13, 1950, Clippings File, "Housing" (Freeport Public Library, Freeport, N.Y.).

51. Freeport Housing Authority, *Howgozit?* 1 (June 1969).

52. Matthew Edel, "Planning, Market or Warfare? Recent Land Use Conflict in American Cities," in *Readings in Urban Economics,* ed. Matthew Edel and Jerome Rothenberg (New York, 1972); also Marc A. Weiss, "The Origins and Legacy of Urban Renewal," in *Federal Housing Policy and Programs, Past and Present,* ed. J. Paul Mitchell (New Brunswick, N.J., 1985), 253–76. For urban renewal in the suburbs, see Yale Rabin, "The Roots of Segregation in the Eighties: The Role of Local Government Actions," *Urban Affairs Annual Reviews* 32 (1987): 208–26.

53. Oscar van Purnell, Oral History, March 12, 1981, Hempstead, New York (Long Island Studies Center, Hofstra University, Hempstead, N.Y.), 4.

54. John R. Logan and Harvey L. Molotch, *Urban Fortunes: The Political Economy of Place* (Berkeley, 1987), 135.

55. New York State Division of Housing, *The Ten-Year Look at State Housing* (1949).

56. Urban renewal in Glen Cove and Manhasset and highway building in Inwood led to black population losses in those communities. On Westchester County, see Danielson, *The Politics of Exclusion,* 42. For racial cleansing in suburban St. Louis, see U.S. Commission on Civil Rights, *Hearings Held in St. Louis, Missouri, January 14–17, 1970,* 384–410.

57. Ehrlich and Wood, "Long Island's Ugly Ducklings," part 5, September 17, 1957, 11C.

Chapter Five

1. Quoted in Dorothy Sutherland Jayne, "First Families: A Study of Twenty Pioneer Negro Families Who Moved into White Neighborhoods in Metropolitan Philadelphia" (M.A. thesis, Bryn Mawr College, 1960), epigraph.

2. The names are pseudonyms. Ibid., see appendix B, 66–70.

3. Ibid., 66–67.

4. Reynolds Farley, "The Changing Distribution of Negroes within Metropolitan Areas: The Emergence of Black Suburbs," *American Journal of Sociology* 75 (January 1970): 345–46; Clarence Dean, "Negroes Facing Test in Suburbs: Major Shift from the City Poses Housing Question," *New York Times,* May 21, 1961.

5. James Felt, "Opportunities of Private Capital in Housing for Negroes," *Opportunity* 24 (summer 1946): 129. To the firm "no" of white suburbanites, of-

ficials, and real estate personnel, African American suburbanization represented a resounding black "yes."

6. Charles Abrams, *Forbidden Neighbors: A Study of Prejudice in Housing* (New York, 1955), 227–43; Kenneth T. Jackson, *Crabgrass Frontier: The Suburbanization of the United States* (New York, 1985), 190–230.

7. Housing and Home Finance Agency (HHFA), "Housing of the Non-White Population, 1940–1950" (Washington, D.C., 1952), 1.

8. U.S. Census of Population: 1960, vol. III, *Selected Area Reports,* part 1D (Washington, D.C., 1963), 2–5.

9. Reynolds Farley and Walter Allen, *The Color Line and the Quality of Life in America* (New York, 1987), 113.

10. The ten metropolitan areas were New York, Chicago, Detroit, Philadelphia, Boston, Pittsburgh, St. Louis, Cleveland, Newark, and Buffalo. U.S. Census of Population: 1960, vol. III, part 1D, 2–5, 49, 71–72, 78, 87–88, 96, 114, 121, 144, 249, 253.

11. Charles Tilly, "What Good Is Urban History," *Journal of Urban History* 22 (September 1996): 711.

12. For cumulative expansion elsewhere, see Farley, "The Changing Distribution of Negroes," 339; New York State Commission Against Discrimination, "Non-Whites in New York's Four Suburban Counties: An Analysis of Trends" (New York, June 1959), 8.

13. Seven areas — Evanston, Maywood, Robbins-Markham, Aurora, Chicago Heights, Waukegan–North Chicago, and Joliet — added 40,764 African Americans. U.S. Census of Population: 1940, vol. II, *Characteristics of the Population,* part 2 (Washington, D.C., 1943), 565, 599, 601, 609, 613–16; U.S. Census of Population: 1960, vol. I, *General Population Characteristics,* part 15 (Washington, D.C., 1961), 105–14, 118, 125–26, 138.

14. "Ten Families Face Eviction and No Place Else to Go," *Evanston Review,* October 14, 1965, 7; "Get Tough Policy on Housing Urged at Interracial Meeting," *Evanston Review,* September 17, 1959; U.S. Census of Housing: 1960, vol. I, *States and Small Areas,* part 3 (Washington, D.C., 1963), 34–35.

15. Area Description, D-21 (Maywood, Illinois), *Security Map of Metropolitan Chicago,* February 1940, box 84, Home Owners Loan Corporation [HOLC] Papers, Record Group 195 (National Archives, Washington, D.C.).

16. Area Description, C-129 (Maywood, Illinois), ibid.

17. U.S. Census of Population and Housing: 1960, vol. I, *Census Tracts,* part 26 (Washington, D.C., 1963).

18. Leslie Wilson, "Robbins, Illinois: The History and Problems of an All-Black Suburb," unpublished paper, 1990, author's possession.

19. U.S. Census of Housing: 1960, vol. I, part 3, 180–82.

20. William Braden, "Negro Suburbia: A Report on the Progress and the Problems," *Chicago Sun-Times,* November 15, 1962, 31; Earl Ray Hutchison Jr., "Black Suburbanization: A History of Social Change in a Working Class Suburb" (Ph.D. diss., University of Chicago, 1984), 118; "Attracting Business a Key Goal for Lollis," *Harvey Star,* May 29, 1988.

21. U.S. Census of Population: 1960, vol. I, part 15, 110; U.S. Census of Population: 1950, vol. II, *Characteristics of Population,* part 13 (Washington, D.C., 1952), 119. New construction accounted for almost half of black suburban growth in metropolitan Chicago during the 1950s. By 1960, 40 percent of African Americans in Chicago's suburbs were living in homes built after 1939 (versus 12 percent in the city). U.S. Census of Housing: 1960, vol. I, part 3, 181.

22. U.S. Census of Housing: 1940, vol. II, *General Characteristics,* part 2 (Washington, D.C., 1943), 764, 793–95; U.S. Census of Housing: 1960, vol. I, part 15 (Washington, D.C., 1963), 180–83.

23. The eight metropolitan areas with the most black suburbanites were New York, Detroit, Philadelphia, Chicago, St. Louis, Newark, Pittsburgh, and Buffalo. U.S. Census of Housing: 1940, vol. II, part 1, 8; part 2, 764; part 3; 576, 869; part 4, 146, 270, 860; U.S. Census of Housing: 1960, vol. I, part 1, 228–33.

24. HHFA, "Housing of the Non-White Population," 2.

25. Ibid., 28; Belden Morgan, "Housing Market Report on the Minority Sector of the Los Angeles Standard Metropolitan Area" (July 1954), box 748, HHFA Papers, Record Group 207 (National Archives, Washington, D.C.), 9.

26. E. Franklin Frazier, *Black Bourgeoisie* (Glencoe, Ill., 1956), 44–59; Bart Landry, *The New Black Middle Class* (Berkeley, 1987), 21–56.

27. Booker T. McGraw, "Wartime Employment, Migration, and Housing of Negroes in the United States," *Midwest Journal* 1 (summer 1949): table 2a. U.S. Census of Population: 1960, vol. I, *U.S. Summary* (Washington, D.C., 1961), 544–47.

28. Forty-one percent of married black women were in the paid labor force in 1960 as compared to 30 percent of white married women. U.S. Census of Population: 1960, vol. I, *U.S. Summary,* 501–2; HHFA, "Housing of the Non-White Population," 11.

29. "Negro Housing: New Vistas Opened for South by Private Industry," *Christian Science Monitor,* October 18, 1948, sec. II, 9; Frazier, *Black Bourgeoisie,* 49.

30. Braden, "Negro Suburbia," 31.

31. On legislative and executive action, see Donald R. McCoy and Richard T. Ruetten, *Quest and Response: Minority Rights and the Truman Administration* (Law-

rence, Ks., 1973), 171–204, 221–50. On local action, see Nina Mjagkij, "Behind the Scenes: The Cincinnati Urban League, 1948–1963," in *Race and the City: Work, Community, and Protest in Cincinnati, 1820–1970,* ed. Henry Louis Taylor Jr. (Urbana, Ill., 1993), 280–94; and Thomas J. Sugrue, *The Origins of the Urban Crisis: Race and Inequality in Postwar Detroit* (Princeton, 1996), 181–207. On the West, see Quintard Taylor, *In Search of the Racial Frontier: African Americans in the American West, 1528–1990* (W. W. Norton, 1998), 278–94.

32. Robert LaFrankie, "The Englewood, New Jersey School Conflict: A Case Study of Decision Making and Racial Segregation, 1930–1963" (Ph.D. diss., Columbia University, 1967); "End Segregation in [Asbury Park] N.J. School," *Chicago Defender,* April 20, 1946, 2; *Taylor v. Board of Education of New Rochelle,* 191 F. Supp. 181 (S.D.N.Y. 1961); *Branche v. Board of Education of the Town of Hempstead, School District No. 1,* 204 F. Supp. 150 (1962); Bruce D. Haynes, *Red Lines, Black Spaces: The Politics of Race and Space in a Black Middle-Class Suburb* (New Haven, 2001), 103–4; Mary E. Crawford, "Bainbridge School Investigation," March 15, 1946, Chagrin Falls Park School File, Cleveland NAACP Papers (Western Reserve Historical Society, Cleveland, Ohio); Shirley Ann Wilson Moore, *To Place Our Deeds: The African American Community in Richmond, California, 1910–1963* (Berkeley, 2000), 102–15.

33. Sherman Beverly Jr., "A Tribute to Edwin B. Jourdain and His Supporters," February 24, 1974 (Evanston Public Library, Evanston, Ill.).

34. Bert Mann, "Pasadena NAACP Weighs New Tactics for Equality," *Los Angeles Times,* September 3, 1978, sec. IX, 1.

35. Kathy Braldhill, "Plunge into Racist City Past," *Pasadena Star-News,* January 12, 1992, A1; also, "CORE, NAACP Picket City Hall," *Crown City Press,* October 4, 1956, 1.

36. Harold M. Rose, "The All-Negro Town: Its Evolution and Function," *Geographical Review* (July 1965): 363; "Ohioans in the News," *Cleveland Call and Post,* September 18, 1948. Residents in Royal Oak Township, Michigan, and Chagrin Falls Park, Ohio, debated but rejected municipal incorporation in the late 1940s. See *Michigan Chronicle,* October 20, 1945.

37. Moore, *To Place Our Deeds,* 100.

38. "Writ Blocks Inkster Split," *Detroit News,* November 1, 1943; "Detroit Suburb's Whites Want All Negroes Barred," *PM Weekly,* n.d., "Housing," vol. I, Clippings Scrapbook (Schomburg Center for Research in Black Culture, New York, N.Y.). In 1960 black residents of Phoenix, Illinois, tried and failed to block the de-annexation of the south side of town, which included the business district and half of the town's white inhabitants. "Phoenix 75th Anniversary: Onward and

Upward" (Phoenix, Ill., 1975). On politics in other suburbs, see Moore, *To Place Our Deeds,* 104–14; and "Three Seek Posts in Suburban Race Tuesday," *Chicago Defender,* April 12, 1947, 1; also see "Twinsburg Voters League in Home Ownership Program," *Cleveland Call and Post,* July 3, 1949, 10; and Ann Morris and Henrietta Ambrose, *North Webster: A Photographic History of a Black Community* (Bloomington, Ind., 1993), 37–46.

39. Wendy Plotkin, "Deeds of Mistrust: Race, Housing, and Restrictive Covenants in Chicago, 1900–1953" (Ph.D. diss., University of Illinois at Chicago, 1999), 2.

40. On the struggle for civil rights in housing, see Stephen Grant Meyer, *As Long as They Don't Move Next Door: Segregation and Racial Conflict in American Neighborhoods* (Lanham, Md., 2000), 79–149.

41. Robert Self, "'To Plan Our Liberation': Black Power and the Politics of Place in Oakland, California, 1965–1977," *Journal of Urban History* 26 (September 2000): 759–92.

42. Steven Gregory, *Black Corona: Race and the Politics of Place in an Urban Community* (Princeton, 1998), 10–19.

43. "Constitution of the National Committee Against Discrimination in Housing," 1953, box 751, HHFA Papers.

44. For a survey, see Meyer, *As Long as They Don't Move Next Door,* 133–49. See also "Interracial Housing: Current News Reports Indicate Variety of Activities in the Field," *Journal of Housing* 12 (June 1955): 200–1.

45. Gloster Current, "NAACP Calls for Restrictive Covenant Campaign," *Michigan Chronicle,* August 18, 1945, 3; "Restrictive Covenant Study Pays Dividends," ibid., January 5, 1946, 13.

46. "Restrictive Covenants Balk Efforts to Get Better Housing," *Michigan Chronicle,* August 25, 1945, 3.

47. Clement E. Vose, *Caucasians Only: The Supreme Court, the NAACP, and the Restrictive Covenant Cases* (Berkeley, 1959), 57–71.

48. "Constitution of the National Committee Against Discrimination in Housing"; Meyer, *As Long as They Don't Move Next Door,* 139.

49. U.S. Commission on Civil Rights, *Housing, 1961,* 119–22.

50. Ibid., 24–25, 62–63; Joseph Ray, "Racial Policy to Govern Administration of HHFA Programs," August 13, 1954, box 961, HHFA Papers.

51. Dorothy Sutherland Jayne, "First Families: A Study of Twenty Pioneer Negro Families Who Moved into White Neighborhoods in Metropolitan Philadelphia," summary report, Philadelphia Commission on Human Relations (Philadelphia, 1960), 1.

52. Jayne, "First Families" (thesis); see also Eunice Grier and George Grier, *In Search of Housing: A Study of Experiences of Negro Professional and Technical Personnel in New York State* (New York, 1958); Eunice Grier and George Grier, *Buyers of Interracial Housing* (Philadelphia, 1957); and Henry G. Stetler, *Racial Integration in Private Residential Neighborhoods in Connecticut* (Hartford, 1957).

53. Jayne, "First Families" (thesis), 23, 29.

54. Philadelphia Commission on Human Relations, "Some Factors Affecting Housing Desegregation" (Philadelphia, December 1962), 3.

55. Quoted in Jayne, "First Families" (thesis), 23.

56. Quoted in Eunice Grier and George Grier, *Negroes in Five New York Cities: A Study of Problems, Achievements, and Trends* (New York, 1958), 78.

57. Reginald Johnson, "Discrimination in Private Housing and Its Resulting Hardship on Minority Group Families," Statement before Senate Committee on Public Health, Albany, New York, January 27, 1960, box 246, Atlanta Urban League [AUL] Papers (Robert Woodruff Library, Special Collections, Atlanta University, Atlanta, Ga.).

58. Grier and Grier, *In Search of Housing,* 45.

59. George Snowden, Address to the Mortgage Bankers of America, September 29, 1954, box 745, HHFA Papers.

60. Quoted in Jayne, "First Families" (summary), 33.

61. Quoted in Moore, *To Place Our Deeds,* 117–18.

62. "Racists Again Set Fire to Negro's Long Island Home," *New York Post,* November 23, 1953; "Negro Selling Long Island House at a Loss — 'Neighbors Don't Want Me,'" ibid., January 22, 1954; "Police Guard Home of Long Island Negro after Threat to Burn It," ibid., May 8, 1956. See Clipping Scrapbook, "Housing: New York State" (Schomburg Center for Research in African Cultures, New York, N.Y.).

63. Quoted in James Haskins with Kathleen Benson, *Nat King Cole* (New York, 1984), 81.

64. Harold Goldblatt, "Open Occupancy Housing in Westchester County," Report to the Housing Committee of the Urban League of Westchester County (November 1954), 35–40, box 96, HHFA Papers; Jayne, "First Families" (thesis), 55.

65. Vose, *Caucasians Only,* 71–73. For examples, see Current, "NAACP Calls for Restrictive Covenant Campaign"; "Mass Meeting on Covenants," *Michigan Chronicle,* February 2, 1946, 3; "Covenants Bar Negroes from ¾'s of Cleveland," *Cleveland Call and Post,* November 22, 1947, 1A; "Banking Policies Keep Negroes in Ghettoes," *Cleveland Call and Post,* November 29, 1947, 1–2A.

66. "Woodmere Homebuilder Arrested on Building Code Violations," *Cleveland Call and Post,* August 16, 1946, 9A; "Vandals Bomb Negro Homes," ibid., May 30, 1953, 1; "NAACP Seeks to Rebuild Birmingham Home Blasted by Prejudiced Whites," ibid., October 4, 1947, 14B; "Two Crosses Burned," *Crown City Press,* March 21, 1957, 1; "Fear and Loneliness Haunt Negro Family in Chicago's Race War," *Ebony* 9 (June 1954): 18–24.

67. See responses to attacks on the Percy Julian family in Oak Park, Illinois. "Hunt on for Julian Bombers," *Chicago Defender,* June 16, 1951, 1; George S. Harris, *Hearings before the U.S. Commission on Civil Rights: Hearings Held in Chicago, May 5–6, 1959* (Washington, D.C., 1959), 746–47. For incidents involving black celebrities, see "Good Neighbors: California Judge Knocks out Race Restrictive Covenant as Unconstitutional," *Architectural Forum* 84 (January 1946), 20; "Colored Stars to Keep Homes in Hollywood," *Michigan Chronicle,* December 15, 1945, 1; "U.S. Grabs King Cole's Home," *Chicago Defender,* March 17, 1951, 1; Jackie Robinson, *Hearings before the Commission on Civil Rights: Housing, Hearings Held in New York, New York, February 2–3, 1959* (Washington, D.C., 1959), 269; Haskins with Benson, *Nat King Cole,* 77–83; Willie Mays with Lou Sahadi, *Say Hey: The Autobiography of Willie Mays* (New York, 1988), 147; Joseph Moore, *Pride against Prejudice: The Biography of Larry Doby* (Westport, Conn., 1988), 87–88; and Lena Horne and Richard Schickel, *Lena* (New York, 1986), 156–57.

68. George S. Harris, letter to Dwight D. Eisenhower, January 22, 1954, box 745, HHFA Papers.

69. National Association of Real Estate Brokers, press release, August 11, 1954, box 745, HHFA Papers.

70. William J. Roberts, Address on "Listings," Proceedings of the Fourth Annual NAREB Mid-Winter Conference, February 12–13, 1951, box 8, Long-Rucker-Aiken Papers (Atlanta History Center, Atlanta, Ga.); Henry W. Morison, "Selling on Today's Market," ibid.; William Calloway, interview by author, Atlanta, Georgia, June 10, 1997.

71. "New Frontiers," *Amsterdam News,* January 6, 1962, 30.

72. For example, "Alex Dean Opens Arlington to Colored Buyers!" *Michigan Chronicle,* August 4, 1945, 2. See also "Freedom Homes," ibid.; and "Pioneer Real Estate Pays First Dividends," 1946 highlights, *Cleveland Call and Post,* January 4, 1947.

73. Theodore Bartlett, taped interview, 1984, Pasadena Black History Project (Pasadena Historical Society, Pasadena, Calif.).

74. "William H. Gill," obituary, *Evanston Review,* July 27, 1961, 96.

75. Abrams, *Forbidden Neighbors,* 237.

76. See Jackson, *Crabgrass Frontier,* 190–230; also see George Lipsitz, "The Possessive Investment in Whiteness: Racialized Social Democracy and the 'White' Problem in American Studies," *American Quarterly* 47 (September 1995): 218–36.

77. For a more balanced analysis of federal housing policy, see Arnold Hirsch, "Containment on the Home Front: Race and Federal Housing Policy from the New Deal to the Cold War," *Journal of Urban History* 26 (January 2000): 158–90.

78. Sugrue, *Origins of the Urban Crisis,* 10.

79. B. T. McGraw and Frank Horne, "The House I Live In," *Opportunity: The Journal of Negro Life* 24 (summer 1946): 122–27; "Participation by Negroes in the War Housing Program by Racial Occupancy Patterns," March 31, 1954, box 748, HHFA Papers; "Disposition of Lanham Act Housing," September 30, 1950, ibid.

80. McGraw, "Wartime Employment, Migration, and Housing of Negroes"; Felt, "Opportunities of Private Capital," 129. On white resistance, see Dominic Capeci, *Race Relations in Wartime Detroit: The Sojourner Truth Housing Controversy of 1942* (Philadelphia, 1982); and Arnold Hirsch, *Making the Second Ghetto: Race and Housing in Chicago, 1940–1960* (New York, 1983).

81. Kristin Szylvian Bailey, "Defense Housing in Greater Pittsburgh, 1945–1955," *Pittsburgh History* 73 (1990): 16–28; Henry L. Taylor Jr., *From Ghetto to Suburb: City Building and the Formation of a Black Town,* unpublished manuscript, author's possession, 241–45; Gretchen Lemke-Santangelo, *Abiding Courage: African American Migrant Women and the East Bay Community* (Chapel Hill, N.C., 1996), 86–88; Maximilian Martin, "Housing Problems of the Philadelphia Non-White Population," typescript, 1953, 22, box 96, HHFA Papers.

82. The Detroit Housing Commission built 2,760 permanent and temporary housing units for blacks in the suburbs. Betty Smith Jenkins, "The Racial Policies of the Detroit Housing Commission and Their Administration" (M.A. thesis, Wayne State University, 1950), 20–25; Detroit NAACP, *Forward with Action: Annual Report, 1943* (Detroit, 1943).

83. Simeon Booker Jr., "Cleveland's Seville Homes Becomes Northern Ohio's Model GI Village," *Cleveland Call and Post,* January 25, 1947, 1B.

84. Frank Horne, "Disposition Policy for Lanham Act Housing, Richmond, California and Bay Area," May 26, 1954, box 748, HHFA Papers.

85. Lemke-Santangelo, *Abiding Courage,* 89.

86. Quoted in ibid., 89.

87. Booker, "Cleveland's Seville Homes."

88. Horne, "Disposition Policy for Lanham Act Housing"; Frank Horne to Raymond Foley, "Bi-Weekly Report," May 23, 1952, box 8, HHFA Papers.

89. Lemke-Santangelo, *Abiding Courage,* 90–93; Moore, *To Place Our Deeds,* 88–89; U.S. Commission on Civil Rights, *Hearings before the U.S. Commission on*

Civil Rights: Hearings Held in San Francisco, California, January 27–28, 1960 (Washington, D.C., 1960), 622–31.

90. "New Homes for You," *Cleveland Call and Post,* September 2, 1950, 4B.

91. "Operation Bootstrap," *Journal of Housing* 12 (June 1955): 198–99; "Inkster Solving Problems—A Decent Town to Live In," *Detroit Times,* October 30, 1957, Clippings File, "Inkster" (Burton Historical Library, Detroit, Mich.); "Planning a New Home?" *Cleveland Call and Post,* April 1, 1950, 10B; "Muskegon, Michigan Brief," box 745, HHFA Papers; Charles Tilly, Wagner Jackson, and Barry Kay, *Race and Residence in Wilmington, Delaware* (New York, 1965), 54–55.

92. FHA and VA programs worked by limiting risk for private builders and lenders. Thus, decisions regarding who would benefit from federal programs remained largely in private hands. Jackson, *Crabgrass Frontier,* 203–18; U.S. Commission on Civil Rights, *Housing: 1961,* 59.

93. Albert Cole to Sid Mack, December 12, 1954, box 96, HHFA Papers.

94. Robert Weaver and Hortense Gabel, "To Friends of the HHFA Racial Relations Service," press release, September 23, 1953, box 257, AUL Papers; also Robert Weaver, *The Negro Ghetto* (New York, 1948), 148–54.

95. Federal Housing Administration, *Fourteenth Annual Report of the Federal Housing Administration* (Washington, D.C., 1948), 5; Charles Abrams, letter to the editor, *New York Times,* August 23, 1955, 22.

96. Raymond Foley, "Memo Re: Racial Relations Advisors," August 15, 1947, Bi-Weekly Reports, box 7, HHFA Papers. For activities of the service, see Frank Horne, "Bi-Weekly Reports," 1947–1952, ibid.

97. Roland Sawyer, "FHA Program Aids Minorities," *Insured Mortgage Portfolio* 16 (4th quarter, 1951): 6–9; Margaret Kane, "A Wider Field for Mortgage Lending," ibid. 14 (4th quarter, 1949); Albert L. Thompson, "Negro Mortgagees and Builders in the South," ibid. 18 (3rd quarter, 1953): 9–11.

98. "Interracial Projects, FHA Insured, 1950–1953," December 10, 1953, box 748, HHFA Papers.

99. Warren Cochrane, Butler Street YMCA, Atlanta, Georgia, to Raymond Foley, June 13, 1947, box 6, HHFA Papers.

100. Horne to Foley, "Bi-Weekly Reports," May 11–August 31, 1951.

101. Sawyer, "FHA Program Aids Minorities."

102. Morgan, "Housing Market Report"; R. A. Winkler et al., "Some Aspects of the Negro Housing Market in the Chicago Area," in *Open Occupancy vs. Forced Housing under the Fourteenth Amendment,* ed. Alfred Avins (New York, 1963), 269–70; Braden, "Negro Suburbia," 30–32; Martin, "Housing Problems of the Philadelphia Non-White Population," 22–23; Sawyer, "FHA Program Aids Minorities."

103. U.S. Commission on Civil Rights, *Housing: 1961,* 61–63, 68–69. In 1950, 96.2 percent of "nonwhites" in the United States were African American. Margaret Kane, "The Non-White Housing Market," *Insured Mortgage Portfolio* 16 (4th quarter, 1951): 23.

104. Total represents 2 percent of 5 million FHA-insured loans between 1946 and 1959 (100,000), plus 2.9 percent of 5.5 million VA-guaranteed loans between 1944 and 1960 (159,000), plus approximately 5 percent of 900,000 units in multifamily cooperative and rental projects (45,000). U.S. Commission on Civil Rights, *Housing: 1961,* 61, 68. Forty percent of 674,000 new housing units occupied by African Americans during the 1950s. U.S. Census of Housing: 1960, vol. IV, *Components of Inventory Change,* part 1A (Washington, D.C., 1962), 26–27.

Chapter Six

1. "Average Home Sold to Negro," *Christian Science Monitor,* October 18, 1948, sec. 2, 9.

2. On African American efforts to use domestic space symbolically to challenge white supremacy in the nineteenth and early twentieth century, see Barbara Burlinson Mooney, "The Comfortable Tasty Framed Cottage: An African American Architectural Iconography," *Journal of the Society of Architectural Historians* 61 (March 2002): 48–67.

3. Earl Lewis, "Connecting Memory, Self and the Power of Place in African American Urban History," *Journal of Urban History* 21 (March 1995): 358.

4. Housing and Home Finance Agency, "The Housing of Negro Veterans: Their Housing Plans and Living Arrangements in 32 Areas" (Washington, D.C., June 1948), 9–10.

5. Frederick Gutheim, "Failure to Build for Negroes Will Create New Blight Areas," *New York Herald Tribune,* July 4, 1948, sec. VI, 1.

6. Robert Kleiner, Seymour Parker, and Haywood Taylor, "Social Status and Aspirations in Philadelphia's Negro Population," prepared for the Philadelphia Commission on Human Relations (June 1962), 9.

7. Philadelphia Commission on Human Relations, "Some Factors Affecting Housing Desegregation: A Summary and Analysis of Five Papers concerning Non-white Attitudes and Behavior" (Philadelphia, December 1962), 1.

8. See chapter 5, note 23.

9. Clydie Smith, interview by author, July 1986.

10. City of Pasadena, Department of Planning and Permitting, letter to owner

of 523 Pepper Street, April 4, 1952, Building Permit Files (Hall Building, Pasadena, Calif.). Also, letters to owners of 525 and 545 Hammond Avenue, ibid.

11. David Doles, interview by Elizabeth Langley, October 25, 1979, "Black History in Mount Vernon, New York" (Local History Room, Mount Vernon Public Library). On gardening in other suburbs, see Harold Rose, "The All Black Town: Suburban Prototype or Rural Slum?" *Urban Affairs Annual Reviews* 6 (1972): 414; David J. Dent, *In Search of Black America: Discovering the African American Dream* (New York, 2000), 69; and Felix James, *The American Addition: History of a Black Community* (Washington, D.C., 1979), 58–60. Even newly wealthy entertainers like Pearl Bailey, Eartha Kitt, and Josephine Baker indulged working-class roots by keeping chickens on estate properties. Pearl Bailey, *The Raw Pearl* (New York, 1968), 141–44; Eartha Kitt, *Alone with Me: A New Autobiography* (Chicago, 1976), 234; "Josephine Baker, Modern Cinderella," *Baltimore Afro-American Magazine*, October 25, 1947, 1.

12. Lorraine Hansberry, *A Raisin in the Sun* (New York, 1959), 41, 78.

13. U.S. Census of Housing: 1940, vol. I, *Block Statistics, Evanston, Illinois* (Washington, D.C., 1942), 5, 8–9; U.S. Census of Housing: 1950, vol. V, *Block Statistics,* part 61, *Evanston, Illinois* (Washington, D.C., 1952), 3–11; ibid., part 17, *Berkeley, California,* 3–17; ibid., part 56, *East Orange, New Jersey,* 3–8; ibid., part 124, *New Rochelle, New York,* 3–10; part 138, *Pasadena, California,* 3–17.

14. "Get Tough Policy on Housing Urged at Interracial Meeting," *Evanston Review,* September 17, 1959.

15. See "Lots for Sale," *Chicago Defender,* May 11, 1946, 11; "Special Sale, Choice Homesites, Morgan Park," ibid., October 13, 1945, 11; "$10 a Month Pays for a Large Lot," ibid., May 25, 1946, 8; and "It's Cheaper to Own than to Pay Rent," ibid., October 13, 1945, 2. For New York, see "Gordon Heights, L.I.," *Amsterdam News,* December 31, 1949; "Help Me, I Want to Own My Own Home," ibid.; and "Bungalow, Farm or Homesite," ibid., July 12, 1947. For Detroit, see "Little Farms, 90' x 126'," *Michigan Chronicle,* October 13, 1945, 4.

16. "Farm Homesites," *Amsterdam News,* July 12, 1947.

17. "You Too Can Beat the High Cost of Living," *Chicago Defender,* January 31, 1948, 4.

18. Smith, interview; William Hagler, interview by author, August 11, 1986; Clara Adams, interview by author, July 29, 1986.

19. E. P. Stephenson, U.S. Commission on Civil Rights, *Hearings before the U.S. Commission on Civil Rights: Hearings Held in San Francisco, January 27–28, 1960* (Washington, D.C., 1960), 622; Harold O. Lindsey, "From Fields to Fords, Feds to Franchise: African American Empowerment in Inkster, Michigan" (Ph.D. diss., University of Michigan, 1993); James, *The American Addition,* 58–60.

20. "Port-o-Cottage," *Chicago Defender,* August 14, 1948, 9; "Phoenix, Ill. Properties . . . Owner Completed or Finished Homes on Your Paid Up Lot," ibid., April 1, 1950, 19; "Quonset Makes an Attractive Home," *Cleveland Call and Post,* December 21, 1946, 13B; Floris Barnett Cash, "Long Island by Design, Segregation's Brand of Housing," *New York Newsday,* December 29, 1997, A25.

21. Eunice Grier and George Grier, *In Search of Housing: A Study of Experiences of Negro Professional and Technical Personnel in New York State* (New York, 1958), 18.

22. Dorothy Sutherland Jayne, "First Families: A Study of Twenty Pioneer Negro Families Who Moved into White Neighborhoods in Metropolitan Philadelphia," summary report, Philadelphia Commission on Human Relations (Philadelphia, 1960), 1–4; idem, "First Families: A Study of Twenty Pioneer Negro Families Who Moved into White Neighborhoods in Metropolitan Philadelphia" (M.A. thesis, Bryn Mawr College, 1960), 22.

23. "St. Alban's: New York Community Is Home for More Celebrities than Any Other U.S. Residential Area," *Ebony* 6 (September 1951): 34.

24. "Period Styles for Elegance: Detroit's Dr. Saulsbury Chooses 18th Century Motif to Furnish Home in Restful Tone," *Ebony* 6 (December 1950): 64; "Louis Jordan Birthday Party," ibid. (November 1950): 91–92; "Rochester: Radio Star Finds Long Greens Buy Lots of Comfort and Ease," ibid. (November 1945): 13–20; "Push Button Home," ibid. (November 1954): 42–46; "The White House," ibid. (April 1946): 3–7.

25. "St. Alban's," 34–39.

26. Ibid.

27. On equality through consumption, see Lizabeth Cohen, "Citizens and Consumers in the Century of Mass Consumption," in *Perspectives on Modern America: Making Sense of the Twentieth Century,* ed. Harvard Sitkoff (New York, 2001), 152–58. On middle-class suburban dreams, see Kenneth T. Jackson, *Crabgrass Frontier: The Suburbanization of the United States* (New York, 1985), 243–45; Barbara Kelly, *Expanding the American Dream: Building and Rebuilding Levittown* (Albany, 1993), 59–88; and Elaine Tyler May, *Homeward Bound: American Families in the Cold War Era* (New York, 1988), 3–6, 16–20.

28. "Hempstead Park Detached," *Amsterdam News,* July 12, 1947.

29. "Pacoima's Quality Circle," *Pasadena Crown City Press,* February 7, 1957, 5.

30. Adams, interview.

31. Jayne, "First Families" (summary), 1, 4.

32. "Interracial Unit Ready," *New York Times,* August 22, 1950; advertisement, *New York Daily News,* October 14, 1951; Eardlie John, "Bring Up Your Children in This Suburban Paradise," *Amsterdam News,* December 31, 1949, 25.

33. "It's Cheaper to Own than to Pay Rent," 2.

34. Quoted in Grier and Grier, *In Search of Housing,* 17.

35. Quoted in Chelsea Carter, "Unlikely Musical Mecca: Jazz Fans Take Journey through Neighborhoods Where the Greats Lived," *Cedar Rapids Gazette,* January 10, 1999, 2G.

36. On black middle-class values related to children, see St. Clair Drake and Horace Cayton, *Black Metropolis: A Study of Negro Life in a Northern City* (New York, 1945), 663–68.

37. U.S. Commission on Civil Rights, *Hearings before the U.S. Commission on Civil Rights: Hearings Held in New York, February 2–3, 1959* (Washington, D.C., 1959), 272.

38. "Poitier Says Bias Exists on Coast," *New York Times,* August 19, 1960, 14.

39. Winston Richie, "Pro-Integrative Policy and Incentives," transcript, National Federation for Neighborhood Diversity Conference, Cleveland, Ohio, June 15, 1990.

40. Mary Patillo-McCoy, *Black Picket Fences: Privilege and Peril among the Black Middle Class* (Chicago, 1999), 19.

41. U.S. Commission on Civil Rights, *Hearings before the U.S. Commission on Civil Rights: Hearings Held in Los Angeles, January 25–26, 1960* (Washington, D.C., 1960), 260–61. See also John Kain, "Housing Market Discrimination, Home-ownership and Savings Behavior," *American Economic Review* 62 (June 1972): 263–77.

42. Eunice Grier and George Grier, *Negroes in Five New York Cities: A Study of Problems, Achievements, and Trends* (New York, 1958), 78; U.S. Commission on Civil Rights, *Hearings before the U.S. Commission on Civil Rights: Hearings Held in Detroit, Michigan, December 14–15, 1960* (Washington, D.C., 1961), 259; Jayne, "First Families" (summary), 3; Council for Civic Unity of San Francisco, *San Francisco's Housing Market—Open or Closed?* (San Francisco, 1960), 9.

43. Grier and Grier, *In Search of Housing,* 41–42; Council for Civic Unity, *San Francisco's Housing Market,* 9. Gwendolyn Brooks also pointed to the internalization of harm caused by housing discrimination in the poem "Beverly Hills, Chicago." Gwendolyn Brooks, *Selected Poems* (New York, 1963).

44. Quoted in Jayne, "First Families" (thesis), 68–69.

45. Quoted in ibid.

46. Quoted in ibid., 37, 40–41, 57.

47. Quoted in ibid., 32, 70. Also see Marvin Bressler, "The Myers' Case: An Instance of Successful Racial Invasion," *Social Problems* 8 (fall 1960): 126–42.

48. Jayne, "First Families" (thesis), 45, 70.

49. Ibid., 48, 73.

50. Drake and Cayton, *Black Metropolis,* 531.

51. Jayne, "First Families" (thesis), 52; Harold Goldblatt, "Open Occupancy Housing in Westchester County," Urban League of Westchester County, New York (November 1954), 36, box 96, HHFA Papers.

52. Philadelphia Commission on Human Relations, "Some Factors Affecting Housing Desegregation," 1–6.

53. Ossie Davis and Ruby Dee, *With Ossie and Ruby: In This Life Together* (New York, 1998), 302–3.

54. Philadelphia Commission on Human Relations, "Some Factors Affecting Housing Desegregation," 5.

55. See, for example, Molly McCarthy, "North Amityville: Where Freed Slaves Could Make a Home," *New York Newsday,* February 22, 1998, sec. H, 7–8; U.S. Commission on Civil Rights, *Hearings Held in Los Angeles,* 244, 279–80.

56. Philadelphia Commission on Human Relations, "Some Factors Affecting Housing Desegregation," 5.

57. May, *Homeward Bound,* 3. See also Margaret Marsh, *Suburban Lives* (New Brunswick, 1990); and Mary Corbin Sies, *The American Suburban Ideal: A Cultural Strategy for Modern American Living, 1877–1917* (Philadelphia, forthcoming).

58. Bart Landry, *The New Black Middle Class* (Berkeley, 1987), 59.

59. "St. Alban's," 34–39; "Period Styles for Elegance," 64; "Louis Jordan Birthday Party," 91–92; "Designer for Living: America's Ace Architect Paul Williams Attains Fame and Fortune Blueprinting Stately Mansions," *Ebony* 1 (February 1946): 24–28.

60. "St. Alban's," 34–39.

61. Willard B. Gatewood, *Aristocrats of Color: The Black Elite, 1880–1920* (Bloomington, Ind., 1990), x, 182–90.

62. Ibid.

63. Drake and Cayton, *Black Metropolis,* in Patillo-McCoy, *Black Picket Fences,* 26; Gatewood, *Aristocrats of Color,* 194–95. See also Steven Gregory, *Black Corona: Race and the Politics of Place in an Urban Community* (Princeton, 1998), 17–18; and Arthur S. Evans Jr., "The New American Black Middle Classes: Their Social Structure and Status Ambivalence," *International Journal of Politics, Culture, and Society* 7 (winter 1993): 209–28.

64. Patillo-McCoy, *Black Picket Fences,* 23, 27.

65. Quoted in Grier and Grier, *In Search of Housing,* 17.

66. U.S. Commission on Civil Rights, *Hearings Held in San Francisco,* 575.

67. Quoted in Goldblatt, "Open Occupancy Housing in Westchester County," 23.

68. Grier and Grier, *In Search of Housing,* 17; Clarence Q. Pair, *The American Black Ghetto* (New York, 1969), 13; Joseph Moore, *Pride against Prejudice: The Biography of Larry Doby* (New York, 1988), 88.

69. Leslie Gourse, *Unforgettable: The Life and Mystique of Nat "King" Cole* (New York, 1991), 104.

70. Quoted in Jayne, "First Families" (thesis), 35, 50.

71. Quoted in ibid., 46.

72. Preston H. Smith II, "The Quest for Racial Democracy: Black Civic Ideology and Housing Interests in Postwar Chicago," *Journal of Urban History* 26 (January 2000): 133; Carl Fuqua, executive secretary, Chicago NAACP, U.S. Commission on Civil Rights, *Hearings before the U.S. Commission on Civil Rights: Hearings Held in Chicago, May 5–6, 1959* (Washington, D.C., 1959), 828.

73. Fred E. Case and James H. Kirk, *Housing Status of Minority Families, Los Angeles, 1956,* Los Angeles Urban League (Los Angeles, 1958), 78.

74. Grier and Grier, *In Search of Housing,* 17.

75. U.S. Commission on Civil Rights, *Hearings Held in San Francisco,* 575.

Chapter Seven

1. Sam Fulwood III, *Waking from the Dream: My Life in the Black Middle Class* (New York, 1996), 7–8.

2. Donald T. Wyatt, "Better Homes for Negro Families in the South," *Social Forces* 28 (March 1950): 297–303; Elizabeth L. Virrick, "New Housing for Negroes in Dade County, Florida," in *Studies in Housing and Minority Groups,* ed. Nathan Glazer and Davis McEntire (Berkeley, 1960), 135–43; Forrest LaViolette et al., "The Negro in New Orleans," in ibid., 110–35; "What Builders Are Doing about Minority Housing," *House and Home* 6 (April 1955): 146–47; "Private Builders Provide Better Negro Housing in Oklahoma City," *American Builder* (February 1947): 142–43.

3. Fulwood, *Waking from the Dream,* 8.

4. On black community growth in the postwar South, see Ronald Bayor, *Race and the Shaping of Twentieth-Century Atlanta* (Chapel Hill, N.C., 1996), 53–92; Christopher Silver and John Moeser, *The Separate City: Black Communities in the Urban South, 1940–1968* (Lexington, Ky., 1995), 125–62; and William H. Wilson, *Hamilton Park: A Planned Black Community in Dallas* (Baltimore, 1998).

5. This approach to improving African American housing choices contrasted with prevailing trends in the North and West, where African Americans' assault against housing discrimination coincided with an ideology of racial integration. Perhaps more than anything else, the politics of "Negro housing" in the South reveals the importance of historical context and local-regional power relations in shaping local outcomes as well as patterns of negotiation and the contours of resistance and aspiration themselves.

6. "Compromise Housing Plan," *Atlanta Daily World*, January 29, 1950. On southern housing conditions, see Gunnar Myrdahl with Richard Sterner and Arnold Rose, *An American Dilemma: The Negro Problem and Modern Democracy* (New York, 1944), 376–78.

7. Robert A. Thompson, memorandum to Phillip Hammer, "Atlanta Urban Renewal Survey," June 25, 1957, box 243, Atlanta Urban League [AUL] Papers (Robert Woodruff Library, Special Collections, Atlanta University, Atlanta, Ga.).

8. Silver and Moeser, *The Separate City;* Raymond Mohl, "Making the Second Ghetto in Metropolitan Miami, 1940–1960," *Journal of Urban History* 21 (March 1995): 395–427; Bayor, *Race;* Wilson, *Hamilton Park*. By 1970, Thomas Hanchett points out, nineteen of the twenty most segregated cities in the United States were in the South. Thomas Hanchett, *Sorting Out the New South City: Race, Class, and Urban Development in Charlotte, 1875–1975* (Chapel Hill, N.C., 1998), 261.

9. Arnold R. Hirsch, *Making the Second Ghetto: Race and Housing in Chicago, 1940–1960* (New York, 1983).

10. Daniel M. Johnson and Rex R. Campbell, *Black Migration in America: A Social Demographic History* (Durham, N.C., 1981), 132.

11. Joseph K. Heyman, press release, March 26, 1950, box 244, AUL Papers.

12. U.S. Census of Housing: 1960, vol. IV, *Components of Inventory Change,* part 1A (Washington, D.C., 1962), 64, 86, 108, 130.

13. Citizens Advisory Committee for Urban Renewal, "The Story of Negro Housing in Atlanta," n.d. (1959–60), box 3, Atlanta Bureau of Planning [ABP] Papers (Atlanta History Center, Atlanta, Ga.).

14. U.S. Census of Population and Housing: 1960, vol. I, *Census Tracts,* part 63 (Washington, D.C., 1962), tables H-1, H-3; ibid., parts 8, 89, 90, 99, 111, 113, 140, 156; U.S. Census of Housing: 1960, *Block Statistics* (Washington, D.C., 1962). For examples, see Jack E. Dodson, "Minority Group Housing in Two Texas Cities," in *Studies in Housing and Minority Groups,* ed. Glazer and McEntire, 98–109; Virrick, "New Housing for Negroes in Dade County"; Albert L. Thompson, "Negro Mortgagees and Builders in the South," *Insured Mortgage Portfolio* 18 (3rd quarter, 1953): 9–11; "Orlando—A New Subdivision Is Created," *Journal of*

Housing 12 (October 1955): 320–21; and Tampa Urban League, "League Spurs Development of Negro Housing Expansion Areas in Tampa," September 10, 1948, box 7, Housing and Home Finance Agency [HHFA] Papers, Record Group 207 (National Archives, Washington, D.C.).

15. Paul F. Coe, "Non-white Population Increases in Metropolitan Areas," *American Statistical Association Journal* (June 1955): 296–97; Karl E. Taeuber and Alma F. Taeuber, *Negroes in Cities: Residential Segregation and Neighborhood Change* (Chicago, 1965): 124–25.

16. Fulwood, *Waking from the Dream,* 8.

17. Frank Horne, "Bi-Weekly Report," August 31, 1951, box 8, HHFA Papers; "College Hill Housing Development," prospectus, "Correspondence, 1950, Sept.–Dec., 1950," box 4, Long-Rucker-Aiken [LRA] Papers (Atlanta History Center, Atlanta, Ga.); LaViolette, "The Negro in New Orleans"; I. E. Saporta to Housing, Incorporated, n.d., box 244, AUL Papers; and Wilson, *Hamilton Park,* 62.

18. Earl Lewis, *In Their Own Interests: Race, Class, and Power in Twentieth-Century Norfolk, Virginia* (Berkeley, 1991), 66–88; Howard M. Rabinowitz, *Race Relations in the Urban South, 1865–1900* (New York, 1978), 125–225; Zane Miller, "Urban Blacks in the South: 1865–1920: The Richmond, Savannah, New Orleans, Louisville and Birmingham Experience," in *The New Urban History: Quantitative Explorations by American Historians,* ed. Leo F. Schnore (Princeton, 1975), 198.

19. William Chafe, *Civilities and Civil Rights: Greensboro, North Carolina, and the Black Struggle for Freedom* (New York, 1980), chap. 2; Bayor, *Race,* 10, 132–33; Walter Weare, "Charles Clinton Spaulding: Middle-Class Leadership in the Age of Segregation," in *Black Leaders of the Twentieth Century,* ed. August Meier and John Hope Franklin (Urbana, Ill., 1982), 167–90.

20. On earlier racial planning, see Bayor, *Race,* 53–58, 81; Michael J. O'Connor, "The Measurement and Significance of Racial Residential Barriers in Atlanta, 1890–1970" (Ph.D. diss., University of Georgia, 1977), 100–12; and Hanchett, *Sorting Out the New South City,* 115–44.

21. Bayor, *Race,* 19–29. The landmark white primary case was *Smith v. Allwright,* 321 U.S., 649 (1944).

22. Thomas Parham, "Report of the Housing Coordinator," August 26, 1960, ABP Papers. On neighborhood violence, see Robert Thompson, Hylan Lewis, and Davis McEntire, "Atlanta and Birmingham: A Comparative Study of Negro Housing," in *Studies in Housing and Minority Groups,* ed. Glazer and McEntire, 26–27, 62–64; Mohl, "Making the Second Ghetto," 395–97, 404–10; Glenn T. Eskew, *But for Birmingham: The Local and National Movements in the Civil Rights*

Struggle (Chapel Hill, N.C., 1997), 53–84; and Stephen Grant Meyer, *As Long as They Don't Move Next Door: Segregation and Racial Conflict in American Neighborhoods* (Lanham, Md., 2000), 98–114.

23. Robert C. Weaver, "Integration in Public and Private Housing," *Annals of the American Academy of Political and Social Science* (March 1956): 93.

24. For annexation statistics, see Clarence Ridling and Orin Nolting, eds., *The Municipal Year Book*, editions 1948–60 (Chicago, 1948–60). For historical context, see Kenneth T. Jackson, *Crabgrass Frontier: The Suburbanization of the United States* (New York, 1985), 144–46; and Jon Teaford, *City and Suburb: The Political Fragmentation of Metropolitan America, 1850–1970* (Baltimore, 1979), 76–104.

25. Bayor, *Race*, 85–91; Silver and Moeser, *The Separate City*, 146, 151.

26. Wilson, *Hamilton Park*, 49; Wyatt, "Better Homes for Negro Families in the South," 301; Silver and Moeser, *The Separate City*, 146.

27. On resistance to African American housing outside Atlanta, see "Fulton County and Negro Housing," *Atlanta Daily World*, February 1, 1950; also see Robert A. Thompson, interview by author, June 6, 1997, Atlanta, Georgia. On Dallas, see Wilson, *Hamilton Park*, 10–32. For concerns about "Negro expansion" and black political influence, see Bayor, *Race*, 71–72.

28. William L. Calloway, *The "Sweet Auburn Avenue" Business History, 1900–1988* (Atlanta, 1988).

29. "Urban League Outlines Its Role in Locating New Expansion Areas," *Atlanta Daily World*, April 18, 1951.

30. Booker T. McGraw, "Wartime Employment, Migration, and Housing of Negroes in the United States," *Midwest Journal* 1 (summer 1949): table 2a; Bayor, *Race*, 110.

31. Dana F. White, "The Black Sides of Atlanta: A Geography of Expansion and Containment, 1870–1970," *Atlanta Historical Journal* 26 (summer/fall 1982): 210–11.

32. Walter H. Aiken, Joint Committee on Housing, *Study and Investigation, Hearings before the Joint Committee on Housing, 80th Congress, Proceedings at Atlanta, Georgia, October 29, 1947* (Washington, D.C., 1948), 1254.

33. "Statement of the Atlanta Urban League," in ibid., 1263, 1261–66; "Locating New Housing Sites for Negroes Challenges Planning Body," *Atlanta Daily World*, April 17, 1952.

34. Today this neighborhood comprises the Martin Luther King, Jr., National Historic Site.

35. Thompson, Lewis, and McEntire, "Atlanta and Birmingham," 19–20.

36. Silver and Moeser, *The Separate City*, 23–24.

37. Thompson, Lewis, and McEntire, "Atlanta and Birmingham," 40–41; "To the Commissioners of Roads and Revenue of Fulton County Georgia," April 6, 1949," box 251, AUL Papers.

38. Calloway, *"Sweet Auburn Avenue" Business History,* 4; "Men of the Month," *Crisis* (April 1915): 65–66.

39. Quoted in Thompson, Lewis, and McEntire, "Atlanta and Birmingham," 19.

40. Timothy J. Crimmins, "Bungalow Suburbs: East and West," *Atlanta Historical Journal* 26 (summer–fall 1982): 83–94; Thompson, Lewis, and McEntire, "Atlanta and Birmingham." See purchases by H. E. Perry, September 7, 1923, *Grantee Index* (Fulton County Recorder of Deeds, Atlanta, Ga.). After Perry's collapse, other black Atlantians followed his lead. In 1927 members of the Chennault family opened a subdivision just west of Ashby Street. A decade later, several Auburn Avenue businessmen who had once worked for Perry opened the Fountain Heights subdivision in the same section. Calloway, *"Sweet Auburn Avenue" Business History,* 4.

41. "Walter H. Aiken," biographical sheet, box 7, LRA Papers; "Housing Is His Business," *Headlines and Pictures* 3 (August 1946): 5–8; "W. H. Aiken Biographies," box 7, ibid.; "Tiger Flowers," box 8, ibid.; "Aiken Biography," n.d. (1953?), box 7, ibid.

42. "Produce to Prove Equality," *Pittsburgh Courier,* clipping (1950?), box 7, ibid.; "Housing Is His Business," 8; "Ideas for Keynote Address," National Builders Association, n.d., box 16, ibid.

43. Weare, "Charles Clinton Spaulding."

44. Barbara Burlinson Mooney, "The Comfortable Tasty Framed Cottage: An African American Architectural Iconography," *Journal of the Society of Architectural Historians* 61 (March 2002): 48–67.

45. Calloway, *"Sweet Auburn Avenue" Business History,* 4. Mildred Warner et al., *Community Building: The History of Atlanta University Neighborhoods* (Atlanta, 1978), 9; Alvin White, "Fairview Terrace," January 1944, box 7, LRA Papers; Hylan Lewis and Robert Thompson with Carl Coleman, "Housing for Negroes in Atlanta and Birmingham: Report Prepared for the Commission on Race and Housing," draft, 1956, in the possession of Robert A. Thompson; B. Q. Chennault from Owen Collum, May 21, 1943, *Grantee Index,* 1943–47 (Fulton County Recorder of Deeds); Carrie Andrews from Thomas L. Cofer, February 8, 1944, ibid.; L. R. Aiken from P. T. Logan, October 30, 1944, ibid.

46. Sources list Aiken's total housing production between two thousand and five thousand units. "One-Man Housing Boom," *Chicago Defender,* January 14, 1950, 13; "Housing Is His Business," 5–8.

47. "Housing Is His Business."

48. Walter H. Aiken, "Report on the Committee on Housing for Negroes," February 15, 1949, box 254, AUL Papers.

49. Temporary Coordinating Committee on Housing [TCCH], "Minutes," December 4, 1946, box 254, ibid.

50. TCCH, "The Community Housing Corporation," n.d. (1948), box 252, ibid.

51. "American Veterans Committee Proposal on Housing," summer 1946, box 255, AUL Papers; TCCH, "Minutes," December 4, 1946, box 254, ibid.; Atlanta Housing Council, "Proposed Areas for Expansions of Negro Housing in Atlanta, Georgia," May 1947, box 244, ibid.

52. Atlanta Housing Council, "Proposed Areas for Expansions."

53. Ibid. On segregated expansion planning in other cities, see HHFA Race Relations Advisors' Field Reports from Macon, Orlando, Savannah, Dallas, and Miami, HHFA Papers. Also Mohl, "Making the Second Ghetto," 398–99; Wilson, *Hamilton Park,* 33–66; and Silver and Moeser, *The Separate City,* 125–62.

54. Minutes, Meeting between Atlanta Housing Council and Officials from Fulton and Dekalb Counties, May 14, 1948, box 254, AUL Papers.

55. Bayor, *Race,* 29–32, 59–60.

56. Aiken, Joint Committee on Housing, *Study and Investigation,* 1254–56; Robert A. Thompson, quoted in Bayor, *Race,* 59. Official concerns with racial violence remained apparent through the 1950s, giving blacks continuing leverage in the struggle to build new housing. See "Bombings," ca. April 1958, box 1, ABP Papers. To minimize racial violence, Atlanta officials orchestrated the racial turnover of whole neighborhoods at once. In 1952 Mayor Hartsfield created the West Side Mutual Development Committee, with representatives from Atlanta's black and white real estate boards, to manage this process. Silver and Moeser, *The Separate City,* 136–44. For an insider view, see T. M. Alexander Sr., "Atlanta: The Negro Oasis in the 'Hot South,' Why?" box 1, ABP Papers.

57. Alexander, "Atlanta: The Negro Oasis."

58. Thompson, Lewis, and McEntire, "Atlanta and Birmingham," 26–33.

59. Ibid., 25–28.

60. Bayor, *Race,* 15–52; Lewis and Thompson with Coleman, "Housing for Negroes in Atlanta and Birmingham"; L. D. Milton to Atlanta Housing Council, June 13, 1947, box 238, AUL Papers.

61. Thompson, Lewis, and McEntire, "Atlanta and Birmingham," 41. On financing by black institutions, see Albert L. Thompson, "Negro Mortgagees and Builders in the South," *Insured Mortgage Portfolio* 18 (3rd quarter, 1949): 9–11.

62. Thompson, Lewis, and McEntire, "Atlanta and Birmingham," 45–46.

63. "Whites Protest Re-zoning Move for Negro Housing," *Atlanta Daily World,* January 19, 1950, 1; "Fulton Commissioners Approve Plan for Negro Housing Units," ibid., February 9, 1950, 1. "South's Smartest Apartments," ibid., June 1, 1950.

64. Robert A. Thompson, "A Report of the Housing Activities of the Atlanta Urban League," revised June 18, 1951, box 244, AUL Papers; Thompson, Lewis, and McEntire, "Atlanta and Birmingham," 26.

65. Thompson, interview.

66. Thompson had earlier played an instrumental role in the 1946 voter registration drive, which had increased black political clout in the city. Bayor, *Race,* 24; Thompson, interview.

67. Robert Thompson to Earl Metzger, Atlanta Housing Authority, October 28, 1952, box 238, AUL Papers.

68. Ibid.

69. E.g., "Compromise Housing Plan Approved Here," *Atlanta Daily World,* January 26, 1950.

70. "Robert Thompson to W. R. Ulrich, Re: 'Land Ownership Analysis,'" September 16, 1947, box 254, AUL Papers; "Project X, Plats of Property Owners Who Own Land in More than One Land Lot," March 21, 1951, box 251, ibid.

71. Atlanta Urban League, "Project X Report," 1951, box 252, AUL Papers.

72. Members of the TCCH discussed land in western Fulton County at their second meeting in April 1947. Negro Coordinating Committee on Housing, "Minutes," April 24, 1947, box 254, AUL Papers.

73. Atlanta Urban League, "Project X Report."

74. Robert Thompson to Velma McEwen, Fort Worth Urban League, March 15, 1951, box 238, AUL Papers; Atlanta Urban League, "Project X Report."

75. Thompson, interview. The development of new black neighborhoods also accelerated the transfer of existing housing to African Americans, which the city managed through the West Side Mutual Development Corporation. Silver and Moeser, *The Separate City,* 126–27, 136–44.

76. "See These Beautiful Homes Today," *Atlanta Daily World,* April 13, 1952.

77. "A Report of the Housing Activities of the Atlanta Urban League," June 18, 1951, box 244, AUL Papers.

78. Metropolitan Planning Commission, "Changes in Negro Housing Inventory," April 1, 1950–April 1, 1957, ibid.; Thompson, Lewis, and McEntire, "Atlanta and Birmingham," 36.

79. Atlanta Housing Council, "Proposed Areas for Expansions of Negro

Housing." For restrictions against domestic production elsewhere, see "Private Builders Provide Better Negro Housing in Oklahoma City," 142.

80. "List of Residents of Fair Haven Subdivision, 1952," box 243, AUL Papers; Atlanta City Directory Company, *Atlanta City Directory, 1951–1952* (Atlanta, 1951).

81. Petition from home owners on Penelope Street to County Commissioners, June 19, 1950, box 250, ibid.; letters to A. E. Fuller, Fulton County Manager, box 236, ibid.

82. "Petition to Members of the Municipal Planning Board and Board of Adjustment," December 1952, box 249, AUL Papers.

83. Robert Thompson, "Dear Mr. and Mrs. Home Owner," December 15, 1952, box 243, ibid.

84. Thompson, Lewis, and McEntire, "Atlanta and Birmingham," 33.

85. Ibid.

86. Alexander, "Atlanta: The Negro Oasis."

87. Residents of Penelope Road, "List of Residents of Fair Haven Subdivision, 1952"; *Atlanta City Directory* (Atlanta, 1962); ibid. (Atlanta, 1972); ibid. (Atlanta, 1981).

88. Atlanta Urban League, handwritten descriptions, 1956, box 244, AUL Papers; "Collier Heights Estates," prospectus, box 250, ibid.; "Big Grand Opening, Collier Heights Estates," ibid.

89. Robin D. G. Kelley, "'We Are Not What We Seem': Rethinking Black Working-Class Opposition in the Jim Crow South," in *The New African American Urban History,* ed. Kenneth W. Goings and Raymond A. Mohl (Thousand Oaks, Calif., 1996), 191.

90. Aiken Testimony, Joint Committee on Housing, *Study and Investigation,* 1256.

91. Thompson, interview.

92. Lewis and Thompson with Coleman, "Housing for Negroes in Atlanta and Birmingham," 62–63.

93. HHFA Race Relations Director Joseph Ray contrasted the conviction of northern fair-housing groups, which he described as "a sit-down strike" against all segregated housing, with the attitude of many southern black organizations, which favored "continued building of homes made available to Negroes while the fight goes on to permit all Americans to exercise the right of choice in selecting their place of abode." Joseph Ray, press release, September 9, 1955, box 748, HHFA Papers.

94. Forrester Washington to Robert Thompson, July 30, 1947, box 240, AUL

Papers. Robert Thompson and sociologist Hylan Lewis argued that "the concept of 'Negro area' has no legal validity," but given African Americans' "political and economic weakness" vis-à-vis whites, the strategy was a "necessary device" that "provided easier access to more and better land sites." Lewis and Thompson with Coleman, "Housing for Negroes in Atlanta and Birmingham," 62–63.

95. Robert Thompson to Phillip Hammer, "Re: 'Up Ahead' Plan," May 26, 1952, box 243, AUL Papers; Thompson to Hammer, "Atlanta Urban Renewal Study," June 25, 1957, ibid.

96. Thompson, interview.

97. Ibid.

98. Between 1940 and 1960, indices of racial segregation in Atlanta rose from 87.4 to 93.6, which was fifteenth among southern cities and higher than any major city outside the South. Taeuber and Taeuber, *Negroes in Cities,* 39–41.

99. The 1954 Supreme Court ruling in *Brown v. Board of Education* did not immediately change Atlantians' orientation. Responding to a 1955 questionnaire soliciting local reactions to the *Brown* decision, Robert Thompson wrote that "no action has been taken by the Atlanta Urban League on the question of segregation." Despite the widespread acknowledgment that separate neighborhoods and separate schools went hand in hand, black Atlantians worked for new housing on an implicitly separate basis throughout the 1950s. Separate home building in Atlanta's suburbs remained a major activity through the 1990s. Robert Thompson to Harry Alston, January 12, 1955, box 234, AUL Papers.

100. Robert Fairbanks, "Dallas in the 1940s: The Challenges and Opportunities of Defense Mobilization," in *Urban Texas: Politics and Development,* ed. Char Miller and Heywood Sanders (College Station, Tex., 1990), 141–53.

101. "Statement Submitted by the Dallas Branch of the National Association for the Advancement of Colored People, the Dallas Negro Chamber of Commerce, the Dallas Interdenominational Ministerial Alliance, and the Progressive Voters League, to the Senate and House Joint Committee on Housing in Its Hearing at Dallas, Tex., October 28, 1947, Re Desperate Conditions of Housing for Negro Citizens of Dallas, Tex.," Joint Committee on Housing, *Study and Investigation of Housing, Hearings before the Joint Committee on Housing, 80th Congress, Proceedings at Dallas, Texas, October 28, 1947* (Washington, D.C., 1948), 1518.

102. Ibid., 1518–19.

103. Fairbanks, "Dallas in the 1940s," 151. Also, A. Maceo Smith, "1950 Negro Housing Market Data: Dallas," April 12, 1950, box 750, HHFA Papers; Wilson, *Hamilton Park,* 21.

104. Dallas NAACP et al., Joint Committee on Housing, *Study and Investigation,* Dallas hearings, 1520.

105. Wilson, *Hamilton Park,* 11.

106. G. F. Porter, Joint Committee on Housing, *Study and Investigation,* Dallas hearings, 1513; Fairbanks, "Dallas in the 1940s," 143–44.

107. Dallas NAACP et al., Joint Committee on Housing, *Study and Investigation,* Dallas hearings, 1519; "Report of the Joint Committee of the Dallas Chamber of Commerce and the Dallas Citizens Committee on Negro Housing in Dallas County," August 1950, box 751, HHFA Papers.

108. "Report of the Joint Committee."

109. E. C. Estell, quoted in Dallas NAACP et al., Joint Committee on Housing, *Study and Investigation,* 1514.

110. Dallas NAACP et al., ibid., 1520; G. F. Porter, ibid., 1514.

111. Dallas NAACP et al., ibid., 1520.

112. G. F. Porter, ibid., 1514.

113. Wilson, *Hamilton Park,* 13–24.

114. Ibid., 16.

115. Ibid., 18.

116. Fairbanks, "Dallas in the 1940s"; "Bombers Known, Hansson Declares," *Dallas News,* August 6, 1950.

117. Maceo Smith to Herbert Redman, March 7, 1950, box 751, HHFA Papers. For a similar proposal in Miami, see Ernest Katz to Warren Lockwood, October 28, 1948, box 750, ibid.

118. Quoted in Wilson, *Hamilton Park,* 31.

119. Quoted in ibid., 31. This point is William Wilson's.

120. "Report of the Joint Committee," 6–7.

121. Ibid., 7.

122. Ibid.

123. Dallas's effort reflected a national trend among municipalities to "alleviate . . . unincorporated fringe area problems" through annexation. Clarence Ridling and Orin Nolting, eds., *The Municipal Year Book, 1951* (Chicago, 1951), 94, 102; also see *The Municipal Year Book, 1952* (Chicago, 1952), 41; and *The Municipal Year Book, 1953* (Chicago, 1953), 33–34, 46.

124. "West Dallas," *Journal of Housing* 11 (February 1954): 54; Maceo Smith to James Hicks, November 22, 1950, box 751, HHFA Papers.

125. "Report of the Joint Committee."

126. On race formation in Texas, see Neil Foley, *The White Scourge: Mexicans, Blacks, and Poor Whites in Texas Cotton Culture* (Berkeley, 1997).

127. Fairbanks, "Dallas in the 1940s," 152.

128. For instances of public housing construction on the suburban fringe, see "Orlando—A New Subdivision Is Created," 320–21; Mohl, "Making the Sec-

ond Ghetto," 398; in Savannah, "Bi-Weekly Reports," January 9, 1948, box 7, HHFA Papers; Silver and Moeser, *The Separate City,* 39; Thompson, Lewis, and McEntire, "Atlanta and Birmingham," 35–37.

129. Maceo Smith to E. M. Shepherd, "Ongoing Report on Activities of the Interracial Committee," August 18, 1950, box 751, HHFA Papers; Wilson, *Hamilton Park,* 37–53.

130. Wilson, *Hamilton Park,* map opposite 1.

131. Ibid., 55.

132. Ibid., 67–79.

133. Ibid., 73.

134. Ibid., 67–79; quotes on 77.

135. Ibid., 92–107.

136. Ibid., 121, 137. After closure of the school, Hamilton Park students attended class with whites in nearby Richardson.

137. "Report of the Joint Committee," 7–9; Wilson, *Hamilton Park,* 62, 67–68; U.S. Census of Population and Housing: 1960, vol. I, *Census Tracts,* part 34 (Washington, D.C., 1962), table H-3.

138. Statistics reflect nonwhite-occupied housing constructed 1950–60, census tracts, 27A, 39A, 78, 89, 100–2, 105, 114–15. U.S. Census of Population and Housing: 1960, vol. I, *Census Tracts,* part 34.

Chapter Eight

1. Langston Hughes, *The Panther and the Lash* (New York, 1967), 79–80.

2. Phillip Clay, "The Process of Black Suburbanization," *Urban Affairs Quarterly* 14 (June 1979): 407; U.S. Census of Population: 1960, vol. I, *General Population Characteristics,* part 1, *U.S. Summary* (Washington, D.C., 1962), table 44. U.S. Census of Population: 1980, vol. I, *Characteristics of the Population,* part B, *General Population Characteristics* (Washington, D.C., 1983), 140.

3. U.S. Census of Population: 1980, vol. I, chap. B, part 5, *California,* table 15; part 27, *Missouri;* part 32, *New Jersey;* part 37, *Ohio;* part 45, *Texas.*

4. Andrew Billingsley, *Black Families in White America* (Englewood Cliffs, N.J., 1968); quoted in Elizabeth Huttman, "A Research Note on the Dreams and Aspirations of Black Families," *Journal of Comparative Family Studies* 2 (summer 1991): 147.

5. Harold X. Connolly, "Black Movement into the Suburbs: Suburbs Doubling Their Black Populations during the 1960s," *Urban Affairs Quarterly* 9 (September 1973): 97.

6. "Negro Home in White Area Blasted Again in Cleveland [Cleveland Heights]," *New York Times,* May 15, 1967, 35; Ben A. Franklin, "Louisville Scene of Rights Protest," ibid., April 12, 1967, 29; "Negro Mayor of Flint Decides to Stay," ibid., August 29, 1967, 23; "Milwaukee Gets Housing Warning," ibid., June 25, 1967, 50; Stephen Grant Meyer, *As Long as They Don't Move Next Door: Segregation and Racial Conflict in American Neighborhoods* (Lanham, Md., 2000), 191–96.

7. "Reagan Denounces Open Housing Laws as Rights Violation," *New York Times,* September 27, 1967, 35. On the "home owners' rights" movement, see Thomas Sugrue, *The Origins of the Urban Crisis: Race and Inequality in Postwar Detroit* (Princeton, 1996), 209–29.

8. John M. Stahura, "Suburban Development, Black Suburbanization and the Civil Rights Movement since World War II," *American Sociological Review* 51 (February 1986): 131–44. Clay, "The Process of Black Suburbanization," 409; John R. Logan and Mark Schneider, "Racial Segregation and Racial Change in American Suburbs, 1970–1980," *American Journal of Sociology* 89 (1984): 874–88.

9. National Committee Against Discrimination in Housing [NCDH], *Jobs and Housing: A Study of Employment and Housing Opportunities for Racial Minorities in the Suburban Areas of the New York Metropolitan Region* (New York, 1970), 1. Also see Avery Guest, "The Changing Racial Composition of Suburbs, 1950–1970," *Urban Affairs Quarterly* 14 (December 1979): 195–206; Logan and Schneider, "Racial Segregation and Racial Change," 882–84.

10. Clarence Dean, "Negroes Facing Test in Suburbs," *New York Times,* May 21, 1961, 79.

11. Mark Schneider and John R. Logan, "Suburban Racial Segregation and Black Access to Local Public Resources," *Social Science Quarterly* 63 (1982): 762–70; John R. Logan and Richard D. Alba, "Locational Returns to Human Capital: Minority Access to Suburban Community Resources," *Demography* 30 (May 1993): 243–68; Holly Myers-Jones, "Power, Geography and Black Americans: Exploring the Implications of Black Suburbanization" (Ph.D. diss., University of Washington, 1988).

12. Karl Taeuber, "Racial Segregation: The Persisting Dilemma," *Annals of the American Academy of Political and Social Science* 422 (November 1975): 89.

13. Clay, "The Process of Black Suburbanization," 409.

14. Reynolds Farley, "The Changing Distribution of Negroes within Metropolitan Areas: The Emergence of Black Suburbs," *American Journal of Sociology* 75 (January 1970): 344; Connolly, "Black Movement into the Suburbs," 102–4.

15. Erick Trickey, "Welcome to East Cleveland," *Cleveland Scene,* February 8, 2001, pp. 1+.

16. Larry Ford and Ernst Griffin, "The Ghettoization of Paradise," *Geographical Review* 69 (April 1979): 140–58. New building was a significant factor in a number of fast-growing black suburbs in the 1960s, including Wyandanch and Roosevelt, New York; Harvey and Markham, Illinois; North Shreveport, Louisiana; North Las Vegas, Nevada; Richmond Heights, Florida; and Hollydale, Ohio. Connolly, "Black Movement into the Suburbs," 94–95; Farley, "The Changing Distribution of Negroes," 336, 339; Harold M. Rose, *Black Suburbanization: Access to Improved Quality of Life or Maintenance of the Status Quo?* (Cambridge, 1976), 30.

17. Clay, "The Process of Black Suburbanization," 413. Clay may overstate the extent of integration since what he called "neighborhoods" were census-defined areas containing approximately 5,000 people. By this definition, an all-black community of 600 people isolated by a railroad track from 3,400 whites would constitute a "neighborhood" 15 percent black.

18. Franklin James, Betty McCummings, and Eileen Tynan, *Minorities in the Sunbelt* (New Brunswick, 1984).

19. Andrew Wiese, "Neighborhood Diversity: Social Change, Ambiguity, and Fair Housing since 1968," *Journal of Urban Affairs* 17 (summer 1995): 107–29.

20. For fastest-growing suburbs, see Connolly, "Black Movement into the Suburbs."

21. Earl Caldwell, "The Problems of a Black Suburb," in *Suburbia in Transition*, ed. Louis Masotti (New York, 1974), 79.

22. In 1980, 40 percent of black suburbanites in Los Angeles lived in eight majority black suburbs—each of which had been predominantly or "all" white in 1960. U.S. Census of Population and Housing: 1960, vol. I, *Census Tracts,* table 1; U.S. Census of Population and Housing: 1980, vol. I, *Census Tracts,* table P-7.

23. Connolly, "Black Movement into the Suburbs," 93.

24. Miami's ten black suburbs housed 48 percent of the black suburban population in 1980. An equal percentage lived in three majority-black suburbs of Newark. Two mostly black communities near Cleveland accounted for 47 percent of black suburbanites. U.S. Census of Population: 1980, vol. I, part B, table 15.

25. Bart Landry, *The New Black Middle Class* (Berkeley, 1987), 76–77.

26. Ibid., 77; Victor Perlo, *The Roots of Black Inequality in the U.S.A.* (New York, 1975), 53; The fraction of African Americans earning $25,000 or more (in 1982 dollars) increased from 10.4 percent in 1960 to 24.5 percent in 1982. William Julius Wilson, *The Truly Disadvantaged: The Inner City, the Underclass, and Public Policy* (Chicago, 1987), 109.

27. U.S. Census of Population: 1960, vol. I, part 1, 544–47; Mary Patillo-

McCoy, *Black Picket Fences: Privilege and Peril among the Black Middle Class* (Chicago, 1999), 27; Wilson, *The Truly Disadvantaged,* 109, 110–11.

28. Landry, *New Black Middle Class,* 78–90.

29. U.S. Census of Population: 1960, vol. I, part 1D, *Detailed Characteristics, U.S. Summary* (Washington, D.C., 1963), 501–2; U.S. Census of Population: 1980, vol. I, chap. D, *Detailed Characteristics,* part 1, *U.S. Summary* (Washington, D.C., 1984), 142–46. Suburban black women played an even more important role; in a variety of fast-growing black suburbs, as many as 65 to 75 percent of married black women were employed outside the home. Connolly, "Black Movement into the Suburbs," 105.

30. Landry, *New Black Middle Class,* 67; William Julius Wilson, *The Declining Significance of Race: Blacks and Changing American Institutions* (Chicago, 1980); Thomas A. Clarke, *Blacks in Suburbs: A National Perspective* (New Brunswick, N.J., 1979), 7–10.

31. Stahura, "Suburban Development, Black Suburbanization and the Civil Rights Movement," 131–44.

32. George Cable Wright, "Bias Fight Grows in Lower Jersey," *New York Times,* September 16, 1962, 74; Milton Bracker, "Integration Forces in Suburbs Mount Drive on a Broad Front," ibid., March 19, 1962, 1.

33. Bracker, "Integration Forces in Suburbs Mount Drive," 42.

34. NCDH, *Report of the National Conference on Equal Opportunity in Housing: Challenge to American Communities* (Washington, D.C., 1963), 24. For legal action, see *Taylor v. Board of Education of New Rochelle,* 191 F. Supp. 181 (S.D.N.Y. 1961); *Blocker v. Board of Education of Manhasset,* 229 F. Supp. 709 (1964); *Branche v. Board of Education of the Town of Hempstead, School District No. 1,* 204 F. Supp. 150 (1962); *Bryant v. Board of Education of Mount Vernon,* 274 F. Supp. 270 (1967); and *Schults v. Board of Education of the Township of Teaneck,* 86 N.J. Super. 29 (1964). For examples of direct action, see "Mount Vernon Negroes Criticize Rezoning," *New York Times,* March 24, 1962, 8; and "200 Negroes Stage Port Chester March to Protest Housing," ibid., September 25, 1962, 39.

35. "Muslim Charges Englewood Sham," *New York Times,* August 6, 1962, 27.

36. "Muslim May Join Englewood Drive," *New York Times,* August 5, 1962, 55. For demonstrations in Albany, Georgia, see Clayborne Carson, *In Struggle: SNCC and the Black Awakening of the 1960s* (Cambridge, 1981), 56–65. On *Taylor v. Board of Education of New Rochelle,* see John Kaplan, "Segregation Litigation and the Schools — Part I: The New Rochelle Experience," *Northwestern University Law Review* 58 (1963).

37. "Discrimination in Housing Called 'Number One City Problem,'" *Evan-*

ston Review, July 4, 1963; "Minister Says Number One Race Problem in Evanston Is 'Invisible Fence,'" ibid., March 14, 1963, Clippings Files, "Housing VI" (Evanston Public Library, Evanston, Ill.).

38. On the Freedom Rides, see Carson, *In Struggle,* 31–44. On CORE activities outside the South, see August Meier and Elliot Rudwick, *CORE: A Study in the Civil Rights Movement* (New York, 1973), 182–210.

39. On Operation Windowshop, see Gladwin Hill, "Negroes on Coast Fight for Housing," *New York Times,* July 9, 1962, 1; and Roy Silver, "L.I. Realty Men Accused of Bias," ibid., August 7, 1962, 18.

40. "33-day Sit-in Wins Home for Negro Physicist in All-White Los Angeles Tract," *House and Home* 21 (May 1962): 58; "CORE Sit In at Monterey Park Development," *New York Times,* March 4, 1962, 73.

41. "Whites to Aid [Dearborn] Rally by Detroit Negroes," *New York Times,* June 23, 1963, 57; "Color Line Scored in Detroit Suburb [Warren]," ibid., August 4, 1963, 64; "Romney Leads Detroit [Grosse Pointe] Racial Demonstration," *Los Angeles Times,* June 30, 1963, 14.

42. Eileen Shanahan, "Negro Initiates Home Policy Test," *New York Times,* June 9, 1963, 58; Eileen Shanahan, "Builder Bids U.S. End Racial Curb," ibid., August 15, 1963, 15.

43. Grace Simons, "1,000 Tell Torrance Integration's Coming," *California Eagle,* July 4, 1963, 1; Bill Becker, "Negroes on Coast March at Project," *New York Times,* June 30, 1963, 46.

44. Paul Weeks, "700 March for Integration in Torrance Tract," *Los Angeles Times,* June 30, 1963, 1; "Coast Builder Bows to Demands and Sells Home to Negro Family," *New York Times,* July 13, 1963, 7; "CORE Shifts Major Southern California Demonstrations from Housing to Employment," *New York Times,* August 27, 1963, 27; Meier and Rudwick, *CORE,* 186.

45. Meyer, *As Long as They Don't Move Next Door,* 166.

46. Quoted in "'Ain't Scared of Your Jails,' 1960–1961," *Eyes on the Prize: America's Civil Rights Years* film series (Blackside Productions, 1985).

47. Meyer, *As Long as They Don't Move Next Door,* 169; Juliet Saltman, *Open Housing: Dynamics of a Social Movement* (New York, 1978), 51–52.

48. Beth J. Lief and Susan Goering, "The Implementation of the Federal Mandate for Fair Housing," *Urban Affairs Annual Reviews* 32 (1987): 232.

49. The states were California, Colorado, Connecticut, Indiana, Massachusetts, Oregon, Michigan, Minnesota, New Jersey, New York, Pennsylvania, Rhode Island, Wisconsin, and Washington. Davis McEntire, *Residence and Race: Final and Comprehensive Report to the Commission on Race and Housing* (Berkeley, 1960), 266–68.

50. U.S. Commission on Civil Rights, *Housing: 1961 Commission on Civil*

Rights Report (Washington, D.C., 1961), 120–22; Thomas Ennis, "Panic Promoters Facing Penalties," *New York Times,* May 28, 1961, sec. 8, 1. Also *Summer v. Township of Teaneck,* 53 N.J. 548 (1969).

51. Edward Brooke, quoted in Alexander Polikoff, "Sustainable Integration or Inevitable Resegregation: The Troubling Questions," in *Housing Desegregation and Federal Policy,* ed. John M. Goering (Chapel Hill, N.C., 1986), 48.

52. Meyer, *As Long as They Don't Move Next Door,* 206–9.

53. Civil Rights Act of 1968, Public Law 90-284, April 11, 1968, 82 Stat. (Title VIII, Fair Housing) *U.S. Statutes at Large, 90th Congress, 1968;* Leif and Goering, "The Implementation of the Federal Mandate for Fair Housing," 235, 261.

54. Thomas Ennis, "1866 Rights Law Tested in St. Louis," *New York Times,* February 26, 1967, 8: 1; Meyer, *As Long as They Don't Move Next Door,* 209–10; *Jones v. Alfred H. Mayer Co.,* 392 U.S. 409 (1968).

55. John Yinger, "The Racial Dimension of Urban Housing Markets in the 1980's," *Urban Affairs Annual Reviews* 32 (1987): 43–67; George Galster and Mark Keeney, "Race, Residence, Discrimination and Economic Opportunity: Modeling the Nexus of Urban Phenomena," *Urban Affairs Quarterly* 24 (September 1988): 87–117.

56. U.S. Commission on Civil Rights, *The Federal Fair Housing Enforcement Effort: A Report of the U.S. Commission on Civil Rights* (Washington, D.C., 1979), 230, quoted in Robert Bullard, "The Black Family: Housing Alternatives for the 1980s," *Journal of Black Studies* 14 (March 1984): 341–51.

57. Robert W. Lake, "Postscript: Unresolved Themes in the Evolution of Fair Housing," in *Housing Desegregation and Federal Policy,* ed. Goering, 316; Lief and Goering, "The Implementation of the Federal Mandate for Fair Housing," 236–58.

58. Douglas Massey and Nancy Denton, *American Apartheid: Segregation and the Making of the Underclass* (Cambridge, 1993), 195.

59. George Bowens, U.S. Commission on Civil Rights, *Hearing before the U.S. Commission on Civil Rights: Hearing Held in Washington, D.C., June 14–17, 1971* (Washington, D.C., 1971), 408.

60. Larman Williams, ibid., *Hearings Held in St. Louis, Missouri, January 14–17, 1970* (Washington, D.C., 1970), 301.

61. Fair Housing Council of Delaware Valley, "A Survey of the Housing Experiences of Negro Professional Industrial Employees" (Philadelphia, 1967); LeRoy M. Collins, interview by Laurie Collins-Thomas and Jennifer Palacio, in *The Civil Rights Movement on Long Island: A Local History Curriculum Guide for Middle School and High School,* ed. Alan Singer (Hempstead, N.Y., 1997), 31.

62. Fair Housing Council of Delaware Valley, "A Survey of the Housing Experiences"; "Housing Sit-in Staged," *New York Times,* May 30, 1961, 6.

63. Quoted in Byron Porterfield, "Negroes Describe Frustrations of Entry into White Suburbia," *New York Times,* April 16, 1965, 57.

64. Fair Housing Council of Delaware Valley, "A Survey of the Housing Experiences."

65. Juliet Saltman, *A Fragile Movement: The Struggle for Neighborhood Stabilization* (New York, 1990), 354.

66. Meyer, *As Long as They Don't Move Next Door,* 179–82.

67. "Laws to Bar Bias in Housing Gain," *New York Times,* March 21, 1965, sec. 8, 12.

68. On the property rights movement and white disaffection with liberalism, see Sugrue, *Origins of the Urban Crisis,* 209–29; On Prop. 14 and the politics of race, see Becky M. Nicolaides, *My Blue Heaven: Life and Politics in the Working-Class Suburbs of Los Angeles, 1920–1965* (Chicago, 2002), 308–27.

69. "Laws to Bar Bias in Housing Gain," 12; "Home Sale Curbs Opposed in Texas," *New York Times,* March 2, 1965, 57. For a contemporary analysis of white attitudes, see Herbert Aurbach, John R. Coleman, and Bernard Mausner, "Restrictive and Protective Viewpoints of Fair Housing Legislation: A Comparative Study of Attitudes," *Social Problems* 8 (fall 1960): 118–25. In a 1960 survey by the National Opinion Research Center, 60 percent of whites agreed with the statement: "White people have the right to keep blacks out of their neighborhoods, and blacks should respect that right." Quoted in Reynolds Farley and William H. Frey, "Changes in the Segregation of Whites from Blacks during the 1980s: Small Steps toward a More Integrated Society," *American Sociological Review* 59 (February 1994): 27.

70. Silver, "L.I. Realty Men Accused of Bias."

71. Ibid.; also see Hill, "Negroes on Coast Fight for Housing," 31; and Massachusetts Advisory Committee to the U.S. Commission on Civil Rights, *Report on Massachusetts: Housing in Boston* (December 1963), 21.

72. Silver, "L.I. Realty Men Accused of Bias."

73. Fair Housing Council of Delaware Valley, "A Survey of the Housing Experiences."

74. Ibid.; also see Porterfield, "Negroes Describe Frustrations," 57.

75. Fair Housing Council of Delaware Valley, "A Survey of the Housing Experiences."

76. Quoted in NCDH, *Affirmative Action to Achieve Integration* (New York, 1966), 31.

77. Diana M. Pearce, "Black, White, and Many Shades of Gray: Real Estate Brokers and Their Racial Practices" (Ph.D. diss., University of Michigan, 1976).

For an example, see Horacio D. Lewis, *"I Might As Well Move to the Moon": A Case Study of Housing Discrimination and a Legal Manual* (Bloomington, Ind., 1972).

78. Donald L. Foley, "Institutional and Contextual Factors Affecting the Housing Choice of Minority Residents," in *Segregation in Housing,* ed. Amos Hawley and Vincent Rock (Washington, D.C., 1973), 86.

79. Ronald E. Wienk, Clifford E. Reid, John C. Simonson, and Frederick J. Eggers, *Measuring Racial Discrimination in American Housing Markets: The Housing Market Practices Survey* (Washington, D.C., 1979); H. Newberger, *Recent Evidence on Discrimination in Housing* (Washington, D.C., 1984). For instances of discrimination, see *Bush v. Kaim,* 297 F. Supp. 151 (1969); *Smith v. Sol D. Adler Realty Co.,* 436 F. 2d 344 (1970); *U.S. v. Youritan Construction Co.,* 370 F. Supp., 643 (1973); and *Williams v. Mathews,* 499 F. 2d 819 (1974).

80. Bernard J. Frieden, "Blacks in Suburbia: The Myth of Better Opportunities," in *Minority Perspectives,* ed. Lowden Wingo (Washington, D.C., 1972), 162.

81. Quote in NCDH, *Jobs and Housing,* 55.

82. Ibid. See *UAW, et al., v. Township of Mahwah, New Jersey,* 119 N.J. Super. 389 (1972). Class-based zoning was not restricted to white suburban areas. See Bruce D. Haynes, *Red Lines, Black Spaces: The Politics of Race and Space in a Black Middle-Class Suburb* (New Haven, 2001), 110–13.

83. The landmark case was *James v. Valtierra,* 402 U.S. 137 (1971). Jonathan Entin, "Race and the Origins of Zoning in the Chicago Suburbs," in *Contested Terrain: Power, Politics and Participation in Suburbia,* ed. Marc L. Silver and Martin Melkonian (Westport, Conn., 1995), 71.

84. *Village of Arlington Heights v. Metropolitan Housing Development Corporation,* 429 U.S. 252 (1977). See also David L. Kirp, John P. Dwyer, and Larry A. Rosenthal, *Our Town: Race, Housing, and the Soul of Suburbia* (New Brunswick, N.J., 1995).

85. "Effect, and not motivation, is the touchstone, in part because clever men may easily conceal their motivations, but more importantly, because whatever our law was once, we now firmly recognize that the arbitrary quality of thoughtlessness can be as disastrous and unfair to private rights and the public interest as the perversity of a willful scheme." *U.S. v. City of Black Jack* 508 F. 2d 1179 (1975).

86. My point is not to impugn the specific goals of these movements, but to note that racists have freely concealed their aims in the ostensibly race-neutral cover they provide. See Kirp, Dwyer, and Rosenthal, *Our Town,* 108–10, 115–16.

87. See Yale Rabin, "The Roots of Segregation in the Eighties: The Role of Local Government Actions," *Urban Affairs Annual Reviews* 32 (1987): 208–26; and Yale Rabin, "Expulsive Zoning: The Inequitable Legacy of *Euclid,*" in *Zoning and the American Dream: Promises Still to Keep,* ed. Charles M. Haar and Jerold S. Kayden (Washington, D.C., 1981), 103–6. See also Richard Babcock and Fred

Bosselman, *Exclusionary Zoning: Land Use Regulation and Housing in the 1970s* (New York, 1973); and Michael Danielson, *The Politics of Exclusion* (New York, 1976).

88. "Housing and Race Stir Court Fight," *New York Times,* April 1, 1973, 70; for exclusionary zoning in Chicago suburbs, see Entin, "Race and the Origins of Zoning in the Chicago Suburbs," 71–82.

89. *U.S. v. City of Black Jack*.

90. Roberta L. Raymond, "The Challenge to Oak Park: A Suburban Community Faces Racial Change," (M.A. thesis, Roosevelt University, Chicago, 1972), 75–76.

91. Porterfield, "Negroes Describe Frustrations," 57.

92. For examples of attacks against blacks in white suburbia, see "Home Negro Was Buying Burns in Suspicious Blaze in Fairfield [Conn.]," *New York Times,* June 22, 1963, 8; William G. Weart, "Negroes Are Jeered at New [Folcroft,] Pennsylvania Home," ibid., August 31, 1963, 6; "[Oceanside,] L.I. Negro Homeowner Offers to Sell House after Bombing," ibid., November 19, 1967, 44; "Blast Rocks Two Homes in a Cleveland Suburb [Cleveland Heights]," ibid., October 19, 1965, 47; Porterfield, "Negroes Describe Frustrations," 57; Raymond, "The Challenge to Oak Park," 98–101; "Unpleasant experiences," Adel Allen, U.S. Commission on Civil Rights, *Hearings Held in St. Louis,* 308.

93. U.S. Commission on Civil Rights, *Hearings Held in St. Louis,* 307.

94. Reynolds Farley, Howard Schuman, Suzanne Bianchi, Diane Colasanto, and Shirley Hatchett, "'Chocolate City, Vanilla Suburbs': Will the Trend toward Racially Separate Communities Continue?" *Social Science Research* 7 (1978): 330–44; Clifford Wurdock, "Neighborhood Racial Transition: A Study of the Role of White Flight," *Urban Affairs Quarterly* 17 (1981): 75–89. A 1990 survey uncovered that just 10 percent of whites expressed a favorable reaction to the possibility of living in a neighborhood that was "half white and half black." See Joe R. Feagin, "A House Is Not a Home: White Racism and U.S. Housing Practices," in *Residential Apartheid: The American Legacy,* ed. Robert D. Bullard, J. Eugene Grigsby, and Charles Lee (Los Angeles, 1994), 43.

95. Quoted in Singer, ed., *The Civil Rights Movement on Long Island,* 23.

96. Charles L. Leven, James T. Little, Hugh O. Nourse, and R. B. Read, *Neighborhood Change: Lessons in the Dynamics of Urban Decay* (New York, 1976).

97. Clay, "The Process of Black Suburbanization"; Rose, *Black Suburbanization;* Farley, "The Changing Distribution of Negroes"; Guest, "The Changing Racial Composition of Suburbs"; Richard D. Alba and John R. Logan, "Variations on Two Themes: Racial and Ethnic Patterns in the Attainment of Suburban Residence," *Demography* 28 (August 1991): 431–53.

98. Allen, U.S. Commission on Civil Rights, *Hearings Held in St. Louis,* 302; Harriette Robinet, "I'm a Mother—Not a Pioneer," *Redbook* 130 (February 1968): 12; Clarence Q. Pair, *The American Black Ghetto* (New York, 1969), 13–14.

99. Robinet, "I'm a Mother," 16.

100. Quoted in Michele Derus and Lee Hawkins Jr., "A Dream Deferred: Wide Open Spaces Beckon Black Families," *Milwaukee Journal Sentinel,* September 14, 1997, 1.

101. Williams, U.S. Commission on Civil Rights, *Hearings Held in St. Louis,* 300.

102. Quoted in Rosalyn Baxandall and Elizabeth Ewen, *Picture Windows: How the Suburbs Happened* (New York, 2000), 180.

103. Helena White, quoted in ibid., 181; Robinet, "I'm a Mother," 12.

104. "Will the Suburbs Beckon?" *Ebony* 26 (July 1971): 112.

105. Williams, U.S. Commission on Civil Rights, *Hearings Held in St. Louis,* 302.

106. Percy Sutton, U.S. Commission on Civil Rights, *Hearings Held in Washington, D.C,* 279.

107. Theodore "Ted" Wheeler, interview by author, July 27, 2001.

108. Ibid. ACT refers to American College Test, a college aptitude test similar to the more popular SAT.

109. "What I was looking for was the same kind of environment that could permit me to do the same for my children in the sense of their dignity." Wheeler, interview.

110. Carole Goodwin, *The Oak Park Strategy: Community Control of Racial Change* (Chicago, 1979), 33.

111. Wheeler, interview.

112. On the Julians' move to Oak Park, see "Hunt on for Julian Bombers," *Chicago Defender,* June 16, 1951, 1.

113. Raymond, "The Challenge to Oak Park," 65–66, 79.

114. Ted Wheeler, interview by author, November 4, 2000.

115. The mortgage and title to the Wheelers' home remained in the name of their straw buyer for two years until they found a bank to refinance the mortgage. Wheeler, interview, July 27, 2001. Third-party purchases were not uncommon among early black buyers in Oak Park; see Raymond, "The Challenge to Oak Park," 66–67.

116. Support for open housing among a vocal minority of whites coalesced in a number of upper-middle-class suburbs during the late 1950s and 1960s. Saltman, *Fragile Movement;* see also Wiese, "Neighborhood Diversity: Social Change, Ambiguity, and Fair Housing since 1968." For examples, see "Fair Housing Pledge

Being Circulated," *New Rochelle Standard Star,* January 24, 1963; "700 in Montclair Advertise for Equal Housing Rights," *New York Times,* June 14, 1963, 14; and Doris Faber, "I'm Not Against It, But—," ibid., October 27, 1963, part 6, 58.

117. Raymond, "The Challenge to Oak Park," 65.

118. Wheeler, interview.

119. Raymond, "The Challenge to Oak Park," 64–69.

120. Goodwin, *The Oak Park Strategy,* 108.

121. Raymond, "The Challenge to Oak Park," 78–79.

122. Ibid., 76–84; Roberta "Bobbie" Raymond, interview by author, June 14, 1989; Oak Park Housing Center, *Annual Report, 1990* (Oak Park, Ill., 1990).

123. "Soul Searching in a Pioneering Town," *Newsweek,* March 3, 1988, 32–33, 37; Richard Firstman, "Trying Hard to Keep that Racial Mix," *New York Newsday,* December 9, 1990, 7, 31–32; U.S. Census of Population and Housing: 2000, vol. I, *Summary of the Population and Housing Characteristics,* part 15, *Illinois* (Washington, D.C., 2002), 142.

124. Yvonne Simmons, quoted in Baxandall and Ewen, *Picture Windows,* 186; Hazel Dukes, quoted in ibid., 180.

125. Wheeler, interview, July 27, 2001.

126. Ibid.

127. Jackie Robinson, U.S. Commission on Civil Rights, *Hearings before the U.S. Commission on Civil Rights: Hearings Held in New York, February 2–3, 1959* (Washington, D.C., 1959), 271.

128. Logan and Schneider, "Racial Segregation and Racial Change," 875–76; Rose, *Black Suburbanization,* 250–63.

129. Quoted in Haynes, *Red Lines, Black Spaces,* 112.

130. *Racial Transition in the Inner Suburb: Studies of the St. Louis Area,* ed. Solomon Sutker and Sara Smith Sutker with the assistance of Karen A. Plax (New York, 1974), 21–79.

131. U.S. Census of Population: 1980, vol. I, part B, part 22, *Maryland,* 185; U.S. Census of Population: 1960, vol. I, part 22, *Maryland,* 66; Clay, "The Process of Black Suburbanization," 413.

132. George Bradley, U.S. Commission on Civil Rights, *Hearings Held in Washington, June 14–17, 1971* (Washington, D.C., 1971), 92.

133. Rose, *Black Suburbanization,* 262–63.

134. John R. Logan, "Growth, Politics, and the Stratification of Places," *American Journal of Sociology* 84 (1978): 404–15.

135. See Edward Orser, *Blockbusting in Baltimore: The Edmondson Village Story* (Lexington, Ky., 1994), 84–98.

136. Sophia Robison, John Morsell, and Edna Merson, "Summary of Survey on Country-Wide Instances of Open Occupancy Housing," Committee on Civil Rights in Manhattan, in Atlanta Urban League Papers, box 250, file 6 (Robert Woodruff Library, Special Collections, Atlanta University, Atlanta, Ga.), 19.

137. Hillel Levine and Lawrence Harmon, *Death of an American Jewish Community* (New York, 1992), 195–96; quoted in Baxandall and Ewen, *Picture Windows,* 184.

138. Arnold Hirsch, *Making the Second Ghetto: Race and Housing in Chicago, 1940–1960* (New York, 1983), 32.

139. Ibid., 31; on redlining, see Harriet Taggart and Kevin Smith, "Redlining: An Assessment of the Evidence of Disinvestment in Metropolitan Boston," *Urban Affairs Quarterly* 17 (1981); also see Robert Schafer and Helen F. Ladd, *Discrimination in Mortgage Lending* (Cambridge, 1981).

140. Norris Vitchek, "Confessions of a Block Buster," *Saturday Evening Post* (undated), quoted in Raymond, "The Challenge to Oak Park," 80.

141. Hirsch, *Making the Second Ghetto,* 32.

142. Ibid., 33.

143. Ibid., 35.

144. Luigi Laurenti, *Property Values and Race* (Berkeley, 1959). See Donald Phares, "Socioeconomic Transition and Housing Values: A Comparative Analysis of Urban Neighborhoods," *Urban Affairs Annual Reviews* (1974), 183–208; Harold Aldrich, "Ecological Succession in Racially Changing Neighborhoods: A Review of the Literature," *Urban Affairs Quarterly* 10 (March 1975): 327–48; and Thomas J. Phelan and Mark Schneider, "Race, Ethnicity, and Class in American Suburbs," *Urban Affairs Review* 31 (May 1996): 659–81.

145. Allen, U.S. Commission on Civil Rights, *Hearings Held in St. Louis,* 303–14.

146. Ibid., 303.

147. Ibid., 304–5.

148. Ibid., 304.

149. On real estate brokers and racial transition, see Hirsch, *Making the Second Ghetto,* 34–35; also see Rose Helper, *Racial Policies and Practices of Real Estate Brokers* (Minneapolis, 1969), 41–42, 182–84.

150. There appears to be no academic study of black real estate brokers. The role of black blockbusters is even more obscure.

151. "The Hour of Our Discontent," *East Cleveland Leader,* May 12, 1966, quoted in W. Dennis Keating, *The Suburban Racial Dilemma: Housing and Neighborhoods* (Philadelphia, 1994), 86.

152. For rates of racial change without "white flight," see Harvey Molotch, "Racial Change in a Stable Community," *American Journal of Sociology* 75 (September 1969): 226–38.

153. Connolly, "Black Movement into the Suburbs," 96.

154. In 1980, 79,422 (84 percent) of 94,299 black suburbanites in greater Cleveland lived in seven east-side suburbs: East Cleveland, Warrensville Heights, Shaker Heights, Cleveland Heights, Euclid, Bedford Heights, and University Heights. U.S. Census of Population: 1980, vol. I, chap. B, part 37, 18–26.

155. Trickey, "Welcome to East Cleveland."

156. U.S. Census of Population: 1960, vol. I, *Characteristics of the Population,* part 37B (Washington, D.C., 1962), 133; U.S. Census of Population: 1970, vol. I, *Characteristics of the Population,* part 37 (Washington, D.C., 1973), 235.

157. Arthur D. Little, Inc., *East Cleveland: Response to Urban Change* (East Cleveland, 1969), 3.

158. Trickey, "Welcome to East Cleveland."

159. Keating, *The Suburban Racial Dilemma,* 89–90. On rioting, white flight, and white avoidance elsewhere, see Richard Elman, *Ill-at-Ease in Compton* (New York, 1967).

160. U.S. Census of Population: 1980, vol. II, *Census Tracts,* part 123, *Cleveland, Ohio, SMSA* (Washington, D.C., 1983), 99–100; Little, *East Cleveland,* 60–61.

161. Little, *East Cleveland,* 30–38.

162. Keating, *The Suburban Racial Dilemma,* 92.

163. Paul Delaney, "The Outer City: Negroes Find Few Tangible Gains," *New York Times,* June 1, 1971, 28, quoted in ibid.

164. In 1970 the median income of East Cleveland was 7 percent lower than the Cleveland median, and about 11 percent of the suburb's residents lived in poverty. Keating, *The Suburban Racial Dilemma,* 91.

165. Trickey, "Welcome to East Cleveland."

166. Ibid.; Paula M., interview by author, June 7, 1989.

167. Clay, "The Process of Black Suburbanization," 407, 416; Logan and Schneider, "Racial Segregation and Racial Change," 875–76.

Chapter Nine

1. U.S. Census of Population and Housing: 2000, data posted on the website of the Lewis Mumford Center at the State University of New York at Albany, http://mumford1.dyndns.org/cen2000/data.html — 1990: 8.5 million; 2000: 11.9 million.

2. Patrick T. Reardon, "Life in the Suburbs Is Becoming More of a Trend," *Chicago Tribune,* February 5, 1992, 3C.

3. William P. O'Hare and William H. Frey, "Booming, Suburban, and Black," *American Demographics* (September 1992): 30–38; U.S. Census of Population, vol. I, *Characteristics of the Population,* chap. B, *General Population Characteristics,* part 1, *U.S. Summary* (Washington, D.C., 1983), 201–46.

4. O'Hare and Frey, "Booming, Suburban, and Black"; Jon Sall, "More Blacks Choose Suburbs; City Residents Outward Bound," *Chicago Sun-Times,* September 14, 1992, 1.

5. Delbert Ellerton, "Tensions of Transition: North Clayton Adapts to Racial Shifts, Growing Pains," *Atlanta Journal and Constitution,* April 5, 1998, 8D; Sall, "More Blacks Choose Suburbs," 1; Frances Taylor and John Moran, "More Black Families Calling Suburbs Home," *Hartford Courant,* December 18, 1994, A1; "Racial Pioneers Reap Benefits," *USA Today,* March 4, 1993, 3D; also see Joel Garreau, *Edge City: Life on the New Frontier* (New York, 1991), 145.

6. Garreau, *Edge City,* 146.

7. Doug Cumming, "Bright Flight; A New Term and Trend: Middle-Class Blacks Heading for the Suburbs and Private Schools," *Atlanta Journal-Constitution,* April 20, 1997, 1R.

8. Ibid.; Hollis Towns, "The New Black Power," *Atlanta Journal-Constitution,* July 14, 1997, 1E. On home building for blacks near Chicago, see Janita Poe, "Blacks Finding Places to Call Their Own in Suburbs," *Chicago Tribune,* September 29, 1992, 1.

9. Michael Abramowitz and Richard Morin, "Prince George's: Views in Black and White," *Washington Post,* August 7, 1994, 1A.

10. Michael Fletcher, "The Changes: Over 30 Years, the Washington Region's Black Population Has Been Redefined by Its Education and Affluence," *Washington Post,* February 1, 1998, W11.

11. Garreau, *Edge City,* 144, 153.

12. Lawrence DeGraaf, "The Unheralded Triumph: Residential Integration and Its Consequences for Blacks in California Suburbs, 1960–1990," paper delivered at the Annual Meeting of the Pacific Coast Branch of the American Historical Association, August 8, 1998.

13. Quintard Taylor, comment, at ibid.

14. "Whites Own 10 Times the Assets Blacks Have, Census Study Finds," *New York Times,* July 19, 1986; "Survey Shows Racial Bias in Home Loans," *Cleveland Plain Dealer,* January 22, 1989. Also see Joe R. Feagin, "The Continuing Significance of Race: Anti-Black Discrimination in Public Places," *American Sociological Review* 56 (February 1991): 101–16; and Robert D. Bullard, J. Eugene

Grigsby, and Charles Lee, eds., *Residential Apartheid: The American Legacy* (Los Angeles, 1994), 1–11.

15. Thomas J. Phelan and Mark Schneider, "Race, Ethnicity and Class in American Suburbs," *Urban Affairs Review* 31 (May 1996): 659–71; Mark Schneider and Thomas J. Phelan, "Black Suburbanization in the 1980s," *Demography* 30 (May 1993): 269–79; also see John R. Logan and Brian Stults, "Racial Differences in Exposure to Crime: The City and Suburbs of Cleveland in 1990," *Criminology* 37 (May 1999): 251–76.

16. Sheryl McCarthy, "White Flight Follows Blacks' Move to Suburbs," *New York Newsday,* June 26, 1997, A46; George Galster, "Black Suburbanization: Has It Changed the Relative Location of the Races?" *Urban Affairs Quarterly* 26 (June 1991): 621–28.

17. David J. Dent, "The New Black Suburbs," *New York Times Magazine,* March 17, 1994, 24.

18. Barry Bluestone and Bennett Harrison, *The Deindustrialization of America: Plant Closings, Community Abandonment, and the Dismantling of Basic Industry* (New York, 1982).

19. Ibid.; Saskia Sassen, *Global Cities: New York, London, Tokyo* (Princeton, 1991); Bennett Harrison and Barry Bluestone, *The Great U-Turn: Corporate Restructuring and the Polarizing of America* (New York, 1988); Katherine Newman, *Declining Fortunes: The Withering of the American Dream* (New York, 1991).

20. Kevin Phillips, *The Politics of Rich and Poor: Wealth and the American Electorate in the Reagan Era* (New York, 1990).

21. Sassen, *Global Cities,* 245–310.

22. Douglas S. Massey and Nancy Denton, *American Apartheid: Segregation and the Making of the Underclass* (Cambridge, Mass., 1993); Douglas S. Massey and Mary J. Fischer, "How Segregation Concentrates Poverty," *Social Forces* 23 (July 2000): 670–92.

23. Susan S. Fainstein and Norman I. Fainstein, "The Racial Dimension in Urban Political Economy," *Urban Affairs Quarterly* 25 (December 1989): 187–99; "A City [East St. Louis] without Bootstraps," *Time,* June 12, 1989; Robin D. G. Kelley, "Playing for Keeps: Pleasure and Profit on the Post-Industrial Playground," in *The House that Race Built,* ed. Waheema Lubiano (New York, 1997), 195–231.

24. David Masci, "Middle-Class Blacks Still Face Obstacles," *Cleveland Plain Dealer,* February 17, 1998, 6A.

25. Sam Fulwood III, *Waking from the Dream: My Life in the Black Middle Class* (New York, 1996), 224.

26. Ronald Smothers, "For Long Island Blacks, Prosperity Is a Relative Term," *New York Times,* August 1, 1985, B 1–2.

27. Garreau, *Edge City,* 153.

28. On "linked fate," see Michael C. Dawson, *Behind the Mule: Race and Class in African American Politics* (Princeton, 1994), 76–80; also see Bruce D. Haynes, *Red Lines, Black Spaces: The Politics of Race and Space in a Black Middle-Class Suburb* (New Haven, 2001), 150–53.

29. Jennifer Hochschild, *Facing Up to the American Dream: Race, Class, and the Soul of the Nation* (Princeton, 1995), quoted in Mary Patillo-McCoy, *Black Picket Fences: Privilege and Peril among the Black Middle Class* (Chicago, 1999), 44.

30. Theodore "Ted" Wheeler, interview by author, July 27, 2001.

31. Steven A. Holmes and Karen DeWitt, "Black, Successful and Safe and Gone from Capital," *New York Times,* July 27, 1996, 1; Gayle P. Williams, letter to the editor, *New York Times Magazine,* July 12, 1992, 6.

32. Nate Parker, letter to the editor, *Chicago Tribune,* May 3, 1994, 18.

33. Quoted in Cumming, "Bright Flight," 1R.

34. Quoted in Sall, "More Blacks Choose Suburbs," 1.

35. Quoted in Karen DeWitt, "Minorities Departing U.S. Cities," *Dallas Morning News,* August 21, 1994, 1A.

36. Tony Massengale, interview by author, July 15, 1989.

37. David Montgomery, "BET Sees a Hungry P.G.; Video Age Restaurant to Cater to Black Suburbs," *Washington Post,* October 27, 1995, B1; Sall, "More Blacks Choose Suburbs," 1; Ford Fessenden, "Pattern of Bias; Study: Segregation Marks Long Island Housing," *New York Newsday,* May 18, 1992, 5; Sue Ellen Christian, "Affluent Blacks Opt Out of City; New Study Finds Many Choosing the Suburbs," *Chicago Tribune,* May 21, 1995, 1C.

38. Louis Freedberg, "A Different Kind of Chicago 'Housing Project,'" *San Francisco Chronicle,* February 22, 1993.

39. William A. Wheeler, interview by author, June 16, 1989.

40. Quoted in J. Linn Allen, "Living Apart; Anxieties Perpetuate Pattern of Segregation," *Chicago Tribune,* November 21, 1993, 1C.

41. Towns, "The New Black Power"; O'Hare and Frey, "Booming, Suburban, and Black."

42. Quoted in Cumming, "Bright Flight," 1R.

43. Quoted in DeWitt, "Minorities Departing U.S. Cities."

44. Quoted in Montgomery, "BET Sees a Hungry P.G.," B1.

45. Freedberg, "A Different Kind of Chicago 'Housing Project,'" A1; Holmes and DeWitt, "Black, Successful and Safe and Gone from Capital," 1; Harold

McNeil and Susan Schulman, "Suburbs Prompt Question: Why Are They So White?" *Buffalo News,* December 3, 1992, 1.

46. Quoted in Garreau, *Edge City,* 157.

47. Quoted in Christian, "Affluent Blacks Opt Out of City," 1C.

48. Quoted in ibid.

49. Quoted in Cumming, "Bright Flight."

50. Bill Bryan, "St. Louis High in Murders; Violence Pushes City to Third in Nation, Says Report by FBI," *St. Louis Post Dispatch,* August 30, 1992, 1D; Joseph Gambardello, "Murder Rate May Drop," *New York Newsday,* December 10, 1992, 33; Ruben Castaneda, "Our Killing Streets: Did Fulwood Have a Chance?" *Washington Post,* September 13, 1992, C1.

51. Dennis Cauchon and Desda Moss, "Murder, a National 'Epidemic,'" *USA Today,* June 10, 1992, A1.

52. On social control and crime in a middle-class black neighborhood, see Patillo-McCoy, *Black Picket Fences,* 68–90.

53. Patrick Reardon, "Second City to Suburbs; More Chicagoans Find It Isn't Their Kind of Town," *Chicago Tribune,* November 28, 1993, 1C.

54. Quoted in ibid.

55. Quoted in DeWitt, "Minorities Departing U.S. Cities," 1A.

56. Quoted in Craig Horowitz, "The Upper West Side of Suburbia," *New York* 29, November 18, 1996, 43–49; see also Darryl Fears, "To Stay or Not to Stay in L.A." *Los Angeles Times,* December 4, 1998, 1.

57. Quoted in McNeil and Schulman, "Suburbs Prompt Question," 1.

58. J. Linn Allen, "Civil Wrongs; As Blacks Go House Hunting, Too Often the Door Is Closed," *Chicago Tribune,* November 14, 1993, C1. On housing discrimination, see Margery Turner, Raymond Struyk, and John Yinger, *Housing Discrimination Study: Synthesis* (Washington, D.C., 1991); and Joe R. Feagin, "A House Is Not a Home: White Racism and U.S. Housing Practices," in *Residential Apartheid,* ed. Bullard, Grigsby, and Lee, 25–40.

59. Mike Leachman, Phil Nyden, Bill Peterman, and Darnell Coleman, *Black, White and Shades of Brown: Fair Housing and Economic Opportunity in the Chicago Region* (Chicago, 1998), 22–26.

60. "Survey Shows Racial Bias in Home Loans," 1A; Feagin, "A House Is Not a Home," 35. Also see "Banks Fail Blacks Seeking Home Loans," *New York Times,* October 7, 1997, B8; Scott Minerbrook, "Blacks Locked Out of the American Dream," *Business and Society Review* 87 (fall 1993): 23–28.

61. Adel Allen, U.S. Commission on Civil Rights, *Hearings before the U.S. Commission on Civil Rights: Hearings Held in St. Louis, Missouri, January 14–17,*

1970 (Washington, D.C., 1970), 308; Christian, "Affluent Blacks Opt Out of City"; Allen, "Living Apart."

62. Mary Johnson and Don Hayner, "Changing Areas; Diversity Brings Disillusionment in City, Hope in the Suburbs," *Chicago Sun-Times,* January 13, 1993, 16.

63. Quoted in J. Linn Allen, "Race Remains Housing's Main Dividing Line," *Chicago Tribune,* February 22, 1998, 1.

64. Quoted in Steve Inskeep, "Segregated Suburbs," *Morning Edition,* National Public Radio, April 20, 1998.

65. Quoted in Allen, "Living Apart."

66. Robert Thomas, "Black Suburbanization and Housing Quality in Atlanta," *Journal of Urban Affairs* 6 (winter 1984): 19–20; Christopher Silver, "Housing Policy and Suburbanization: An Analysis of the Changing Quality and Quantity of Black Housing in Suburbia since 1950," in *Race, Ethnicity and Minority Housing in the United States,* ed. Jamenid A. Momeni (New York, 1986), 77; Nancy Denton, "Are African Americans Still Hypersegregated?" in *Residential Apartheid,* ed. Bullard, Grigsby, and Lee, 49–81.

67. Christian, "Affluent Blacks Opt Out of City."

68. The 1990 index of racial segregation in suburban Chicago was 88.9, just two points below the index level in Chicago. The index measures the percentage of people of one race or another who would have to move for the races to be equally distributed throughout a given area. An index of 100 would reflect complete racial separation. Allen, "Living Apart."

69. Fessenden, "Pattern of Bias," 5.

70. Allen, "Race Remains Housing's Main Dividing Line"; Schneider and Phelan, "Black Suburbanization in the 1980s"; Leachman, Nyden, Peterman, and Coleman, *Black, White and Shades of Brown.*

71. Quoted in Lee Bey, "Suburbs Attract Middle Class; African Americans' Incomes Frequently Exceed Neighbors'," *Chicago Sun-Times,* May 21, 1995, 16.

72. Holmes and DeWitt, "Black, Successful and Safe and Gone from Capital," 1.

73. Ibid.

74. Journalist and Prince George's County resident Sam Fulwood described his neighbors' flashy cars as "buppie mobiles," suggesting their importance as emblems of membership in a group defined by both race and class. Fulwood, *Waking from the Dream.*

75. Fletcher, "The Changes," W11; Abramowitz and Morin, "Prince George's: Views in Black and White," A1.

76. Fletcher, "The Changes."

77. Retha Hill, "Prince George's County; Curry Victory Caps Historic Shift in Power," *Washington Post,* November 9, 1994, A38; John Rivera, "Curry Already Changing Prince George's History," *Baltimore Sun,* December 27, 1994, A1.

78. Karen Williams Gooden and Alvin Thornton, *Like a Phoenix I'll Rise: An Illustrated History of African Americans in Prince George's County, Maryland, 1696–1996* (Virginia Beach, Va., 1997), 132–37.

79. Bianca Floyd, *Records and Recollections: Early Black History in Prince George's County, Maryland* (Upper Marlboro, Md., 1989), 100–23; Frank Harold Wilson, *Footsteps from North Brentwood: From Reconstruction to the Post–World War II Years* (Upper Marlboro, Md., 1997); Susan G. Pearl, *Glenarden: The Past in Perspective* (Upper Marlboro, Md., 1995); see also T. J. Calloway, "Lincoln [Maryland]," *Crisis* 10 (March 1915): 240–42; and "High Ridge Park, the Land of Promise," *Baltimore Afro-American,* August 15, 1925, 19.

80. Rivera, "Curry Already Changing Prince George's History," A1; Fletcher, "The Changes."

81. Harold Rose, "The All Black Town: Suburban Prototype or Rural Slum?" *Urban Affairs Annual Reviews* 6 (1972): 403, 421–22; Susan G. Pearl, *Historical Survey of North Brentwood, Maryland* (Upper Marlboro, Md., July 1991); Susan G. Pearl, *Fairmount Heights, Maryland: A History from Its Beginnings (1900) to Incorporation (1935)* (Upper Marlboro, Md., July 1991).

82. Quoted in Kevin Merida, "Privilege and Privation," *Washington Post Magazine,* March 10, 2002, 8.

83. Prince George's black population grew by 217,000, from 31,000 to 248,000, between 1960 and 1980, compared to total black suburban growth of 310,000. By 1990 the metropolitan area reported 619,000 black suburbanites (excluding Arlington). U.S. Census of Population: 1980, *Census Tracts,* table P-7; U.S. Census of Population: 1990, *Summary Population Characteristics and Housing Characteristics, U.S.,* CPH 1-1 (Washington, D.C., 1993), table 2.

84. Merida, "Privilege and Privation," 8.

85. Frank Ahrens, "A Minority of One; Sylvester Vaughns Still Believes in Busing. In P.G. County He's Almost Alone," *Washington Post,* September 4, 1996, B1; Sandra Gregg, "Group of Black Officers Quitting Union," ibid., July 28, 1983, C2; "P.G. Council Amends Charter," ibid., April 3, 1980, 9.

86. Joel Garreau, "The Emerging Cities; Blacks: Success in the Suburbs," *Washington Post Reprints* (November 29–December 1, 1987), 22.

87. Prince George's County, 1960: total population, 357,395, black population, 31,011 (9 percent); 1970: total population, 660,567, black population, 91,808 (14 percent); 1980: total population, 656,071, black population, 247,860

(38 percent); 1990: total population, 729,268, black population, 369,791 (51 percent).

88. Hill, "Prince George's County; Curry Victory Caps Historic Shift of Power," A38.

89. Merida, "Privilege and Privation."

90. On the making of empowering group territory, see Manuel Castells, *The City and the Grassroots: A Cross-Cultural Theory of Urban Social Movements* (Los Angeles, 1983), 155–58.

91. Patriot Homes, a white-owned venture founded in Columbia, Maryland, was one of the state's largest builders in the 1990s, specializing in midmarket homes in the state's booming suburban fringes. "Patriot Homes," promotional brochure (Columbia, Md.); Douglas Hanks, "Miami-based Firm Acquires Maryland Home Builder," *Miami Herald,* November 15, 2001.

92. Fulwood, *Waking from the Dream,* 189.

93. Ibid., 238.

94. Ibid.

95. Ronald Handy, quoted in Abramowitz and Morin, "Prince George's: Views in Black and White."

96. Quoted in Dent, "The New Black Suburbs," 20.

97. Quoted in ibid.

98. Quoted in ibid., 25.

99. Betty Winston Baye, "Inside Sam Fulwood's 'Buppie Cocoon,'" *Louisville Courier-Journal,* May 17, 1994.

100. Quoted in Dent, "The New Black Suburbs," 20.

101. Quoted in Rosalind Bentley, "Cronkite Focuses on Black 'Self-Segregation,'" *Minneapolis Star Tribune,* October 18, 1993, 9E.

102. Baye, "Inside Sam Fulwood's 'Buppie Cocoon.'"

103. Dent, "The New Black Suburbs," 25.

104. Stokely Carmichael and Charles V. Hamilton, *Black Power: The Politics of Liberation in America* (New York, 1967), 54–55.

105. Quoted in Holmes and DeWitt, "Black, Successful and Safe and Gone from Capital."

106. Ibid.

107. Quoted in ibid.

108. Quoted in Juan Williams, "Area's Hottest Campaign; P.G.'s Mudslinging Hides Dueling Visions," *Washington Post,* August 28, 1994, C1.

109. Quoted in Rivera, "Curry Already Changing Prince George's History."

110. Quoted in ibid.

111. Abramowitz and Morin, "Prince George's: Views in Black and White."

112. Quoted in Dent, "The New Black Suburbs," 21.

113. Quoted in Garreau, "The Emerging Cities," 22.

114. Quoted in Abramowitz and Morin, "Prince George's: Views in Black and White."

115. Quoted in Paul Schwartzman, "Prince George's Executive Stakes Out Legacy," *Washington Post,* March 23, 2002, B5.

116. Holmes and DeWitt, "Black, Successful and Safe and Gone from Capital"; Jackie Spinner, "Resort Plan Finds Strong Support Close to Home," *Washington Post,* February 23, 1998, D3.

117. Quoted in Abramowitz and Morin, "Prince George's: Views in Black and White"; Montgomery, "BET Sees a Hungry P.G."

118. Clyde W., conversation with author, October 29, 2001.

119. Montgomery, "BET Sees a Hungry P.G."

120. Jonathan Fletcher, "Increase Availability of Credit," *National Mortgage News,* November 8, 1993, 4.

121. Quoted in Jackie Spinner, "Prince George's 'Shop at Home' Campaign Means Tough Choices for Many," *Washington Post,* January 18, 1998, B1; Montgomery, "BET Sees a Hungry P.G."

122. Tracey Reeves, "A P.G. Education; Iris Metts Never Thought Things Could Go So Bad with the Board," *Washington Post,* April 3, 2002, C1.

123. Howard Libit, "Prince George's Pins Hopes on New Funds," *Baltimore Sun,* January 23, 2002, 1A.

124. Eric Lipton, "School System Beset by Problems," *Washington Post,* June 21, 1998, A1.

125. Libit, "Prince George's Pins Hopes on New Funds," 1A.

126. Reeves, "A P.G. Education," C1.

127. Libit, "Prince George's Pins Hopes on New Funds," 1A.

128. Quoted in Paul Schwartzman, "In Pr. George's, a Different Kind of Campaign," *Washington Post,* April 28, 2002, A1.

129. Lipton, "School System Beset by Problems."

130. Reeves, "A P.G. Education"; Lisa Frazier, "Where There's Never Enough; Students Lack Continuity, Resources, Involved Parents," *Washington Post,* June 23, 1998, A1.

131. Reeves, "A P.G. Education"; Frazier, "Where There's Never Enough."

132. Frazier, "Where There's Never Enough."

133. Patillo-McCoy, *Black Picket Fences.*

134. Merida, "Privilege and Privation," 8.

135. R. A. Zaldivar, "Deadly Drug War Turning D.C. and Its Suburbs into Battle Zone," *Miami Herald,* March 20, 1988, 1A.

136. Jon Jeter, "Loosening the Grip of Crime in Glenarden; P.G. Town Pulls

Together, Becomes a Model for Curbing Violence," *Washington Post,* May 7, 1995, A1.

137. Frazier, "Where There's Never Enough."

138. Merida, "Privilege and Privation."

139. Garreau, "The Emerging Cities," 23.

140. Holmes and DeWitt, "Black, Successful and Safe and Gone from Capital," 1.

141. Quoted in Terry M. Neal and David Montgomery, "School Board in P.G. Seeks End to Busing," *Washington Post,* July 26, 1996, B1.

142. Holmes and DeWitt, "Black, Successful and Safe and Gone from Capital," 1.

143. Susan Saulny, "On the Inside and Looking Out; Black Suburb Rebuffs Uninvited Black Visitors," *Washington Post,* July 8, 1996, A1.

144. Quoted in ibid.

145. Quoted in ibid. Perrywood was not the only local subdivision where the suburban mania for property values led to a restriction on black teenagers' use of public space. In one Lake Arbor neighborhood, "large groupings of teenagers and older children" gathered in various culs-de-sac where residents had erected portable backboards. The local civic association forced residents to remove them each evening.

146. Ibid.

147. See Dawson, *Behind the Mule,* 45–68, 76–80.

148. Charles Thomas, interview by author, June 15, 1989.

149. Patillo-McCoy, *Black Picket Fences,* 6.

150. Phelan and Schneider, "Race, Ethnicity, and Class in American Suburbs"; Schneider and Phelan, "Black Suburbanization in the 1980s"; Diana Jean Schemo, "Suburban Taxes Are Higher for Blacks Analysis Shows," *New York Times,* August 17, 1994, A1.

151. Schemo, "Suburban Taxes Are Higher," A1.

152. Andrew Beveridge, quoted in ibid.

153. Patillo-McCoy, *Black Picket Fences,* 3.

154. Schemo, "Suburban Taxes Are Higher for Blacks"; Phelan and Schneider, "Race, Ethnicity, and Class in American Suburbs."

155. Sean Shong Hwang and Steve H. Murdock, "Racial Attraction or Racial Avoidance in American Suburbs?" *Social Forces* 77 (December 1988): 541–65; also Taylor and Moran, "More Black Families Calling Suburbs Home," A1.

156. Parker, letter to the editor, 18; Timothy Egan, "On Posh Island [Mercer Island, Washington], Black Means Suspect," *San Diego Union Tribune,* May 10, 1998, A3; Kenneth Noble, "Race Issue Rattles Celebrity Haven [Beverly Hills, California]," *New York Times,* April 23, 1996, 14.

157. Taylor and Moran, "More Black Families Calling Suburbs Home"; Marianne Rohrlich, "Feeling Isolated at the Top, Seeking Roots," *New York Times,* July 19, 1998, sec. 9, 1; Diego Ribadeneira, "Gathering Together; City Churches Serve Suburban Flock," *Boston Globe,* March 10, 1996, Metro, 1; David Sharos, "Roselle Church Reaching Out Across Suburbs: Christian Tabernacle Helping Its Members Make a Connection," *Chicago Tribune,* January 12, 1996, Metro, 8.

158. Feagin, "A House Is Not a Home," 40.

159. Shelley Parks, conversation with author, College Park, Maryland, October 29, 2001.

160. Catherine Hughes, quoted in I. Austin, "In a Class of Their Own," *Maclean's,* January 20, 1986, 20.

161. A recent exception is Rick Famuyiwa's 1999 film *The Wood,* which looks back with nostalgia at three young men growing up in Inglewood, California.

162. Gloria Naylor, *Linden Hills* (New York, 1985).

163. Henry L. Taylor Jr., quoted in Trevoor Coleman and Corey Williams, "Black Flight to Suburbs Hurts Those Left Behind," *Detroit News,* February 25, 1992; in the view of historian Manning Marable, black suburbanites' commitment to central city African American communities required more than "lip service," ibid.

164. William Julius Wilson, *The Truly Disadvantaged: The Inner City, the Underclass, and Public Policy* (Chicago, 1987), 56.

165. Thomas J. Sugrue, *The Origins of the Urban Crisis: Race and Inequality in Postwar Detroit* (Princeton, 1996), 207. Arnold Hirsch points out that, even if only implicitly, Sugrue blames middle-class suburbanites for "distancing themselves physically and symbolically from the African American poor" and for the resulting "isolation of the urban black poor in deteriorating center-city areas." Arnold Hirsch, "Race Space Race," *Journal of Urban History* 26 (May 2000): 519–29.

166. Quoted in Coleman and Williams, "Black Flight to Suburbs Hurts Those Left Behind." For criticism of the "golden age of segregation," see Robin D. G. Kelley, "'We Are Not What We Seem': Rethinking Black Working-Class Opposition in the Jim Crow South," *Journal of American History* 80 (June 1993): 75–112.

167. See Robert E. Park, Ernest W. Burgess, and Roderick D. McKenzie, *The City* (1925; reprint, Chicago, 1967).

168. For a discussion of contemporary uses of the ecological model, see Richard D. Alba and John R. Logan, "Variations on Two Themes: Racial and Ethnic Patterns in the Attainment of Suburban Residence," *Demography* 28 (August 1991): 431–53.

169. For a careful review of this literature, see Joe William Trotter Jr., *Black Milwaukee: The Making of an Industrial Proletariat* (Urbana, Ill., 1985), 64–77;

examples of critical work within the ecology paradigm include Charles Johnson and Herman Long, *People versus Property: Race Restrictive Covenants in Housing* (Nashville, 1947); Luigi Laurenti, *Property Values and Race* (Berkeley, 1959); Morton Deutsch and Mary Evans Collins, *Interracial Housing: A Psychological Evaluation of a Social Experiment* (Minneapolis, 1951); and Robert Weaver, *The Negro Ghetto* (New York, 1948).

170. Trotter, *Black Milwaukee*, 273, 265.

171. Richard Walter Thomas, "From Peasant to Proletarian: The Formation and Organization of the Black Industrial Working Class in Detroit, 1915–1945" (Ph.D. diss., University of Michigan, 1976); Peter Gottlieb, *Making Their Own Way: Southern Blacks' Migration to Pittsburgh, 1916–30* (Urbana, Ill., 1987); James R. Grossman, *Land of Hope: Chicago, Black Southerners, and the Great Migration* (Chicago, 1989); Elizabeth Clark-Lewis, *Living In, Living Out: African American Domestics in Washington, D.C., 1910–1940* (Washington, 1994); Gretchen Lemke-Santangelo, *Abiding Courage: African American Migrant Women and the East Bay Community* (Chapel Hill, N.C., 1996); Kimberley L. Phillips, *AlabamaNorth: African-American Migrants, Community, and Working-Class Activism in Cleveland, 1915–45* (Urbana, Ill., 1999).

172. Phillips, *AlabamaNorth*, 7.

173. Earl Lewis, *In Their Own Interests: Race, Class, and Power in Twentieth-Century Norfolk, Virginia* (Berkeley, 1991).

174. Earl Lewis, "Connecting Memory, Self, and the Power of Place in African American Urban History," *Journal of Urban History* 21 (March 1995): 347–71.

175. Henri Lefebvre, in *The Production of Space,* describes the production of social space in three "moments": *spatial practice,* which is human activity in the world; *representations of space,* intellectual conceptions of space, ideologies, and the language of planners, architects, subdividers, academics, etc.; and *representational spaces,* the images, symbols, and other mental states related to lived experience in particular spaces. Steven Gregory, *Black Corona: Race and the Politics of Place in an Urban Community* (Princeton, 1998); Bobby M. Wilson, *Race and Place in Birmingham: The Civil Rights and Neighborhood Movements* (New York, 2000); Haynes, *Red Lines, Black Spaces;* Clyde Woods, *Development Arrested: The Blues and Plantation Power in the Mississippi Delta* (London, 1998); Robert Self, "'To Plan Our Liberation': Black Power and the Politics of Place in Oakland, California, 1965–1977," *Journal of Urban History* 26 (September 2000): 759–92.

176. Castells, *The City and the Grassroots,* 311.

177. Toni Morrison, "Home," in *The House that Race Built: Black Americans, U.S. Terrain,* ed. Wahneema Lubiano (New York, 1997), 5.

Index

Dekalb County, GA, 257. *See also*
  Atlanta, GA
Democratic Party, 128, 222–23,
  234–35
Denson, Estella, 79, 86
Denson, Sallie, 87
Denton, Nancy, 224
Denson family (Chagrin Falls Park,
  OH), 87–88
Denver, CO (metropolitan area), 214
Department of Justice, U.S., 223
depression, 57, 72, 135, 140, 178,
  249; and black employment, 56;
  urban conditions during, 89
Detroit, MI (metropolitan area), 20,
  22, 34, 45, 46, 87, 103, 114, 139,
  145, 265, 287, 308–9n72; home
  ownership, 123, 318–19n56;
  housing statistics, *170;* open-
  housing protests, 220; population statistics, 23, *116, 171, 212;*
  war housing in, suburbs, 135–36,
  137; working-class suburbanization of, *12,* 23, 28, *29,* 43–50,
  91, 147. *See also specific places and
  institutions*
Detroit River (Detroit, MI), 44,
  45, 46
Detwyler, Fannie, 89
Devon, PA, 21
DeWitt, Karen, 277, 282
Dillard University, 169
Dirks, Nicholas, 297n26
Dixmoor, IL, *62, 119,* 121, 122
Doby, Larry, 132
Doles, David, 146
domestic employment, 35, 52, 75,
  79, 82, 90, 104, 310n97; black
  women and, 55, 61, 63; impor-

tance of, in affluent suburbs, 54–
55, 64; link to social and spatial
inequality, 25–27, *26,* 65, 219;
live-in work, 21, 46, 56, 57–58,
309–10n88, 309n87; men and,
56, 63; and race relations, 64,
219, 302n53; and rhythms of
suburban life, 57, 63; role in suburban migration, 20, 21, 56, 61,
63, 105; in South, 26
domestic production, 66, *78,* 79,
125, 151, 153, 202; of alcohol,
77; and class, 85, 91, 146–47; as
cushion against urban insecurity,
8, *14,* 86–87, 145–147; foraging,
19, 77; gardens, 8, 12, 19, 55,
67, 69, 72, *73, 75,* 77, *78,* 79, 85,
88–89, 91, 93, 145–47 passim,
148, 153, 184, 207; home-based
business and labor, 79, *83,* 85–
86; livestock, 8, 19, 69, 72, *73,
75, 77, 78, 83,* 85, 88–89, 93,
145–47 passim, *148,* 151, 153,
336n11; owner building (*see*
owner building); in postwar suburbs, 145–47, *148;* in real estate
advertising, 72, *73,* 146–47, *148,*
153; renting domestic space, 8,
52, 55, 69, 79, 85, 86, 146; restriction of, after World War II,
91–92, 97, southern roots of,
86–87, 88–89, 146
domestic service employment
suburbs. *See* domestic service
suburbs
domestic service suburbs, 25–27, 34–
36, 54–65, 301–2n49, 310n97;
attractions of, to women, 55,
56–58; discrimination and

Lee-Harvard neighborhood (Cleveland, OH), 249, *250*
Lefebvre, Henri, 290, 373n175
leisure and recreation, 49–50, 53–54, 57–58, 79, 90–91; church-based, 49, 57, 90; home-centered, 157, 158–59; as a marker of class, 159; and masculinity, 53–54; in postwar suburbs, 144, 149–50, 151, 156, 205, 269, 274, 282–83; "sporting life," 54; sports, 53, 80, 90
Levitt, William, 220–21, 230
Levittown, PA, *94,* 156
Levittown (PA) Betterment Committee, *94*
Lewis, Earl, 171, 290
Lewis, Hylan, 194, 348n94
Lewis, Robert, 283
Lexington, KY, 18
Lilydale (Chicago, IL), *62, 119,* 147
Lincoln, Abraham: use of name in real estate developments, 5, 72, *73,* 126, 153, 277, 316n18
Lincoln, MD, 277
Lincoln Elementary School (Englewood, NJ), 219–20
Lincoln Heights, OH, 5, 126
Lincoln Manor subdivision (Robbins, IL), 153
Linden Hills (Naylor), 287
Lipsitz, George, 98–99
Live Oak, FL, 37
Locke, Alaine, 53
Logan, John R., 107
Lomita, CA, 43
Long Beach, NY, 105
Long Island, NY, 139, 224, 229; housing discrimination, 131,

226; population, 106; prevalence of historic black communities, 104–5; segregation on, 268; unplanned subdivisions on, 147, *148;* urban renewal, 104–7. *See also* New York, NY; *and specific places*
Look (magazine), 209–10, *210,* 212
Loop, the (Chicago, IL), *62,* 118, *119*
Los Angeles, CA (metropolitan area), 44, 114, 131, 154, 211, 263, 310n93; central city "spillover," 215; crime in, and suburbanization, 265; discrimination and segregation in suburbs, 42–43; home-ownership rates, 123, 318–19n56; housing construction for blacks, 139, *152;* housing statistics, *170;* open-housing movement in, 220, 221; population statistics, 20, *116, 171, 212;* socioeconomic statistics, 124; suburban landscape, 11. *See also specific places and institutions*
Lottier, Pat, 264
Louisville, KY, 41
Lynbrook, CA, 42
Lynchburg, VA: disadvantageous location of black neighborhoods, 18

Macon, GA, 172
Madison, IL, 54
Magnolia, AR, 37
Main Line (Philadelphia, PA), 25
Malcolm X, 220
Manayunk, PA, 21
Manhasset, NY, 105, 326n56
Manhattan Beach, CA, 43

367n68; link between housing and school, 63, 172–73, 252, 348n99; in public facilities and accommodations, 40–41, 43, 48–49, 50, 60–61, 63, 66, 126, 158–59, 166, 171–72, 218–19, 312n119; and race, 7–8, 60, 65, 99, 142, 258, 268, 287; real estate industry and, 41–43, 64, 247 (*see also* housing discrimination); role of government in, *22,* 40–43, 60–63 passim, 92, 100–101, 113, 127, 134–35, 165–66, 167, 181, 198, 200, 202–3, 206, 207, 221; in schools, 8, 40, 48, 49–50 60–61, 63–64, 76, 80, 126, 166, 171–73, 205–6, 219–20, 252, 270, 291; white attitudes toward, 42, 98–99, 165–66, 196, 198, 201, 206, 230

Self, Robert, 127

Seville Homes (Cleveland, OH), 136, 137

Shahn, Ben, 12

Shaker Heights, OH, *71,* 154, 249, *250,* 362n154; support for integration, 215

Shannon, James, 268

Shelley v. Kraemer, 128, 131, 172. *See also* Supreme Court: and restrictive covenants

Shreveport, LA (metropolitan area), 172, 214

Simmons, Clarence, 265

Simpson Heights subdivision (Atlanta, GA), 182

Skokie, IL, 15, *62*

Smith, A. Maceo, 198, 199–200, 203

Smith, Clydie, 145, 147

Smith, Lessie, 89

Smith, Preston, 162

Smith v. Alwright, 342n21. *See also* voting rights: invalidation of white primary

Snow, Gwen, 262, 265

Snowden, George, 103

social networks: and child care, 58, 59; and employment, 38, 39; and race, 156–57, 258–59, 262, 286; role in suburban migration and settlement, 36, 38–40, 58–59, 65, 68, 82, 113, 114, 116, 154, 158; and segregation, 158; women and creation of, 57–58, 60, 85, 136. *See also* family

Social Security, 91, 125

South (region), 10, 17–19, 26, 40, 65, 68, 86, 93, 112, 114, 118, 123, 124, 134, 140, 220, 222, 232, 233, 244, 290, 298–99n11; black politics in urban, 171–74, 182–83, 208, 290; disadvantageous location of black neighborhoods in, 18, 201; dispersal of black neighborhoods in urban, 17–19, 29, 163, 169, 174, 186, 203; domestic service suburbs in, 25–26, *26;* employment patterns in, 17, 26, 55, 174; and home ownership, 8, 31, 67, 69–70, 84, 90, 93, 145; housing and neighborhood conditions in urban, *14,* 17, 19, *26,* 27, 174–75, *175,* 185, 189, *190, 193,* 194–95, 197–99; housing statistics, *170;* industrial suburbs in, *14,* 23–24, 54; migration to urban, 18, 37, 168, 176, 196–97; postwar

subdivisions, unplanned. *See* unplanned subdivisions
suburban dreams, 2, 142, 145–54,
  288; contemporary, 1; defined,
  315n10; elite and middle-class
  white, 4–5, 25, 69, 88–89, 98–
  99, 108–9; middle-class black, 9,
  31, 111–12, 142, 143–44, 147–
  54, 156–59, *150, 152,* 160–63,
  166–67, 188–89, 190–91, 195–
  96, 204–6, 207–8, 211, 218,
  230–31, 232, 233–35, 240–43,
  258–59, 261–65, 266, 274–79,
  286; reflected in real estate advertising, 72, *73,* 146–47, *148,* 150–
  53, *152,* 191, *192,* 207; southern
  roots of black, 10, 69, 83–90
  passim, 93, 147; white supremacy and, 9, 42, 144; working-
  class black, 8–9, 66, 67–70, *78,*
  82–90, 92–93, 145–47, *148;*
  working-class white, 6, 91, 109.
  See also suburbanites, African
  American
suburbanites, African American: aspirations for children, 144, 147,
  153–54, 156, 161, 233–35, 240–
  41, 242, 262, 264, 276–77, 286;
  attitudes toward cities, 66, 69,
  88, 89–90, 93, 263, 264–65,
  266, 277; attitudes toward crime
  and personal safety, 230–31, 233,
  262, 264, 265–67, 284 (*see also*
  suburbanization, African American: crime and); attitudes toward
  home ownership, 31, 66, 67, 68,
  69, 82, 83–85, 92–93, 144, 145–
  47, 148, 149, 204, 241; attitudes
  toward integration, 39, 153–54,

156, 157–58, 162, 232, 242–43,
  276–77, 286 (*see also* integration:
  African American attitudes
  toward); attitudes toward schools
  and education, 31, 39, 69, 147,
  148, 153, 162, 205–6, 230–31,
  232, 233–35, 240, 241, 262,
  263, 264, 265, 280 (*see also* suburbanization, African American:
  schools and); attitudes toward
  segregation, 61, 65, 201, 205–6,
  276–77 (*see also* segregation:
  African American attitudes
  toward); attitudes toward services and infrastructure, 17, 76,
  88, 89, 188, *190,* 205, 230, 262,
  263, 264–65; and civil rights activism (collective), 112–13, 126–
  27, 129–32, 212, 219–20, 224,
  234–35, 238–40, 272, 288; and
  civil rights activism (individual),
  95–96, 112–13, 129–32, 133–
  34, 224, 234–38, *239,* 241–42,
  254 (*see also* black pioneers);
  commuting patterns, 18, 19, 21,
  63, 77–78, 90, 104, 188; critical
  views of, 87, 286–87, 372n163;
  efforts to maintain black social
  networks, 9, 90–91, 234, 241,
  258–59, 262, 286; home-
  ownership rates, 122–23, *123;*
  political and civic activities, 31,
  80, 126–27, 136, 157, 189, 205;
  population, 1, 5, 15, *16,* 20, 95,
  114, *115, 116,* 211, *212,* 217,
  255, *256,* 295n16, 293n2,
  298n8, 304n10; preferences for
  black communities, 8, 9, 69–70,
  157–58, 207, 213, 258–59, 262,

suburbanites, African American
(*continued*)
275–77; preferences for family-
based communities, 9, 68, 83,
93, 143, 157; preferences for
housing and landscape, 7, 8–9,
31, 66, 67–70, *78,* 88–90, 93,
111–12, 132, 142, 143–44, 145–
50, *150,* 157, 158–59, 166, 188–
89, *190,* 190–91, 195, 204–5,
207–8, 218, 224, 230, 231, 254,
261–65, 274–77; preferences for
middle-class neighborhoods,
144, 147–48, 160–63, 204–5,
207–8, 258–59, 263, 275–77;
socioeconomic composition of,
5–6, 10, 15, 31, 47, 65, 112,
124, 125, 189, 205, 213–14,
255–57; urban frame of reference, 261–62, 264–67. *See also*
suburban dreams: working-class
black; suburban dreams: middle-
class black; *and individual suburbs
and suburban types*
suburbanization, African American,
209–10, *210;* black migration
and, 1, 5, 22–23, 34–36, 37, 38–
40, 65, 114, 136–37, *137,* 140,
168 (*see also* Great Migration; migration); central city "spillover"
and, 211, 215, 240, 244–45,
249–54, *250, 251, 253,* 272; children and, 39, 144, 151–54, 156–
57, 161, 164, 204, 230–31, 35,
56, 58, 59, 93, 233–35, 262–67
passim, 276–77, 286; civil rights
movement and, 125–29, 140–
42, 143, 156, 211, 219–25, 241,
254 (*see also* civil rights move-

ment; open-housing movement);
and class, 4, 9, 69, 91, 112, 132,
142, 143–54, 159–63, 166–67,
188–91, *190, 192,* 204–5, 211,
241, 257–59, 261–67, 282–86;
crime and, 230–31, 264, 265–
67, 272; critical views of, 67–68,
87, 266, 287, 372n165; economic restructuring and, 10,
211, 265; as expression of racial
politics, 9, *111–12,* 131–32, 144,
150, 162–63, 166, 224, 241–42;
gender and, 44, 50–54, 56–60,
66 (*see also* gender); as geographically cumulative process, 2, 3–4,
18, 22, 29–31, *30,* 66, 92, 113,
114–17, 118–22, 135–38, *137,*
142, 157–58, 162–63, 169–71,
213, 214, *215,* 215, 244, 247,
249–51, *250,* 271–72, 288, 291;
growth of middle class and, 2,
10, 112, 124–25, 140, 142, 210,
211, 254, 217–19, 260, 272 (*see
also* black middle class); home
ownership and (*see* home ownership); overlapping influence of
race and class, 91, 142, 144–45,
159–60, 163, 166–67, 258–59,
261–67, 283–84; and race, 2, 4,
21, *22,* 35, 40–43, 44, 48–50,
61, 63–65, 66, 69–70, 72, 90–
91, 113, 44–45, 117, 142, 144–
45, 154–59, 162–63, 166–67,
190, 203, 205–6, 211, 241–42,
254, 257–59, 268, 284–86, 291;
and racial struggle for space, 3,
185–87, 211, 213, 225, 230,
286, 288, 291; role of employment, 20, 23–25, 43–44, 50–53,